Triumphs and Tragedies of the Modern Presidency

Triumphs and Tragedies of the Modern Presidency

Case Studies in Presidential Leadership

Second Edition

MAXMILLIAN ANGERHOLZER III,
JAMES KITFIELD,
NORMAN ORNSTEIN, AND
STEPHEN SKOWRONEK, EDITORS

CENTER FOR THE STUDY OF THE
PRESIDENCY & CONGRESS

PRAEGER™

An Imprint of ABC-CLIO, LLC
Santa Barbara, California • Denver, Colorado

About the Center for the Study of the Presidency & Congress

Established in 1965, the Center for the Study of the Presidency & Congress is a unique non-partisan, non-profit 501(c)(3) organization in Washington, D.C., that collaborates with the best minds in government, the private sector, and academia to apply strategic thinking and the lessons of history and leadership to today's most critical policy challenges.

Other CSPC publications of interest:
Triumphs and Tragedies of the Modern Congress (Praeger, 2014)
Presidential Studies Quarterly (ISSN 0360-4918)
A Call to Greatness: Challenging Our Next President, by David M. Abshire (Rowman & Littlefield, 2008)
Saving the Reagan Presidency, by David M. Abshire (Texas A&M University Press, 2005)

Library of Congress Cataloging-in-Publication Data

Names: Angerholzer, Maxmillian, editor.
Title: Triumphs and tragedies of the modern presidency : case studies in presidential leadership / edited by Maxmillian Angerholzer III, James Kitfield, Norman Ornstein, Stephen Skowronek, editors.
Description: Second edition. | Santa Barbara : Praeger, 2016. | Includes bibliographical references and index.
Identifiers: LCCN 2015044133| ISBN 9781440840227 (hardback) | ISBN 9781440840500 (paperback) | ISBN 9781440840234 (eBook)
Subjects: LCSH: Presidents—United States—History—20th century. | Political leadership—United States—Case studies. | United States—Politics and government—1933-1945. | United States—Politics and government—1945-1989. | United States—Politics and government—1989- | BISAC: POLITICAL SCIENCE / Government / Executive Branch. | POLITICAL SCIENCE / Political Process / Leadership.
Classification: LCC E176.1 .T775 2016 | DDC 973.09/9—dc23
LC record available at http://lccn.loc.gov/2015044133

ISBN: 978-1-4408-4022-7
Paperback ISBN: 978-1-4408-4050-0
EISBN: 978-1-4408-4023-4

20   19   18   17   16   1   2   3   4   5

This book is also available on the World Wide Web as an eBook.
Visit www.abc-clio.com for details.

Praeger
An Imprint of ABC-CLIO, LLC

ABC-CLIO, LLC
130 Cremona Drive, P.O. Box 1911
Santa Barbara, California 93116-1911

This book is printed on acid-free paper ∞

Manufactured in the United States of America

Board of Trustees

Contents

Introduction

When President Dwight D. Eisenhower encouraged R. Gordon Hoxie to establish what would become the Center for the Study of the Presidency & Congress (CSPC), the Supreme Allied Commander turned president lamented the lack of historical case studies to prepare him for civilian political leadership. As a military leader, he could pore over analyses of previous battles, deployments, and international crises, yet no similar repository of institutional memory existed for the equally complex arts of governing and legislating.

In 2000, the Center for the Study of the Presidency & Congress published *Triumphs and Tragedies of the Modern Presidency*, a collection of case studies focused on the complexities of presidential leadership—a modern fulfillment of President Eisenhower's wish. Now, fifteen years later and on the eve of the 2016 election, we update this anthology to provide new analyses and lessons for today's leaders and those of future generations.

Historians have often debated how individual leaders have shaped the course of history, and the study of the U.S. presidency certainly demonstrates the profound impact one individual can have, especially if working in the Oval Office. However, in these case studies, we also see the critical role played by the cast of characters who surround the president—some working with the president, others opposing his agenda. Whether a president is successful is not determined by only the sheer force of his will; rather, it often depends on his ability to work with others—inside the administration, in Congress, within his party, and with foreign leaders. Perhaps most important is a president's ability to connect with the American people.

In these case studies, it becomes evident that presidential leadership also depends on the formulation of sound strategy—setting goals, determining ways and means, and developing plans for the successful execution of policy. In this regard, we find that a president's strategic vision must be accompanied by a unique combination of guile and compromise, determination, and pragmatism.

In Section I, the opening chapters of this anthology deal with the fundamental structure of the modern presidency. We learn how in the 19th century Congress dominated national policy making except in times of war, and how presidents became dominant in the 20th century beginning with the New Deal and its expansion of the scope of the federal government. World War II further extended the role of the federal government in the economy and thrust the United States into a leadership role in world affairs that during the decades-long Cold War greatly expanded the powers the Commander in Chief wielded over national security and foreign policy. By the 1970s, the historian Arthur Schlesinger, Jr. had coined the term the "imperial presidency" to describe this fundamental shift in power.

Section I also explores the role of other primary actors in American politics and their relationships with the chief executive: the White House staff and executive branch, the Congress, the Supreme Court, the media, and the president's own political party. We learn how in modern times vice presidents have steadily gained in stature and influence. Despite the fact that there are no set playbooks for building a White House staff, we see how mistakes made in this critical early stage of a presidency can have profound repercussions. Although the American public elects only one person to lead from the White House, much of the actual work of policy making is conducted instead in the executive branch bureaucracy—the corps of departments headed by Cabinet Secretaries. Every president also shares responsibility for management of the economy with an independent Federal Reserve System, dubbed simply "the Fed."

The often tense relationship between presidents and Supreme Court Justices has helped shape American history and is explored in the chapter "No Friends in Black Robes: Presidents and the Supreme Court." Each president has also brought his own identity and personal background to the critical relationship between the White House and Congress, where success is measured in wins and losses on major pieces of legislation that help define a presidency. In the age of the Internet and social media, the relationship between presidents and the White House Press Corps has also fundamentally changed, with the chief executive increasingly able to go around the press corps and take his or her message more directly to the public. Even the relationship between presidents and their own political party is often fraught with tension—strong, popular presidents can usually ride herd on a fractious party, but the minute a president is seen as weak or unpopular, party divisions come to the fore.

Section II explores the "First One Hundred Days" of modern Presidencies beginning with President Franklin D. Roosevelt, who set the modern standard and an impossibly high bar for achievement. These case studies provide a window into how each of the modern presidents set his agenda and the tone for his term in office from the earliest days of his administration. Much can be learned about a president from this aspirational period when they are at the height of their power and their agendas have yet to be buffeted by political headwinds and unforeseen crises. These brief windows inevitably close as presidents lose popularity over time, and their parties almost always lose congressional seats in midterm elections. Master legislator Lyndon Johnson said it best in explaining his push for immediate congressional action in his first hundred days as president: "I keep hitting hard because I know this honeymoon won't last," said Johnson. "Every day I lose a little more political capital."

In Section III, we examine how the president has played a key role in setting the course of U.S. domestic policy. In this section, we see how the presidents' domestic agendas have shaped the modern United States and defined American life as we know it today. We are this country in large part because Dwight Eisenhower was determined to construct the interstate highway system; John F. Kennedy decided to put a man on the moon, launching the modern space program; Lyndon Johnson advanced the civil rights movement, and strengthened the social safety net with Medicare and Medicaid; Richard Nixon pushed the Clean Air and Clean Water Acts, and fourteen other pieces of critical environmental legislation; Bill Clinton and Al Gore laid the groundwork for the Internet, giving America a head start on the freewheeling Information Age; and George W. Bush launched the "No Child Left Behind" federal education reform.

Furthermore, while the Congress controls the power of the purse, the markets control the price of resources, and much of the economy is in the private sector domain. Case studies in Section III thus also examine how the president plays a key role in federal budgeting and economic policy, in managing the boom-and-bust cycle of energy prices and policy, and in managing major economic recessions.

In Section IV, we describe how the national security and foreign policy decisions made by modern presidents of the past seven decades have built the "American Century." For a public accustomed to the idea of "American exceptionalism," it may seem that the nation has always cast an oversized shadow over world affairs, but as recently as the first half of the 20th century, the United States was largely a strategic ward of the British Empire on which the sun famously never set. Only at the end of World War II in 1945, with Europe in ruins and Great Britain exhausted by two world wars, did the United States truly assume the mantle of Western leadership.

Victory in the Cold War and success in building and sustaining a liberal world order were never foreordained, and coupled with the imperative to avoid a potentially devastating World War III, the effort has weighed heavily on every commander-in-chief of the modern era. Nearly all of them would send troops into harm's way only to have some return in flag-draped coffins, and each man emerged from his tenure in the White House prematurely aged. Such are the burdens of global leadership.

In Section V, we end by examining some of the darkest days of the modern presidency through the prism of the Watergate, Iran-Contra, and the Clinton Impeachment scandals. These scandals have had a major impact in shaping the power and perceptions of the office of the presidency. As these case studies make clear, the character of a president is equally as important as his vision and determination.

Finally, as you read these case studies, we remember the words of the late David M. Abshire, who led the Center for the Study of the Presidency & Congress from 1999 to 2012. In 2000, in the introduction of the original *Triumphs and Tragedies of the Modern Presidency*, addressed to the president-elect, Dr. Abshire wrote:

> By reading this, a President can be fortified for the long look forward by better understanding the long view backward. This vantage may help nourish the character, wisdom, and vision we associate with Washington, Adams, Jefferson, Lincoln, the Roosevelts, and Truman—all readers of history. These lessons will be different and surely more valuable than the advice of pollsters and spin masters or the evening news.

David Abshire's vision of how the lessons of history can be applied to the challenges of today and shape a more hopeful future inspires us to continue the Triumphs and Tragedies series.

Maxmillian Angerholzer III, James Kitfield,
Norman Ornstein, and Stephen Skowronek

SECTION I

The Modern Presidency

1. The Constitution and Presidential Prerogative

by Richard M. Pious

The Framers left an ambiguous legacy: James Madison wanted checks and balances and enumerated powers that would define and confine executive power; Alexander Hamilton wanted vague general terms that would permit the exercise of presidential prerogative. Madison influenced the draft of the Committee on Detail that provided for separated institutions and checks and balances, but Hamilton's allies controlled the Committee on Style that drafted the final version of the Constitution. Article II can be read through a strict Madisonian or loose Hamiltonian interpretation, but no reading provides a clear blueprint for presidential powers: there are silences (no mention of a removal power or abrogation of treaties), ambiguities and generalities (what is "The Executive Power," and is the commander in chief clause a grant of power or just a title?), and incomplete constructions (there is a presidency but no executive branch, a Supreme Court but no explicit power of judicial review and no lower courts).

The power of prerogative is seen in unilateral actions taken within a governing institution based on constitutional powers (or claims of sovereign and emergency powers not mentioned in the Constitution). Three questions are raised by its use: what are the circumstances under which prerogative power is exercised? How do presidents attempt to legitimize their exercise of prerogatives? What are the possible outcomes?

EXPANDING PRESIDENTIAL PREROGATIVE

The exercise of presidential prerogative was limited through most of the 19th century, as a "Whig" interpretation of the Constitution dominated: Congress was the first branch not only typographically in the Constitution but also politically: it was expected to make policy by legislating, with only the most limited role for the president. There were exceptions: George Washington's Neutrality Proclamation led not only to a political crisis but also to a constitutional debate, with Hamilton defending the prerogative and claiming that all powers (including those granted in international law to every sovereign nation) not specifically assigned to Congress or courts belonged to the president; and Madison asserting that neutrality and all other powers not mentioned in the Constitution belonged to the legislature. President Thomas Jefferson claimed the power to negotiate a treaty to purchase Louisiana, even though the Constitution makes no mention of acquisition of territory; Andrew Jackson asserted a right to veto legislation on policy grounds, and claimed that as a "coordinate branch" of government his interpretation of the constitutionality of laws was not bound by prior court cases; he also claimed a power to remove officials in his administration, although a removal power was never mentioned in the Constitution.

The most significant early assertions of presidential prerogative came from Abraham Lincoln at the start of the Civil War: he claimed the power to conduct hostilities without a declaration of war from Congress; to expand the Army and Navy without statutory authorization; to expend funds to secure secession of western Virginia counties; to suspend the privilege of the writ of habeas corpus without congressional authorization; and to emancipate the slaves in secessionist territory (once freed by the Union armies) without statutory authorization.

Still, uses of presidential prerogative—to gain territory, to destroy national financial institutions and return fiscal power to states, and to secure the Union—were exceptions and did not become institutionalized. Jacksonian assertions were repudiated by the Whigs, for instance, and not defended by the Democrats, especially the removal powers, which were limited by congressional Tenure of Office Acts. In the aftermath of the Civil War, a system of "Congressional government" established on Whig lines was reinstated by the Republican Party, and its jurisprudence distinguished between the powers of "the State" in internal security, diplomacy, and war (in which presidential prerogatives exercised by Lincoln would be upheld) and the powers of a limited "government," which were restricted through court decisions involving the commerce clause and substantive due process.

All this changed at the end of the 19th century with the Spanish-American War. President William McKinley's victory in gaining Senate consent to the Treaty of Paris (which presaged an American empire) over the opposition of some congressional leaders ended a three-decade-long effort to import a quasi-parliamentary system to America and convert the presidency into largely a figurehead position.

Subsequently the presidencies of Theodore Roosevelt, Woodrow Wilson, and Franklin Roosevelt reversed the original constitutional understandings: it was now the presidency in the lead (proposing vast domestic programs) and superior (especially in international affairs), instead of Congress. The "modern presidency," equipped after 1939 with vast institutional resources (the White House Office and the Executive Office of the President), made successful claims of prerogative powers in domestic affairs—by asserting that there was an executive branch and that the president headed it—and by claiming inherent powers as "sole organ" in the making of foreign policy. Congress, in this concept of the modern presidency, was reduced to a reactive and supportive role, relying on checks and balances to assert its own parochial interests, but not interfering in grand presidential plans.

The relationship changed again in the aftermath of the Vietnam War. Lyndon Johnson's Vietnam escalation, founded on the questionable foundation of Congress's 1964 Gulf of Tonkin resolution, ultimately resulted in a military defeat. The Nixon Administration's Paris Peace Accords were followed by the final collapse of the American position throughout Indo-China in 1975. The conflict between a resurgent Democratic-controlled Congress and President Richard Nixon ended with his resignation and with Congress determined to wrest back powers ceded to the executive branch in the post–World War II era.

The presidencies of Gerald Ford and Jimmy Carter in the 1970s were thus supposed to produce a "postmodern" presidency in which presidential prerogative was constrained through "inter-branch policy co-determination." At least that was the view of a majority in Congress.

Contrary to the common interpretation of Article I, the "necessary and proper clause" was seen as not only allowing Congress to pass laws extending its own powers, but also to legislate on "all other Powers vested by this Constitution in the Government of the United States or in any Department or Officer thereof."

According to this interpretation of the Constitution, Congress could therefore legislate on "The Executive Power" of the president. By passing "framework laws," presidential impoundments were to be replaced by congressionally approved rescissions and deferrals. Rather than presidents having the nearly unilateral power to launch hostilities, Congress put in place a system in which specific authorization for hostilities would have to be obtained within sixty days and in which Congress at any time could order a withdrawal of forces to be completed within thirty days. Covert intelligence operations would also have to be reported to Congress through a system of presidential findings. Congress also passed provisions in hundreds of laws requiring the president to report and wait, to ask for judicial warrant or congressional committee clearance, or to submit to a deadline for congressional concurrence and authorization or else face a legislative veto (this last mechanism was found unconstitutional by the Supreme Court in 1983).

Sometimes presidents favor framework laws, because Congress may thereby be willing to delegate more power to the president. Such was the case with the

Lend-Lease Act of 1941; with presidential reorganization powers in the 1960s; and with deals to sell nuclear technology in the 2000s. But often presidents attack the constitutionality of such legislation, as Nixon did with his veto (overridden) of the War Powers Resolution (WPR) described earlier. They avoid compliance or interpret provisions narrowly—the tack taken by presidents from Ford through George W. Bush with the WPR, and by President Reagan with the Intelligence Oversight Act of 1980.

Alternatively presidents may claim a "soft" prerogative: they do not concede the constitutional validity of framework mechanisms, but they seemingly adhere to their provisions, even as they reserve their prerogative to act unilaterally. President Reagan signed the Beirut Resolution, for instance, which Congress had passed to authorize the continued presence of peacekeeping troops in Lebanon after they had come under fire. Supposedly this was acknowledgment of the constitutionality of the WPR—yet at the signing ceremony the White House distributed a "signing statement" indicating that the White House did not believe that provisions of the law could interfere with his powers as commander in chief in making decisions about deploying forces in Lebanon. Presidents can also provide Congress with intelligence information weighted toward their favored position, as George W. Bush arguably did when his administration exaggerated the threat from weapons of mass destruction supposedly in Iraq, and the links between Saddam Hussein's Baathist regime and al-Qaeda before the Iraq War of 2003. Or presidents may simply ignore their obligations to keep Congress informed, as happened when Ronald Reagan secretly authorized arms sales to Iran. The point is that framework legislation and related informal understandings between executive branch officials and congressional committees have failed to create the intended "interbranch policy co-determination." Nor have they prevented presidents from substituting their own prerogative power for statutory authorizations.

And so the pendulum has swung for more than two centuries as presidents and Congresses have wrestled for power: from the 19th-century "Whig" presidency of limited powers; to a 20th-century "modern presidency" closer to Hamilton's model; to an "imperial presidency" of prerogative governance that collapsed in the aftermath of the Vietnam War and Watergate; and on to a postmodern late 20th-century pattern of governance emphasizing collaboration through framework laws.

A STATE WITHIN A STATE

During the 1980s Iran-Contra Affair and later during the post-9/11 Global War on Terrorism, presidents went so far as to use prerogative power to

create their own governing institutions and substitute them for those created
by law. Ironically it was Madison (proponent of strict enumeration of executive power) who opened the way for this tactic. In *Federalist No. 47*, he
observed that if a *complete* separation of power were achieved, the institution
assigned all legislative power would be so powerful it would suck the other
institutions into the "legislative vortex." Madison's way of preventing this
was through a *partial* separation, in which some powers would overlap and
some would blend. The Constitution assigned "the judicial power" to a
Supreme Court, for instance, but Congress has a power of subpoena, it
can hold witnesses at hearings in contempt, and it conducts impeachments
as a trial. The president has a power to issue reprieves and pardons for offenses against the United States, and can issue executive orders, executive
agreements, military orders and proclamations, departmental memoranda
and Office of Management and Budget directives as a substitute for actual
laws (although what weight they are given is ultimately determined by the
judiciary).

Partial separation has allowed presidents to legitimize claims of concurrent
powers, and to counterclaims that they are confined to exercising solely executive powers and statutes. They use concurrent powers to circumvent
Congress and the Courts, on the basis of their commander-in-chief powers,
their claims of inherent and implied executive powers, and their oath of
office. When taken to its extreme, the result is not merely a "unitary executive" in which all executive powers are exercised by the president and his
subordinates, but rather creation of a "state within the state," in which the
executive also exercises legislative and judicial powers sufficient to control
policy without the possibility of effective checks and balances—a system of
parallel governance.

Presidents can also exercise prerogative power to subvert the intent of
Congress through signing statements, as George W. Bush did when he signaled he would enforce a provision in an appropriations measure regarding
background checks of Homeland Security Department officials "in a manner
consistent with the President's constitutional authority to supervise the unitary executive branch."[1] Such a signing statement may assert a dispensing
power if presidents decide not to enforce a provision of law, as President Bush
did when he indicated he would disregard a requirement that the director of
the Federal Emergency Management Agency have five years of experience in
emergency management and homeland security. Presidents have also bypassed
the congressional power of the purse, as Reagan did in the Iran-Contra affair
through Colonel Oliver North's secret arms-for-hostages "enterprise," self-
funded through receipts from arms sales and solicitations to private citizens

and foreign governments (see the essay "Iran-Contra: Saving Reagan's Presidency," Section V, this volume). They have bypassed the declaration of war clause by relying instead on congressional resolutions of support, United Nations resolutions, NATO resolutions, congressional authorizations, and treaty provisions—relying on whatever is at hand, as President Clinton did twice in using military force in the Balkans. They have bypassed military courts-martial established by Congress, as President George W. Bush did through a military order establishing military tribunals with far fewer due process guarantees.

"SOFT" PREROGATIVE

Political scientists distinguish between a claim of "hard" and "soft" prerogative. Presidents rely on "soft" prerogative when they act unilaterally to resolve an issue but later claim that they acted under color of law. They may use delegated powers in ways inconsistent with congressional intent. They may claim that prerogative and law allow them to interpret expansively narrowly drawn delegations of power. They may claim the president has the prerogative to enforce the "mass of legislation" such that he is carrying out congressional intent, even where no specific statutory provision can be found.

Such claims were made by President Grover Cleveland after he put down the Pullman strike, by President Harry Truman after he seized steel mills during the Korean War, and by President Richard Nixon when he impounded funds. A related argument holds that there is a "peace of the United States" that the president is bound to enforce: presidents combine commander-in-chief powers and statutes to claim that they possess quasi-judicial enforcement powers involving strikes, civil insurrection, alleged subversive activities and terrorism and to conduct surveillance without judicial warrant. Presidents claim to be able, in national emergencies, to exercise powers that go beyond or contravene statute law.

Executive power, when combined with a statute, may even permit a president to take action that is not authorized in advance by the law but that involves subsequent "joint concord" of the executive and Congress. The Supreme Court held in *Hirabayashi v. U.S.* that an executive order followed by congressional authorization would constitute such joint concord. Lower federal courts have used the doctrine since the 1970s to uphold presidential war making absent a declaration of war and absent specific congressional authorization. And presidents rely on a combination of "executive power" and the "take care" clause to claim discretion in the exercise of law—what is known in formal terms as the "dispensing power." President Barack Obama unilaterally determined which undocumented aliens would be subject to deportation and which would not, based on the argument that Congress had not provided him with the resources to fully implement its statutes, thus providing him with discretion in implementation. He used that discretion by directing the Department of Homeland Security to issue a departmental memorandum on which categories of undocumented aliens would not face deportation.

FRONTLASH, BACKLASH, AND OVERSHOOT

Presidents must simultaneously defend the wisdom of their policy and thus preserve their authority, as well as the constitutionality and legality of their actions, thus preserving their legitimacy. When their authority is preserved, their legitimacy is not at risk. When their authority is successfully questioned, however, the legitimacy of their actions will be questioned as well.

There are generally three outcomes that flow from a prerogative governance. If the policy works, there will often be a "frontlash" effect. Success quiets the critics and enables the president to retain support of party and public. His own party unites while the opposition splits. Congress passes laws "perfecting" the president's initiatives: broad delegations, supportive resolutions, retrospective authority and funding, subsequent authorization, and immunity or indemnification of officials if there were a question of the legality of their actions. Presidents gain both political strength and an expansion of their powers through this kind of precedent. The institutional self-confidence of the executive branch tends to increase in such cases, while that of Congress decreases.

Backlash tends to occur when the presidential initiative succeeds, but at a high cost, or when the policy fails altogether. Attacks on a presidential policy lead critics to attack the associated prerogatives. The president's party becomes dispirited and divided, while the opposition is emboldened. There may be investigations and tough oversight, Congress may follow on with framework legislation that promotes inter-branch policy collaboration. It may pass obstructive or prohibitory legislation, funding cutoffs or conditions, or make cuts. It may pass resolutions condemning the presidential action. It may require additional reporting and consultation for future decisions. It may take reprisals, such as holding up nominations, failing to pass unrelated legislation, or holding up reorganization plans until they are modified to suit congressional interests. Courts may resuscitate the doctrine of separation of powers and find presidential transgressions. Private parties may sue for damages on the grounds that presidents and their subordinates did not act according to

law. Prosecutions of presidential agents may result, involving the original offense or cover-ups. The precedent becomes not the exercise of power, but
the check against it. The president's exercise of prerogative, if failed, affects his
reputation in the Washington community, his public standing, and consequently limits his options and weakens his leadership.

At times, presidential assertions of prerogative so overshoot the accepted
bounds of legality and constitutionality that a crisis of legitimacy ensues, and
the policy in question collapses. The impeachment of Andrew Johnson over
the removal power; the resignation of Richard Nixon over the Watergate
cover-up; and the paralysis in the latter stages of the Reagan Administration
over the Iran-Contra Affair represent examples of presidential assertions of
prerogative that led to a crisis of legitimacy and subsequent collapse. The
president loses the battle for public opinion and some of his party deserts
him. High-ranking officials are investigated by Congress and grand juries for
criminal offenses. The president and his top aides are distracted with the investigations, there is turnover in the ranks, and eventually the president seeks
resignations of top officials and replaces them with others who have the confidence of Congress. This occurred in the aftermath of the Watergate and
Iran-Contra affairs, in effect creating for a time a quasi-parliamentary system.
During these scandals there is a sharp drop in presidential approval ratings,
which is accompanied by a similar drop in approval scores on administration-
sponsored legislation. Impeachment may occur as happened with Andrew
Johnson or Bill Clinton (whose transgressions were mostly personal but did
involve charges of perjury), or to forestall them, the president may resign, as
Nixon did (see the essays on Watergate and the Lewinsky Scandal in Section
V, this volume).

IT'S MY PREROGATIVE

History suggests that presidents should invoke prerogative powers with caution. Prerogative governance should be instituted only in the national interest and when national security is at risk, for instance, and not for partisan
or personal advantage. It should never be used against legitimate political
opponents. Presidents take a huge risk if their lawyers argue that emergency
powers are unlimited (or that the emergency defines the scope of the power),
or that the courts do not have jurisdiction. Judges tend to take a dim view
of such assertions of prerogative power. Certain decisions and actions may
need to be kept secret, but it will usually go badly for the White House if it
keeps these secrets from congressional committees authorized to conduct
oversight. Parallel governance may seem to provide the advantage of unity,

secrecy, and dispatch, but its use is likely to delegitimize the administration, because the idea of separation of powers and checks and balances is hard-wired into the American political culture. There are also lessons to be drawn from framework legislation, usually designed by Congress to rein in presidential excess and in response to presidential fiascos, and those who do not learn the lessons are destined to repeat the fiascos.

Perhaps the most important lesson is that the key to defending prerogative governance and preserving presidential authority is to *get the policy right*. To the extent that prerogative governance is tempting because it will enable the White House to avoid explaining and justifying its policies to Congress, the courts, and the public, it is a temptation that is best resisted by presidents and those who advise them. Presidents must institute decision processes that lead to good decisions. Good decisions in turn lead to successful policies that by definition can be defended before public opinion, congressional committees, and, if necessary, in court. The successful defense of a decision, in turn, leads to a successful defense of the prerogatives necessary to implement it. That is what defines the great presidents, all of whom did not hesitate to rely on their prerogative powers to implement policies of supreme national interest.

◆ ◆ ◆ ◆ ◆

2. White House Rules: The Post–World War II Presidency

by James P. Pfiffner

When the Framers of the Constitution met in Philadelphia in 1787 to draft the Constitution, they faced a dilemma: how to provide for an effective national government in a polity that feared concentrated power. One of the main reasons they called the Constitutional Convention was the scant attention to the executive function in the Articles of Confederation. But they had also chaffed at what they saw as the tyranny of King George III and were thus distrustful of power in the executive. After the Revolution the thirteen states had weak executives, and the state legislatures often abused their powers. So the Framers attempted to create an executive that was strong enough to be effective, but not so strong as to abuse powers. They made the executive independent of Congress, but guarded against tyranny by balancing presidential power with congressional and judicial authority. In creating a separation of powers system, they clearly rejected the "king in Parliament" structure of British government.

In the 19th century, Congress dominated national policy making except in times of war. But in the 20th century, presidents became much more assertive in both domestic and national security policy making. The New Deal had expanded the scope of the federal government, and over ensuing decades, Congress delegated considerable discretion to the executive branch in general, and to the president in particular. The Executive Office of the President was first created in 1939 to help the president manage this vastly enlarged executive branch. World War II further extended the role of the federal government in the economy and thrust the United States into a leadership role in world affairs that expanded the powers the commander in chief wielded over national security policy.

When President Eisenhower came to office in 1953, he did not plan to pursue an active domestic policy agenda; yet after 20 years of activist presidents, members of Congress expected that the president would have some policy agenda, albeit not of the same scope as Roosevelt and Truman. Thus, Eisenhower created the Office of Legislative Liaison in the White House, which has played an increasingly important role ever since. In the end, Eisenhower in fact did pursue many major domestic initiatives, including the federal highway system and the National Defense Education Act. In effect, he institutionalized the activist presidency.

POWER IN THE MODERN PRESIDENCY

Presidential power was increased substantially by the initiatives of several presidents to improve White House capacity in policy development, at the expense of the departments and agencies of the executive branch. Presidents Kennedy and Johnson began to centralize policy control in the White House. President Nixon institutionalized that control with the creation of the domestic policy staff and the expansion of the National Security Council staff. The new Office of Management and Budget (reorganized from the existing Bureau of the Budget in 1970) would control budget and managerial issues. These presidential units drew control of policy into the White House by giving the president the staff resources to develop policy without having to depend on the departments and agencies of the executive branch for information, analysis, and advice.

The increased size and capacity of the White House staff undercut the role of cabinet secretaries as the primary policy advisers to the president. Despite attempts by Presidents Ford and Carter to restore the traditional role of the cabinet, they too came to the conclusion that to ensure presidential direction of government policy, they needed personal control of policy development in the White House. No president since Nixon has significantly reduced the role of the White House staff vis-à-vis the rest of the executive branch. This new presidential capacity gave presidents more control of policy, but also enabled White House staffers to undertake dubious activities, as seen through the Watergate scandal and the Iran-Contra Affair.

In addition to their formal constitutional authority, presidents can wield a number of unilateral powers in making policy and directing the executive branch. They can issue executive orders, executive agreements, and proclamations, for instance, as long as these unilateral actions do not conflict with their constitutional duty to faithfully execute the laws.

In national security policy presidential power also increased dramatically with the emergence of the Cold War. Plans had to be made for possible war with the Soviet Union, with the knowledge that diplomatic clashes could lead to nuclear war. Rapid response was at a premium in the nuclear age, and the president was the one national leader who had the capacity to act quickly. A vast national security apparatus thus developed to meet the needs of the Cold War.

President Truman's decision in June 1950 to engage U.S. troops in a "police action" in Korea without calling on Congress for its consent created an important constitutional precedent; despite several significant conflicts since then, Congress has not formally declared war since World War II. Congress did acquiesce in sending U.S. troops into battle on numerous occasions, however, including with the Gulf of Tonkin Resolution in 1964, the Persian Gulf War authorization of 1991, and Authorizations for the Use of Military Force against al-Qaeda in 2001 and in Iraq in 2002.

In 1973, Congress asserted itself and tried to rein in the president's war-making powers. Enraged by what many members saw as a deliberate attempt to mislead them into supporting the Gulf of Tonkin Resolution to justify an expansion of American involvement in Vietnam and by President Nixon's secret bombing in Cambodia, Congress enacted the War Powers Resolution (overriding President Nixon's veto). This act sought to provide for presidential consultation with Congress and to limit unilateral deployments to sixty days. If at the end of that time period Congress had not passed an authorization for war, the president was to withdraw the troops (with a thirty-day extension if necessary for an orderly withdrawal).

Although presidents since then have notified Congress "consistent with" (rather than "pursuant to") the WPR when deploying U.S. troops, no president has accepted the constitutionality of the War Powers Resolution, and

Congress has yet to actually force a president to withdraw troops under the Resolution. Congress also passed several other laws intended to hold the "imperial presidency" in check, to include the Freedom of Information Act; the Case Act (requiring the president to report executive agreements to the Senate); the Hughes-Ryan Amendment (requiring a formal presidential "finding" for the authorization of covert activities); and the Foreign Intelligence Surveillance Act (requiring warrants for domestic surveillance).

Despite undertaking a more active role in domestic policy making, presidents have not been as successful in convincing Congress to cede power on that front. Since the New Deal, presidents have often had active domestic policy agendas, but even when they get Congress to address those proposals, they are often unsuccessful in winning congressional approval. A few presidents enjoyed impressive successes with Congress in their first years in office: Franklin Roosevelt's famous "Hundred Days," President Johnson's Great Society initiatives, and President Reagan's initial policy agenda all stand out; but even these successful presidents suffered decreasing legislative success after their first years, and other presidents have had mixed success in compelling Congress to pass their respective legislative agendas.

9/11 INCREASED PRESIDENTIAL POWER

The partisan and ideological polarization of Congress intensified in the last decades of the 20th century, and along with divided government, that has hampered presidential leadership of Congress, particularly in the George W. Bush and Barack Obama Administrations.

In the national security policy arena, however, presidential power has continued to increase, particularly since the terrorist attacks of 2001. At the end of the Cold War, George H.W. Bush and Bill Clinton used their executive powers fully and asserted the authority of the president to take military action without consulting Congress. Still, neither president fundamentally challenged congressional constitutional powers in unusual ways.

In the 21st century, however, President George W. Bush began to assert executive power in unprecedented ways. At the beginning of his administration, he and Vice President Dick Cheney felt that previous presidents had let Congress impinge on constitutional executive prerogatives, and that presidential powers had to be reasserted. The attacks of 9/11 provided the opportunity for them to greatly enhance presidential power through national security.

On several fronts, President Bush took direct action secretly and without seeking congressional approval. He created military commissions in his military order of November 13, 2001; authorized the National Security Agency to monitor the communications of Americans, without complying with the Foreign Intelligence Surveillance Act; approved the use of "enhanced interrogation techniques," some of which amounted to torture, in violation of U.S. law and the Geneva Conventions; and issued signing statements that asserted the authority not to execute more than 1,000 provisions of laws that he signed, more than all other previous presidents combined.

Several Supreme Court decisions reversed Bush's actions on military commissions and the suspension of the Geneva Convention treaties. But Congress later passed laws that backed the surveillance programs of the National Security Agency. President Bush also used the state secrets privilege to stop litigation challenging some of his actions in office, such as renditions of terrorism suspects to be interrogated in foreign countries.

Presidential candidate Barack Obama criticized some of President Bush's uses of executive power as abuses, and shortly after taking office, President Obama issued executive orders forbidding the CIA from using any interrogation techniques not included in the U.S. Army field manual on interrogation, which all complied with the Geneva Conventions. He also ordered any remaining secret prisons in foreign countries closed.

On the other hand, Obama continued many of President Bush's national security programs. He still confronted the fact that a number of detainees remained at Guantanamo Bay, Cuba, who could not be released. Some had to await trial on charges of war crimes. But some of those detainees had been subject to torture (or evidence against them had been obtained through coercion) and thus could not be prosecuted. Since some of these detainees, if they were released, would pose threats to Americans, Obama decided that they would be detained indefinitely without trial.

Although Obama issued many fewer signing statements than President Bush, he still used some of them to claim that he did not need to comply with provisions in some laws. He continued forcefully to use the state secrets privilege to stop litigation that challenged Bush Administration practices on interrogation and extraordinary rendition.

With respect to the National Security Agency's surveillance of Americans, Congress had made changes to laws that legally authorized the programs President Bush conducted. President Obama supported those changes and continued the programs, despite constitutional objections to some of them (particularly gathering bulk metadata on Americans' communications without warrants). President Obama also sharply increased the use of armed drone strikes in Pakistan and several other countries to attack terrorist targets, including several American citizens. Despite Justice Department legal justifications, critics argued that the drone strikes were illegal extra judicial killings.

In 2014, President Obama sent U.S. forces to attack the Islamic State in Iraq and Syria (ISIS) and sent American troops as advisers to the Iraq government, which was trying to defend itself from ISIS. Rather than asking Congress for authorization, he relied on the Authorization to Use Military Force (AUMF) of 2001, even though its direct relevance was questionable.

In summary, since World War II, presidential power has continued to increase in the national security arena, particularly since 9/11. Like Republicans before him, President Obama's actions once in office demonstrated that increasing executive power is not a partisan issue. The Framers of the Constitution were right: executives naturally tend to accumulate power.

Executive assertions of power are understandable; they want to fulfill campaign promises and achieve policy goals within a system that consciously limits executive power. Polarization in Congress has often thwarted attempts to address important policy issues, making unilateral executive actions tempting to presidents. But the Framers of the Constitution understood this and created a separation of powers system designed to limit such power. The Framers expected that Congress would act to protect its own constitutional power, but they did not foresee the development of strong political parties and particularly the partisan polarization of politics. Thus, congressional abdication of its own prerogatives has aided and abetted presidential assertions of power.

Precedents set in the Bush and Obama presidencies have created more leeway for subsequent presidents to assert the same powers, and if history is any guide, to stretch them to suit their own purposes. The Framers of the Constitution would not recognize the institutional presidency as it exists today; they would be surprised by the extent of contemporary presidential power; and they would be disappointed by the political paralysis that sometimes results from polarized parties in Congress. Nevertheless, they would recognize the dynamic tension that continues to define American politics, an inevitable result of the separation of powers system they designed.

◆ ◆ ◆ ◆ ◆

3. The 21st-Century Imperial Presidency

by Andrew C. Rudalevige

The "imperial presidency" entered the political lexicon with Arthur M. Schlesinger, Jr.'s 1973 book of that name and came back into fashion thirty years later. One editorial even upgraded the 2007 Bush White House to "The Imperial Presidency 2.0."[1] The idea, hardly new, is to evoke executive excess, as a way to suggest not the literal reincarnation of Nero or Caligula, but rather an empire's annexations over porous borders. The borders in this case are between the branches of government, and the annexation is of another branch's authority. As such the "imperial presidency" implies a usurpation of authorities and responsibilities by the executive branch that, in the American system of government, are rightly shared. In that sense the idea of an "imperial presidency" is as potent today as ever.

Although presidential overreach is hardly limited to foreign affairs, nowhere has it been more pronounced in modern times than in what Schlesinger refers to as the "rise of presidential war," often conducted in secret and free of congressional authorization.[2] "Exhibit A" are the years after the terrorist mass murders of September 11, 2001, which reinvigorated executive claims to expansive authority that were made by two very different presidents. Their successors, building on today's precedents, will find ample opportunity for their own imperial overreach. It's worth stressing, however, that an imperial presidency requires an invisible Congress.

A PAGE OF HISTORY

The Framers worried a good deal about executive power, and the war powers were thought particularly problematic. No one doubted the president's authority to defend the country against sudden attack, nor the need for a unified chain of command in wartime. But as James Madison summarized, "the constitution supposes, what the history of all governments demonstrates, that the executive is the branch of power most interested in war and prone to it. It has accordingly with studied care, vested the question of war in the Legislature."[3] Congress was given the power to declare war, and thus to activate the forces the president would direct as commander in chief; to raise and regulate fleets and armies; to make rules regarding the conduct of warfare and the use of the militia; to ratify treaties; and even to govern foreign trade.[4]

That was the idea, but as Supreme Court Justice Oliver Wendell Holmes, Jr., once observed, "a page of history is worth a volume of logic."[5] In practice, enough was left vague—notably in the vesting of an undefined "executive power" in the president—that presidents quickly proved skilled at interpreting constitutional ambiguity in their own favor. The huge growth in governmental capacity over time, cemented by the expansive national security apparatus built up during and after World War II in particular, tended to empower the executive branch. If nothing else, the large, standing army and vast arsenal of nuclear weaponry maintained during the Cold War meant that presidents always have forces ready to command.[6] The unitary structure of the executive branch, as Hamilton recognized in the *Federalist*, also has strong advantages over the collective decision making of the legislature, especially when it comes to foreign policy.[7] And for its part, Congress, especially after its embarrassing isolationism in the 1930s, was happy to delegate discretion to the presidency. Harry Truman never sought its approval to prosecute the Korean War, while a series of "blank check" resolutions authorizing presidents to respond to world events culminated in the 1964 Gulf of Tonkin Resolution—and 58,000 American war deaths in Vietnam.

Vietnam and Watergate finally prompted a legislative backlash that sought to rein in presidential autonomy.[8] For instance, intelligence oversight acts sought to ensure consultation with Congress when presidents planned covert action. The 1978 Foreign Intelligence Surveillance Act (FISA) required the intelligence community to obtain judicial approval for its efforts within the United States. And the War Powers Resolution (WPR) aimed to constrain the unilateral use of force by presidents. Presidents were given authority to introduce U.S. troops into ongoing or imminent "hostilities" only under a specific legislative authorization, or in "a national emergency created by attack upon the United States . . . or its armed forces." Deploying troops or using force would also trigger a "clock" that would require the troops be removed by a fixed deadline unless Congress had agreed to a longer deployment.

Today's imperial presidency is defined by the reaction to—and the crumbling of—that "resurgence regime." Over the next two decades, presidents pushed back against the constraints described in the WPR and met surprisingly little resistance. Only once, in 1975, was the WPR even invoked by a president. At best, presidents reported their actions (in Iran, Grenada, Panama, etc.) "consistent with" the WPR but not admitting its constraining authority. Indeed, one critic termed Bill Clinton's military intervention in the Balkans in 1999 "one of the most flagrant acts of usurpation of the war power in the history of the republic."[9]

TODAY'S IMPERIAL PRESIDENCY

The September 11 attacks put a brutal exclamation point on this evolution. Within days of the attacks, Congress passed a sweeping Authorization for the Use of Military Force (AUMF) giving the president the power to identify the attacks' perpetrators and to take action to punish them and to forestall their future actions. The Bush Administration pushed further, asserting that the boundaries of what it called the president's "zone of autonomy" would be determined by the president himself. The administration's Office of Legal Counsel (OLC) said the AUMF was nice, but not necessary:

> It is clear that Congress's power to declare war does not constrain the President's independent and plenary constitutional authority over the use of military force. . . . [W]e think it beyond question that the President has the plenary constitutional power to take such military actions as he deems necessary and appropriate. . . . Force can be used both to retaliate for those attacks, and to prevent and deter future assaults on the Nation.

Indeed, in contrast to the AUMF, the OLC argued that "military actions need not be limited to those . . . that participated in the attacks on the World Trade Center and the Pentagon."[10] And President Bush, in short order, unilaterally approved a wiretapping program that bypassed the warrant requirements of FISA; designated and detained hundreds of "unlawful enemy combatants," including American citizens arrested within the United States; issued orders limiting the applicability of the Geneva Conventions and setting up a system of military tribunals; and approved interrogation techniques that many thought constituted torture and were thus prohibited both by treaty obligation and U.S. law. Much of this was kept secret at the time.[11] In each case, the action was justified as flowing from battlefield exigency—only the battlefield now was literally everywhere—and executive power itself.

In another advance, the administration declared that Congress's constraining actions might even be unconstitutional: "in order to respect the President's inherent constitutional authority to manage a military campaign," one report proclaimed, "[the laws against torture] as well as any other potentially applicable statute must be construed as inapplicable to interrogations undertaken pursuant to his Commander-in-Chief authority."[12] Thus, when Congress passed an amendment banning torture in the course of such interrogations, President Bush said the administration would enforce the law only to the extent it was "consistent with the constitutional authority of the President to oversee the unitary executive branch and as Commander in Chief."[13]

Eight years later, Barack Obama pledged a new approach, rejecting Bush's very expansive "executive power" rationale. In May 2009, Obama said that his predecessor had "established an ad hoc legal approach for fighting terrorism that was neither effective nor sustainable"[14] and pledged to act instead only in accordance with specific constitutional and statutory authority.

And yet, despite some important early reversals,[15] the Obama Administration wound up making many of the same claims of autonomy, suggesting the "imperial" boundaries had hardened and that where you stood on the issue of executive authority depended very much on whether you sat in the Oval Office. How did this occur?

A COMPLIANT CONGRESS

First, over time Congress had blessed many things President Bush had claimed to be able to do by himself. The PATRIOT Act (2001); the Military Commissions Act (2006); the "Protect America Act" (2007); the FISA Amendments Act (2008)—all these gave the president enhanced and sometimes amorphous powers over national security. The scope of the surveillance allowed by the PATRIOT Act and the FISA Amendments, for example, became clear when whistle-blower Edward Snowden released a cache of National Security Agency documents starting in 2013.

Another legislative workhorse also helped: the 2001 AUMF described earlier. Combined with a broad interpretation of the laws of war, Obama wound up using that AUMF as authority to act against targets only tangentially related to 9/11 itself. This justified, for instance, the use of unmanned drones carrying out military operations in far-flung countries such as Yemen and Somalia. And in 2014 the administration argued that attacks against the terrorist group calling itself the Islamic State of Iraq and the Levant (ISIL) had also been authorized by the AUMF—even though ISIL had broken away from, and was even repudiated by, al-Qaeda. This argument had potentially unlimited reach: how many degrees of separation would it permit from al-Qaeda and the original terrorist architects of 9/11?[16]

Indeed, the administration was quite willing to interpret extant statutes in creative ways. In November 2011, for instance, drones targeted and killed at least two American citizens in Yemen. The attorney general, claiming that "the Constitution guarantees due process, not judicial process," argued that a criminal trial was unnecessary.[17] Instead, the administration renewed broad claims about the unbounded geographic scope of the war on terror and defined "imminence" (as in imminent threat) more or less out of existence.

Another instance of sustained institutional aggrandizement is found in the prisoner swap that freed American soldier Bowe Bergdahl in exchange for several Taliban prisoners held at Guantanamo Bay. The 2014 defense authorization act that President Obama signed into law had required thirty-day notification to Congress in advance of a transfer of such detainees. The administration did not notify Congress. It decided instead that legislators "did not intend" to bar such action: "the notification requirement should be construed not to apply to this unique set of circumstances" because it would "interfere" with "functions that the Constitution assigns to the president."[18] The difference between this and a claim of presidential over congressional prerogative was hard to distinguish.

A third example came with the 2011 operation in Libya, where the United States and the NATO alliance sought first to protect refugees against dictator Muammar Gaddafi, and then to protect militias seeking to overthrow him. Obama first invoked Article II, noting he was acting "pursuant to my constitutional authority to conduct U.S. foreign relations and as Commander in Chief and Chief Executive." This notification, he said, was "consistent with" the WPR. But as the WPR "clock" ticked, the administration changed course: it argued that the law did not apply here at all because the engagement did not constitute "hostilities," never mind that U.S. war planes were dropping real bombs, and real people were being killed. That term "hostilities," the president stressed, was meant for the next Vietnam: "half-a-million soldiers . . ., tens of thousands of lives lost, hundreds of billions of dollars spent."[19]

This rewriting of the WPR was blatant, but presidents had long skirted the WPR in what they considered "police" actions (for instance, when Ronald Reagan authorized "imminent danger" pay for sailors in the Persian Gulf but denied there were "imminent hostilities" that would invoke the WPR). It has taken a large-scale contemplated intervention, as in the 1991 and 2003 wars with Iraq, to persuade presidents to seek advance authorization for the use of force. Even in those cases they did not admit the *need* for such approval. As George H.W. Bush said, "I didn't have to get permission from some old goat in Congress to kick Saddam Hussein out of Kuwait."[20]

Typically, modern presidents invoke one of two broad conditions as justifying the unilateral use of force: a grounding in self-defense or in an international endorsement that justifies the action. In the first, presidents rely on the WPR's permission to use force without specific authorization in an "attack upon the United States." Some of these cases are clear, as with the (failed) rescue attempt of the American hostages in Iran in 1980 or the 1998 missile strikes retaliating for the bombing of U.S. embassies in Africa. In others, presidents have been more creative. The 1989 invasion of Panama was explained by President Bush as a response to "an imminent danger to the 35,000 American citizens" there.[21] In 1983, President Reagan justified the Grenada operation likewise: "American lives are at stake."[22]

The blessing of the international community, often on humanitarian grounds, can also be invoked. In Grenada, Reagan stressed that its neighbors had invited the United States to respond and that "this collective action has been forced on us by events that have . . . no place in any civilized society." Likewise in Somalia (1992), Kosovo (1999), and even in Obama's Libyan and anti-ISIL operations, presidents cited both humanitarian concerns and treaty obligations, normally to the United Nations or NATO. The WPR specifically says such obligations do not bypass the need for congressional action. Nonetheless, they muddy the legal waters.

In Syria in 2013, President Obama publicly stated his intent to ask Congress to authorize the use of force against the Syrian regime for using chemical weapons against its own civilian population. But he had neither of the preceding conditions working in his favor. When it looked like Congress would reject his request, Obama instead reached a face-saving deal engineered by Russia that involved the removal or destruction of Syria's remaining chemical weapons. This case, then, highlights the boundaries of the imperial presidency—as the exception that proves the rule.

INVISIBLE CONGRESS, RELIANT COURTS

Members of Congress frequently rail against executive overreach—but the institution as a whole has done little since the 1970s WPR to push back against it. Indeed, as noted earlier, Congress has granted additional powers to the president as the "war on terror" continues and morphs. Legislators have long enjoyed the luxury of blame avoidance in this regard. Worse, increased polarization has made it politically difficult for the president's party to oppose him, while encouraging kneejerk criticism from an opposition with little ability to conduct substantive oversight.[23] While in 2014 the House sought to sue Obama over some of his executive actions, punting to the judiciary was itself an admission that Congress as a whole was too paralyzed to act. As 2015 dawned, it seemed increasingly unlikely that some sort of AUMF regarding ISIL—or, equally importantly, an update of the 2001 AUMF— would receive attention in the 114th Congress.

The judicial branch has taken intermittent steps into the oversight void. The executive branch has resisted these efforts too, arguing (in the *Hamdi* case) that the court must not "intrude upon the Constitutional prerogative of the Commander in Chief." The Bush and Obama Administrations both argued that the "state secrets" doctrine prevented other cases from coming to court at all because trials could result in the release of information critical to national security.[24]

In a series of cases dealing with the rights of "enemy combatants," the Supreme Court did rein in executive discretion somewhat—ultimately ruling in *Hamdi*, for instance, that "a state of war is not a blank check for the

President." American citizens were found to be entitled to a fair trial, even outside the civilian court system.[25] Subsequent cases extended due process rights to detainees in Guantanamo Bay and limited the scope of military commissions.[26] The Foreign Intelligence Surveillance Court in 2007 refused to sign off on warrantless wiretapping without congressional authorization. Congress, however, promptly provided just that, bringing the process full circle.[27]

CONCLUSION

As the Obama Administration winds down, then, the prerogatives of the imperial presidency remain largely in effect. The Obama Administration shifted the rationale for its actions from those of the Bush years, but not all of the actions themselves. The Obama Administration did ban "enhanced interrogation techniques" that most of the world considered torture, and it has attempted to close the military prison at Guantanamo Bay, Cuba, without success because of a balky Congress. But the administration still claims the authority to unilaterally use lethal force against enemy combatants, including American citizens, far from any declared war zone. The breadth of the post-9/11 laws empowering the executive to wage the "global war on terror," by plain text or creative interpretation, have thus given cover for a wide array of unilateralism.

That state of affairs is fine with this president—as it will be with the next one. You don't need to attribute malign intent to any chief executive to understand that he will seek to expand his autonomy; as longtime Washingtonian Leon Panetta has put it, "I don't think any president walks into their job and starts thinking about how they can minimize their authority."[28] And that is not all bad. The myriad challenges of governing a much smaller country, in what seemed a much larger world, were enough to persuade the Framers to submerge their fear of monarchy and empower a single person as president. Presidents are rightfully constrained by the Constitution, but it does not follow that the country would be better off with an institutionally feeble executive branch.

Those sanguine about the Constitutional balance of power argue that the political process, broadly speaking—to include the press and public opinion—is sufficient to rein in presidential overreach and ensure accountability.[29] Still, the Senate report on torture released in 2014 shows how far executive action can go even within those constraints. And outright abuse aside, presidential insistence on unilateralism can forfeit the consensus and credibility needed to make the American constitutional system function. That, in turn, can weaken rather than strengthen those in the Oval Office.[30] If only in their own self-interest, then, presidents should be cautious about claiming the imperial mantle. In short, as Schlesinger suggested long ago, we should work for a strong presidency *within* the Constitution.

◆ ◆ ◆ ◆ ◆

4. The Nature of Presidential Leadership

by George C. Edwards III

It is natural for new presidents, basking in the glow of an electoral victory, to focus on creating, rather than exploiting, opportunities for change. It may seem quite reasonable for leaders who have just won the biggest prize in American politics by convincing voters and party leaders to support their candidacies to conclude that they should be able to convince members of the public and Congress to support their policies. Thus, they need not focus on evaluating existing possibilities when they think they can create their own. Yet, assuming that the White House can persuade members of the public and Congress to change their minds and support policies they would otherwise oppose is likely to lead to self-inflicted wounds.

Influencing others is central to most people's conception of leadership, including those most focused on politics. In a democracy, we are particularly attuned to efforts to persuade, especially when most potentially significant policy changes require the assent of multiple power holders.

But the American political system is not a fertile field for the exercise of presidential leadership. Most political actors, from the average citizen to members of Congress, are free to choose whether to follow the chief executive's lead; the president cannot force them to act. At the same time, the sharing of powers established by the Constitution's checks and balances prevents the president from acting unilaterally on most important matters and gives other power holders different perspectives on issues and policy proposals. Thus, the political system compels the president to attempt to lead while inhibiting his ability to do so. It seems as though the president has to rely on persuasion.

The view that presidents not only need to persuade but also that they can succeed at it has led observers of the presidency to focus on the question of *how* presidents persuade rather than the more fundamental question of *whether they can do so*. As a result, for example, many scholars and other commentators on the presidency have fallen prey to an exaggerated concept of the potential for using the "bully pulpit" to go public or pressure members of Congress to fall into line with the White House. We should not *assume* the power to persuade.

The issue is not *whether* major policy changes that presidents desire occur. They do. The fundamental question is *how* presidents achieve these changes. Do they have the potential to create opportunities for change by persuading others to follow them?

The tenacity with which many commentators embrace the persuasive potential of political leadership is striking. They routinely explain historic shifts in public policy, such as those in the 1930s, 1960s, and 1980s, in terms of the extraordinary persuasiveness of Franklin D. Roosevelt, Lyndon Johnson, and Ronald Reagan. Equally striking is the lack of evidence of the persuasive power of the presidency. Observers in both the press and academia base their claims about the impact of such leadership on little or no systematic evidence. There is not a single systematic study that demonstrates that presidents can reliably move others to support them.

LEADING THE PUBLIC

Presidents invest heavily in leading the public in the hope of leveraging public support to win backing in Congress. Nevertheless, there is overwhelming evidence that presidents rarely move the public in their direction. Most observers view Ronald Reagan and Bill Clinton as excellent communicators. Nevertheless, pluralities and often majorities of the public opposed them on most of their policy initiatives. Moreover, public opinion typically moved away from rather than toward the positions they favored.[1]

Despite the national trauma resulting from the September 11 terrorist attacks, the long-term disdain of the public for Saddam Hussein, and the lack of organized opposition, George W. Bush made little headway in moving the public to support the war in Iraq, and once the initial phase of the war was over, the rally resulting from the quick U.S. victory quickly dissipated.[2] Despite his eloquence, Barack Obama could not obtain the public's support for his initiatives that were not already popular.[3] For example, his health care reform lacked majority support even six years after it passed.

Even Franklin D. Roosevelt, the president often viewed as the greatest politician of the 20th century, faced constant frustration in his efforts to move the public to prepare for entry into World War II. His failure to persuade the public regarding his plan to pack the Supreme Court effectively marked the end of the New Deal.[4] George Washington, who was better positioned than any of his successors to dominate American politics because of the widespread view of his possessing exceptional personal qualities, did not find the public particularly deferential.[5]

More broadly, public opinion usually moves contrary to the president's position. Because public officials have policy beliefs as well as an interest in reelection, they are not likely to calibrate their policy stances exactly to match those of the public. Thus, a moderate public usually receives too much liberalism from Democrats and too much conservatism from Republicans.[6]

There are many impediments to leading the public,[7] including the following:

- the difficulty of obtaining and maintaining the public's attention;
- dependence on the media to reach the public;
- the need to overcome the public's policy and partisan predispositions;
- a frequently misinformed public that resists correction;
- distrust of the White House created by partisan media; and
- the public's aversion to loss and thus wariness of policy change.

As a result, presidents usually fail to move the public to support them and their policies.

LEADING CONGRESS

Presidents invest an enormous amount of time trying to lead Congress. They know that their legacies are highly dependent on their proposals passing the legislature. Are presidents persuasive with senators and representatives? The best evidence is that presidential persuasion is effective only at the margins of congressional decision making. There is little relationship between presidential legislative leadership skills and success in winning votes. Even presidents who appeared to dominate Congress understood their own limitations and explicitly took advantage of opportunities in their environments. Working at the margins, they successfully guided legislation through Congress. When their opportunities lessened, they reverted to the stalemate that often characterizes presidential–congressional relations.[8]

Three of the most famous periods of presidential success in Congress illustrate the point.[9]

THE HUNDRED DAYS

Perhaps the 20th-century's most famous and successful period of presidential–congressional relations was the Hundred Days of 1933, when Congress passed fifteen major pieces of legislation proposed by President Franklin D. Roosevelt. FDR won a clear electoral victory, and the Democrats gained large majorities in both houses of Congress. Five days after his inauguration in 1933, FDR called a special session of Congress to deal with the economic crisis. All he planned to ask from Congress was to pass legislation to regulate the resumption of banking (he had closed the banks one day after taking office), amend the Volstead Act to legalize beer (a very popular policy), and cut the budget. He expected to reassemble the legislature when he was ready with permanent and more constructive legislation.

The first piece of legislation Roosevelt proposed was a bill regarding the resumption of banking. He found that he did not have to persuade anyone to support his bill, which passed unanimously in the House after only thirty-eight minutes of debate and without a roll-call vote (although few members had seen the bill—there was only one copy for the chamber) and by a margin of seventy-three to seven in the Senate, which simply adopted the House bill while waiting for printed copies. An hour later, the bill arrived at the White House for the president's signature. The whole affair took less than eight hours.

Much to his surprise, the president found a situation ripe for change. The country was in such a state of desperation that it was eager to follow a leader who would try something new. Thus, FDR decided to keep Congress in session and exploit the favorable environment by sending it the legislation that became known as the "New Deal."

FDR went on to serve in the White House longer than anyone else, but most of these years were not legislatively productive. James MacGregor Burns titled his discussion of presidential–congressional relations in the late 1930s "Deadlock on the Potomac." Either Roosevelt had lost his persuasive skills, which is not a reasonable proposition, or other factors were more significant in determining congressional support. By 1937, despite the president's great reelection victory, his coalition was falling apart.[10]

THE GREAT SOCIETY

The next great period of legislative productivity for a president was Lyndon Johnson's success with the 89th Congress in 1965 through 1966. The 1964 presidential election occurred in the shadow of the traumatic national tragedy of the assassination of John F. Kennedy, and Johnson won reelection overwhelmingly. With it, opposition to his proposals melted. As Lawrence O'Brien, his chief congressional aide, put it, Johnson's landslide "turned the tide."[11] For the first time since the New Deal, liberals gained majorities in both houses of Congress.

Johnson did not have to convince these liberals to support policies that had been on their agenda for a generation.[12] Nor did he have to convince the public of much. His policies were popular.[13] Both congressional leaders and

White House aides felt they were working in a period of remarkable unanimity in which, as one member of LBJ's domestic staff put it, "some of the separation got collapsed. It seemed we were all working on the same thing."[14]

No one understood Congress better than LBJ, and he knew that his personal leadership could not sustain congressional support for his policies. The president understood the opportunity the large, liberal majorities in the 89th Congress presented to him, and he seized it, keeping intense pressure on Congress. In O'Brien's words, with LBJ, "Every day, every hour it was drive, drive, drive."[15] It is telling that virtually all the participants in the legislative process during Johnson's presidency agree that his tenaciousness and intensity in pushing legislation and exploiting his opportunities were his great talents, not his persuasiveness.[16] According to then House Majority Leader Carl Albert, Congress was not rubber-stamping the president's proposals but doing what it wanted to do. "We had the right majority," he recalled.[17]

In the 1966 midterm elections, the Democrats lost forty-seven seats in the House and four in the Senate. Legislating became much more difficult as a result. Sixteen months later, in March 1968, the president declared that he would not seek reelection. Johnson had lost neither his leadership skills nor his passion for change. Instead, he had lost the opportunity to exploit a favorable environment.

THE REAGAN REVOLUTION

It was the Republicans' turn in 1981. Ronald Reagan beat incumbent Jimmy Carter by ten percentage points, and the Republicans won a majority in the Senate for the first time since the 1952 election. The unexpectedly large size of Reagan's victory and the equally surprising outcomes in the Senate elections created the perception of an electoral mandate. Reagan's victory placed a stigma on big government and exalted the unregulated marketplace and large defense budgets. He had won on much of his agenda before Congress took a single vote.

The new president also benefited from the nature of the times. Although 1981 was hardly a repeat of 1933, there was a definite sense of the need for immediate action to meet urgent problems. David Stockman, a principal architect and proponent of Reagan's budgeting and tax proposals, remembers that when the president announced his "Program for Economic Recovery" to a joint session of Congress in February 1981, "the plan already had momentum and few were standing in the way." Reagan was "speaking to an assembly of desperate politicians who . . . were predisposed to grant him extraordinary latitude in finding a new remedy for the nation's economic ills . . . not because they understood the plan or even accepted it, but because they had lost all faith in the remedies tried before."[18]

The president's advisers recognized immediately that they had a window of opportunity to effect major changes in public policy. Like LBJ, the White House knew it had to move quickly before the environment became less favorable. Thus, the president was ready with legislation, even though it was complex and hastily written. Moreover, within a week of the March 30, 1981, assassination attempt on Reagan, his aide Michael Deaver convened a meeting of other high-ranking officials at the White House to determine how best to take advantage of the new political capital the shooting had created.

The Reagan Administration also knew it lacked the political capital to pass a broad program. Thus, it enforced a rigorous focus on the president's economic plan and defense spending, its priority legislation. Reagan essentially ignored divisive social issues and tried to keep the issue of communist advances in Central America on the back burner. By focusing its political resources on its priorities, the administration succeeded in using the budget to pass sweeping changes in taxation and defense policy.

It was wise for Reagan to exploit his opportunities. The going was much tougher the next year as the United States suffered a severe recession, and for the rest of his tenure, commentators frequently described Reagan's budgets as DOA: Dead on Arrival.

SUMMARY

Despite the prestige of their office, their position as party leader, their personal persuasiveness, and their strong personalities, presidents often meet resistance from members of Congress to their appeals for support. Personal appeals by themselves are useful but unreliable instruments for passing legislation. As a result, one-on-one lobbying by the president is the exception rather than the rule. The White House conserves such appeals for obtaining the last few votes on issues of special significance, recognizing that presidents cannot personally persuade members of Congress with any frequency.

Thus, presidential leadership of the legislature is more useful in exploiting discrete opportunities than in creating broad possibilities for policy change. Congress operates in an environment largely beyond the president's control, and the chief executive must compete with other factors that affect voting. These include ideology, personal views and commitments on specific policies, and the interests of constituencies. By the time a president tries to exercise influence on a vote, most members of Congress have made up their minds on the basis of these other factors.

As a result, a president's legislative leadership is likely to be critical only for those members of Congress who remain open to conversion after other influences have had their impact. Although the size and composition of this group varies from issue to issue, it will almost always be a small minority in each chamber. Whatever the circumstances, the impact of persuasion on the outcome will usually be relatively modest. Therefore, conversion is likely to be at the margins of coalition building in Congress, rather than at the core of policy change.

In sum, the most effective presidents do not create opportunities by reshaping the political landscape. Instead, they exploit opportunities already present in their environments to achieve significant changes in public policy.

CONCLUSION

Although it may be appealing to explain major policy changes in terms of persuasive personalities, public opinion is too biased, the political system is too complicated, power is too decentralized, and interests are too diverse for one person, no matter how extraordinary, to dominate. Recognizing and exploiting opportunities for change—rather than creating opportunities through persuasion—are the essential presidential leadership skills. As Edgar declared in *King Lear*, "Ripeness is all."

To succeed, presidents have to evaluate the opportunities for change carefully, and orchestrate existing and potential support skillfully. Successful leadership requires that the president have the commitment, resolution, and adaptability to take full advantage of opportunities that arise. When the various streams of political resources converge to create opportunities for major change, presidents can be critical facilitators in realizing alterations in public policy. But the president's power to achieve policy change hinges on correctly sizing up opportunities. It rarely, if ever, depends on the power to persuade.

◆ ◆ ◆ ◆ ◆

5. Rise of the Vice President

by Richard M. Yon and Joseph Amoroso

Thomas R. Marshall once compared his position as vice president to "a man in a cataleptic fit; he cannot speak; he cannot move; he suffers no pain; he is perfectly conscious of all that goes on, but has no part of it."[1] The Office of the Vice President (OVP) has always been an easy target of political mockery. It seems history has offered more quips about the position's irrelevance than arguments in support of its utility. This is not all that surprising, given the office's peculiar conception during the final days of the Constitutional Convention. The Framers primarily created the nation's number two position for procedural purposes: as a means to avoid conflict in the election of the president and prevent anticipated gridlock in the Senate.[2]

Today, the office has evolved into a prominent and highly influential position within presidential administrations. The selection of a vice presidential candidate is regarded as the most important decision made by presidential contenders. To the American public, candidates for vice president are most commonly viewed in terms of presidential succession, and how they balance the party's national ticket. The 25th Amendment and the eight historical precedents in which vice presidents were elevated to the presidency make vice presidential choices a legitimate concern to the voting public, a concern keenly recognized by presidential campaigns.

As technology, media, capital, and global interdependence reshaped the national political environment over the course of the last century, the executive branch, and the OVP in particular, experienced tremendous growth. The jokes about vice presidential insignificance are now punch lines used for self-deprecation or coy attempts to downplay political ambition. The reality is that a position once labeled by John Adams as "most insignificant," has proven to be one of the most critical players in presidential administrations.

This chapter reassesses the vice presidency, highlighting basic roles that have evolved over the past few decades with expanded duties. These include the duties of advisor, administrator, and ambassador. Along with institutional developments related to these roles, this chapter discusses the public perception of modern vice presidents and the inimitable partnership between a president and his vice. Although the vice president can still be regarded as the colloquial "bench warmer," Vice President Marshall might truly be surprised with how the position has changed.

VICE PRESIDENTIAL MODELS

Even some of the men who held the position have blamed the authors of the Constitution for their hasty creation of the vice presidential office, with its lack of tangible institutional structure. But the great potential of the office lies in the absence of constitutional stipulations and limits. The lack of specificity has bestowed on occupants the flexibility to acquire the additional responsibilities evident today.

A commonly discussed criterion in vice presidential selection is the need to "balance" the ticket for the presidential campaign. This tactic has been employed numerous times in modern presidential elections, and the balancing can be conducted on several dimensions, including age, region, experience, and diversity.[3] A common example of a balanced duo was the John F. Kennedy–Lyndon B. Johnson ticket in 1960. Kennedy was a young, northeastern Democrat from a wealthy Irish and Roman Catholic family. In contrast, Johnson was an older Democrat from Texas who had a modest upbringing in the southern Protestant tradition. President Kennedy knew that if he wanted to win the national election, he needed to effectively quell the concerns about his religion and win the state of Texas. Lyndon Johnson helped in achieving both objectives.

While Johnson's balancing effect might have helped Kennedy secure the White House, not all vice presidential candidates have been as successful in deciding the electoral success of a ticket. In the 2004 and 2012 presidential elections, John Edwards and Paul Ryan, respectively, were unable to carry their own home states. Conventional political strategy seems to suggest that the litmus test for vice presidential nominees is that, at a minimum, they do no harm to the presidential candidate. The traditional interest in balance, however, hints at other concerns that extend beyond Election Day. Once the winning administration takes office, a complementary vice president can have substantial impact on an administration's governance, supporting the new president where he/she is weakest, and solidifying the vice president's role as chief advisor.

Vice President Walter Mondale set the tone for the advisory function of the office in his memorandum to President Jimmy Carter. He wrote, "The position of being the only other public official nationwide, not affected by specific obligations or institutional interests of either the congressional or executive branch, and able to look at the government as a whole, does put me in a unique position to advise."[4] Mondale believed that the lack of departmental responsibility and its associated biases allowed him to offer opinions and challenges without reservations. His experience in Washington and his work on various domestic and foreign policy initiatives at the national level provided him with operational expertise that well served Carter, who had only held state-level offices before running for president.[5]

Similarly, when former Arkansas Governor Bill Clinton ran for office, he chose as his vice presidential running mate Senator Al Gore, who was steeped in the ways of Washington after serving many years in Congress (both in the House and Senate). In what would become a norm in the modern presidency, Clinton involved Gore in high-level decision making and gave him the lead in key administrative initiatives involving government reform, expansion of the Internet into an "information superhighway," and environmental issues associated with climate change.

In much the same way, Barack Obama constantly battled public perceptions of being too inexperienced to handle the office when he ran for president in 2008. Early in the election season, a Gallup poll found that the chief concern of 39 percent of American voters was that Obama was "inexperienced or unprepared."[6] When it came time to choose a running mate, Obama selected another Washington veteran, Senator Joe Biden. Although polling showed relatively insignificant improvements to Obama's favorability when Biden was announced, the selection appeared to be a good balance for a young candidate who represented change but lacked experience.[7]

The real benefit to selecting Biden came after the election. His unparalleled experience in Congress, specifically on areas relating to foreign policy, the judiciary, and domestic issues affecting the working class, offered President Obama a wise political ally and confidant. In a 2008 preinaugural interview on ABC's *This Week*, Biden offered that a vice president should give "the best, sagest, most accurate, most insightful advice and recommendations he or she can make to a president to help them make some of the very, very important decisions that have to be made."[8] Biden has exemplified the counselor model throughout his time as vice president. Seizing on this potential, Obama, like Carter, enhanced the office of his number two. From his commitment to including Biden in "every critical decision" to the private lunches with Biden that are a staple of the president's weekly schedule, President Obama has elevated Biden's status as "general counselor."

INSTITUTIONAL POWER

Before the 1970s, the OVP consisted of around twenty permanent staff members, office space in five to six locations, no formal budget, and limited access to the West Wing. Today more than seventy professionals work for the vice president. The vice president and his staff maintain their own annual budget and occupy office space in three critical locations: the West Wing, the Eisenhower Executive Office Building next door, and the U.S. Capitol.[9] These institutional changes, crucial in their own right, are structural expressions of a more extensive transformation in the role of the office. Taken together, these innovations have enabled vice presidents to assume key administrative duties within the executive branch. Three such developments have been especially instrumental in this regard: inclusion of the vice president as a member of the National Security Council; placement of the vice president within the executive chain of command; and maintenance of joint staffs and staff collaboration.

Harry Truman, one of the eight vice presidents to eventually ascend to the presidency, recognized his lack of preparedness in the foreign policy arena after the death of Franklin Roosevelt. Truman, who met with Roosevelt only eight times during his vice presidency, was never informed of the atomic bomb or of diplomatic details surrounding the end of World War II. Truman believed that the wide information gap that he faced after Roosevelt's death negatively impacted his first few months as commander in chief. He recognized the need for the vice president to be intimately involved in the foreign policy discussion as a matter of national security in the event of future succession. With the passage of the National Security Act of 1947, Truman's personal experience as vice president influenced the decision to formally include the vice president as a statutory member of the National Security Council (NSC).[10]

Truman's recommendation was perhaps the most significant institutional move made by a president to elevate the role of his vice president. He paved the way for other presidents to enhance the integration of the vice president into the policy-making process. In 1970, President Nixon established the Office of Policy Development, which was the precursor to the current Domestic Policy Council (DPC). Under the Ford Administration, Vice President Nelson Rockefeller chaired the council and used the position to drive the domestic policy agenda. The vice president has been a consistent member of the council as it evolved into its current form.[11]

In addition to these prominent positions in both foreign and domestic policy, vice presidents are frequently tasked to lead commissions, councils, and programs that are commonly referred to as "line assignments." Examples of these line assignments include Spiro Agnew's leadership of the Office of Intergovernmental Relations; Dan Quayle's supervision of George H.W. Bush's Task Force on Regulatory Relief; and Dick Cheney's controversial stewardship of the National Energy Policy Development Group.[12] Modern vice presidents have sometimes tried to avoid these line assignments because they consume a great deal of time and energy, and diminish their capacity to weigh in on other issues important to the president. Nonetheless, line assignments and membership on the NSC and DPC are critical elements of the vice president's modern administrative function.

President Carter entered the White House concerned about the treatment of former vice presidents by senior presidential staffers. In the past, senior officials were known to subvert vice presidents in an effort to maintain control of certain aspects of the administration. Judging this a dangerous practice, Carter directed that all staffers "respond to a request from the vice president as if it had come from the president, and anyone attempting to undercut the vice president in any way could not expect a long tenure in his administration."[13]

Carter's directive to his staff at the start of his administration effectively operationalized the vice president's role as "second in command." Succession was no longer an emergency or ceremonial concept. Vice President Mondale was to be viewed as a member of the command structure. This position was bolstered further when Carter signed an executive order placing the vice president second in line for the control of nuclear weapons.[14] The steps taken by Carter set a standard for presidential–vice presidential relations that has been maintained in subsequent administrations. Before Joe Biden officially agreed to join President Obama's ticket, his chief stipulation was that in "every critical decision, economic and political, as well as foreign policy, I'll get to be in the room."[15] The now-routine expectation of sharing operational responsibilities reflects the new view of modern vice presidents as administrators.

EXPANDING POWER AND INFLUENCE

The vice president's staff grew along with the responsibilities of the office in policy formulation and executive leadership. The Carter Administration can again be credited for its work in building executive staff cohesion. Vice presidential scholar Paul Light highlights four steps taken by the Carter Administration that led to the proper integration of the White House staff. The first was characterized by Mondale's open invitation to attend any of the president's meetings. While Mondale exercised this right judiciously; members of his staff had complete access to the president's schedule and used their knowledge of the president's activities to set Mondale's priorities and schedule. This type of synchronization kept Mondale informed and relevant.[16]

Second, in efforts to further synchronize the two staffs, Mondale's senior aides attended the president's daily staff meetings. These collaborative morning meetings became critical in achieving a third change, which called for Mondale's midlevel aides to attend meetings with the president's deputies. This integrated the two staffs in daily operations of the White House. The fourth step was Carter's appointment of Bert Carp to the Domestic Policy Staff and David Aaron to the National Security Council. Carp and Aaron had been legislative aides to Mondale during his time in the Senate and their appointments to Carter's senior staff sealed their political alliance.[17]

The standards of staff interoperability established during the Carter years have continued to serve as the model for modern administrations. During the Bush–Cheney Administration, staff integration reached unprecedented levels. Before taking office, Bush assigned Cheney the task of making provisional appointments to the president's senior staff. Cheney took advantage of this latitude by appointing personal political allies to deputy posts in major executive departments. For instance, Stephen Hadley and Sean O'Keefe, Cheney's colleagues from his time as Secretary of Defense, were named deputy national security advisor and deputy director of the Office of Management and Budget, respectively.[18] Additionally, multiple members of Cheney's senior staff simultaneously held named positions in President Bush's inner circle. Scooter Libby, Cheney's chief of staff, and Mary Matalin, a counselor to Cheney, both held the powerful rank of assistant to the president.[19] The steps taken by Cheney brought staff integration to such unprecedented levels that his influence was highly criticized by the media, public, and political adversaries.

The reach of the modern presidency goes far beyond anything imagined by those who created the office and is, as a practical matter, a lot for one person to handle. This reality has worked to the advantage of vice presidents. During recent administrations, presidents have enlisted their political partners to share this ever-expanding burden and to maximize executive control. The ambassadorial function of the modern vice presidency, for instance, has become much more than ceremonial wreath-laying. Although there are still many of these obligations, vice presidents have filled the role of executive ambassador in more critical capacities: internationally, domestically, and politically.

The day after his inauguration, for instance, President Carter made a public demonstration of his confidence in his vice president and the ambassadorial role he would play. Carter sent Mondale on an important international expedition to introduce the newly elected administration to other leaders of the world. For the first time in presidential history, a vice president departed from the White House south lawn. At the end of his four years in office, Mondale had visited thirty-six countries in fourteen trips abroad.[20]

Mondale was not the first vice president, and certainly not the last, to represent the president abroad. The substance of these trips depends on how much the vice president and his staff is trusted to carry out the wishes of the administration. Richard Nixon was given immense foreign policy license by President Eisenhower on his 1959 trip to Russia. Throughout his trip, Nixon used every opportunity presented to engage the Russian Premier, Nikita Khrushchev, on substantive issues. These visible face-offs were referred to by the media as the "Kitchen Debates" and cast Nixon as an authoritative international emissary. George H.W. Bush and Bill Clinton relied more heavily on their secretaries of state to fulfill the ambassadorial function, but Dan Quayle and Al Gore both played a substantial, although more limited, ambassadorial role.[21]

EMISSARIES TO CONGRESS

The constitutional responsibility as president of the Senate offers the vice president not only real estate within the corridors of the Capitol but a seat at the legislative negotiating table. Many vice presidents have also been former members of Congress, and they tend to know their way around Capitol Hill. This role as liaison to Congress has been crucial to the effectiveness of vice presidents in pursuing the administration's agenda.

Joe Biden is viewed by most pundits to be the consummate domestic negotiator and envoy to Congress. His long career in the Senate has proven to be of great value to the Obama Administration, especially in the effort to pass the American Recovery and Reinvestment Act in 2009. Biden was successful in pushing the Act through the Senate by persuading Senator Susan Collins of Maine to vote for passage.[22] Biden also proved to be a valuable asset in dealing with the 111th lame-duck Congress, after the Republicans' stunning electoral gains in the House of Representatives. With the connections he had built on both sides of the aisle, Biden was able to lobby Republicans to approve President Obama's disputed START Treaty, reach a consensus regarding the future of the Bush tax cuts, and build support for the repeal of the "Don't Ask Don't Tell" policy on gays in the military.[23] Biden not only has a way with congressional colleagues, but he also interacts with average Americans in a way that makes him a useful substitute for the cooler but rhetorically more gifted Obama.

The president's role as party leader, and the temporal extension of campaign seasons, have also enhanced the political value of the vice presidency. The White House must not only concern itself with furthering the administration's platform, but also with the future electoral success of the party and political allies. Vice presidents are called on to aid the president in this function.

George H.W. Bush, Dan Quayle, and Al Gore have all been credited for their tireless efforts as political emissaries. Quayle would make a "political trip somewhere around the country at least once or twice a week . . . his job was to touch the dozens of reelection bases that Bush [did] not have time to visit." It is estimated that these trips to more than 200 cities raised over $20 million for the Republican Party. Similarly, Bush was well equipped to hit the campaign trail while he was vice president. His previous service as the

Chairman of the Republican National Committee in 1973, and his own political ambition, powered his political diplomacy.[24]

The vice president's performance as a political ambassador serves multiple functions. Vice presidents often serve as the political attack dogs for the executive branch, exerting influence throughout the political debate. At the same time, they keep the president a safe distance from directly engaging in campaign maneuvers that might seem beneath the dignity of the office. And political ambassadorship serves as a means for vice presidents to build their own constituencies for a possible future run at the Oval Office.

An unknown Reagan aide was once quoted, "Twenty years ago, I wouldn't have advised my worst enemy to take the Vice-Presidency. It was God's way of punishing bad campaigners, a sort of political purgatory for the also-rans. Now you'd be crazy not to take the job."[25] The vice presidency of today is much different than the office disparaged by Thomas Marshall. It has grown into a position of unique relevance and subtle authority, built by the ambitious men who worked tirelessly to enhance its authority and prestige within modern presidential administrations. As the nation looks toward 2016, another American will be called to serve as the next president's advisor, administrator, and ambassador and to further solidify the vice president's place in national government.

BIBLIOGRAPHY

Baker, Peter. *Days of Fire: Bush and Cheney in the White House*. New York, NY: Doubleday, 2013.

Baumgartner, Jody C. *The American Vice Presidency Reconsidered*. Westport, CT: Praeger Publishers, 2006.

Connolly, Katie. "Why Liberals Have Grown to Love Joe Biden." *Newsweek* (Mar. 30, 2010). http://www.newsweek.com/why-liberals-have-grown -love-joe-biden-69131?piano_t=1 (accessed Nov. 22, 2014).

Gallup. "Gallup's Quick Read on the Election." (Oct. 22, 2008). http://www .gallup.com/poll/109759/Gallups-Quick-Read-Election.aspx (accessed Nov. 17, 2014).

Gallup. "Presidential Candidates' Weaknesses in Depth." (Apr. 2, 2008). http://www.gallup.com/poll/105994/Presidential-Candidates -Weaknesses-Depth.aspx (accessed Nov. 18, 2014).

Goldstein, Joel K. *The Modern American Vice Presidency: The Transformation of a Political Institution*. Princeton, NJ: Princeton University Press, 1982.

Kengor, Paul. "The Vice President, Secretary of State, and Foreign Policy." *Political Science Quarterly* 115, no. 2 (Summer, 2000): 175–99.

Light, Paul C. *Vice-Presidential Power: Advice and Influence in the White House*. Baltimore, MD: Johns Hopkins University Press, 1984.

Moe, Richard. "The Making of the Modern Vice Presidency: A Personal Reflection." *Presidential Studies Quarterly* 38, no. 3 (September 2008): 390–400.

Mondale, Walter F. "Memorandum to Jimmy Carter Regarding the Role of the Vice President in the Carter Administration." Walter F. Mondale Papers. Minnesota Historical Society. December 9, 1976. http://www.mnhs.org/collections/upclose/Mondale-CarterMemo-Transcription.pdf (accessed Nov. 19, 2014).

Nelson, Michael. *A Heartbeat Away: Report of the Twentieth Century Fund Task Force on the Vice Presidency*. New York: Priority Press Publications, 1988.

Rathbone, Mark. "The US Vice Presidency Today." *Political Insight* (Dec. 2011): 28–31.

Stephanopoulos, George. "Interview with Joe Biden." *This Week with George Stephanopoulos*. (Dec. 21, 2008). http://abcnews.go.com/blogs/politics/2008/12/biden-ill-get-t/ (accessed Nov. 17, 2014).

Yon, Richard M. "Vice President Joe Biden: Perpetuating Influence or Restoring Historical Insignificance?" In *The Obama Presidency: A Preliminary Assessment*, Robert P. Watson, Jack Covarrubias, Tom Lansford, and Douglas M. Brattebo, Eds. New York: SUNY Press, 2012.

◆ ◆ ◆ ◆ ◆

6. In the Shadow of the Oval Office: The White House Staff

by Kenneth M. Duberstein

In the American political system, the people elect one person to lead them, but a president's success will depend greatly on his or her ability to assemble a smoothly functioning White House staff. There are no set playbooks or established blueprints for building a staff. Incumbents will put their own personal stamp on the process, and mistakes made in this critical stage of a presidency can have profound repercussions later on. As someone who participated in this little-understood process from the inside as a member of Ronald Reagan's White House staff, and ultimately as Reagan's Chief of Staff, I'd like to offer some observations and lessons learned.

In the heady days after a successful election campaign, it's easy to lose sight of the fact that a White House staff cannot serve just as a refuge or reward for campaign workers. The art of campaigning and the art of governing are two very different disciplines. In a political campaign, the goal is to annihilate your opposition. To a certain degree in the rough and tumble of American politics, that means demonizing your opponent in order to win. By contrast, the art of governing sometimes requires you to say "no" to your most ardent supporters and "yes" to your most strident opponents. Those are very different talents, and there are some people who are excellent at political campaigns who lack the instinct for compromise that is essential to governing.

In fact, I think one of the problems in the American political system today is the phenomenon of the "perpetual campaign" that accentuates the role of the campaign operative over the White House staffer whose goal is to get things done. During Ronald Reagan's two-term presidency in the 1980s, for instance, his pollster would conduct public opinion polls roughly once a month. The polls were not designed to indicate in which direction President Reagan should lead, but rather to let him know whether his message was getting through to the public. By contrast, today the process is driven by a constant cycle of overnight polling, focus groups, and "word testing" to shape the White House's course. That breeds a campaign psychology as opposed to a governing psychology. Combined with the constant need for fundraising in modern politics and the growing influence of interest groups, I think that the tendency for White Houses to stay in a constant campaign mode has contributed to the obvious dysfunction in Washington, D.C.

BALANCING A STAFF

A key attribute of a successful White House staff is balance. In the case of President Reagan, he chose as his first Chief of Staff James Baker, who had served in the Ford Administration, knew his way around Washington, and had a reputation as someone who could get things done. For the job of White House Counselor, Reagan chose Ed Meese, who was from Reagan's California clique and was very familiar with the president's ideology and policy goals. As his Deputy Chief of Staff, Reagan chose Mike Deaver, who had known the president personally for many years and understood exactly how to stage Reagan at major events and to create backdrops that conveyed to the American people the message that President Reagan wanted to send. Those three formed the core leadership of the White House staff in the first term, and although they took their share of criticism, they were successful because each brought a needed dimension to the staff. They provided a mix of talents that included a deep understanding of how to get things done in Washington, familiarity with the president's policy priorities, and ties to the campaign and the supporters back home in California. It also didn't hurt that they all fundamentally got along well with each other.

Reagan's closeness with his top White House team proved important because they were able to be frank with him. What you learn very quickly in the White House is that most people who walk into the Oval Office get cotton in their mouth. They tell the president what they think he wants to hear, rather than what he needs to know. The role of the White House Chief of Staff and senior staff is to tell the president the harsh realities—to explain that if he goes down a certain path, there are likely some problems and risks he will encounter at various potential forks in the road. Senior staff discussions with the president have to be about what I call "reality therapy." You have to tell the president uncomfortable truths in a way that is constructive, but not confrontational. The very last thing a president needs is a White House staff full of sycophants.

As a White House staff member, you also want to avoid picking losing battles or giving the president Don Quixote–like moments in which he is essentially "tilting at windmills." Every president possesses only a limited number of chips in terms of political capital, and you can't afford to waste them. Your job as a staff is to know where the president wants to go and to lay out a clear agenda for getting there that anticipates the plausible alternatives and thinks through all the options. You always have to consider what catnip will entice congressional support. Any time the president makes a decision, the White House staff is responsible for ensuring that he or she is doing so with the very best information available.

Because presidents only have so much political capital, and there is only so much political and policy bandwidth in Washington for pushing a presidential agenda, it's important that a White House staff sets clear priorities. In the case of President Reagan, that was easy, because he was very much an "outbox" president. From the day he was elected, Ronald Reagan knew what he wanted to accomplish: reduce taxes on the American people; cut the rate of spending increases of the federal government; reduce over-burdensome government regulation and red tape; and build up a depleted U.S. military. Because all of the senior White House staff clearly understood President Reagan's governing philosophy and major priorities, we were able to act on his behalf, knowing that what we were doing fit into the president's core agenda. I would contrast that to "inbox" presidents and White House staffs who tend to get so consumed dealing with pressing events of the day that they lose sight of the overarching goals that the president was elected to achieve. You always have to remember as a White House staffer that you're there not simply to make the trains run on time, but to make sure that the trains are running in the direction that the president desires.

CRITICAL RELATIONSHIPS

There is creative tension in every White House. That goes with the territory. You inevitably have a mix of different kinds of people, most of them driven, Type A personalities. You manage it through close cooperation. As the White House Chief of Staff, I was the gatekeeper to the Oval Office, for instance, but on the organizational chart, the National Security Adviser also had a direct line to the president. We worked that by agreeing that former National Security Advisers Colin Powell and Frank Carlucci would never go to the Oval Office without touching base with my office first. Powell and I would meet each morning before I briefed President Reagan, for instance, and then Powell would typically come in and brief him on national security issues. You quickly learn that for most foreign policy and national security issues, there is a domestic overlay. In many domestic policy issues, there are also international ramifications. In those instances, Colin Powell and I would often discuss the matter first and decide in advance who was best to set up the subject and which issues were best for each of us to handle, and then walk down the hallway to the Oval Office together to brief the boss. So it's very important that the White House Chief of Staff and National Security Adviser coordinate closely.

There are many other critical relationships on the White House staff. Many people don't realize the importance of the Staff Secretary, for instance, but that person controls the all-important flow of paper and electronic communications into the Oval Office. The White House Counsel is obviously a key player on all legal questions. From the very beginning of an administration, the White House Personnel Director is responsible for teeing up the names of potential candidates to fill important jobs, not only on the White House staff but in the cabinet as well. Obviously, the relationship between the White House Chief of Staff and the vice president and his chief of staff is important as well.

One area of critical importance that is too often overlooked is the White House staff's sensitivity to the First Lady. You quickly learn in the White House that the First Lady knows her husband better than anyone else, and you need to take that into account. In the case of President Reagan, his wife, Nancy Reagan, understood his rhythms, personality, and fundamental beliefs better than anyone else. Because my job was to make President Reagan successful, it was important that Nancy Reagan shared that insight with me. I'm sure it's the same with Michelle Obama, just as it was with Laura Bush, Hillary Clinton, and Barbara Bush. The First Lady knows her husband best, and those insights are important for a White House staff.

Another critical relationship is between the White House staff and the Cabinet. As Chief of Staff, I was very sensitive to the fact that Cabinet Secretaries needed to be included in our deliberations and plans, and not just the State, Defense, and Treasury Secretaries, but also the Secretaries of Agriculture, Labor, Interior, and so forth. So every couple of weeks, I would invite several Cabinet Secretaries to lunch in my office, and invariably I would work it out so that President Reagan came down and had dessert with us.

I would also chair a breakfast once a month in the Cabinet Room that didn't include the president, and I would give Cabinet Secretaries an opportunity to vent and air whatever frustrations they had with the White House staff. I always got useful feedback from those breakfasts with the cabinet, because members of Congress and other stakeholders would tell cabinet officials about problems before they would tell the president.

It's important that Cabinet Secretaries get regular face time with the president because then they can say, "I met with President Reagan yesterday, and he said 'X' or 'Y.'" That proximity to the president gives them more clout. There is also a common belief that after a year or two, Cabinet Secretaries tend to be captured by whatever constituency they oversee and regulate, and regular meetings between them and the president tend to delay that phenomenon, which can be helpful.

As an example of this relationship, I remember a case in which there was a severe drought in the Midwest and I had Agriculture Secretary Dick Lyng come to the White House and walk me through the crisis over lunch. I realized right away that a disaster was brewing, so I had Secretary Lyng spend fifteen minutes briefing President Reagan as well, who decided on the spot to take a trip to the Midwest. The photograph and media coverage of President Reagan and Secretary Lyng standing in the middle of a dried-out cornfield conveyed to the public just how seriously the administration took the problem and that they were on top of the issue. Time and again we were able to stay ahead of problems like that by being closely engaged with Cabinet Secretaries and officials.

A successful presidency also requires that the White House staff stay closely engaged with Congress. Early in Reagan's first term, then White House Chief of Staff James Baker established the Legislative Strategy Group in the White House. President Reagan had wisely determined that to be successful, he would have to win key battles on Capitol Hill. At that time Republicans controlled the Senate for the first time in twenty-five years, but only by a very narrow fifty-two to forty-eight margin. In the House we only had 191 Republicans. That meant that to successfully push legislation through Congress, we had to keep all of the House Republicans in line and pick off twenty-seven Democrats to prevail over (former Speaker of the House Thomas) Tip O'Neill, D-Mass., and the liberal Democrats. Reagan and the White House staff used the Legislative Strategy Group to develop strategies to build coalitions that could move various pieces of legislation. It was so useful that it quickly grew to handle most of the policy issues that landed on the president's desk. The strategy group proved absolutely fundamental to President Reagan's success.

GATEKEEPING, COMPROMISING, AND BUBBLE BURSTING

The close interplay between a president, the White House Chief of Staff and a member of his cabinet was revealed when Ronald Reagan was scheduled to deliver an especially important speech in Berlin. As Chief of Staff, I reviewed all of the president's major speeches, and this one had a notation in it that the State Department objected to a particular phrase. I read the speech, and I had no problem with the paragraph, but when I gave it to President Reagan, I duly noted that the State Department had that one objection. Later when President Reagan and I were going over the speech, I got a call from Secretary of State George Shultz, who asked me to convey to President Reagan that he shared the State Department's objection to the one phrase. I knew at that moment that Shultz was actually okay with the reference because if he really objected Shultz would have asked to see Reagan personally, which he did many times. Shultz was really saying that the speech was okay with him, but if it caused trouble the problem would be on my shoulders. The next day President Reagan and I were in his limousine riding to the Brandenburg Gate in Berlin to deliver the speech, and he turned to me and said, "I know this is going to drive those State Department boys crazy, but I'm leaving the paragraph in."

And that's how Reagan came to deliver his iconic line at the Berlin Wall, "Mr. Gorbachev, tear down this wall!"

Part of the inevitable creative tension on the White House staff is between those people focused on the "art of the possible," and the "true believers" who think compromise is a dirty word. You need a process where both sides can frankly debate the issues, and then put options on the table for the president to decide. Those debates can get lively, because you don't usually have a lot of shrinking violets on the White House staff. One side might be arguing that a certain option is simply the right thing to do. But how do you get it done? What if the votes aren't there on Capitol Hill, or the American people are not in favor? Are you willing to mount a massive campaign to convince the public, and thus force action in Congress? How long will that take, and how much political capital will it require? Is it better to spend that political capital on this issue, or the other three or four issues jockeying for priority and attention?

At the end of that process is often a compromise. People often forget that President Reagan succeeded largely on his willingness to compromise. He would tell the White House staff, "I'll take 80 percent of what I'm trying to accomplish any time, and then I'll come back next year and try and get the final 20 percent." Some on the far right and left will criticize any compromise, but President Reagan taught me that people on the far political flanks are professional complainers anyway. They bitch because that's how they build their following and raise their money. Reagan would do what he felt was right, take his 80 percent solution, and come back the next year looking for the rest. That's what governing is all about.

Staff must also avoid being caught in the White House "bubble," an echo chamber that can isolate a president and his team from the everyday realities of the rest of the country. One of the things I encouraged President Reagan to do when I was head of White House Legislative Affairs was to pick up the phone on a regular basis and call senators and congressmen who were back home in their districts. Reagan would call them and ask what the lawmakers were hearing in town hall meetings. What was the local media saying? What does the White House need to know that lawmakers are hearing from people as they drive around their districts? That's not White House lobbying, but rather gathering of critical information.

When I served as White House Chief of Staff, I also would return to Lancaster, Pennsylvania, where I had gone to Franklin & Marshall College, and visit my favorite submarine sandwich shop. I would go up there on Sundays and sit at the counter eating a steak and cheese, and just listen to what the people were talking about. I never let on that I worked in the White House, because as soon as people hear that they talk to you differently. You have to make a conscious effort to get away from the White House on a regular basis, because that's the only way you get to the unvarnished truth about things. Inside the White House bubble, you are viewed and treated differently depending on your title, and it's easy to forget that all of the attention you get is not because of your personality and good looks, but simply because of your title.

Another occupational hazard for White House staff is burnout. You may be working around the clock trying to get an appropriations bill passed in Congress, and as soon as it's passed, you have to move right on to the next issue. It's not unusual for White House staffers to work fourteen and sixteen hours a day, and ten hours on Saturdays. And as White House Chief of Staff, there are also many times when the phone rings in the middle of the night. The old campaign ad that Hillary Clinton ran in the 2008 campaign about the president having to answer the phone call at 3 AM had it wrong. It's the White House Chief of Staff that takes those calls, and then you have to ask yourself whether the crisis is important or dire enough to wake the president. Then you try and go back to sleep for a couple of hours, and the routine starts all over again the next morning.

So burnout can be a problem. On the other hand, for a kid from a modest family from Brooklyn to grow up to sit at the right hand of the President of the United States is incredibly rewarding. I had actually left the White House when I got a call that President Reagan wanted to see me about returning to become Deputy and then White House Chief of Staff. When I walked into the Oval Office, Reagan got up from behind his desk to greet me, and he said that "Nancy and I want you to come home!" I had been reluctant to accept the position at first, because the saying goes that you accept that kind of job the first time because you're a patriot, and the second time because you're a glutton for punishment. But agreeing to serve as Ronald Reagan's White House Chief of Staff was the smartest professional decision I ever made. Only in America!

◆ ◆ ◆ ◆ ◆

7. Behind the Scenes Policy Makers: The Executive Branch

by Sean Gailmard

"How a bill becomes a law," the classic textbook account of government policy making, actually describes just a way station in the process of making public policy in the United States today. The designs of Congress do not take effect simply or automatically by dint of passing a bill that garners the president's signature. Nor do the president and his agents merely "execute" or bring into effect the writ of Congress with selfless fidelity to Congress's aims.

Much of the work of policy making is done instead in the executive branch bureaucracy—the corps of departments headed by cabinet secretaries, and the looser groupings of agencies and commissions that comprise the "independent agencies."

The executive branch does not merely "fill up the details" left vague by congressional directives, as polite legal fiction sometimes has it, so as to square federal agency activity with the constitutional stipulation that only Congress can make law. The Federal Communications Commission, in charting a policy course toward "net neutrality"—and picking a particular version of that concept to codify in regulation—is not working out the minutiae of a broad policy architecture articulated by Congress. In this instance and innumerable others, federal agencies themselves set the policy, in the sense of choosing among competing interests and values in society, in a legally authoritative way. Absent the reach and expertise that federal agencies bring to bear, the scope of modern public policy would be inconceivable.

In this essay I review how federal agencies come to exercise the power to make policy, some of the channels through which they exercise it, and the possibilities for higher-level, constitutionally enumerated branches (Congress, the president, and federal courts) to check and control policy making in federal agencies.

POLICY MAKING BY FEDERAL AGENCIES

The classical theory of policy making by bureaucratic agencies holds that they exercise this authority by virtue of delegation under law from Congress. The Federal Trade Commission has legal authority to hammer out exactly what is meant by "business combination" in the restraint of trade, and therefore, to make trade-offs between the welfare of consumers and the profits of firms— because Congress granted that authority, and the federal courts have interpreted the delegation as consistent with the Constitution. The president plays a formal role in this delegation as well, inasmuch as he typically signs the bill that spells out the delegating.

Congress and the president choose to delegate policy-making authority to federal agencies due to agencies' dual advantages of focus on a specific issue and expertise on issues in their domain. Agencies focus much more deeply on a smaller number of problems than Congress, whose members are, comparatively speaking, generalists on policy matters. This expertise gives agencies an advantage in anticipating the consequences of alternative policy choices. The agencies have a greater degree of information that can be brought to bear on policy, enabling them to make more reasoned policy on various issues than if Congress made all policy itself. The politics of legislative enactment do not themselves prove that this delegation of policy-making authority is in the general public's interest, if there is such a thing, but given that policy will be made on an issue, reasoned consideration by relative experts seems beneficial.

On the other hand, delegations by Congress and the president to federal agencies give rise to what political scientists call "principal-agent problems." Congress and the president are understood here as "principals" who wish for their common "agent," the agency, to exercise a skill or utilize some expertise on the principals' behalf. Precisely because the principal does not possess that expertise, it cannot always be sure that the agent was faithful to its intent. Asymmetric information can lead to principal-agent problems, as can conflicting goals or visions of good public policy. Although the career staff in federal agencies is typically composed of relatively public-spirited individuals, they cannot be expected to have the same sense of the best resolution of public policy trade-offs that members of Congress or the president have.

One presumes, in particular, that employees of the National Labor Relations Board, the Environmental Protection Agency, and the State Department are more concerned about union organization rights, environmental protection, and diplomacy, respectively, than the average member of Congress or political appointee. Political scientists interpret the actions of Congress and the president with respect to federal agencies as an attempt to mitigate principal-agent problems—for example, Congress's design of administrative procedures—but by their very nature, these problems can never be entirely extirpated.

Although Congress and the president are both principals with respect to bureaucratic agents, this does not imply that they have a common interest in the agents' policy choices. On the contrary, the degree of conflict between them can imply greater discretion for the agency to steer its own course. Just as control is most effective and authoritative when Congress and the president speak in unison, divided interests between these principals create space for independent bureaucratic policy making. Political scientists refer to this as "bureaucratic drift." More will be said later in this chapter about specific approaches Congress and the president use to mitigate principal-agent problems with respect to federal agencies.

THE RULEMAKING PREROGATIVE

Rulemaking is the process through which executive branch agencies write regulations that have the force of law. Rulemaking is itself governed by an extensive body of law, some of it statutory and much of it case law. The watershed statute on rulemaking is the Administrative Procedure Act (APA) of 1946. The APA and subsequent amendments define several forms of rulemaking and the procedures federal agencies must use for regulations to stand up to legal scrutiny. Probably the canonical form of APA rulemaking is "informal," or "notice and comment," rulemaking.

In brief, "notice and comment" rulemaking begins when an agency publishes a Notice of Proposed Rule Making (NPRM) in the Federal Register. In the NPRM, the agency notifies the public of the draft regulation it intends to enact, and solicits comments from interested parties and the public. Commenters do not have to demonstrate any special expertise on the rule or that they are likely to be affected by its content. The agency then revises the NPRM into a final rule, which it publishes in the federal register, and adds to the stock of rules in the Code of Federal Regulations (CFR)—the federal agency analogue to the U.S. Code. Other types of rulemaking include formal "on the record" rulemaking and "negotiated rulemaking."

The procedural steps in rulemaking were established by Congress to help ensure the sensitivity of agencies to public input and to reflect available information as adduced in comments. But promulgation of a "final rule" by an agency after receiving and processing public comment does not in any sense make the rule a "final say" on policy. Instead, agencies can be sued in federal court by parties adversely affected by their rules and by other parties granted standing in specific statutes by Congress. Congress, indeed, can manipulate grants of standing as a method of obtaining "cheap" oversight of agency activities by interested parties.

When agency rules are challenged in federal court, courts review the agency's finding of facts that supported the specific content of the rule and the agency's finding of law that give the agency the legal right to address the issue by taking action. Review of agency fact finding in court review of regulations is much different than in criminal cases: far from "beyond a reasonable doubt," agencies must only show that their rules are consistent with the preponderance of the evidence adduced in the record as a whole. This provides a check on rules that are "arbitrary and capricious"—they must have some evidentiary basis—but gives agencies wide latitude to interpret the evidence as they determine. Review of agency finding of law is designed to ensure that the agency actually has the legal authority it claims to regulate.

In the famous case *Chevron v. Natural Resource Defense Council* (1984), the Supreme Court ruled that (i) if a statute has specifically addressed an issue of regulatory choice, the agency much follow it; (ii) if a statute has not specifically addressed an issue of regulatory choice, the agency can choose any reasonable interpretation of the statute (and the reviewing court will not demand the agency utilize the court's own preferred interpretation).

Court review is not the only channel of control of rulemaking by Constitutional actors. In 1996 Congress passed the Congressional Review Act, which specifies procedures by which Congress and the president can act in concordance to invalidate an agency rule. Of course, a combination of both houses of Congress and the president could pass a law to invalidate any specific action of an agency not mandated by the Constitution, and the Congressional Review Act was not necessary to confer this power. The CRA in fact specifies a particular legislative vehicle, the joint resolution of disapproval, that receives favorable parliamentary consideration in Congress compared with an ordinary bill or joint resolution. If both houses pass and the president signs the joint resolution of disapproval within a specific period of time after the agency's publication of the final rule in the Federal Register, the agency's rule is invalidated, and it is prohibited from promulgating a substantially similar rule in the future.

Of course, given that important final rules will rarely be promulgated by agencies over presidential objection, the CRA's requirement of congressional *and* presidential disapproval of a regulation implies that it will rarely be invoked. One high-profile case was the invalidation in 2001 of workplace ergonomics regulations by the Department of Labor. Nearly a decade in the making, the ergonomics rules were published in the waning days (and with the support) of President Bill Clinton's Administration; the George W. Bush Administration took power within the window of review under the CRA. The unified Republican Congress and Republican President agreed to invalidate the ergonomics rules under the CRA's procedure.

The president has even more potent tools to manage, shape, and control the policy made through rulemaking by cabinet departments. This power was claimed for the first time in 1981 by President Ronald Reagan, in Executive Order 12,291. Specifically, under the aegis of his responsibility for management of the executive branch in general, President Reagan claimed the authority to review, and if desired to veto, "major" agency regulations[1] before their final publication. This authority is referred to as "regulatory review." It is carried out by the Office of Information and Regulatory Affairs (OIRA) in the Office of Management and Budget (OMB), a critical part of the Executive Office of the President (EOP). Presidents Bill Clinton and George W. Bush elaborated and extended this presidential authority, and all presidents since Reagan have availed themselves of the power.

OIRA (and OMB) are staffed with close presidential advisors and carry the analytical capacity to scan the whole executive branch. They are not "line" agencies that carry out specific laws; instead, they help the president manage the executive branch in general and, in practice, help guard the interests of the president (and perhaps the presidency). OIRA cannot claim the authority to write regulations itself on behalf of agencies; when a statute delegates authority to the Administrator of the EPA to promulgate regulations for controlling emission of pollutants from electric utilities, the president and the president's agent cannot simply seize the authority. But through their constitutional obligation to execute laws, and implicitly to manage the executive branch, presidents have claimed the authority to implement a coherent regulatory agenda—and therefore to invalidate or return to agencies for further consideration any regulations they (or OIRA agents) deem inconsistent with that agenda.

OIRA regulatory review confers significant authority on the president to manage the content of agency regulations. But presidents have only claimed that it extends to rules issued by departments in the cabinet (either by statute or presidential designation; thus, the EPA is included). No presidents have claimed to extend OIRA review to "independent" agencies such as the Securities and Exchange Commission, the Federal Communications Commission, or the Federal Trade Commission.

REINING IN AGENCIES

Because agencies are not elected, they lack the democratic legitimacy of Congress or the president. Moreover, they are not granted specific policy-making powers by the Constitution. Yet they make important trade-offs among social interests, embodied in policy that has the force of law. This juxtaposition poses a potential threat to the concepts of popular sovereignty and constitutionalism. The threat can be alleviated to the extent that constitutional elites, the president and Congress, have effective tools to control policies enacted by agencies. Apart from such theoretical niceties, principal-agent problems between federal agencies and Congress and the president imply that the latter principal actors have strong incentives to use available tools to influence what agencies do.

A potent channel of such control is influence over personnel. Influence over executive branch personnel lies more with the president than with Congress, and presidents have made increasingly broad use of this power in recent years. Specifically, presidents work hard to ensure that appointees to leadership positions within the cabinet departments are not only competent but ideologically consistent with their bosses. This became clear in the 1980s with President Reagan's appointment of conservatives James Watt as Secretary of the Interior and Anne Gorsuch Burford as Administrator of the EPA. Use of this strategy has not abated, as revealed by the George W. Bush Administration's preference for Republicans as U.S. Attorneys.

But presidents can exercise this tool well beyond the top levels of federal agencies, all of which are subject to Senate confirmation. Increasingly, presidents have made use of "schedule C," non–Senate-confirmed, appointments to influence midlevel staff at the agencies. In this way, handpicked presidential appointees help determine the fine details of policy (not just overall direction at the most senior secretarial level) made by federal agencies in the first place, and then review those policies under the auspices of OIRA. Personnel and regulatory review combine to give presidents a relatively high degree of control over the policy enacted as rules in cabinet departments.

In addition, presidents also have the formal authority to dismiss presidential appointees in cabinet departments without specific cause; that is, these agents serve at the pleasure of the president. Although this exact issue of presidential removal was the reason for impeachment of President Andrew Johnson in 1868, the president's unilateral authority to dismiss senior cabinet staff at his pleasure has been settled since at least a 1924 Supreme Court case. On the other hand, presidents, at least since a 1936 Supreme Court case, do not have the formal authority to dismiss at will the senior staff of independent agencies. (Career, nonappointed staff subject to merit system protection cannot be dismissed at the pleasure of the president, either in cabinet departments or independent agencies.)

Congress also may avail itself of other levers of influence or control, although they are less formal than those previously named. Congress can threaten recalcitrant agencies with budget reductions, but inasmuch as Congress actually values the services produced by the agency, this threat may not prove credible. Even the highly visible Republican critique of EPA regulation and enforcement in the early 1980s, and attendant calls for budget cuts, led only to short-term reductions in the EPA's budget. Essentially all of the sizeable 1982 budget cuts were restored by 1983. Congress can also engage in strict oversight of agency actions. Any committee of Congress can hold hearings on virtually any program in any agency of the government. Oversight hearings, once relatively rare, have become quite common in recent decades. They serve to communicate both ways between agencies and Congress, and agencies have every incentive to take them seriously. Oversight hearings influence agencies by communicating the will of Congress, or at least the preferences of individual members of Congress, but rarely take the form of "punishment" of an agency for a wayward policy choice.

CONCLUSION

Federal agencies play a crucial role in making public policy. Agencies give structure to the general designs of Congress and the president, and they often exercise authority by articulating trade-offs between competing social interests or values without specific direction to do so by Congress or the president. Yet agencies are restricted by the procedures they must follow to make policy; by federal court review; by presidential control over personnel; and by congressional oversight. When that process works as intended, the expertise and focus that federal agencies possess is directed by constitutionally named actors to ideally connect agency policy-making activity to a broader public interest.

◆ ◆ ◆ ◆ ◆

8. Independent Money Managers: Presidents and the Federal Reserve

by John T. Woolley

Every president shares responsibility for management of the economy with a prestigious independent agency, the Federal Reserve System. Dubbed "the Fed," this institution is responsible for monetary policy—the management of money supply, interest rates, and inflation—and for regulating financial institutions and maintaining financial stability. All of these duties have proved critical in coping with the recent financial crisis.

Presidents have broad responsibilities for the national economy, and the state of the economy looms large in public judgment of presidential performance. Although the Fed's independence makes cooperative engagement difficult, presidents have an abiding interest in its decisions and smooth operation. At times, the Fed has acted contrary to executive preferences, and tensions have flared; for instance, the Fed kept interest rates higher than a president might prefer to prevent inflation. In recent years, however, presidents have been more appreciative of the Fed's independence and its willingness to act decisively in the face of gridlock among elected officials.

In the financial crisis of 2007–2008, the Fed with other financial regulators devised and implemented a host of novel policy strategies. These approaches were widely credited with stopping incipient panics and averting a devastating depression. Still, these policies were controversial, prompting renewed congressional oversight of the Fed. After two hundred years of operation, the Fed finds itself a more transparent institution, but one that has also become more openly involved in policy conflict.

PRESIDENTS AND THE FED

Presidents have significant influence over the Fed. One source is the power of appointment to the Federal Reserve Board, particularly the ability to nominate the Chair. Normally, presidents expect to have a close working relationship with the Fed Chair, and their appointment authority enables the executive to shape the makeup of the Federal Reserve Board. Another source of influence is the president's legislative role as agenda-setter. By setting the agenda, a chief executive can diminish or enhance the responsibilities of the Fed. The president also wields the constitutional power of the veto. Through veto, the president can protect the Fed or prevent legislation that might weaken the administration's role in monetary policy. Finally, presidents and their economic advisors can directly communicate with the Fed at various levels.

The basic structure of responsibilities in the Federal Reserve has been stable since the 1930s. At the apex of the system is the Board of Governors with seven members, nominated by the president and confirmed by the Senate. Board member appointments are for staggered fourteen-year terms, but members rarely serve a full term. The president designates the Chair and Vice-Chairs among the Board members for four-year terms, and their confirmation is also approved by the Senate. The Board has exclusive responsibility for setting two instruments of monetary policy: the discount rate (the interest rate for lending funds to qualified financial institutions) and reserve requirements (the percentage of bank deposits that must be held in cash rather than converted into loans). The Board also sets regulations for many banks, bank holding companies, and large financial institutions designated as "systemically important."

The Fed's second main policy-making venue is the Federal Open Market Committee (FOMC). The FOMC is responsible for policy concerning the purchase and sale of securities by the Federal Reserve. Traditionally, these "open market operations" have been the primary means of influencing interest rates and the money supply. They operate in an interbank market, known as the Federal Funds market. At full strength, the FOMC has twelve voting members, including all the members of the Board of Governors plus five of twelve presidents of Federal Reserve District Banks, each of whom serve in rotation. The Board Chair is chair of the FOMC. The New York Federal Reserve Bank conducts open market operations; thus, the president of that bank serves as FOMC vice-chair. A controversial feature of the system is that district bank boards of directors, mostly private bankers, and select district bank presidents, are subject to veto by the Federal Reserve Board.

FED INDEPENDENCE

The Fed is designed to be independent of partisan politics. Central bank independence is widely regarded as essential to following noninflationary monetary policy. The Fed's independence flows from several factors. The system is not subject to congressional appropriations, for instance, or included in the Executive Budget. No outside agency audits the Fed's activities with respect to their monetary policy impact or efficiency. The Fed's primary funding source is its earnings on the System open market account—the assets the Fed buys and sells to pursue its policy objectives. Furthermore, the president cannot dismiss top Fed officials, who are appointed for terms of up fourteen years (although since 1980, Board appointees have served only 5.5 years on average). Over the years, a powerful norm has also evolved, which holds that it is inappropriate for presidents to apply explicit public pressure on the Fed over monetary policy.

The implementation of monetary policy has reinforced the Fed's independence. Historically, the Fed acted in very broad, short-term markets and did not directly purchase Treasury debt. Together, these operating principles reduced pressures to monetize government debt or to support particular sectors of the economy.

The Fed's independence has long been associated with a tradition of secrecy. Defenders of secrecy argue that it is necessary to ensure full and frank deliberation within the institution, and, in turn, good policy. They also argue that secrecy is necessary to protect valuable private economic information shared with the Fed. However, secrecy has been controversial. The Fed's secrecy reinforces many of the doubts and fears about the Fed, including conspiracy theories.

The Fed's independence limits presidential influence compared with major cabinet agencies. Presidents are normally able to designate a Fed Chair early in their term, an important moment to secure favorable monetary policy. There have been reports suggesting, for instance, that both Bill Clinton and George W. Bush used Alan Greenspan's reappointment to dictate the future course of monetary policy. Although Greenspan served for nearly two decades, it is unlikely that many future Fed Chairs will have such long tenures. Further, more frequent turnover on the Board will enhance the role of the Fed staff in creating monetary policy.

Given the high rate of turnover on the Board, recent presidents have certainly had many opportunities to shape the composition of the Board. Presidents feel that they must nominate candidates, however, who are seen as well qualified or who have detailed knowledge of the financial industry. In periods of crisis, presidents also tend to stick with incumbent Chairs who are viewed favorably by financiers. Because of the need for Senate confirmation and credible policy, presidents have almost never proposed nominees who are extreme either in their economic views or in their politics. These constraints tend to keep policy anchored solidly within the mainstream.

THE FINANCIAL CRISIS: GOOD POLICY, BAD POLITICS

For nearly 25 years prior to the financial crisis of 2008, there was remarkable stability in economic growth and inflation—what economists have called "the great moderation." For most of this period, Alan Greenspan served as Fed Chair. Economists broadly agreed about how to approach monetary policy. Undergirding that consensus was a confidence in the ability of markets to recognize risks and to reflect them appropriately in prices. While some say that the great moderation resulted from good monetary policy, others believe that it was merely good luck. In any case, the financial crisis of 2008 undermined such faith in the economic system. In short order major financial institutions failed, and markets critical to the overall economy collapsed. The Fed's key interest rates approached 0%, leaving the Fed with little ability to stimulate the economy by reducing interest rates. In those circumstances, the Fed, working in close collaboration with the Treasury and other financial regulators, undertook a set of sweeping reforms.

Through so-called special purpose vehicles, for instance, the Fed took ownership of billions of dollars of debt from failing financial giants. The new intervention methods, known popularly as "quantitative easing," involved massive purchases of debt in a variety of financial markets—markets for securitized mortgages, for other asset-backed securities, for commercial paper, and for long-term Treasury bonds. The Fed also provided special lending facilities for a variety of specialized markets.

Qualitative easing began as an effort to provide liquidity for markets that had substantially failed due to lost trust in the solvency of trading partners. Qualitative easing evolved into a mechanism for providing economic stimulus by directly providing bank reserves (i.e., funds available to use for loans) and by lowering longer-term interest rates. By lowering rates, the Fed hoped that households and others could refinance debt at much lower interest rates and reduce their fixed costs. By lowering rates across the board, qualitative easing also drove investors to pursue higher yields by making riskier investments—especially in equities. Stock markets soared, and because stock ownership is highly unequal, the wealthy disproportionately benefitted.

Several critiques emerged from this innovation, often with partisan tones. Throughout the Great Recession, there were questions about the Fed's failure to recognize and address growing problems before they reached crisis levels. For instance, it was clear that the Fed had not effectively used its authority with respect to mortgage loans. Eventually, evidence also emerged showing that Fed regulators chose to relax enforcement standards on big banks. Critics even argued that the Fed had been "captured" by the banks and that the Fed's regulatory role clashed with its duties to stabilize the overall economy. Influential lawmakers asked whether the Fed had betrayed the trust represented by its special grant of independence. Did it need to be more open to scrutiny and criticism?

The Fed's innovative crisis response was also controversial. Some argued that it shifted the Fed toward engaging in capital allocation, thus demanding more political involvement and oversight. Others argued that the bailouts were unwise in the long term, despite their short-term successes in defusing the short-term crisis. They taught financial market participants to believe that failures would be handled in ways that protected some investors, especially bondholders. More than unfair, this practice undercuts market discipline and raises "moral hazard" concerns.

Others criticized qualitative easing because it effectively provided a massive subsidy to Wall Street banks, worsening already troubling inequalities. Critics also claimed that qualitative easing facilitated dysfunction in Washington, D.C., by mitigating economic pain attributable to political gridlock. Others worried that the generous liquidity the program provided would cause future inflation and harm the international position of the dollar. In the program, the volume of assets the Fed owned more than quintupled, from around $800 million to more than $4.5 trillion. That was, in effect, a massive exercise in printing money. As long as the economy was in a slump, such liquidity was not a problem. However, when the economy began to recover, could the Fed muster the political resolve to reverse such a large stimulus in an orderly and timely way?

The problem of "tapering" the stimulus and gradually returning to more traditional operating procedures preoccupied markets and policy makers starting as early as 2013. In an effort to avoid causing panic in markets as policy changed, Fed officials utilized public communications. Post-meeting press conferences by the Fed Chair, first started in 2011, became a central feature in "forward guidance" to shape market expectations.

DODD-FRANK REFORM

For many years, proposed reforms of the U.S. financial regulatory system emphasized two ideas. One was to unify financial regulators, so that giant and highly diversified financial firms could be examined as a whole rather than according to their functional parts. The second was to assign one institution to assess and maintain overall financial system stability. A prominent postcrisis reform proposal called for a transformed Fed to combine monetary policy and responsibility for system stability. Yet another proposal was to merge parts of several agencies, including the Fed, to create a new financial regulator altogether. However, many lawmakers were unwilling to confer powerful new responsibilities on the Fed given its failures to anticipate and foreclose unsustainable financial speculation. The Fed itself resisted giving up its regulatory responsibilities.

The eventual financial reform law, a large and complex piece of legislation, known popularly as the Dodd-Frank Act, created a new body responsible for system stability that includes Fed representatives, called the Financial Stability Oversight Council (FSOC). Among other powers, the FSOC can designate large, nonbank financial firms as "systemically important." Those firms are then subject to special regulatory oversight by the Fed, including requiring that they participate in periodic "stress tests" to estimate how well they might fare in a future crisis.

Virtually all provisions of the Dodd-Frank Act have proven controversial. As a central implementer of the act, the Fed has come under renewed scrutiny and criticism. Observers from both the progressive-left and the libertarian-right have expressed concerns about the Fed's inherent secrecy, budgetary independence, "capture" by banks, and its expanding regulatory responsibilities. The potential for conflict between the Fed's responsibilities as an industry regulator and as a defender of systemic stability has also caused concerns.

One provision of Dodd-Frank called for designating a second Fed Vice-Chair responsible for financial institutions supervision. There had long been a board member with special responsibility for bank regulatory affairs, but more than four years after the passage of Dodd-Frank, President Obama has not appointed a regulatory Vice-Chair. The reason for the delay is unclear.

In conclusion, the Fed is a powerful economic actor of great concern to presidents, yet largely outside of their direct control. During the financial crisis, the Fed's aggressive innovation helped mitigate the economic downturn in the United States and accelerate recovery. The Fed's economic stimulus provided, in effect, a detour around congressional gridlock, creating a harmonious relationship between the Fed and the White House, different from the usual tensions. In the future, under more normal circumstances, strain between the executive and the Fed are likely to reemerge.

♦ ♦ ♦ ♦ ♦

9. No Friends in Black Robes: Presidents and the Supreme Court

by Stuart S. Taylor, Jr.

The often tense relationship between presidents and Supreme Court justices has helped shape American history, especially since World War II. The Court has issued a number of momentous rulings—including at least three since 1945—to block presidential actions that the Court deemed lawless. For their part, presidents have sought to influence Supreme Court decisions in both the short and the long term by choosing ideologically compatible men and women to fill vacancies.

James Madison, often called the father of the Constitution, foresaw the Court's role reining in presidential as well as congressional power when he explained in *Federalist No. 51* the need for the executive, legislative, and judicial departments of the federal government to provide checks on one another. "Ambition must be made to counteract ambition," Madison wrote, "supplying, by opposite and rival interests, the defect of better motives."

Post–World War II justices have certainly taken that role of counterbalance to heart, issuing profoundly important rulings against Presidents Harry Truman, Richard Nixon, Bill Clinton, and, to a lesser extent, Barack Obama. Truman, Nixon, and Clinton were rebuffed even by some or all of their own appointees. Most memorably, the Court helped drive Nixon from the presidency in 1974 and installed George W. Bush in 2000.

Modern presidents have hardly been passive bystanders in those dramas. Truman, Nixon, Clinton, and Obama all tried to use their appointment power to shape the Court's ideological direction, with varying degrees of success. The Supreme Court nevertheless decided in 1952 that Truman had usurped congressional power in his effort to win the Korean War, a ruling that two of his appointees joined; in 1974, the Court ordered Nixon to hand over incriminating White House tapes to the Watergate Special Prosecutor, a ruling that three of his appointees joined; a 1997 Supreme Court decision was instrumental in getting Clinton impeached, a ruling that both of his appointees joined; and in 2010, the Court's campaign finance decision so upset

Obama that he launched an extraordinary attack on the Court's conservatives during a State of the Union address.

NO FRIENDS IN ROBES

When Vice President Harry Truman, a Democrat, became president in 1945, on the death of President Franklin Roosevelt, he had every reason to expect smooth sailing with the Supreme Court justices. All nine had been appointed by the long-serving Roosevelt. And Truman would replace four of them with personal friends before leaving office in 1953. He chose his Senate pals Harold Burton, a Republican, and Democrat Sherman Minton; his Attorney General, Tom Clark; and his Treasury Secretary, Fred Vinson, as Chief Justice. They were later described by Harvard Law Professor Laurence Tribe as "perhaps the least distinguished group of appointments made by any President in [the 20th] Century."

Truman's appointees did what he wanted for the most part. They supported broad government regulatory authority; they cautiously expanded the civil rights of African Americans; and during the early Cold War years, they upheld tough internal security measures that were said by civil libertarians to violate the rights of Communists and other political dissidents.

But the justices delivered a major shock to Truman in 1952, in *Youngstown Sheet & Tube Co. v. Sawyer*. A 6–3 majority struck down as unconstitutional the president's effort to seize the nation's steel mills without congressional authorization to avert a strike that he feared could do grave damage to the Korean War effort. Truman was furious, especially at his appointees Clark and Burton for joining the majority. He called Clark a "damn fool" and "about the dumbest man I think I've ever run across." Years later, in 1959, he lamented: "Packing the Supreme Court simply can't be done. . . I've tried it and it won't work. . . . Whenever you put a man on the Court he ceases to be your friend."

For all of Truman's complaining, the Steel Seizure decision, as it came to be called, has stood well the test of time. Indeed, in Senate confirmation testimony John Roberts, the current Chief Justice, and others have cited Justice Robert Jackson's concurrence as the most important constitutional analysis of the president's war powers ever written by a justice.

HISTORIC CONFRONTATIONS

Richard Nixon won the presidency in 1968 after a "law and order" campaign assailing Chief Justice Earl Warren and the other liberal justices for coddling criminals. In choosing his own four appointees, Nixon sought conservative jurists who would roll back the Warren Court's limits on police powers to search, seize, wiretap, bug, and interrogate criminal suspects, and its expansion of defendants' rights to counsel and due process. After Warren retired in 1968, Nixon appointed Warren Burger as Chief Justice in 1969 and Harry Blackmun, Lewis Powell, and William Rehnquist as associate justices. These four narrowed the Warren Court's liberal innovations but did not overrule them.

Meanwhile, Powell and especially Blackmun proved to be surprisingly moderate in other areas, especially as time passed. In 1973, for example, Blackmun, Powell, and even the conservative Burger joined the 7–2 majority to create an almost unlimited right to abortion in *Roe v. Wade*, which became the most reviled (by conservatives) Supreme Court decision in modern history. And Blackmun, who wrote the opinion, kept moving leftward, becoming the Court's most liberal member by the time he retired in 1994.

The hardest blow ever dealt by the Supreme Court to a president came in 1974, in *United States v. Nixon*, a landmark 8–0 decision authored by Burger and joined by Blackmun and Powell as well as the more liberal justices (Rehnquist recused himself). Rejecting Nixon's broad claim of "executive privilege," the Court ordered him to turn over to Watergate Special Prosecutor Leon Jaworski highly incriminating tapes of his conversations with aides. The president, facing almost inevitable impeachment and removal, resigned fifteen days later, on August 9, 1974.

After he was elected in 1992, Bill Clinton became the first Democratic president to appoint a justice since 1967. He sought to use his two appointments to move the Supreme Court to the left on abortion, racial affirmative action preferences, and other issues—but not so far as to provoke a big Senate confirmation battle. He succeeded by choosing moderately liberal, widely respected federal appeals court Judges Ruth Bader Ginsburg and Stephen Breyer, respectively, when Byron White and Harry Blackmun retired in 1993 and 1994. Ginsburg and Breyer were easily confirmed. They have done largely what Clinton would have wanted, with Ginsburg—who had been the leading women's rights lawyer of her era—moving further to the left in recent years.

Clinton nonetheless ran afoul of the Court in 1997, when he sought to freeze until after his presidency all proceedings in a sexual harassment lawsuit against him by Paula Jones. The justices, including both Clinton appointees, ruled against him unanimously, and somewhat surprisingly. They held for the first time that a sitting president could be sued for actions outside the scope of his official duties.

That decision led to a lower court order that Clinton testify in a civil deposition about his relations with various women, including twenty-three-year-old

White House intern Monica Lewinsky. Clinton's subsequent sworn denial that he had ever had sexual relations with Lewinsky led in turn to months of criminal investigation by Independent Counsel Kenneth Starr (and bitter attacks on Starr by the Clinton team), followed by a report by Starr to Congress citing evidence that Clinton had obstructed justice and perjured himself both in the deposition and before Starr's grand jury. The Starr Report led to Clinton's impeachment by the Republican House and thus the Senate trial that acquitted Clinton in February 1999.

A FACE-TO-FACE ENCOUNTER

President Obama, unlike Truman, Nixon, and Clinton, has not been on the receiving end of a direct personal rebuff from the Court. But his relations with the five more conservative justices have been extraordinarily confrontational. Most dramatically, during his second State of the Union address, on January 27, 2010, Obama surprised the justices sitting in the first two rows by denouncing the Court's highly controversial, six-day-old decision in *Citizens United v. Federal Election Commission*. It held that corporations have First Amendment rights to spend unlimited amounts of money endorsing and opposing federal candidates. The five Republican-appointed justices had outvoted the four Democratic appointees.

Looking directly at the justices, Obama declared: "With all due deference to separation of powers, last week the Supreme Court reversed a century of law that I believe will open the floodgates for special interests—including foreign corporations—to spend without limit in our elections." After a thunderous standing ovation from Democrats, he added: "I don't think American elections should be bankrolled by America's most powerful interests or, worse, by foreign entities."

This face-to-face rhetorical assault by the president on the Supreme Court was unprecedented. And the reaction was angry. Justice Samuel Alito—whose nomination Obama had voted to reject, as he had that of Roberts—shook his head and mouthed "not true" the moment after the president's assertion. This was apparently a reference to the fact that the Court had not decided whether foreign corporations would enjoy the same political-spending rights as U.S. corporations. Justice Antonin Scalia later called it "a juvenile spectacle."

Chief Justice Roberts hurled his own retort about six weeks later. He said that he had "no problems" with the president's criticizing the Court but suggested that Obama had chosen the wrong setting. "The image of having the members of one branch of the government standing up, literally surrounding the Supreme Court, cheering and hollering while the Court—according to the requirements of protocol—has to sit there expressionless, I think is very troubling," he said. Roberts also suggested that "the State of the Union has degenerated into a political pep rally." The White House responded by taking another shot at the Court.

This was far from the only clash between President Obama and the Court's Republican appointees. For example, in June 2013 he said he was "deeply disappointed" when the five conservatives struck down a key provision of the Voting Rights Act of 1965. A year earlier, Roberts had averted what could have been a monumental clash with Obama when he sort-of sided with the four more liberal justices by casting the fifth vote in June 2013 to uphold the central provisions of Obama's Affordable Care Act, widely known as Obamacare.

APPOINTMENT DISAPPOINTMENT

Although all modern American presidents have been occasionally displeased with Supreme Court decisions, not all had such dramatic confrontations with the justices. But like Truman, Nixon, Clinton, and Obama, all sought to use their appointment power to shape the Court's direction, with the exception of Jimmy Carter, who served from 1977 to 1981 without ever having a Supreme Court vacancy to fill.

The modern president who was most disappointed in his Supreme Court appointees—at least, in two of the five—was the centrist Dwight Eisenhower, who in 1952 broke twenty years of Democratic control of the presidency and served for eight years. He appointed longtime Republican California Governor Earl Warren Chief Justice after Vinson's unexpected death in 1953, and New Jersey Judge William Brennan, a Democrat, in 1957. Eisenhower chose Warren, who had helped him win the 1952 Republican nomination, in part to pay a debt. He chose Brennan because a well-regarded Northeastern Catholic Democrat might play well politically. But to Eisenhower's dismay, the "Warren Court" became famous for its liberal activist decisions, with Warren and the passionately progressive, charmingly persuasive Brennan leading the charge. Brennan continued as the Court's leading liberal strategist until his retirement in 1990.

The most famous and controversial Warren Court decision was *Brown v. Board of Education* in 1954, which struck down as unconstitutional state-sponsored segregation of public schools by race. Notably, the decision was unanimous, which increased its moral authority, and was a testament to Warren's persuasive powers with his often-warring colleagues. The Court also ordered that school segregation be ended "with all deliberate speed" and laid the groundwork for lower courts to strike down all other forms of government-sponsored racial segregation and discrimination against minorities.

Eisenhower was not happy about the desegregation decisions, which he thought exceeded the limits of the Court's constitutional power, although he did not publicly assail them. Indeed, he sent National Guard troops to Little Rock, Arkansas, in 1957 to overcome Governor Orval Faubus's defiance of a unanimous Supreme Court order to allow black students to enter Little Rock Senior High School. But Eisenhower complained privately that the Court had overextended its powers in ordering desegregation and in some other areas. He was especially displeased with several decisions striking down Cold War programs that limited the free speech, due process, and other rights of Communists, suspected Communists, and other political dissidents.

When asked, after leaving office, whether he had made any mistakes as president, Eisenhower famously (and perhaps apocryphally, some scholars suggest) responded: "Yes, two, and they are both sitting on the Supreme Court." The two were Warren and Brennan. Eisenhower's other appointees were John Marshall Harlan II and Potter Stewart, both moderate Republicans with distinguished legal minds, and Charles Whittaker, who resigned in 1962 after five unremarkable years. Presidents John F. Kennedy, elected in 1960, and Lyndon Johnson, who took office when Kennedy was assassinated in 1963 and was elected in 1964 to a full term, were largely bystanders to a succession of hugely important decisions by what was still the Warren Court. The Justices decreed that election districts must be reapportioned on the "one person, one vote" principle; worked the revolution in criminal justice cases that Nixon later sought to undo with scant success; pushed for more aggressive school desegregation; greatly expanded the First Amendment free speech rights of the news media, authors, political dissidents, accused pornographers, as well as others; and upheld congressional power to adopt broad civil rights laws.

Meanwhile, Kennedy appointed his Labor Secretary, Arthur Goldberg, who strengthened the Warren Court's liberal wing for three years before leaving to become Ambassador to the United Nations, and former football luminary Byron White. Although White largely shared Kennedy's political views, which were never as liberal as has been widely supposed, his moderate to conservative voting record on some issues caused many to label him a conservative for most of his years on the Court.

President Johnson appointed his close adviser Abe Fortas, an extremely able lawyer, to the Court in 1965 and made Thurgood Marshall, who had been the nation's leading civil rights lawyer, the first African American justice in 1967. Both men, like Goldberg, were liberal stalwarts. Marshall continued to carry the liberal banner, along with Brennan, until his retirement in 1991, a year after Brennan's.

Johnson's 1968 nomination of Justice Fortas to succeed the retiring Earl Warren as Chief Justice failed in the Senate, however, amid controversies over the nominee's continuing close-adviser relationship with Johnson and alleged ethical transgressions. This left the vacancy in the center chair to be filled with Warren Burger after Richard Nixon succeeded Johnson in 1969. Fortas resigned in 1969 and Nixon replaced him with Blackmun.

DRIFTING LEFT

Vice President Gerald Ford, who became president when Nixon resigned in 1974, had only one appointee to the Supreme Court, federal appeals court Judge John Paul Stevens. He proved to be a somewhat unpredictable moderate in his early years; over time, like Blackmun, he moved to the liberal end of the Court's ideological spectrum. President Carter, who beat Ford in 1976, had no Supreme Court vacancies to fill before he lost to Ronald Reagan in 1980.

Reagan, the most conservative president since the 1920s, had sought during his 1980 campaign to counter complaints about his conservative positions on abortion and women's rights by vowing to appoint the first woman to the Supreme Court. And so he did, in 1981, when Justice Potter Stewart retired. Reagan chose Sandra Day O'Connor, a respected Republican former Arizona legislative leader and judge. Reagan also set out to make the Court more conservative on issues including abortion, court-ordered busing to desegregate schools, and racially preferential affirmative action.

Reagan had mixed success in this effort. O'Connor's voting pattern was fairly conservative until the 1990s, when she began drifting gradually to the left, as had Justice Powell, although not as far as Blackmun and Stevens. (This pattern of ideological drift among some conservative appointees has no counterpart among liberal appointees.) Most dramatically, O'Connor joined a 1992 decision to reaffirm what she called the "core holding" of *Roe v. Wade*, protecting broad abortion rights. From 2000 or so until her retirement in 2005, she voted with the liberals in many big cases.

Reagan's two 1986 appointments, after Burger retired, had a more lasting impact on the Court's ideological balance. He chose Rehnquist, long the Court's most conservative member, to replace Burger as Chief Justice, and Antonin Scalia, an outspokenly conservative federal appeals court judge with an acid pen, to fill the associate-justice seat vacated by Rehnquist. Both Rehnquist and Scalia remained conservative. But in 1987, when the moderate

Powell retired—leaving the Court at an ideological tipping point, with four conservatives and four liberals—Reagan fell short of his goal of shifting the balance sharply to the right.

Reagan nominated another strong conservative, Judge Robert Bork. But liberal senators and interest groups erupted in a firestorm of opposition, stressing and often distorting the nominee's long record of well-argued but highly controversial public assaults on the constitutional foundations of abortion rights, racially preferential affirmative action, and other liberal causes. After a titanic confirmation battle, the Senate rejected Bork by a vote of 58–42, to the bitter disappointment of his many admirers.

A second Reagan pick for the Powell seat washed out when it was revealed that he had smoked marijuana as a law professor. In the hope of avoiding another donnybrook, Reagan then chose Anthony Kennedy, a federal appeals court judge from Sacramento. With a record markedly less conservative than Bork's or Scalia's and a reputation for fairness, Kennedy was confirmed in 1988 by a vote of 97–0. He has turned out to be quite conservative on some issues, including gun rights and state's rights; quite liberal on others, including gay rights and the death penalty; and in the middle on still others, including abortion and racial preferences.

Reagan's vice president and successor, George H.W. Bush, was elected in 1988. When the liberal Brennan and Marshall retired in 1990 and 1991, Bush came under strong pressure from his conservative base at last to move the Court decisively to the right. But Bush knew he might not be able to get a known conservative through the Democratic Senate. So he chose little-known federal appeals court Judge David Souter—a "stealth nominee," some called him—in 1990 to fill the Brennan vacancy. Bush had been privately assured by admirers from Souter's home state of New Hampshire that he would be a "home run" for conservatives; some liberals warned that he would destroy abortion rights and set back civil rights. But Souter was easily confirmed (by 90–9) because his record was both respectable and unrevealing. And before long, Souter surprised both the president and the liberal critics, becoming a fairly consistent member of the Court's liberal bloc. The most dramatic sign of this evolution was his joint opinion with O'Connor and Kennedy in that 1992 abortion decision. Before long, conservative Court-watchers were vowing "no more Souters."

DRIFTING RIGHT

Clarence Thomas, Bush's 1991 nominee to succeed Marshall, was the second African American justice in history. He was no Souter, and no Marshall. After growing up poor in rural, segregated Pin Point, Georgia, he had made it to and through Yale Law School. As the Reagan-appointed Chairman of the Equal Employment Opportunity Commission, he had strongly opposed racial preferences, an article of faith for liberals. Although his views on other issues were largely unknown, Thomas became a pariah to liberals after a former subordinate, Anita Hill, accused him of sexual harassment, which he angrily denied. Thomas won confirmation by a narrow, 52–48 vote. He soon proved to be a fervent conservative on race, voting rights, abortion, religion, the death penalty, crime, gay rights, gun rights, campaign finance regulation, environmental regulation, and a wide range of other hot issues.

Eight years after Bill Clinton beat the first President Bush in 1992, the Supreme Court made his son, George W., the second President Bush. The December 12, 2000, ruling was one of the most bitterly denounced (by Democrats) of all time. Overturning a Florida Supreme Court decision that had kept hope alive for then-Vice President Al Gore, Bush's opponent, the Court ended the recounting of disputed votes in Florida that had riveted the nation since the November 7 election. Seven justices agreed that the Florida recount process was so unreliable as to violate the Constitution. Two of those—Breyer and Souter—would have given the state more time to try to count all the disputed ballots. But the other five, all appointed by Republicans, held that no recount could be done both fairly and fast enough to meet "minimal constitutional standards."

Justices Stevens and Ginsburg dissented, thundering that the Court's action "can only lend credence to the most cynical appraisal of the work of judges throughout the land." Defenders of the decision said the Court had to avert the risk that Inauguration Day might arrive before the presidential election had been settled. But squadrons of law professors, most of them liberal, denounced the Court's decision as a naked power-grab with no basis in law. Even some conservatives said that the justices should have deferred to Congress's constitutional power to settle disputed presidential elections.

President George W. Bush appointed two conservative federal appeals court judges, Roberts and Alito, after Rehnquist died and O'Connor announced her retirement in 2005. Alito was considerably more conservative than the by-now moderately liberal O'Connor. This made the Court—with its ideological center of gravity now occupied by the usually conservative but sometimes liberal Justice Kennedy—perhaps the most conservative in modern history on many issues.

President Obama's two appointees—federal appeals court Judge Sonia Sotomayor, the Court's first Hispanic American, in 2009, and Solicitor General (and former Harvard Law School Dean) Elena Kagan, in 2010—did not change the ideological balance much. Both were liberals like the men they replaced, the Republican-appointed Souter and Stevens.

Obama's appointments did, however, produce another first in modern history: all five of the more conservative justices had been appointed by Republican presidents and all four of the liberals by Democrats. This highlighted the Court's polarization into Republican-conservative and Democratic-liberal camps, with Kennedy in the middle—a precarious ideological balance that may be a formula, the next time a justice retires, for a Senate confirmation battle that could make the scourging of Robert Bork look tame.

◆ ◆ ◆ ◆ ◆

10. At Opposite Ends of Pennsylvania Avenue: Presidents and Congress

by Richard E. Cohen

Presidents regularly send to Congress their proposals for new legislation. If Congress responds, it typically will take months or even years to hold hearings, draft proposals, debate and vote on the measures, and resolve differences between the House- and Senate-passed versions. Only then will clerks deliver a printed bill to the White House for the signature of the president, who may bring the process full circle with the flourish of a signing ceremony. Some committee chairs or leaders from each party might stand behind the president as props—to applaud or, if they are fortunate, receive a pen that the president used in signing the bill. But it will be the president's moment, with the legislation to be added to the presidential talking points and perhaps to become a major part of the president's legacy.

Notice, for example, what President George H.W. Bush said as he enacted the far-ranging amendments to the Clean Air Act in November 1990: "As we used to say in the Navy, 'Mission defined. Mission accomplished.'" At a White House event, President Bush signed the top page of a stack of paper that represented two years of congressional work in crafting the legislation, claiming much of the credit for the new law's broad principles. Even though Congress might have made countless decisions or written hundreds of pages of legislative language, the outcome typically becomes known as the president's health care policy, the president's tax cut policy, and so on. In part, that emphasis reflects the national news media's preoccupation with the

White House, where it's easy to identify who is in charge and represents the single face of the institution, rather than the 535-person rabble on Capitol Hill. In the century since Presidents Woodrow Wilson and Franklin D. Roosevelt proposed and won enactment of their "New Freedom" and "New Deal" agendas, presidents typically have sat atop the legislative process like colossuses. Congress, whose constitutional structure and responsibilities have been described as those of the "First Branch," instead has become more reactive than envisioned by the Founding Fathers or than was practiced during the 19th century.

Each president has brought his own identity and personal background to the critical relationship between the White House and Congress. Ultimately, the performance of chief executives in dealing with Congress has been measured by their wins and losses. In the past century, little major legislation has been enacted without the president taking the initiative and pressing for subsequent action, often by urging public support to pressure Congress. "The president proposes, Congress disposes" is a simplified, but common, adage. There are other ways in which Congress can influence presidential action—including the Senate's power to confirm high-ranking nominees to the executive branch and the judiciary, plus its authority to ratify treaties. Both the House and Senate also conduct oversight of federal agencies, which can often be disruptive. But these are largely reactive steps by Congress.

On the relatively few occasions when Congress has taken the legislative initiative, the result often has been disastrous or otherwise unproductive. That was the case, for example, when Newt Gingrich became House Speaker in 1995 and sought approval of the "Contract with America" on which Republicans had successfully campaigned the previous year. When President Bill Clinton mostly objected to those sweeping policy changes from the Republican-controlled Congress, Gingrich and his allies deadlocked with Clinton after lengthy negotiations, an escalating showdown that ultimately led to a shutdown of the federal government and a retreat by Republicans.

Certainly, the details that Congress adds to presidential proposals may be significant. Lawmakers in the House and Senate remain relevant players in the federal government. But they offer notes for the music, while the president typically acts as conductor of the grand legislative symphony.

As we have witnessed recently, there are also stretches of months and even years when the president and Congress produce little legislation of significance. In part, that was the intent of the Framers of the Constitution who insisted on carefully crafted checks and balances on power. Granted, the Founding Fathers didn't envision the level of polarization and constant bickering that have become routine in Washington, but that may decline when a future president wins an overwhelming electoral mandate for a specific agenda.

OBAMA AND CONGRESS

When he was elected president in November 2008, Barack Obama brought strengths and weaknesses to his dealings with Congress. His 53 percent of the popular vote was the strongest performance by a Democrat since Lyndon Johnson in 1964. His rhetorical skills and background as the first racial-minority president had stirred unusual enthusiasm from the public, especially at a time when the nation was mired in a deep recession. But Obama had limited experience in Washington, having served only four years in the Senate, much of which he spent running for president. His first campaign for president relied more on broad themes than on specific proposals. Somewhat surprisingly for a former senator, Obama also kept his political distance from Congress—including its Democratic leaders.

The 2008 election centered less on specific issues and more on demographic changes, including Obama's race and the big increase in young voters. As journalists Dan Balz and Haynes Johnson wrote in their book, *The Battle for America 2008*, the campaign "did not answer the question of whether the public wanted a return to big government—or to the principles of government as the neutral umpire."[1] During the Democratic primary, for example, Obama and Hillary Clinton had bickered over the details of health reform. But candidate Obama never offered an outline, let alone the specifics, of a health reform plan. Likewise, despite a surge in unemployment and with the nation's banking and financial systems in crisis on the eve of the election, Obama did not detail how he planned to revive the economy.

With Obama providing inspirational rhetoric in his inaugural address, it was Democratic leaders in Congress who moved quickly to fill in the specifics. With an economic "stimulus" bill as the initial urgent priority, House Speaker Nancy Pelosi took charge of its preparation after the election. She, in turn, named House Appropriations Committee chairman David Obey to coordinate the House's handling of the bill. Obey placed his imprint on the measure when he revealed the details of the $825 billion proposal to reporters in his Capitol office five days before Obama was sworn in. "Indeed, it was Mr. Obey, the third most senior member of the House, who, in large measure, shaped the bill, in concert with other House Democratic leaders," the *New York Times* reported at the time.[2] When reporters asked him about Obama's contribution to that proposal, Obey sarcastically referred to him as "the crown prince"—with the clear implication that the congressional baron had crafted the details. The completed measure was sent to Obama a month later, with modest reductions to accommodate a few Republican supporters in the Senate.

A similar script characterized the yearlong and far more complex handling of the health reform bill, which became law in March 2010 as the Affordable Care Act. Again, Obama offered only broad outlines for how the Democratic-controlled Congress should proceed. The details were first set by Speaker Pelosi in close coordination with the chairman of the three House committees that worked on health care issues. The sausage making in the House and later in the Senate, under the direction of Majority Leader Harry Reid, took place largely behind the scenes among Democrats. Obama and his aides largely deferred on the specifics, although they were comfortable with the results. "While Obama used his bully pulpit to try to rally support for the broad outlines of an overhaul, he left it largely to congressional leaders to work out the details," *Congressional Quarterly* reported.[3]

With strong Democratic majorities in each chamber, the House and Senate approved these and other initiatives during the hectic first two years of Obama's presidency. Obama and his team basked in taking credit. But the perceived lack of bipartisanship had major consequences in Obama's dealings with Republicans in Congress, culminating in a painful political setback for Democrats in the November 2010 congressional elections. Republicans picked up sixty-four seats in the House, the biggest turnover from one party to the other since 1948, and Republican John Boehner replaced Pelosi as Speaker. Republicans also made gains in the Senate, although Democrats narrowly kept control until 2014. The political earthquake was fueled by grassroots "Tea Party" opposition to Obama and the legislation that he had encouraged and signed. Obama retained the reins of power, but his clout on Capitol Hill had been diminished. The 2010 election provided a stinging rebuke of his big win two years earlier.

WHEN PRESIDENTS SUCCEED

There are cautionary lessons in President Obama's often fraught relationship with Congress, as well as lessons to be gleaned from the most successful relationships between the White House and Capitol Hill. In the seven decades of the modern, post–World War II political era, for instance, two presidents are widely credited with achieving the most successful legislative record. They were Lyndon Johnson in 1965 and Ronald Reagan in 1981. One was a liberal Democrat who passed his "Great Society" program to expand government. The other was a conservative Republican who achieved his goal of lower federal taxes and spending. One had spent more than thirty years in Washington, and the other had spent most of his career in California—first as an actor and then as governor. But the circumstances of their legislative successes were strikingly similar.

Both Johnson and Reagan, for instance, firmly articulated their agendas. In the 1964 campaign, Johnson was clear in describing his goals. "I ask the American people for a mandate—not to preside over a finished program— not just to keep things going, I ask the American people for a mandate to begin," he told the Democratic convention in accepting his nomination. "This Nation—this generation—in this hour, has man's first chance to build the Great Society—a place where the meaning of man's life matches the marvels of man's labor."[4] Reagan's acceptance speech at the 1980 Republican convention took a very different direction, but he too was clear and compelling. "We are going to put an end to the notion that the American taxpayer exists to fund the federal government. The federal government exists to serve the American people. On January 20th, we are going to re-establish that truth."[5]

Both Johnson and Reagan also enjoyed overwhelming party unity. Just as most Democrats in 1964 were eager to enact a program that their party had long advocated, so too were Republicans largely unified behind Reagan's tax cuts. In each case, members of Congress of those respective parties had spent years preparing the details of the Johnson and Reagan agendas. Some party members were more enthusiastic than others. But, in each case, the presidential nominee was speaking for his party, and its congressional corps was on board.

Johnson and Reagan also benefitted from election landslides. In November 1964, Johnson won 61 percent of the popular vote and took forty-five states in the Electoral College. Democrats that year gained thirty-six seats in the House and two in the Senate, cementing roughly two-thirds majorities in each chamber. In November 1980, Reagan won 51 percent of the popular vote to 41 percent for Democratic President Jimmy Carter and 7 percent for independent John Anderson. Reagan won forty-four states, and Republicans gained thirty-three seats in the House and 12 in the Senate, taking firm working control in each chamber, even though Democrats remained the nominal majority in the House in 1981. Following their elections, both presidents also prepared for quick congressional action in the critical first few months in office (see essays on Carter and Reagan in Section II, "The First Hundred Days," this volume), leveraging the momentum from the election and largely achieving their goals.

Other presidential nominees during the post–World War Two have skillfully defined their objectives in dealing with Congress, and some have had comparable victory margins. But their success may have been more personal for them than for their party, or their objectives may have been more limited. What made the 1964 and 1980 campaigns unique is that Johnson and Reagan each passed legislation that had a huge and lasting impact on the nation.

"Presidential agenda-setting requires a well-planned and consistent political message that can withstand the inevitable bumps in the road and other complications," I wrote in an earlier essay about successful presidential campaigns. "If the national leader wants to change public policy, he must reach out from the start to the lawmakers whose support will be essential."[6]

TENSIONS WITH CONGRESS

In our constitutional system of separation of powers, tensions are inevitable. Even the most successful presidents have faced major traumas with Congress. For Johnson, it was Senate hearings and growing opposition to his handling of the war in Vietnam. Reagan faced harsh hearings from a joint Senate–House committee on his handling of what became known as the Iran-Contra Affair—the secret sending of weapons to Iran in exchange for aid to "Contra" guerrilla fighters in Nicaragua. Johnson and Reagan also encountered later in their presidencies legislative conflicts with members of their own party—chiefly, in budget showdowns.

So every president can expect to face tensions and confrontations with Congress. When Bill Clinton took office in 1993, for example, his policy goals—economic revival and health reform—were remarkably similar to Obama's plans sixteen years later. But it turned out that the earlier large Democratic majorities in Congress were not committed to quick action or to locking arms with the president. Clinton won a scaled-down version of his economic plan, and his health care plan died a slow death. Those contrasts may have been due at least as much to the congressional leaders and rank-and-file attitudes at the time, rather than presidential actions.

Probably the worst conflicts that presidents recently have faced in dealing with Congress were the impeachment of President Nixon by the Democratic-controlled House in 1974 (see "Watergate: Dirty Tricks and Cover-Ups," Section V, this volume), and the impeachment of Clinton by the Republican-controlled House in 1998 (see "The Clinton Impeachment: Washington's Scorched Earth Politics," Section V, this volume). In each case, the president was the focus of lengthy congressional investigations. Nixon resigned before nearly certain House and Senate votes to impeach and then convict him. Clinton survived after the Senate failed to approve charges that had been brought by the House, but his subsequent dealings with Congress were limited and fractious.

Other presidents have had showdowns with the Senate on Supreme Court nominations. Both Nixon and Reagan suffered defeats of their nominees by a Democratic-controlled Senate, or else withdrew them from further consideration to avoid sure defeat. Occasionally, presidents have encountered problems even when their own party controls Congress. Jimmy Carter, who had mostly campaigned separately from congressional Democrats in his successful 1976 contest, found little support from congressional Democrats for his proposals on health care, energy, and taxes. When President George W. Bush in 2005 submitted Social Security reform to the Republican-controlled Congress, his plan was mostly ignored.

Both branches of government must respond to other demands and pressures. Presidents manage the nation's economy and foreign policy and serve as commander in chief of the armed forces. Members of the House run for reelection every two years and often have their eyes focused on the political near horizon. Senators run for election only every six years and often have their own agendas independent of the White House. Presidents serve a maximum of two terms, while individual lawmakers often serve with more than one president. Presidents usually get the most support when Congress is controlled by their own party, but since 1968, seventeen of twenty-four elections have resulted in divided party control of Washington.

SEEKING COMMON GROUND

Presidential elections provide opportunities to reset the relationship between the White House and Congress. But it's up to the candidates to offer policies that are compelling and popular. For effective governing, successful presidents must seek early support from their party's members of Congress and show a willingness to engage with Congress in search of common ground. That burden is mutual. Lawmakers must be responsive and willing to recognize that only the president speaks for the entire nation.

Even in the best of circumstances, the relationship between the White House and Congress is complex. That has been the rule throughout the nation's history. The conflicts in recent years have become starker, however, notably in Obama's dealings with congressional Republicans. To some extent, those tensions reflect broader underlying factors. Contributing factors include the movement of both Democrats and Republicans away from the center of the political spectrum, where compromise is most often found; the decline of states and local jurisdictions that are competitive political battlegrounds, producing lawmakers who must have crossover appeal; the growing partisanship within the nation's news media; and the political polarization that has resulted from all those trends. There also has been vastly increased spending in politics, much of which has grown outside the control of candidates and their parties and a lot of which is spent on negative advertising that only exacerbates the political partisanship.

"The parties began to sort themselves out ideologically," as a result of these changes, former Republican Congressman Tom Davis of Virginia recently wrote. "Along the way, the minority party began to act less as a minority shareholder in government and more like an opposition party. Compromises became rarer and bipartisanship a dirty word.[7]

These are important factors that presidents must face as they deal with Congress. But they should not serve as excuses. In many ways, the ability of the two branches to deal constructively with each other is vital to effective governance of the nation. To the extent that they have faced difficult times in the past, that should not dictate what happens in the future. Nor should the public view continued failures as unavoidable or acceptable.

♦ ♦ ♦ ♦ ♦

11. Social Media Jousting: Presidents and the Modern Media

by Major Garrett

On November 19, 2014, the power of the presidency, legacy media, and social media intersected in the equivalent of a total eclipse. Historians may well look back at the day as the dawn of a new era in presidential communication and the moment when the power of legacy media to influence, let alone intimidate, the White House began to decisively wane.

At 3:05 PM that afternoon the White House posted a video on Facebook of President Obama sitting at the edge of his uncluttered Resolute Desk— only a coffee cup and saucer, black telephone, and two pieces of paper visible. Obama spoke to a White House camera operator brought into the Oval Office to produce the fifty-nine-second taxpayer-funded video. The president wore no suit jacket; his light blue dress shirt matching his solid blue-gray tie and blue suit slacks. He spoke casually under natural Oval Office light augmented by the afternoon sun streaming through the window over his right shoulder.

From the Oval Office the president detailed executive actions he would soon take to provide temporary protection from deportation and legal work status to upward of 5 million undocumented adults. On Facebook. With a government cameraman. And without a single White House correspondent in sight.

President Obama's use of Facebook to communicate a major policy pronouncement was not the issue in this case. The White House had used Facebook, Twitter, Flickr, Instagram, and other social media for years, the better to circumvent major national broadcast networks, cable news channels, newspapers, and wire services. Neither was the issue the White House's deploying a taxpayer-funded propagandist to produce the Facebook video. Rather, the Facebook video was historic precisely because of what it represents in the long tug-of-war between the White House and the media over what news gets covered, and how.

The Obama White House was furious that the major broadcast networks— ABC, CBS, NBC, and Fox—were unwilling to interrupt prime-time "sweeps week" programming for the president's immigration address. White House officials never formally requested prime-time coverage because they knew through a variety of back-channel conversations that the request would be denied. Instead of stewing in silence or complaining publicly—the spindly tactical pushback of a different media era—the White House scorned the networks and the White House correspondents who cover the president. Instead, it took control of the announcement with Obama's unfiltered presentation to the nation.

"In under an hour the video reached more than 1.2 million users on Facebook—227,000 people had viewed it, another 12,000 people had shared it," White House Press Secretary Josh Earnest said that day. "This is a pretty effective way of the president communicating with the American public."[1]

In less than two months, Obama's Facebook post had 4.3 million "views," nearly 31,000 "likes," and nearly 60,000 "shares." Previous presidents would have drooled at the prospect of ignoring the dominant media outlets of their time and speaking instead directly, cheaply, efficiently, and—importantly— repetitively to the nation. Certainly the White House correspondents grasped the import of the press secretary's message.

FIRESIDE CHATS TO FACEBOOK

Yes, Franklin Delano Roosevelt had his fireside chats, and Ronald Reagan had his Saturday radio addresses. Each gave the president his voice and unique leadership style, and made his interpretation of events memorable and vital to millions of Americans. And those tools, especially the fireside chats, held America in thrall in ways Facebook and its social media brethren cannot. But the messages broadcast through those older media megaphones were still filtered and shaped by the powerful media cluster that covered the White House. By contrast, the Obama White House cherishes social media precisely because it allows for greater control of the message and the sidestepping of impertinent White House correspondents.

In previous White Houses, correspondents served the twin roles of conveying and questioning information. They critiqued and analyzed speeches, policy decisions, and legislative actions. Obama's is the first White House that can, and routinely does, ignore these established conventions of press relations. When possible, it controls the president's image by denying White House reporters access that was once considered vital to both roles and to their credibility with the public.

Part of this debate is garbled by the persistent misunderstanding of the difference between transparency and accessibility. Transparency is about visibility. Accessibility is about giving skeptical reporters the means to question a president about his actions, rhetoric, and record. Every White House decides what the public sees and determines the degree of transparency based on the standard set by previous presidents. By definition, transparency is thus the preserve of the presidency, not the public or the journalists who operate and scrutinize on their behalf.

The Obama White House argues that it is more transparent than any previous administration. It cites two innovations: publishing a searchable list of White House visitors and publishing salaries of White House staff. Both are nods in the direction of more visibility but do not, as suggested by the White House, significantly illuminate the inner workings of government.

The visitor log is published three months after the fact, for instance, and senior officials waved into the complex are not included on the list. The White House also scrubs the list for national security and law enforcement reasons and excludes any notation that might reveal interviews for significant government posts (such as the Supreme Court). The list also does not identify whom the visitor is meeting with, merely the low-level aide who acts as the escort. And the list is utterly silent on sensitive meetings between top officials and lobbyists conducted off White House grounds—interactions that have increased dramatically since publication of the White House visitor list. In fairness, a three-judge panel of the U.S. District Court of Appeals ruled unanimously in 2013 that no White House was legally bound to release a full list of White House visitors.

As for White House salaries, that was information previous administrations were required by law to send to the relevant congressional committees, where it was dutifully and routinely leaked. That the White House labels this nod toward transparency historic does not make it so.

DISAPPEARING PRESS CONFERENCES

There is a temptation to think in conventional terms about journalistic access to the president, looking for metrics to judge the daily give-and-take between White House correspondents and those in the West Wing. Of the many ways to numerically assess how accessible a president is to the beat reporters who cover his every move and utterance, the press conference is the favored metric.

As far as press conferences go, however, presidents haven't done very many since Harry Truman, who held 324 press conferences for a monthly average of 3.48. Most presidents in the modern era have averaged less than 2.5 press conferences a month. Ronald Reagan has the lowest average in the modern era—a paltry .48 per month. Richard Nixon follows closely with an average of .59 press conferences per month. The rest fall in between.

In terms of judging accessibility, I believe press conferences are fast becoming a false metric. Presidents hold relatively few of them and increasingly find ways to get around them. Although it's true that a White House press conference is still a place of potential fireworks between a president and a reporter (I have sparred with all three presidents I have covered, most memorably with Obama), presidents can now use Twitter, Google, Reddit, and a variety of other social media to "go to the people" and answer their questions directly, rather than deal with less pliable and gullible reporters.

Presidents simply no longer need the White House Press Corps to communicate with the public the way they used to. Increasingly, the White House can use its vast technological dexterity to short-circuit White House reporters from the communications process. Just as Obama told the country about his new immigration policy via Facebook, for instance, he also used the WhiteHouse.gov website to announce a major environmental initiative to protect Bristol Bay in Alaska from oil and gas leasing. Another innovation in direct communication is the White House-produced video "West Wing Week," which frequently includes video and audio of Obama, shot by taxpayer-funded videographers, at events that independent photo-journalists or videographers were never permitted to see and that print and radio reporters were not allowed to witness. There is a name for this phenomenon, and it is becoming more common—*Propaganda*. Its increased use points ominously to a future where White House communications blur the lines not only between visibility and accountability but also between news and propaganda.

COMMUNICATIONS INFLECTION POINT

Early in the Obama Administration, top officials became enamored of the phrase "inflection point." In White House argot it means a point of significant shift in the direction of policy or politics. We are, I believe, living through an inflection point in relations between the presidency and the press. Technology now empowers the president and the White House to ignore, circumvent, and marginalize reporters—all while generating the deceptive appearance of accessibility.

For instance, my CBS colleague Mark Knoller counted, as of January 2015, seventy-four town-hall events during Obama's presidency. Nine were conducted entirely online via social media platforms: two on YouTube, three Google Hangouts, one on Twitter, one on Facebook, one on Zillow, and one open virtual town hall. Town halls are typically tightly scripted events where nary a question or bit of choreography is left to chance. They have become a low-wattage staple of presidential communication, a venue where things look spontaneous but are not. Internet town halls give the White House and the preselected moderator even more control, cutting reporters still further out of the process. They also pass for accessibility when they are, in fact, just another part of the White House messaging factory.

Still, the immigration announcement on Facebook represents the apex of this phenomenon. It advanced a White House policy of keeping reporters and photo-journalists away from news events of public interest. One might argue that there is no practical difference between a White House press release on paper and an in-house video posted to Facebook. However, I believe a White House press release would, by its very nature, eventually flow through the reporting and editing process of news organizations that have a responsibility to include historical context and apply appropriate skepticism. Such reporting might even include commentary from a lawmaker from an opposing political party. It almost certainly would include more than unadulterated White House spin. The difference is important and the implications deeply troubling in a society that cherishes the adversarial relationship between those in power and those responsible for monitoring the application or misapplication of power. A press release begins a process of reporting. A Facebook video post circumvents it. White House manipulation that blurs that distinction is rapidly becoming an art form.

JOURNALISTS NOT WELCOME

Let me cite a couple of other examples. On November 5, 2013, the Obama Administration reopened the White House to public tours. As one might expect, President Obama and First Lady Michelle Obama greeted tourists lucky enough to be first in line on that semihistoric day (the tours had been suspended as part of White House belt-tightening stemming from across-the-board budget cuts).

Unfortunately no journalist was allowed to observe the First Family's inaction with the American public. The White House forbade all reportorial access. No print reporters. No TV cameras. No radio reporters. But it did make room for a White House videographer and sound technician to "cover" the event, which was streamed live on WhiteHouse.gov. This was a dispiriting and infuriating surprise to beat reporters who assumed the "most transparent" White House in American history would allow reporters to observe a president interacting with fellow Americans in the White House. The bigger surprise? That taxpayer-funded White House employees—whose job it is to serve the political aims of the president—were given unfettered access while reporters were kept locked outside the White House doors.

Perhaps the Obama White House uses this tactic for low-level events like announcements of addresses to the nation or the return of public tours to the White House. One might imagine this to be a minor realignment of journalistic and White House communications conventions. Surely the White House would not employ these tactics to exclude reporters or photographers from a genuine news event—one where the presence of independent journalists would in the past have been considered vital

On August 9, 2011, President Obama traveled to Dover Air Force Base to salute thirty-one U.S. Special Forces personnel killed in an August 6 helicopter crash in Afghanistan. Under Pentagon policy, reporters and photographers are forbidden from base grounds when military remains are returned if family members object to media coverage. In this case, families of nineteen of the thirty-one military personnel objected. This meant no independent media coverage. But President Obama's White House photographer Pete Souza was there and snapped a solemn, powerful silhouette of Obama saluting the returning caskets. That photo, released by the White House, was used nationwide as a news photograph before editors realized it was, essentially, a government press release photo. The concept of barring reporters and photographers from a newsworthy event but releasing White House photos that look like photojournalism, was so utterly unprecedented it took newsrooms by surprise. Yet again.

THE NEW NORMAL

This is not just about the current White House. Every president and those who work for them have tried to control their image and message. Fencing with reporters has always been part of that give-and-take. In the 19th century, the partisan press helped presidents burnish their images, acting as a counterweight to White House critics elsewhere in the ink-stained trenches of daily newspapering. The propaganda was bought and paid for, and the audience became part of the transaction by deciding which partisan paper to purchase.

That model disappeared in the early 20th century with the rise of journalism as a profession, and objectivity as a prized journalistic principle and marketing hook. At the same time, urbanization increased the clout of newspapers as journalistic and commercial powers. Radio and TV followed, and both grew under the same umbrella of professionalism and credibility.

Consider the power of mainstream media at its pinnacle. In 1950, total daily newspaper circulation saturated 124 percent of U.S. households (meaning there were lots of daily newspapers, and plenty of customers bought more than one). In 2012, total daily newspaper circulation is equivalent to one-third of American households. Newspaper daily circulation peaked in raw numbers in 1984 at 55 million and fell below 40 million in 2012—even as the population increased by 78 million people.[2]

Corporate ownership of broadcast TV and cable news has created new, unrivaled cost pressures on news organizations pinched by declining audience shares, the rising costs of coverage, and unrelenting shareholder demands for quarterly profits. Following the slide in the newspaper industry, audiences for network news coverage have declined steeply. Since 1980, the evening news broadcasts have lost, on average, 1 million viewers per year. News on cable TV has captured some of that audience, but the total numbers of viewers remains a fraction of the nightly news broadcasts of old. If those trends continue, then legacy media are on an irreversible march toward commercial and cultural oblivion.

That fracturing of the media landscape means that major news organizations have fewer resources to draw on in their attempt to service ever smaller audiences. When President Obama flew to China, Burma, and Australia for the Asia-Pacific Economic Cooperation and G-20 summits, for instance, the press charter flying reporters on the trip thus had seventeen empty rows. Little wonder: the per-seat cost to each organization was $90,000. American presidents used to fly with a press charter filled with reporters from wire services, newspapers, magazines, still photographers, network and cable TV reporters, producers, videographers, and sound technicians. Every trip had coverage of this kind. Now cost pressures have rendered even charter flights on foreign trips cost-prohibitive.

Even as those dynamics make the modern presidency too expensive for most news organizations to cover, social media and other communications tools that allow the White House to sidestep traditional journalists have never been more powerful. White House correspondents are thus being squeezed from both ends, facing intimidating commercial challenges from below and power challenges from above.

These trends are real and every future occupant of the White House will exploit them to maximum advantage. That's the nature of the adversarial relationship between presidents and the press. You can see that shift in power dynamics happening every day on Facebook. Or Twitter. Or Flickr. You can see it in the declining ratings for network and cable broadcasts, and in the incredible shrinking American newspaper. That transformation is happening every day in subtle and distinctive ways. Call it the "new normal" in relations between the modern presidency and the press.

◆　◆　◆　◆　◆

12.　An Uneasy Alliance: Presidents and Their Party

by Alexis Simendinger

Weeks after the midterm elections of 2014 diminished the heft and hopes of the Democratic Party, President Obama was still trying to sort out voters' rebukes of his party at every level, from state legislatures, to governorships, to Congress. Somehow a president credited for his long coattails when he made history by becoming the first African American elected to the nation's top job in 2008 was now being blamed for straitjacketing Democratic candidates, tying them to his blemished record and diminished popularity with the electorate after six years. Not since the twilight of the 1920s has an election left the House Democratic minority so minute.

Asked in an interview about his impact on congressional races, Obama pointed to 2016 and said he would do everything possible to help his party hold the White House, even if it meant remaining on the sidelines. The distance that can grow between a president in the White House and his own political party was evident even in Obama's body language.

"I think the American people are going to want, you know, that new car smell," Obama said during an interview[1] with ABC News. If the economy has rebounded in two years, "not only will I be serving the American people well, I think I will be serving a potential successor well," he continued. Democratic candidates, he added, "are probably not going to be looking at me to campaign too much."

The Democrats' defeats in the midterm elections of 2010 and 2014 have hardly been a surprise, at least not in the context of modern midterm-year outcomes.[2] But the magnitude of the 2014 results packed a wallop that has the party smarting: the GOP gained control of two-thirds of state legislatures, thirty-one of fifty governorships, the largest majority in the House since 1929, and control of the Senate.

Even in the best of circumstances it is difficult for a president and his party to buck "sixth-year-itis," the tendency for presidents in second terms and facing lame duck status to drag down the fortunes of their own party.

Political analysts, crunching data months in advance, have found that in midterm years during second terms, presidents' job approval[3] numbers foreshadow the actual verdict after Election Day. Voters' perceptions of the economy also play an outsized role in such polling.

In 2014, Obama's job approval hovered in the low 40s as voters weighed their ballot choices in October, and in many states, Democrats were buried under a barrage of attack ads tying them directly to an unpopular president. National voter turnout, already projected to be so-so (especially among young and minority supporters seen as key Democratic constituencies), proved to be the lowest[4] in a midterm election since 1942. Republicans, who campaigned to send a string of long-pending conservative measures to Obama's desk, rallied enough of the GOP base and independent voters to expand their ranks in the House while comfortably seizing a majority of 54 seats in the Senate.

The Republican wave instantly set off soul-searching and finger-pointing among Democrats about whether they fumbled their economic message, but there is plenty of historical evidence of frayed relations between presidents and their own political parties. In the sixth year of their own presidencies, GOP Presidents Dwight D. Eisenhower, Ronald Reagan, and George W. Bush also had low job approval ratings, and in each case, their parties experienced big losses in midterm congressional elections.[5] In his sixth year, Bill Clinton was impeached by the House of Representatives for lying under oath about a sexual relationship with an intern (see "The Clinton Impeachment: Washington's Scorched Earth Politics," Section V, this volume), and his own vice president, Al Gore, ran away from Clinton during his 2000 campaign for the White House.

"Sixth year-itis" does not fully explain, however, the often tense relationship between presidents and their party. When sitting presidents are seen as vulnerable or weak, they have been challenged by establishment figures in their own party. That happened when Senator Robert Kennedy ran against Lyndon Johnson in the Democratic primary of 1968, and when his brother Edward Kennedy ran against President Jimmy Carter in the 1980 Democratic primary. Richard Nixon's fate was ultimately sealed when a group of prominent Republican politicians came to the White House during the impeachment drama of 1973 and told him that a prolonged impeachment would inflict too much damage on the party. Many Republicans were furious at President George H.W. Bush for breaking his "read my lips, no new taxes" pledge, blaming it for Bill Clinton's election in 1992. Democrats were similarly miffed at Clinton early on for fumbling universal health care and abandoning a promised cut in middle class taxes, missteps that they blamed for the "Republican Revolution" that bought a Republican majority to the House in 1994 for the first time in decades. After the Iraq War sapped George W. Bush of much of his popularity, his own party opposed him on signature initiatives such as immigration and social security reform.

What emerges from that list is a relationship between presidents and their parties that, at its core, revolves around a highly contingent leader–follower dynamic. Strong, popular leaders can often ride herd on a fractious party, aligning party interests with their agendas and keeping outliers in check. At times they may also have to sacrifice congressional followers to the greater good.

But the minute the president is seen as weak and unpopular, the inherent party divisions and imbalance in the relationship come to the fore. Followers seek to distance themselves from the leader; they charge betrayal and hold the leader responsible for all the ills that have befallen the party cause. Although the nominal leaders of their parties, presidents have proven to be highly vulnerable to political isolation when their popularity begins to wane.

PARTY OF ONE

Since 2009, many senior Democrats[6] have groused that Obama prefers a party of one. They charge him with insufficient sympathy for candidates' challenges in the face of shifting demographics, regional divides, wearying economic hurdles, and the permanent and exhausting hunt for campaign cash. But that complaint is not unique to this incumbent.

"All presidents—Teddy Roosevelt, FDR, and everyone since—put themselves before their parties. They really have no choice," George C. Edwards,[7] author and presidency scholar at Texas A&M University, said. "Few presidents leave much impact on the party operation. They use the party to support themselves."

After more than eighty years, the reasons for this unbalanced relationship are clear: power and efficiency. "FDR's leadership was the principal ingredient in a full-scale realignment of the political parties, the first in history that placed executive leadership at the heart of its approach to politics and government," explained Sidney M. Milkis, politics professor at the University of Virginia's Miller Center of Public Affairs, in his book about the transformation of the American party system.[8] An executive-centered nation state, viewed by its backers as a modern improvement on the traditional party system, evolved beyond the New Deal era and eventually attracted conservatives as well, including Presidents Nixon, Reagan, and George W. Bush.

Divided government, now a routine occurrence, reinforces the notion of the president as a party of one. Obama's muscular reliance on executive authority, for instance, often has him charting an agenda unilaterally. He points to an incentive system outside the traditional party structure that limits legislative collaboration to moments of national crisis or brief interludes usually following presidential elections when public activism is especially high. The Constitution and legal precedent, the president argues, all steered him toward implementing the Affordable Care Act at his own discretion; pursuing a progressive environmental agenda primarily through the regulatory process; deploying U.S. troops without waiting for congressional declarations of war; and temporarily deferring enforcement of immigration laws. By and large, his party signed on.

Republicans, who themselves expanded executive power in years when they controlled the White House, have had a different perspective when relegated to a majority in either the House or Senate. Much to their frustration, the weapons they can wield from Capitol Hill are politically problematic. "This is a serious breach of our Constitution," House Speaker John Boehner[9] said of Obama's decision to extend deportation relief and other benefits to more than 4 million undocumented migrants in the United States. "It's a serious threat to our system of government. And frankly, we have limited options and limited abilities to deal with it directly."

As GOP leaders test the boundaries of unity within their expanded caucuses, it remains unclear how they plan to dominate in the public square, even when confronting a weakened Democratic president. Republican majorities want to build a conservative record that buoys their party and rallies the public in anticipation of a GOP presidential nominee in 2016. Democrats in the minority, meanwhile, are already looking beyond Obama and considering who will carry their standard in the next presidential election cycle.

GETTING STUFF DONE

Obama's most significant legislative achievements occurred in his first two years in office, when he leaned on Democratic majorities in the House and Senate to pass measures lifted from his campaign platform, plus others improvised to respond to an economic cataclysm.

He signed an $800 billion stimulus measure after unemployment shot above 10 percent; approved a second round of the Troubled Asset Relief Program, launched by President Bush before he exhausted his political capital to complete it; hailed the mammoth and controversial Patient Protection and Affordable Care Act; and enacted Wall Street reforms designed to curb irresponsible risk taking and weak oversight of the financial markets.

Obama's health care legislation was a Democratic Party creation, drafted with help from legions of special interests during a scramble for Senate votes. Republicans dangled the possibility of support for months and then opposed the bill in lockstep. The resulting measure barely cleared the Senate using a budget strategy that required fifty-one Democratic votes. There was no conference committee to fix problems in the law that later came to light.

Obama celebrated the landmark law as a victory for millions of Americans who had no health insurance or struggled to afford coverage. Certainly the Affordable Care Act realized a goal that had been prominent on the Democratic Party agenda for decades, but at a high cost. In late 2010, many Democratic senators in conservative states who voted for the Act were defeated, Democrats lost control of the House, and "Obamacare" became GOP shorthand for "overreach."

Democrats continue to debate whether they made the right political call on national health care. New York Senator Chuck Schumer, who years ago predicted Democrats would win elections thanks to the law, delivered a prepared speech dissecting[10] the November 2014 election losses in which he called the party's devotion to health reforms "a mistake" that cost them politically.

"After passing the stimulus, Democrats should have continued to propose middle-class-oriented programs and built on the partial success of the stimulus. But unfortunately Democrats blew the opportunity the American people gave them," Schumer said. "We took their mandate and put all of our focus on the wrong problem—health care reform."

Once presidents seize the initiative, they assume ownership of their choices, and time and again, those choices prove politically costly. After President Clinton and his party lost fifty-two House seats and control of Congress in 1994, many political analysts[11] came to believe that if the president, as a New Democrat, had championed a serious, bipartisan welfare reform measure before he tackled health care, different sequencing might have preserved Democrats' majorities in both chambers.

Working with the support of his party in 2005 after his reelection, President Bush believed he had a mandate to deliver a "better deal" on Social Security payroll taxes in the form of private investment accounts. But polls showed that the more he barnstormed to overhaul Social Security, the more the public objected. Marketed as Bush's top domestic priority following a controversial war in Iraq and before the Hurricane Katrina tragedy later that year, private accounts were a conspicuous flop. Many Republican lawmakers distanced themselves from the president and his signature domestic policy reform. By the end of Bush's sixth year, a majority of Americans said they disapproved of the job the president and the GOP-controlled Congress were doing. Democrats captured House and Senate control and gained majorities of governorships and state legislatures. Not a single Democratic incumbent lost a seat in 2006.

FLEETING COALITIONS

Contemporary presidents, with the notable exception of Reagan, have left remarkably fleeting impressions on their parties. Today's presidential candidates build fleeting coalitions around personalities, events, and ideas that can galvanize sufficient votes in key electoral states. Clinton, for all his centrist political instincts, never recast the Democratic Party, which reverted to its liberal orthodoxies after he left office. Moderates in the party today are few in number, seemingly culled with each election.

Bush's "compassionate conservatism" was initially embraced by the Republican Party during his 2000 campaigns, but it left many in the rank and file seething. There is little sign of it in today's GOP, which is more activist and conservative and is hostile to the thinned ranks of moderates. Party leaders eventually distanced themselves from Bush's deficit spending, expansion of a Medicare prescription drug entitlement, and his embrace of immigration reforms. They skewered his No Child Left Behind education program and complained the federal Troubled Asset Relief Program asset-buying plan was an unwarranted expansion of government. Bush's fingerprints are on the Iraq War, the response to Hurricane Katrina, and the Great Recession, but they are little in evidence on today's Republican Party agenda.

In many ways the relationship between a president and his or her party is a marriage of convenience. As long as their interests align and their policy vows are supported by a majority of constituents, the union remains strong. That's why presidents try to launch so much of their policy agendas in their "first one hundred days" in office, while relations with their party are still in the honeymoon phase. Over time, however, presidential popularity wanes, policy execution falters, and political interests diverge, especially during mid-term elections and White House controversies. At that point both sides may just be staying in the relationship for the voters, or until someone better comes along.

The First Hundred Days

13. The First Hundred Days: Myth and Mystique

by James P. Pfiffner

A common yardstick for new presidents is the famed "Hundred Day" marker, but as Richard Neustadt pointed out in a previous edition of this text, the Hundred Days time frame is an unrealistic measuring rod. The term comes from the impressive spate of legislation that Franklin Roosevelt got through Congress to deal with the Great Depression in 1933. The ability of Roosevelt to push sixteen major bills through Congress over the period of 100 days was impressive, but he had the winds of the Great Depression and decisive congressional majorities at his back. That the New Deal marked a turning point in overcoming the Great Depression, made FDR's hundred days of successful legislation historic. No other new president has faced a similar emergency with such large electoral majorities in Congress, although President Johnson had large Democratic majorities and President Obama faced a significant economic crisis.

Despite the unique circumstances in 1933, the modern press and public apply the Hundred Days measuring stick to newly elected presidents whether they like it or not, and presidents cannot afford to ignore public expectations. Although each president faces different historical circumstances, common challenges confront presidents of both parties. A president's political capital is at its highest level, for instance, during the first months of a new administration. As Bruce Miroff points out in this volume, even Franklin Roosevelt did not have a carefully prepared policy agenda but was experimenting with programs meant to relieve the immediate economic distress facing the country. More recent presidents, however, do not have that luxury; they must carefully prepare to take control of a larger government with programs of a much broader scope than in FDR's day. New presidents now must orchestrate elaborate transition bureaucracies to prepare to take advantage of the narrow window of opportunity that opens up after the inauguration of each new president.

In addition to preparing new policy proposals, they must recruit a large White House staff, nominate fifteen cabinet secretaries, choose hundreds of political appointees, prepare a new budget, and, perhaps most challenging, push their policy agenda through Congress. Needless to say, they cannot do this alone, and so they must begin their transitions into office by managing transition operations of hundreds of their supporters.

PLANNING FOR EARLY SUCCESS

In addition to the political, economic, and international circumstances facing a new president, success in the first hundred days depends in good measure on adequate preparation. Before the mid-20th century, newly elected presidents did not spend much time in transition planning. President Kennedy merely asked Clark Clifford and Richard Neustadt to prepare several memos advising him on the first steps he should take as president-elect. But over the past half century, the increasing size of the executive branch and scope of federal programs has made mastering the government more difficult. Congress, with many more staffers and support agencies, has also become more complex and challenging for presidents to influence.

The comparatively casual approach to transitions changed sharply when candidate Jimmy Carter, in part because of his lack of national governing experience, assigned aides to prepare him for transition into office even before he was formally nominated. Ronald Reagan began his transition planning in April 1980, with a sizable personnel recruitment planning operation as well as task forces covering all major executive branch agencies. Since then, every new incoming president has undertaken significant transition operations, now funded by appropriated funds. Success in the first hundred days depends not so much on the number of transition planners, however, but on how well they are organized in preparing the new president's policy agenda.

With a White House staff now comprising hundreds of people, staffing the White House itself is a major challenge. In such a large White House, someone besides the president must be in charge, make the trains run on time, impose order on White House staffers, and control access to the president. This reality was illustrated in the early Carter White House by the lack of clarity of exactly who was in charge. Carter did not want to appoint a chief of staff, but after a disappointing experience with the "collegial model" of White House organization, he realized that it was necessary to appoint a chief of staff to control his advisory system. After his election in 1992, Bill Clinton spent much of his time interviewing and selecting his cabinet secretaries, and he put off appointing his White House staff until late in the transition. Although this may have helped round out his cabinet, the lack of clarity in the authority of White House staffers set back his first hundred days.

The number of positions available for presidential appointment steadily increased in the latter half of the 20th century; each new president must recruit more than 1,000 executive appointments needing Senate confirmation and 600 White House appointees, in addition to hundreds of lower level political appointees. As the number of appointed positions grew, the staff necessary to manage recruitment has grown. President Kennedy's three-person "talent hunt" had increased to a 100 political recruiters in Ronald Reagan's transition offices, and transition personnel recruitment efforts now number closer to 200.

The combination of hundreds of thousands of applicants for political appointments, along with more elaborate vetting and ethics requirements and dilatory Senate confirmations, has created significant delays in getting a new president's team into office to lead the executive branch. The average time to fill top-level positions increased from less than three months for John Kennedy to close to nine months in the 21st century. These delays have made it doubly problematic during the first hundred days. Scandals or difficulties with nominations can deflect attention from the policy agenda, and the predictable delay in appointments can slow policy implementation.

EARLY MISTAKES HINDER NEW PRESIDENTS

Presidents taking office with strong electoral support have a distinct advantage in their first hundred days. As mentioned, FDR was in the best position because of the desperate economic situation of the country. He won in a landslide, and Americans were ready to support any actions that might combat the worst effects of the Great Depression. Panic over the depression along with large Democratic majorities in Congress made FDR's historic hundred days legislation possible. Ronald Reagan benefitted from his clear electoral victory over Jimmy Carter and a feeling that the economy of the late 1970s was in deep trouble. Dwight Eisenhower, Richard Nixon, and Barack Obama benefited from expectations that they would deal with the wars they inherited. Barack Obama benefitted from being the first African American president, but the economic crisis of the Great Recession forced him to deal with it first, rather than the policy priorities he had hoped to pursue.

As Richard Neustadt points out, new administrations are often characterized by hubris and inexperience. They overreact in distancing themselves from the previous administration and sometimes fall into avoidable mistakes. John Kennedy overreacted against Eisenhower's seemingly cumbersome national security policy process by abolishing it, assuming it would be replaced. He did not quickly establish a new policy process, however, and arguably the lack of organization led to the disastrous Bay of Pigs invasion of Cuba in 1961. President Carter, reacting against Nixon's White House–centered administration and domineering chief of staff, H.R. Haldeman, began with hopes of establishing "cabinet government," but he soon changed his mind after cabinet secretaries did not seem to embrace presidential priorities.

President Ford's pardon of Richard Nixon for any Watergate-related crimes, although it might have been best for the country, resulted in falling public approval of his performance in office. In reaction against Nixon and Watergate, Jimmy Carter and Gerald Ford both tried initially to run their presidencies without a chief of staff; they both soon realized that, given the size of the modern White House, this was impossible. Ronald Reagan's proposals for relatively small cuts in Social Security benefits in May 1981 had to be reversed when political reaction was too negative. The failure of the new Clinton Administration to vet carefully enough several potential nominees for Attorney General led to embarrassing delays in appointing his cabinet. His hasty endorsement of the "don't ask, don't tell" policy regarding gays in the military resulted in an embarrassing setback when it was opposed by military leaders.

SUCCESS WITH CONGRESS IS KEY

Good relations with Congress are crucial in general, but particularly for a policy agenda that involves new legislation. New presidents need to designate staffers to coordinate with fellow partisans in Congress, and presidents need to pay their respects in courting Congress. Chances of success with Congress are greatly increased if the president's party enjoys healthy majorities in both Houses, as the presidencies of Roosevelt and Johnson demonstrate. But majorities in Congress are no guarantee of immediate success, as Presidents Carter and Clinton illustrated, and Ronald Reagan was able to achieve significant early victories even with the House controlled by Democrats.

A quick start on a policy agenda can help a new president because the beginning of an administration provides the greatest opportunity to get important policy proposals through Congress (aside from national emergencies, such as the September 11, 2001, terrorist attacks). Executive orders and other unilateral actions by a new president can change policies and attract press coverage, and so a new president should be ready to sign some of these measures shortly after inauguration. Any significant policy agenda, however, usually involves Congress, and that is where the real challenges lie.

Early action is necessary both because presidents have the maximum political capital early in their terms and because of the foreseeable decline in public popularity. Just as important is the reality that the president's party almost always loses seats in both houses of Congress in midterm elections. Master legislator Lyndon Johnson said it best in explaining his push for immediate action with Congress:

> I keep hitting hard because I know this honeymoon won't last. Every day I lose a little more political capital. That's why we have to keep at it, never letting up. One day soon, I don't know when, the critics and

the snipers will move in and we will be at stalemate. We have to get all we can, now, before the roof comes down. [After a few months,] they'll all be thinking about their reelections. I'll have made mistakes, my polls will be down, and they'll be trying to put some distance between themselves and me. They won't want to go into the fall with their opponents calling 'em Lyndon Johnson's rubber stamp.[1]

Perhaps the most illuminating contrast of new administrations' approach to policy agendas in Congress can be illustrated by comparing the first hundred days of Presidents Carter and Reagan. Courting Congress, although primarily symbolic, is an essential task for new presidents. Jimmy Carter came to Washington with a disdain for Congress and was impatient with the small courtesies and social aspects of courting Congress. His attitude was reflected in his staff, and even the Democratic Speaker of the House, Tip O'Neil, felt insulted by the Carter White House. An inexperienced head of congressional liaison did not help. Carter also alienated members of Congress by proposing the elimination (for budgetary reasons) of a number of water projects in congressional districts without warning the members of his plans. Carter finally had to abandon his plan when the water projects were attached to must-pass legislation that he was forced to sign.

Carter came into office with a long list of proposals for specific new legislation, including bills on energy conservation, tax reform, hospital cost control, and welfare reform, among other initiatives. Many of the bills had to pass through the Ways and Means Committee of the House. Members of Congress warned the administration that the president was insisting on too many action issues for Congress to handle at one time. The plethora of legislative proposals was aggravated by Carter's refusal to set priorities. As a result, although President Carter achieved a number of important legislative victories, he might have had a more successful hundred days if he had chosen several major priorities and pursued them assiduously.

In 1981, the incoming Reagan Administration had learned from Carter's mistakes. From the beginning, President Reagan paid his respects to Capitol Hill, even courting Democratic Speaker Tip O'Neill. Reagan's friendly personality contrasted with Carter's "nothing but business" attitude. He was helped by his impressive electoral victory over Carter and the public perception that the economy was in trouble. His administration claimed an electoral mandate to pursue his policy priorities.

Most important, the Reagan transition team decided to focus on three major policy priorities: tax cuts, domestic spending cuts, and increases in military spending. They argued that the first two of these, tax and spending cuts, would turn the economy around and balance the budget. (That this did not happen is not the point; their argument was a unifying theme that focused the first hundred days around economic objectives.) Reagan had also argued during the campaign that it was necessary to increase U.S. military spending. The new administration pursued these three priorities to the exclusion of many other policy preferences, such as the Republican social agenda. This focus, along with skillful political direction, led to impressive legislative victories early in Reagan's first term.

George W. Bush's transition into office was hindered by the recount of election returns in Florida, but the key to his transition was his running mate, Dick Cheney. While much of the future president's staff was in Florida fighting court battles over the election recount, Cheney was, as Peter Baker points out in this volume, up in Arlington, Virginia, recruiting political appointees for the new administration and planning the initial policy agenda. Despite winning fewer popular votes than Al Gore, the new Bush Administration focused its energies on pushing tax cuts through Congress and was successful in doing so.

Barack Obama's transition organization was tightly organized, and the quick designation of his White House staff and recruitment of cabinet secretaries enabled him to begin his administration successfully. In his second full day in office, he signed executive orders to end the coercive interrogation of detainees and to close the detention center at Guantanamo Bay, Cuba. His orders to the military and CIA were quickly implemented, but his inability to close Guantanamo offered a lesson on the importance of Congress during the 100-day window. Through legislation both Republicans and Democrats on Capitol Hill were able to thwart Obama's plans for closing Guantanamo. In a reflection of the polarization in Congress, Obama used up much of his political capital in pushing his $800 billion stimulus bill through Capitol Hill. Liberal and conservative economists agreed that such a large stimulus was necessary to avoid a major depression, but Obama still had to rely almost solely on his narrow Democratic majorities in Congress.

PARTISANSHIP COMPLICATES TRANSITIONS

Since partisan polarization in Congress has greatly increased over the past several decades, the success of future presidents during their first hundred days will increasingly depend on the partisan balance in Congress. As conservative Democratic "Dixiecrats" from the South were replaced by Republicans in Congress, each of the parties became more ideologically homogenous. The increasing number of safe congressional districts reinforced this development, with members of each party having to appeal to the more extreme members of their partisan base who turn out for primary elections. This overall dynamic has resulted in the decline, and almost elimination, of moderates in Congress. In contrast to the overlapping ideologies of the mid-20th century, the most conservative Democrats are now to the left of the most liberal Republicans. This polarization has resulted in much stronger party discipline in which the president's party almost always supports presidential priorities, while the opposing party tries to thwart the president.

New presidents can expect their party to support them, and if they have a majority in the House and a filibuster-proof majority in the Senate, they can expect to win early victories in their first hundred days. They can also expect the opposition party in Congress to use obstructionist parliamentary tactics to thwart their legislative priorities. Barring major calamities such as the 9/11 terrorist attacks, they will also experience the predictable decrease in effectiveness with Congress.

New presidents will thus be best positioned to take advantage of the hundred days window of opportunity if they win by large landslides; pursue policies that are supported by members of both political parties; and take office with large majorities of their party in Congress.

Because it is unlikely that many presidents will enjoy these advantages, newly elected presidents can maximize chances for success during their first 100 days if they begin early, before the election, to organize their transition into office; designate their White House staff leadership quickly, even before choosing cabinet secretaries; have their political recruitment teams working well before the election; and have a focused policy agenda ready to go, including unilateral actions and legislative initiatives.

Taking these actions will not guarantee a successful hundred days, but not doing them will almost inevitably result in failure.

◆　◆　◆　◆　◆

14. The Original Hundred Days: Franklin D. Roosevelt

by Bruce Miroff

The original "hundred days" in presidential politics were extraordinary in two distinct senses of the word. At their center was a display of remarkable energy and talent by a new president, Franklin D. Roosevelt, whom many shrewd observers of politics had previously regarded as an amiable medioc-rity. Their backdrop was an economic crisis so dire that the ordinary obstacles to executive leadership were leveled and the opening for change was im-mense. This rare combination of individual skill and structural opportunity during the first "hundred days" was unlikely to be reproduced in the future, even as the legend it inspired created a standard that pundits would routinely pull out of their files to evaluate each new president after FDR.

"[T]he only thing we have to fear," Roosevelt proclaimed at the outset of his inaugural address on March 4, 1933, "is fear itself—nameless, unreason-ing, unjustified terror which paralyzes needed efforts to convert retreat into advance." The new president appeared indomitable, but the fears of his fel-low citizens were hardly unwarranted. The most productive economy in the world lay prostrate, with enormous numbers of its employers, workers, and farmers stricken by despair. Astoundingly bleak statistics—a quarter of the workforce, for example, was unemployed—were translated in the inaugural address into stark prose: "[T]he withered leaves of industrial enterprise lie on every side; farmers find no markets for their produce; the savings of many years in thousands of families are gone. Most important, a host of unem-ployed citizens face the grim problem of existence and an equally great num-ber toil with little return. Only a foolish optimist can deny the dark realities of the moment."

Omitted from Roosevelt's speech were equally ominous events abroad. Boasting of their superior discipline and efficiency, mocking the parliamen-tary paralyses of liberal democracies, dictatorships on both the right and the left appeared ascendant amid global depression. Fascism in Italy and Stalinism in the Soviet Union, each with its American admirers, were solidly established by 1933. Imperialist Japan had invaded Manchuria in 1931 and was pressing against a fragile China. Only five weeks before Roosevelt took the oath of office, Adolf Hitler became chancellor of Germany and swiftly put into place the foundations of his brutal totalitarian system.

So if the new president was supremely confident, the tasks he faced were supremely daunting. The American people needed relief from mass distress, revival of the engines of economic vitality, and reforms to fix the profound systemic defects that the Great Depression had revealed. And behind these fundamentally material matters lay the critical question of American democ-racy itself. Could democracy combat depression? Could it compete with—and ultimately overmatch—the antidemocratic regimes looming over Europe and Asia?

On the day he was inaugurated, an immediate crisis in the financial system preoccupied Roosevelt: with depositors in a panic, banks across the nation were either failing or were shut down by gubernatorial orders to prevent further collapses. FDR's swift response to the crisis, a "Bank Holiday" to allow the financial system and the public a breather, followed by the Emergency Banking Act to put remedies into place, became emblematic of the new administration. By contrast to the dour Herbert Hoover, ideologically staked to the premise of limited government, here was a president who would employ federal power exuberantly and decisively to avert disaster. Combined with the forceful message of his inaugural address, Roosevelt's initial actions to save the banking system thrilled the American people. As adulatory messages from citizens flooded into the White House, and as a skeptical press for once purred with satisfaction, the new president appeared for the moment as larger than life.

With his jaunty smile and uplifted jaw, Roosevelt was a warm and reassuring leader for a demoralized nation. But beneath the winning surface was an elusive inner core, enigmatic even to his closest associates. Roosevelt was an exceptionally astute politician who kept his motives and maneuvers to himself. Artful, manipulative, sometimes coldly calculating, he played the political game with zest, recruiting a diverse, squabbling corps of advisers, listening to advice from all sides, but intent always on positioning himself at the center of action. A professed liberal in principle, he was adamantly anti-ideological in practice. Experimentation, not systematic thought or action, was his métier; at one of his earliest press conferences during the first hundred days, he compared himself to a quarterback who could not call the next play until he saw how the previous one had worked out.

It was during the hundred days that Roosevelt first established his intimate bond with the mass of Americans through his "fireside chats" on the radio. Although his voice was tinged with the patrician accent of the Hudson River aristocracy and Harvard, his smooth tone and simple language gracefully reached out to a public whose average level of education was far lower than today's. The very first fireside chat, patiently explaining the banking crisis and persuading Americans that it was safe to return their money to the institutions from which they had just withdrawn them now that government safeguards were in place, was a pioneering moment. It forged a direct relationship between the president and the people through the mass media. Just as Abraham Lincoln had described the Union war effort in 1861 as a "people's contest" for democracy, so did Roosevelt's first fireside chat evoke a popular campaign to combat the Great Depression. In a later fireside chat for another tense moment—December 1940—the president recalled how he had imagined his radio audience before delivering his initial one: "I had before my eyes the picture of all those Americans with whom I was talking. I saw the workmen in the mills, the mines, the factories; the girl behind the counter; the small shopkeeper; the farmer doing his spring plowing; the widows and the old men wondering about their life's savings." Absent from his list were the nation's elites; Roosevelt was directing his message at—and beginning to mobilize—what would become the legendary New Deal coalition.

Roosevelt had promised "action, and action now" in his inaugural address, and the way he made good on this pledge became the leitmotif of the hundred days. While some voices were calling for him to assume dictatorial powers to cope with the grim emergency, the president prudently turned instead to a Congress that shared his sense of urgency. Congressional compliance with Roosevelt's requests for legislation was facilitated by the fact that he enjoyed a huge partisan majority: whereas the previous Congress had been narrowly divided, the 1932 elections produced a House in which Democrats outnumbered Republicans by 313 to 117, and a Senate in which Democrats outnumbered Republicans by 59 to 36. Even among the shrunken ranks of Republicans, there was a hardy band of Progressives who were inclined to back Roosevelt.

Called into special session on March 9 by the new president, Congress met for precisely 100 days and produced an extraordinary outpouring of legislation—fifteen major new laws. That sense of urgency on Capitol Hill stood in marked contrast to a legislative process normally prone to delay and tedium. (When Roosevelt first used the phrase "hundred days," he was actually referring to this special session rather than to a period that began with his inauguration.) It was not only the productivity of the special session that struck observers; it was equally the willingness of legislators to follow the president's lead. With their constituents energized by the president and the members themselves eager to break through previous logjams, Congress largely welcomed bills drafted in the executive branch and moved them speedily into law. In a development that would soon prove legally problematic, most of the new laws delegated considerable discretion back to the executive branch that had conceived them in the first place.

Even a partial list of the legislation passed in those fateful hundred days suggests its historic audacity and creativity, along with its striking contradictions. The Emergency Banking Act was followed by the Economy Act to reduce federal spending; creation of the Civilian Conservation Corps (CCC) for unemployed youth; the Tennessee Valley Act, a historic experiment in public power and planning; the Truth in Securities Act to end Wall Street secrecy; and the Glass-Steagall Banking Act to separate commercial from investment banking. Topping the list were the two measures designed to respond directly to the most severe problems of the Great Depression: the Agricultural Adjustment Act (AAA) for the countryside, and the National Industrial Recovery Act (NIRA) for the urban industrial sector.

The agricultural sector in the United States had been suffering long before 1929, but the Great Depression made things much worse, as crashing prices for farm commodities amid abundant crop surpluses led to widespread rural devastation. The AAA aimed above all to lift farm incomes by fixing the imbalance between supply and demand, paying farmers to remove some of their fields from production. If the provisions of the AAA were complex and diffuse, the NIRA was even more of a policy grab bag. Originally, the NIRA was a defensive move by Roosevelt to head off a radical Senate measure, sponsored by Hugo Black of Alabama, to spread employment opportunities by mandating a thirty-hour workweek. Uncertain of what to offer in its place, Roosevelt assembled representatives of the key industrial interests and tasked them to come up with a program. The result was a hydra-headed law: the business sector was to be rescued from ruinous competition and deflationary prices through industrial self-regulation supervised by a National Recovery Administration (NRA) in the executive branch; labor was granted the right of collective bargaining, a landmark for federal law but lacking a mechanism for enforcement; and the jobless were offered employment in large-scale public works.

The unified and fast-moving Congress of Roosevelt's first hundred days has been an object of nostalgia when later generations have bemoaned partisan gridlock. Yet even in 1933 the roots of subsequent discord during the later years of Roosevelt's presidency can be discerned. When the NIRA was adopted by Congress on the last day of the special session, its passage in the Senate came by only seven votes, with opposition mainly from the left due to the bill's suspension of anti-trust law. Roosevelt would increasingly be challenged by the left during the remainder of his first term, most fruitfully in the case of the National Labor Relations Act of 1935. From a later vantage point, even more significant than the initial rumblings on the left was the early support from the right. Representing the most desperately impoverished area of the country, southern Democrats, the most powerful bloc in the president's party, rallied behind the initial New Deal bills for relief and recovery, none of which appeared to present a threat to their region's Jim Crow system. However, once the New Deal moved onto new ground in later years, the southern bloc in Congress became the most important obstacle to its progressive aspirations. Historic reforms in welfare and labor law were accepted by southern Democrats only after they were altered to exclude African Americans from their protections. Roosevelt's efforts to centralize power during his second term in his bid to complete the New Deal were blocked or truncated once southern lawmakers, fearful of a national government that could attack the economic and social order of white supremacy, joined in a coalition with conservative Republicans to hand the president a string of legislative setbacks.

As a moment in time when the American polity, inspired by Franklin D. Roosevelt, entertained so many novel departures from its past amid a mood of unity and with a passion for change, the original hundred days has remained a touchstone for the promise of presidential leadership. What has been largely forgotten in the retrospective uses of Roosevelt's hundred days is how many of its hastily improvised measures lacked staying power. Some, like the Truth in Securities Act, were promptly superseded by more carefully drafted and thoroughgoing legislation. Others, like the CCC (among the most successful of New Deal programs), were terminated once a wartime boom in employment rendered them unnecessary. Most important, the central programs of the hundred days for battling the Depression—the AAA and the NIRA—proved to be short-lived. The enduring New Deal is primarily the product of the "second hundred days" of 1935. The Social Security Act and the National Labor Relations Act surpass in historical importance any of the laws passed during the hundred days both as public policy and as the foundation for a political coalition that dominated American politics for the next four decades.

The shortcomings of the original hundred days are most evident in the law that Roosevelt hailed upon its passage as the most important attempt in American history to conquer the evils of mass unemployment. The NRA was launched amid hoopla and hope; a vast, excited throng paraded down Fifth Avenue in New York City in September 1933 beneath the banners of the program's Blue Eagle symbol. Soon, however, expectations for economic rationalization and industrial harmony gave way to a welter of cross-cutting complaints among the program's four major players: big corporations and their trade associations, small businesses, labor, and consumers. The nation's boldest peacetime departure from the ethos of free-market competition exceeded the capacities of federal administration and underestimated the dogged commitment to self-interest at the heart of American economic life. Most observers concluded that the NRA was on its way to failure even before the Supreme Court voided it in 1935 as an unconstitutional delegation of power from Congress to the executive.

The story of Franklin D. Roosevelt's hundred days, with an exuberant president at its center, banishing the nation's darkened mood and launching an unprecedented flurry of actions to confront its deepest challenges, remains irresistible. But it is essential to look beneath the tale's charmed chapters and recognize the special circumstances that make it a dubious standard for judging later presidents. Fortunately, Roosevelt's successors would not face such dreadful domestic conditions. They would not be favored by such commanding congressional majorities or such a muted partisan opposition. They would not be greeted by a desperate public ready to follow them almost anywhere they chose to lead. Even if one of Roosevelt's successors had possessed his remarkable bundle of talents—and none have—the opening for rapid and dramatic change that he vigorously exploited would not come again save, perhaps, in times of war.

Yet if the original hundred days provides a poor model for scoring the initial accomplishments of presidents, it nonetheless still speaks to fundamental possibilities in democratic governance. As Roosevelt proudly put it in a 1936 campaign address, "In a world which in many places has gone undemocratic, we have gone more democratic." His rejoinder to the dictators of his day still rings true. Roosevelt's hundred days reminds us that American democracy has been capable of finer things than today's dispirited and dysfunctional politics.

◆ ◆ ◆ ◆ ◆

15. The First Hundred Days: Harry S. Truman

by Brian Burnes

On April 12, 1945, Vice President Harry Truman was planning a poker night with pals, having instructed an old Army buddy just where he kept the bourbon stashed in his office. Roughly 100 days later, on July 22, President Truman hosted a much larger party with new friends "Winnie" and "Joe." Winnie and Joe, as Truman referred to them, were British Prime Minister Winston Churchill and Soviet Premier Joseph Stalin. The elbow-bending had been world class. "There were at least 25 toasts," Harry Truman wrote in a letter that same day to his wife, Bess. "So much getting up and down that there was practically no time to eat or drink."[1]

The party he described was one of several formal dinners given during the July 1945 Potsdam Conference, the post–World War II summit near Berlin. Truman, only a few months removed from his poker night with pals, was representing the United States at a critical moment in the shaping of the postwar world. "Tragic fate has thrust upon us grave responsibilities,"[2] Truman had told members of Congress four days after the sudden April 12, 1945, death of Franklin Roosevelt. "Exhibit A" in supporting the truth of that remark was Truman himself.

Much of the appeal of Truman's personal story is the heroic response to monumental challenges by an allegedly average man, one who rose to the occasion and faced down almost cinematic adversity. The same piano-playing failed entrepreneur, who thirty years before was running the family farm south of Kansas City, had to replace a beloved fallen leader near the end of a global war and fill what would have been Roosevelt's chair at Potsdam. "I sure dread this trip, worse than anything I've had to face," Truman wrote Bess on July 12 from aboard the USS *Augusta* on his way to Germany. "But it has to be done."[3]

During his eighty-two days as vice president, Truman had met privately with Roosevelt only twice. And yet during his first hundred days as president, Truman quickly found his sea legs, reassuring the world that Roosevelt's policies and priorities would continue. In delivering his April 16 remarks to Congress—made in part because, as Truman said, "when world events are moving so rapidly, our silence might be misunderstood"—he emphasized that the war would end only with the unconditional surrender of the Axis powers.

The next month Americans accorded Truman an 87 percent Gallup approval rating, higher than Roosevelt had ever received. In fact, almost exactly eighty years after the assassination of President Abraham Lincoln, many citizens had trouble processing the reality of Roosevelt's death. For four days, radio would fail to transmit an advertisement or soap opera.

The idea that Truman could ever replace Roosevelt didn't seem possible to some. "The new president is an average man," wrote Roy Roberts, managing editor of the *Kansas City Star*, in a column after being given an exclusive sit-down with the new president during his first full day in office—Friday, April 13. In the widely syndicated piece, Roberts wrote that Truman was "apparently not a success in life" and reminded readers of how Truman had beheld the rear end of draft animals while guiding a plow across the Truman farm in Grandview, Missouri. Truman, no friend of Roberts, undoubtedly thought his column contained more than a little condescension.

This average man had left the farm to enlist in 1917 and then had led an artillery battery across France in World War I. Truman's men were among approximately 27,000 in the 35th Division, made up of Missouri and Kansas National Guard units. During the Meuse-Argonne offensive, the division suffered about 7,300 casualties, including 1,126 dead. Of the 194 men of

Truman's battery, barely a handful became casualties during the war, and those died of pneumonia or influenza.

After the war—and the failure of his haberdashery—Truman served two terms as presiding judge (or chief executive) of largely urban Jackson County, which included Kansas City and Independence, Missouri. For another eight years, he held a U.S. Senate seat. The performance of his Senate committee investigation into wartime contracts was widely admired, landing him the cover of *Time* magazine in 1943.

In the April 23, 1945, issue of *Time* magazine, the same magazine editors found themselves underwhelmed. Time reported, "Harry Truman is a man of distinct limitations, especially in experience in high level politics. . . . With almost complete unanimity, Harry Truman's friends—in Washington and across the land—agreed last week that he 'would not be a great president.'"

Other editors winced at Truman's flat Missouri accent, in great contrast to Roosevelt's patrician inflections. The *New York Times* noted how Truman sometimes broke up vowels into a diphthong, transforming "fill" into "fih-uhl" or "soul" into "soh-uhl." Several Roosevelt White House administrators, apparently finding Truman so underwhelming in contrast to the memory of their boss, planned their departures.

At the very first, there is even some evidence that Truman was rattled. Historian David McCullough wrote that on April 12, the sixty-year-old senator literally ran from the office of House Speaker Sam Rayburn after receiving a terse telephone message to report to the White House immediately.

But in a series of early 1960s filmed interviews—just released to researchers in 2013—Truman insisted that he had not been entirely stunned by Roosevelt's death. He said that he knew Roosevelt "was a very, very sick man" and desperately needed the rest he would find in Warm Springs, Georgia. But he couldn't be candid about that at the time, Truman added. "I couldn't share the thoughts I had on the subject with anybody," he said, adding that Roosevelt's poor health could diminish the power of the presidency at a moment when the war was still raging.

"I assumed the president sent for me," Truman said, referring to the phone message he received on April 12. "I didn't allow myself to think anything else."

After occupying the Oval Office, Truman seemed to want to convince everyone—and maybe even himself—that he was up to the task. "It won't be long until I can sit back and study the whole picture and tell 'em what is to be done in each department," he wrote Bess on June 6. "When things come to that stage there'll be no more to this job than there was to running Jackson County and not any more worry."[4]

On his first full day in office, Truman instructed Secretary of State Edward Stettinius to have a report on European diplomatic relations on his desk by the end of that day. At noon he left for Capitol Hill for lunch with Senate and House members, in part to tell them that he would return to deliver an address on April 16. Later that same day, he met with former senator and Supreme Court justice James Byrnes, who had accompanied Roosevelt to the February conference in Yalta. Truman's decision to go to Capitol Hill proved shrewd. Not only was his April 16 address well received, the Senate also soon approved U.S. membership in the United Nations by an 89–2 margin. The Roosevelt admirers who initially dismissed Truman soon began changing their minds.

George Elsey, a U.S. Navy intelligence officer assigned to the White House Map Room, later recounted the many times he found Truman transfixed in front of an oversized map of Japan. Some 7,000 American soldiers and Marines and 5,000 sailors had died in the three-month Okinawa campaign, which began just twelve days before Truman became president. The American battle deaths eventually totaled 12,000, which was the worst of any single battle in the Central Pacific campaign, surpassing the 6,800 American deaths on Iwo Jima earlier that year.

In 1945, Truman was only the second 20th century president—besides Theodore Roosevelt—to have led men in close combat. He had personal knowledge of the reality behind such high casualty numbers. On April 25, Truman received a visit from Secretary of War Henry Stimson, who was soon joined by Gen. Leslie L. Groves, head of the Manhattan Project. Only moments after Truman had been sworn in as commander in chief, Stimson briefly mentioned the United States' development of a new weapon of immense and terrible power. After being briefed, Truman agreed with Stimson that an advisory committee should be formed that would consider the device's use.

On June 1, the committee members recommended that the device be deployed. "I have to decide Japanese strategy," Truman wrote in a June 18 note to himself. "Shall we invade Japan proper or shall we bomb and blockade? That is my hardest decision to date. But I'll make it when I have all the facts."

A month later, in a July 18 diary entry, Truman wrote, "Believe [the Japanese] will fold before Russia comes in. I am sure they will when Manhattan appears over their homeland." On July 21, Truman, by then in Potsdam, received a report on the successful test of an atomic bomb in New Mexico five days before. "Now I know what happened to Truman yesterday," Churchill told Stimson the next day, after the war secretary had shown Churchill the New Mexico report.

"I couldn't understand it. When he got to the meeting after having read this report, he was a changed man. He told the Russians just where they got on and off and generally bossed the whole meeting."

On July 25, Truman made another diary entry: "We have discovered the most terrible bomb in the history of the world," Truman wrote. "It may be the fire destruction prophesied in the Euphrates Valley Era, after Noah and his fabulous Ark." The next day the Allies issued their ultimatum in Old Testament terms: unconditional surrender of all Japanese forces or "prompt and utter destruction."

As it turned out Truman's first hundred days would be a mere preamble to the early August bombing of Hiroshima and Nagasaki, decisions that remain fiercely debated today.

There has also been debate about whether Truman really wanted to be vice president, or even president. As late as the 1960s, Truman insisted in interviews that he had discouraged talk of him joining Roosevelt on the ticket during the 1944 Democratic National Convention in Chicago. Historian Robert Ferrell, however, has cited evidence of Truman allowing one Missouri party official to bring up his name during visits to various delegations.

However reluctant, Truman was to assume the mantle of national leadership. His performance once in the White House prompted much rethinking of the definition of "average," the word used by Kansas City editor Roberts almost as a pejorative in April 1945.

"He was a certifiable member of the human race, direct, fallible and unexpectedly wise when it counted," political columnist Mary McGrory wrote following Truman's December 1972 death. "So armed," she added, "he proved that the ordinary American is capable of grandeur. And that a President can be a human being."

♦ ♦ ♦ ♦ ♦

16. The First Hundred Days: Dwight D. Eisenhower

by Fred I. Greenstein

The Rooseveltian notion of the "First Hundred Days" of a presidency as a time for experimentation and highly visible policy achievements did not work for Dwight D. Eisenhower. He spent his first hundred days in a highly deliberate process of reorganizing the presidency, and beginning the process of creating what proved to be the national security strategy of the United States over the course of the Cold War. Still, any new president could profit from studying Eisenhower's assumption of the presidency.

Dwight D. Eisenhower was a highly policy-oriented chief executive, with a sophisticated sense of how to organize collective endeavors. He reluctantly agreed to run for president when he concluded that the Truman Administration did not have a strategy for conducting the Cold War that would be in the nation's interest over the long run. Further, the almost certain Republican nominee, Ohio Senator Robert A. Taft, was unwilling to commit the United States to participate in the collective security arrangements Eisenhower had helped to forge as the first military commander of the North Atlantic Treaty Organization (NATO).

Eisenhower presided over a deliberate process of setting priorities and initiating some of the important, but not highly visible, first-year policies. Once the votes had been counted on Election Day 1952, Eisenhower promptly began constituting his presidency, naming his Budget Director and his White House Chief of Staff, an office that he created. He then promptly selected his cabinet-to-be, including both Republican internationalists and representatives of that party's isolationist-leaning Taft wing. Eisenhower also named his White House staff, relying heavily on experienced Washington professionals with whom he had worked as Army Chief of Staff and NATO Commander. Included were the first Congressional Liaison Director and the first Presidential Special Assistant for National Security in the history of the presidency.

NEW LOOK STRATEGY

Thereupon Eisenhower forged an impressively cohesive team out of very disparate appointees. Two notable team-building and policy-planning activities occurred before he took office. In late November, Eisenhower embarked on the trip to Korea that he had promised to make in his campaign. He also arranged for his appointees to convene on a naval ship at Wake Island, and they spent the voyage to Honolulu engaged in policy deliberations. On that trip Eisenhower first impressed on his aides his strategy for meeting the nation's national security needs—which was to emerge full blown late in 1953 as his administration's New Look strategy. Under the concept the United States would build sufficient military strength (especially in the realm of nuclear weapons) to prevent the Soviet Union from expanding its sphere of influence but would minimize military expenses to foster a vibrantly expanding economy. Early in January 1953, Eisenhower convened his aides-to-be at his New York City campaign headquarters for a similar discussion and to make practical preparations for the inauguration and early period of the presidency.

There was no rapid assault on Capitol Hill in the first months of the Eisenhower Administration. Indeed, Eisenhower chose not to even send a first-year domestic program to Congress, departing from a practice that had begun under Truman. Late in his first year, however, Eisenhower assembled his aides for a two-day conference on domestic policy and hammered out a program that was dispatched to Congress in 1954. Consistent with Eisenhower's hidden-hand leadership style, the early months of his administration were marked by productive, low-profile accomplishments.

By mid-spring, Eisenhower had presided over the creation of an impressively deliberative national security policy planning and policy-making process. Meanwhile, he had begun the deliberations that would lead to the official enunciation of the New Look strategy later in the year. Finally, he was closely involved in the steps that led up to the agreements in the summer of 1953 that in effect ended the Korean War. In short, the Eisenhower Presidency was not ruled by a conventional "Hundred Days" metric, but Eisenhower made systematic use of the period from his election through the end of his first year. He laid the cornerstone of his presidency and created the national security framework that his and later presidencies were to embrace for the remainder of the Cold War.

♦ ♦ ♦ ♦ ♦

17. The First Hundred Days: John F. Kennedy

by Charles Bartlett

His oft-repeated campaign pledge to "get America moving again" was a running theme in John F. Kennedy's preparations to take control of the government in January 1961. But he nevertheless urged his aides to discourage the notion that he intended to emulate the whirlwind pace of Franklin Roosevelt's "First Hundred Days" in 1933. Unlike FDR, Kennedy reasoned, he was not assuming the presidency of a nation in the grips of a dire crisis. True, the economic recession that began in April 1960 needed attention. It had caused unemployment in industrial states, which had hurt the cause of his opponent

Richard M. Nixon and helped Kennedy politically. It promised, however, to be a shallow recession that would serve the great purpose of dampening the inflationary fires.

So the president-elect had time, in his preinaugural days, to relish his victory, to bathe his fatigue in the Florida sun, and to celebrate the birth of his son, John F. Kennedy, Jr. He had the reassuring support of staff aides who had proven themselves in the heat of political battle. They were now launching task forces of distinguished citizens to propose solutions to the problems that the administration would face. It was wisely decided to protect members of these advisory committees from political pressures by neglecting to disclose their identities.

Kennedy had been advised by Harvard's respected expert on the presidency, Richard Neustadt, that he should announce, as soon as he was elected, his intention to retain in office two men whose roles would convey a sense of continuity and assurance to the public. The two men were J. Edgar Hoover, Director of the FBI, and Allen Dulles, Director of Central Intelligence. Kennedy followed Neustadt's advice, and it is interesting and ironic to recall that these two appointments caused him more difficulties than any that he subsequently made.

STAFFING THE PRESIDENCY

In fact the staffing of the Kennedy Administration went amazingly well. The key figures in the Senate and campaign staffs fit neatly into White House niches. Theodore Sorensen was nominally to be the top aide with the title of Special Counsel to the President, but there was to be no commanding figure on the staff.

President Eisenhower had argued for the creation of a post to be known as "First Secretary of the Government." But Kennedy had decided to make a sharp turn away from Eisenhower's highly structured staff. There was to be no Sherman Adams, no top assistant empowered to filter all matters relating to the president. There were no plans for regular staff meetings or for the elaborate structures that the Eisenhower team had erected to conduct national security business.

Cabinet meetings and sessions of the National Security Council were to be rarely called by Kennedy because he felt they were, for most of those involved, a waste of time.

Kennedy's instinctive preference for Secretary of State was a fellow senator, J. William Fulbright of Arkansas, but this choice was heatedly opposed by his brother, Robert Kennedy, who argued that Fulbright's record on civil rights would not conform to the president's commitments in that area. The president-elect then turned to his two most eminent advisers, Robert Lovett and Dean Acheson. They urged the appointment to Secretary of State of Dean Rusk, an establishment figure who had supported Adlai Stevenson for the nomination.

It was harder to find a Democrat with the credentials that would reassure the financial community. The best perceived to be available was a Chicago banker, David Kennedy, but the argument was made that the president would then have too many Kennedys in his Cabinet. With no Democratic possibility in sight, Kennedy turned to a respected Republican, Douglas Dillon, who had served in the Eisenhower Administration and had contributed substantially to the Nixon campaign.

Robert Kennedy deserved any reward his brother could give him for his tireless and frequently brilliant exertions in the campaign. He had not been inspired by his training and experience as a lawyer to seek the post of Attorney General—and the president-elect was keenly aware of the critical reaction that appointment would generate. But this was not to be their decision alone, because their father and family patriarch, Joseph Kennedy Sr., weighed in heavily, arguing strongly and, as it turned out, wisely that Bobby deserved the post and would do well in it.

Nothing matches the exhilaration and optimism of a president taking office with confidence in his team and his intentions. One had the feeling, in talks with the president in those early days, that there was no wrong he did not intend to right, no move he would not make to brighten the luster of the United States. A presidential transition provides a brief euphoric period before the harsh realities of dealing with 535 elected legislators sets in. Great accomplishments seem possible and, in that spirit, Kennedy and his able staff managed to lay before Congress a welter of proposals covering a range of national concerns. By Sorenson's count, there were 277 separate proposals.

The sobering blow in Kennedy's baptism as president was not dealt by Congress, however, but by a tragically short and bloody battle in Cuba's Bay of Pigs. This was a huge miscalculation by the intelligence community, but it carried the stamp of Kennedy's approval. Kennedy softened the public's reaction with a manly assertion of his responsibility. Later reviewing the episode in private, he seemed to count this as an occasion on which he had leaned too heavily on his staff. But he and his staff, when severely tested in later days by the Cuban Missile Crisis, demonstrated that they had drawn wisdom and strength from the humiliation they suffered in the Bay of Pigs.

◆ ◆ ◆ ◆ ◆

18. The First Hundred Days: Lyndon B. Johnson

by Michael Beschloss

During the first six months after his inauguration in January 1965 as president in his own right, Lyndon Johnson achieved one of the richest legislative records in American history. LBJ's Medicare and Voting Rights bills, and other strides toward strengthening education; health care; the fight against crime; the arts and humanities; highways; the environment; and job training all came within this crucial half-year, forming much of what we now admire as his domestic legacy.

In September 1965, the historian William Leuchtenburg told Johnson, "This has been a remarkable Congress. It is even arguable whether this isn't the most significant Congress ever." Irritated, Johnson replied, "No, it isn't. It's not arguable. . . . Never has the American system worked so effectively in producing quality legislation."[1]

How did it happen? LBJ started with a gift that few presidents enjoy. He had been elected with 61 percent of the vote against Barry Goldwater in the greatest presidential landslide in American history. The Johnson landslide gained thirty-nine seats in Congress. Thus, the Democratic majority in 1965 was 68 Senators and 295 Members of Congress. Only FDR in 1936 had attracted greater congressional support. Many of these Democrats knew that they owed their election to Johnson and acted accordingly.

From his long history in Congress, Johnson knew that his influence would never be as great as at the beginning of the first year after his election. From the start, he was running against the clock. In January 1965, LBJ told his congressional liaison men that since Goldwater was no longer around to scare people, he had probably already lost about 3 million of his 16 million popular vote margin: "After a fight with Congress or something else, I'll lose another couple of million. I could be down to eight million in a couple of months."[2] The message: work fast. Even with his majority, Johnson thought it would be "a hard fight every inch of the way."[3]

In May 1964, Johnson had announced his "Great Society" in a University of Michigan commencement speech. That July, he secretly established fourteen task forces made up of experts to flag urgent problems and suggest solutions. "It is very important that this not become a public operation," he told his cabinet. Premature leaks would generate opposition even before his programs were announced. And during the 1964 campaign, although Johnson suggested to Americans that he wanted to launch a sweeping attack on national problems, he wished the voters to think of him more as a frugal centrist than the big-spending champion of Big Government he would suggest himself to be once elected.

SIX KEYS TO LEADERSHIP

Within this framework, there were six keys to Johnson's leadership at the outset of his elected term. First, conviction. As with President Reagan two decades later, members of the Johnson Administration, Congress, and the American people understood that LBJ had strong ideas about the role of government; that these ideas were consistent (allowing lower-level bureaucrats, for example, to imagine with reasonable assurance how the president's philosophy should be applied to a minor matter); and that he would move heaven and earth, if necessary, to carry them out.

Second, timing. Not only did Johnson realize that he would never again have such power over Congress as he did in early 1965, he also knew that 1965 was a liberal moment that would come only once in a generation. The nation was at the apogee of its postwar economic boom. Americans were feeling tolerant, generous, and eager to attack nagging problems like discrimination, health care, education, and poverty. Johnson knew that the moment was rare and that it was not likely to last long. (He was right; the 1966 congressional elections brought a Republican landslide, which was a stinging backlash to the Great Society's spending and social reforms.) LBJ wanted to strike while the iron was hot.

Third, personnel. In the spirit of his hero FDR, Johnson had an uncanny eye for young, fresh talent and the self-assurance to bring strong-minded, independent people into government who in many cases, he realized, knew more than he did. Much of the national Democratic establishment of the late 20th century—individuals such as Joseph Califano, Bill Moyers, John Gardner, Cyrus Vance, and Barbara Jordan—consisted of people that LBJ discovered and promoted.

Fourth, legislative skills. It is almost impossible to overestimate how much LBJ benefited from having served in Congress for twenty-seven years, six years of which he spent as Majority Leader of the Senate. Having witnessed numerous presidential failures with Congress, Johnson designed his programs from the ground up in concert with influential Members of Congress. Having worked intimately with most party leaders, committee chairmen, and ranking Republicans, he had a deep wellspring of personal relationships and knowledge of the players on which to draw. For instance, in 1964, when

Johnson had needed the votes of Republican Senators to overcome the opposition of Southern Democrats to his civil rights bill, he knew just how to appeal to his old friend Minority Leader Everett Dirksen to overcome Dirksen's doubts about the measure and bring the Republican Party along. Once Johnson submitted his programs to Congress in 1965, he was as personally involved in twisting arms as he had ever been as Majority Leader. "Make an effort to get to know the men who sit on the committees that oversee your operations," he ordered his cabinet. "The job of day-to-day contact with Congress is the most important we have. Many battles have been won, and many cases settled 'out of court,' by the right liaison man being there at the right time, with the right approach."

Fifth, Johnson knew how important it was for him to use his bully pulpit to bring the American people along. He was always striving to explain more eloquently how and why he wanted to improve life for Americans. Some of his efforts were failures, because orchestrating speechwriters and reading from prepared texts were not Johnson's strengths. Despite the contributions of John Steinbeck, his 1965 inaugural address was forgettable. So was that year's State of the Union speech. But in March 1965, when LBJ went before Congress to demand a Voting Rights bill declaring, "We shall overcome," he showed how powerfully he was able to move public opinion. In what was probably his best speech, Johnson used the Voting Rights address to campaign for the rest of the Great Society, saying, "I want to be the President who educated young children to the wonders of the world . . . who helped to feed the hungry . . . who helped the poor to find their own way." LBJ went on to say that when he had taught poor young Mexican Americans in 1928, "it never even occurred to me in my fondest dreams that I might have the chance . . . to help people like them all over this country. But now I do have that chance—and I'll let you in on a secret: I mean to use it!"

Sixth, flexibility. In the wake of the 1964 election, Johnson had hoped to give the South and other areas resistant to integration some breathing space as the Civil Rights Act of 1964 was implemented. In 1965, when Martin Luther King and other leaders demanded a separate bill to ensure voting rights, LBJ—although he thought the bill was possibly even more vital than the previous measure banning discrimination in public accommodations—did not want to force another showdown so soon. Nevertheless, when King and other leaders pressed for action at Selma and elsewhere, generating a public groundswell, LBJ was responsive enough to give in and throw himself into an immediate bill, which Congress passed in the summer of 1965.

◆　◆　◆　◆　◆

19. The First Hundred Days: Richard Nixon

by Lee Huebner

Even as Ray Price was helping to draft Richard Nixon's inaugural address, in which the new president would call on his countrymen to "lower our voices" and to reach "beyond government," this senior Nixon speechwriter was also urging the president-elect to lower public expectations by avoiding "those 100 day stunts" that he felt had poorly served earlier presidents.

"The critics' scoring rules are wrong," Price argued in a spirited internal memo. Their approach, he said, had only led to "grandstand-ing."[1] Their frenzies of activity for activity's sake, their extravagant rhetoric, their wars on every real or imagined social ill, their piling of promise on over-promise, their rush of half-baked legislative proposals, their substitution of emotion for reason, their basic premise that to pass a law means to solve a problem, were all counterproductive.

Price's viewpoint was shared by many within the Nixon camp during the transition period, including—in some of his many moods—Richard Nixon himself. Many outside voices agreed that what the nation needed most in 1969, as Walter Lippmann later put it, was "to liquidate, defuse, deflate the exaggerations of the romantic period of American imperialism and American inflation."[2] Even Nixon's most liberal advisor, Daniel Patrick Moynihan, urged that the first Nixon year be one of consolidation, a time to accumulate new political capital rather than to launch a host of new initiatives or even to eliminate failed but symbolic old programs.

On the other hand, as Price noted, another side of Nixon was "like a bull at the rodeo gate, wanting to charge out,"[3] eager to assert command, to make a splash, to surprise his critics, to shape history. Nixon could be romantic about "creative and innovative" ideas—styling himself as a new Disraeli, a "Tory man with Whig principles." And he had assembled a talented, diversified governing team that wanted to make a difference.

Nixon's record in his first months in office reflected the tension between these two sensibilities. It was on the whole a cautious, often reactive period—characterized both by frustrating indecision and by wise restraint. But the deliberative atmosphere was punctuated by bold (and sometimes inconsistent) bursts of action.

Many of the bold strokes were Nixon's doing. Others happened while he looked on—or while he looked away. Some of these steps were taken secretly and came to light only later. Others happened in full public view.

A CHALLENGING TIME

The context in which Nixon launched his presidency was perhaps the most challenging to face any president since Abraham Lincoln. In addition to an interminable foreign war, Nixon, like Franklin Roosevelt, inherited a perilous domestic crisis, one that he described as a "crisis of the spirit"; a questioning of national will; a dangerous sense of racial, social, and generational division. But unlike Roosevelt (or Ronald Reagan, or Dwight Eisenhower, or Lyndon Johnson), Nixon came to office in the weakest political position of any president in a century. Only 43 percent of the electorate had supported him. His controversial career still marred Nixon's credibility—his poll ratings as he took office were the lowest of any president before or since. More than that, the credibility of the presidency itself was at low ebb. When Nixon's daughter Julie returned to Smith College in January of 1969, the campus newspaper featured a picture of her father over a banner headline that read "A Crisis of Legitimacy."

Compounding all of this was Nixon's sense—partly justified and partly exaggerated—that the press, the Congress, and the federal bureaucracy were strongly against him. This disposition turned into a self-fulfilling prophecy. The president compounded his press relations problem, for example, by appointing a young nonjournalist as Press Secretary, freezing out establishment reporters, and creating an overweening public relations machine to fashion a favorable "image." Facing the first Congress in 120 years in which neither chamber was of the same party as an incoming president, Nixon's congressional relations strategy focused defensively on his hard-core supporters and failed to build effective bridges to the Democratic majority. He quickly forced a harsh showdown with the Senate over antiballistic missile deployments, winning by one vote but further straining long-term relationships. Meanwhile, perceiving the federal bureaucracy as "the enemy," Nixon expended enormous energy trying to end-run the departments and agencies.

Nixon did not even have the advantage, in many areas, of clearly delineated programs. In this respect he resembled the pragmatic, experimental FDR and stood in sharp contrast to Johnson and Reagan. His campaign had presented a polarized electorate with sharply described problems but often with fuzzy solutions.

One result was that "process," initially, became more important than "programs." An old cliché argued that "Democrats tend to be fascinated by programs while Republicans are fascinated by structure"—and this was at least partly true in 1969.

FOREIGN POLICY FIRST

Restructuring the foreign policy making process was the most important of Nixon's early actions. Foreign affairs were his passion and preoccupation. ("You don't really need a President for domestic policy," he often declared.) He wanted to be "his own foreign secretary," in part because of his antipathy to the State Department and Central Intelligence Agency. And his National Security Advisor, Henry Kissinger, knew precisely how to act on this ambition. In what was later called "the coup d'état at the Hotel Pierre" (headquarters for the transition), Kissinger designed a series of orders that put him at the center of the policy-making machinery. Later a "back channel" was set up so that the White House could deal directly with the USSR through Soviet Ambassador Anatoly Dobrynin—without bureaucratic knowledge. These and similar measures allowed the president and his expanded National Security Council staff to keep the rest of the government, including the Secretaries of State and Defense, in the dark on many matters. The new procedures undoubtedly enhanced both the confidentiality and the creativity of Nixon's foreign policy, but they also led to errors, omissions, and a "cult of secrecy" in which wiretapping became a frequently used and sometimes misused instrument of power.

From the start, Nixon employed the new machinery to advance a clear set of priorities. Vietnam came first. He quickly eliminated two possibilities—the war was not winnable on the one hand, but he would not "bug out" on the other hand. The president felt that he could end the war quickly through a negotiated settlement and even expected at first that a "peace dividend" would soon allow him to balance the budget and finance his other programs.

To this end, even more than Kissinger, Nixon immediately began to pressure Moscow to push Hanoi to cooperate (seriously overestimating Soviet influence). Furthermore, he worked to "link" progress on arms control with Soviet cooperation on Vietnam and other matters. The president also made an early commitment to phased unilateral troop withdrawals, hoping to turn the South Vietnamese army into a credible long-range force, while calming U.S. domestic opposition. To help in the calming, Nixon moved speedily on a program of draft reform (and eventual draft elimination). But this peace strategy did not foreclose continued military pressure, largely through a 14-month bombing campaign in eastern Cambodia that was launched in response to North Vietnam's offensive in March 1969. (Protecting its secrecy is what motivated the first wave of wiretaps.)

Vietnam was not Nixon's only priority. In his first press conference on January 27, he signaled a considered new posture on arms control by calling for "sufficiency" rather than "superiority." Going against most advice, he insisted on making a February trip to Europe. This not only burnished his presidential image, but also signaled the priority Nixon placed on what he called our "blue chip" European alliances—and especially on close ties with French President Charles DeGaulle. Perhaps most important, and despite Kissinger's initial caution, the president quickly signaled his desire for rapprochement with China.

In domestic affairs, structural reform was also an initial priority, as was evidenced by Nixon's early appointment of the highly effective Ash Council to study government reorganization. Other early innovations included the Urban Affairs Council (which evolved into the Domestic Council), the Cabinet Committee on Economic Policy, the Office of Inter-governmental Relations, the Office of Minority Business Enterprise, and the privatization of the Post Office. Meanwhile, Nixon and his Chief of Staff Bob Haldeman spent endless hours chewing over questions of White House staff structure. (Nixon later said he regretted the personal isolation that these early decisions produced.)

Specific policy choices proved harder to make in the domestic arena. At first, Nixon's inclination was to leave policy choices to the cabinet. He appointed a politically moderate cabinet, made up mostly of people he scarcely knew, and convened it with diminishing frequency. (Nixon said he saw no obligation "to be bored for my country.") At first, he gave Cabinet Secretaries a free hand to appoint their own subordinates, but he quickly came to regret this move—especially as the cabinet failed to clear out bureaucratic enemies. Nixon spent the latter part of his presidency overcompensating for his initial permissiveness.

The president's obsession with foreign affairs, the absence of a clear philosophy, and a challenging set of political constraints (including the so-called Southern Strategy) all contributed to a slower domestic pace. Internal conflicts also slowed things down, epitomized by both the clash over welfare reform between the Moynihan camp and that of the more conservative Arthur Burns and by the tussle over school desegregation policy between John Mitchell's conservative Justice Department and Robert Finch's more liberal Department of Health, Education, and Welfare. In both of these areas, however, the tension would eventually prove to be creative, resulting in the boldest of all of Nixon's domestic initiatives (welfare reform), as well as the quiet but effective desegregation of most southern school districts by the fall of 1970.

DOMESTIC INITIATIVES

In the First Hundred Days, however, bold domestic initiatives were relatively few. One exception came in the first week, when Nixon, angered by newspaper crime stories and in his "bull at the gate" mood, demanded that a program to combat crime in the District of Columbia be on his desk in forty-eight hours. The need to submit a revised budget in March also forced some early economic decisions, including Nixon's determination not to risk sharp spending reductions that might trigger a recession. The budget review also reflected the administration's inclination to keep popular Great Society programs like the Office of Economic Opportunity and Model Cities—much as Nixon personally disliked them.

As he completed his First Hundred Days in April, an impatient president—having decided at the outset not to give a State of the Union address (which would have forced more early decisions)—now issued an omnibus statement on domestic affairs. The message promised a series of later, detailed proposals in areas like tax reform, Social Security, organized crime, revenue sharing, home rule for the District of Columbia, and manpower training.

By summer, despite its piecemeal emergence, the domestic program was, in Bill Safire's words, "in real danger of being described as liberal." And by late 1969, with the emergence of John Ehrlichmann as the arbiter of domestic initiatives, the administration had achieved a fairly dynamic domestic rhythm. Enough was happening, in fact, to allow the public relations team to plausibly present a host of domestic initiatives under the title "Reform is the Watchword." And Nixon's State of the Union addresses in 1970 and 1971 would present an aggressive domestic program (including major reforms in areas like health and the environment) that Nixon claimed would usher in "a great age of reform" and a "New American Revolution."

One factor that prevented this perception from being generally accepted, at the time and since, was the inconsistency of the administration's rhetoric. Even the bolder presentations mentioned above emerged only from a concerted effort—after the fact—to fashion an overarching domestic philosophy that would explain and connect the wide variety of presidential initiatives. Policy in this case preceded philosophy, rather than following it. And it was also true that bursts of progressive language were more than offset by the distinctly conservative cast of much of what the administration had to say. When a liberal group complained to John Mitchell about a lack of progress on civil rights, the Attorney General candidly advised them to "watch what we do and not what we say."

This disparity between rhetoric and policy was another early habit that persisted in later years—helping the administration resolve some of its tortuous political dilemmas, but also obscuring, from that day to this, the scope of its accomplishments.

Nixon's decision not to play the Hundred Days game was certainly consistent with this rhetorical strategy. On the other hand, in the record of those First Hundred Days, one can now discern the foundations of many of the administration's most notable successes. And one can also trace some of the attitudes and actions that would lead to its most conspicuous failures.

◆ ◆ ◆ ◆ ◆

20. The First Hundred Days: Gerald Ford

by Yanek Mieczkowski

On August 9, 1974, Gerald R. Ford took the oath of office to become the nation's 38th president. His was no ordinary inauguration. That same day Richard Nixon, who was mired in the Watergate scandal and confronted with evidence revealing that he had conspired in an illegal cover-up, became the first president in history to resign. His voice brimming with emotion, Ford delivered a brief inaugural address that included the memorable line, "My fellow Americans, our long national nightmare is over."

Ford inherited the White House under some of the most difficult circumstances any president ever faced. Lyndon Johnson's conduct during the Vietnam War had opened a "credibility gap," and Watergate had intensified distrust of the presidency. Moreover, Ford lacked an electoral mandate. He was the nation's first unelected president, having ascended to the vice presidency through the 25th Amendment after scandal forced Vice President Spiro Agnew to resign in 1973. Critics questioned Ford's legitimacy, and he acknowledged the doubts in his inaugural address: "I am acutely aware that you have not elected me as your President by your ballots, and so I ask you to confirm me as your President with your prayers."

Other crises complicated Ford's elevation to power as well. At home, double-digit inflation wracked the economy; abroad, America fought the perception that it was a fading superpower. The Vietnam War had ended in an ignominious American withdrawal, and the Cold War continued unabated.

Ford's first task was to stitch back together the fabric of political and media relationships that had been torn during Watergate. A former House minority leader who represented Michigan's Fifth District for a quarter-century, Ford knew Washington well and set about repairing the presidential-congressional relations that Nixon split asunder. He breathed life into his congressional liaison staff, invited members of Congress to the Oval Office—after Nixon had banished political "enemies"—and pledged "communication, conciliation, compromise, and cooperation" with Capitol Hill.

Ford charted a similar course of openness and communication with the media. He appointed a journalist, Jerry terHorst of the *Detroit Free-Press*, as press secretary. They devised a new seating arrangement for news conferences in which the president used a slim lectern and stood before the open doors of the White House Great Hallway, imparting a more relaxed atmosphere. Ford granted interviews generously and even allowed television cameras into Camp David, the presidential retreat in the mountains of Maryland normally hidden from the public. On August 20, he nominated Nelson Rockefeller as vice president, whom Congress confirmed in December. Nominating the sixty-six-year-old former four-time New York governor—who was five years older than Ford—added stability and gravitas to the executive branch after a scandal-pocked administration.

During Ford's first month on the job, politicians and the media embraced his style. *Time* magazine lauded a president "who worked in his shirtsleeves, who said what he meant and meant what he said, who by his honesty and accessibility was swiftly exorcising the pinched ghosts of the Nixon era from the White House."[1] Cartoonists limned Ford as a muscular, sporty president, playing on his athleticism and University of Michigan football career. (This image contrasted with the media's later depiction of Ford as a klutz after he fell down the rain-slicked steps of Air Force One in June 1975.) While flattered, Ford knew that politics would soon intervene and the praise would end. Friends and adversaries sensed it, too. When Ford invited Democratic House minority leader Tip O'Neill to his inauguration, the latter said, "Jerry, isn't this a wonderful country? Here we can talk like this and we can be friends, and 18 months from now I'll be going around the country kicking your ass in."

A SHORT HONEYMOON

On September 8, 1974, the kicking began. In a national address Ford announced that he was granting a "full, free, and absolute pardon" to Nixon. The pardon stunned Americans, who had not yet digested Watergate and its aftermath. Nixon's critics wanted to see the disgraced leader on trial, and pundits charged Ford with concocting a "deal" to exchange the presidency for a pardon. No evidence for any such arrangement ever surfaced, but the image of impropriety dogged Ford, and his approval ratings plunged from 66 to 49 percent. To protest the pardon, Press Secretary terHorst resigned. (For his replacement, Ford again drew from reporters' ranks, selecting NBC correspondent Ron Nessen.)

Trying to undo the damage, Ford appeared before a House subcommittee on September 24 to answer questions about the pardon. At one point, he vehemently denied allegations of collusion, banging the table while saying, "There was no deal, period, under no circumstances." Ford later explained that his principal reason for granting the pardon was to redirect the nation's attention toward domestic and international concerns, rather than on Nixon's fate. (Presidential science advisor Guyford Stever offered one testimonial that Ford's strategy worked: five days after the pardon, the *Washington Post* front page made no mention of Nixon, after nearly two years of saturation Watergate coverage.)

The Nixon pardon illustrated salient aspects of Ford's presidency. During his first hundred days—indeed, throughout his presidency—an overriding objective was to dispel the lingering Watergate miasma. Following his instincts of decency, Ford called the pardon "the right thing" to do. But its suddenness shocked Americans, who had become cynical about government, and played a role in Ford's relatively low approval ratings (which averaged 46 percent) and in his 1976 election defeat. The pardon's abruptness, and Ford's inability to explain it convincingly, was a testament to the poor public relations machinery that plagued his White House, which struggled to craft a favorable Ford image. Importantly, the pardon also showed Ford's preference for thinking about the long-term consequences of decisions. The "substance" of policies attracted him, he asserted, rather than short-term political gains, and over the decades, public opinion shifted to favor the pardon.

Ford stressed that he granted the pardon largely to focus on pressing policy issues, especially the economy. In 1974, inflation ran at 11 percent, a crippling double-digit rate that robbed consumers of purchasing power and confidence. At Ford's first press conference, on August 28, he declared that if "we take care of inflation," then "most of our other domestic programs or problems will be solved." A week later, Ford assembled the nation's top economists to confer about economic conditions.

For the next three weeks, the White House hosted economic "minisummits" in cities nationwide, inviting participants from government and business. This effort culminated in a Conference on Inflation on September

27–28 in Washington, where some economists emphasized inflation while others called recession the greater danger. These puzzling diagnoses reflected the economy's overall weakness, as it suffered "stagflation," or inflation laced with stagnation. Ford, whose keen interest in economic policy marked a welcome contrast with Nixon, gave institutional expression to his concern with stagflation by forming a new White House Economic Policy Board.

On October 8, 1974, Ford addressed a joint session of Congress to unveil an economic program that distilled advice from his economic summitry. The program's key measure was a proposed 5 percent surtax designed to reduce inflationary pressures. Ford also introduced a voluntary campaign to fight rising prices—"WIN," or "Whip Inflation Now"—to raise public morale and elicit citizen participation.

But Ford's proposals met stiff resistance. The tax increase bombed on Capitol Hill, and some observers called it the wrong medicine. The timing was infelicitous, too, for the proposal came just one month before the 1974 midterm elections and portended poor results for the GOP. Although Ford campaigned heartily for Republicans, Democrats scored thumping victories, gaining forty-three seats in the House and three in the Senate, widening existing majorities. The new 94th Congress was stocked with "Watergate babies," politicians who pledged to cleanse Washington of corruption. They appealed to voters appalled by Nixon Administration scandals and the Ford pardon. Ford's struggles with a resurgent Democratic Congress became a defining aspect of his presidency.

With the midterm elections over, the Ford Administration became blunter in assessing the economy, sending clearer signals that conditions were worsening. For weeks, the White House avoided the politically poisonous word "recession," but on November 12, Press Secretary Nessen acknowledged that the country had slipped into one. While maintaining that inflation was still his top priority, Ford switched gears and abandoned the surtax and WIN program and instead developed antirecession measures. In his January 1975 State of the Union address, he proposed a stimulative tax cut—the opposite of what he had introduced three months earlier—which Congress approved in just two months.

FOREIGN POLICY

In November, Ford also took his first trip abroad. The 17th of that month marked his presidency's 100th day, and it found him in Japan, becoming the first sitting president to visit this Pacific ally. He subsequently flew to the Soviet Union and held a two-day summit with Soviet leader Leonid Brezhnev.

The two men forged the framework for a new Strategic Arms Limitation Treaty (SALT), which the Senate never ratified, a failure that Ford considered his biggest diplomatic disappointment.

Still, the junket abroad presaged future Ford foreign policy endeavors. He continued to focus on Asia, visiting China in 1975, making him only the second president to do so. He met Brezhnev for a second and final time in 1975 at the Conference on Security and Cooperation in Europe, at which thirty-five nations signed the Helsinki Accords, which endorsed the freer movement of people and ideals across borders, thereby weakening communism's Iron Curtain across Eastern Europe. Ford considered Helsinki his greatest diplomatic achievement.

Ford's first hundred days accounted for more than one-tenth of his presidency. This period opened a window to the problems he faced and the principles he would employ to solve them. He regarded rising prices as America's chief challenge, and when he left office he had presided over a substantial drop in the inflation rate, which by then stood at less than 6 percent. The 1974–75 recession helped to squeeze inflation out of the economy, but the downturn also hurt Ford's popularity and contributed to his 1976 election loss. Above all, although the political fallout from the Nixon pardon hovered over his entire presidency, Ford's sincerity and openness helped to restore integrity to the political system.

♦   ♦   ♦   ♦   ♦

21. The First Hundred Days: Jimmy Carter

by Julian E. Zelizer

When Jimmy Carter came to Washington in 1977 following his narrow defeat of President Gerald Ford, many Americans were excited. The new president seemed to be the perfect antidote to the scandal of Watergate. He had campaigned promising voters they could trust him, an appealing message at the time.

The former Georgia governor understood the nation wanted a different kind of leader, one who was not tied to the orthodoxies of either party and who was willing to tackle issues that, until then, had been ignored. "Carter," wrote columnist David Broder, "brings a distinctly different personality heritage, focus and set of goals to the presidency than his predecessors. He promised change in his campaign—and he promised one thing more: personal accountability for bringing it to pass."[1]

After he was sworn in as president, Carter endeared himself to the public when he, his wife, and his daughter decided to get out of the limousine driving them from the Capitol to the White House. Instead of remaining ensconced in the new trappings of power and simply looking out into the crowds through the tinted windows, the Carters walked through the streets, waving to excited crowds who couldn't believe their eyes. When he stepped out of the car, Carter recalled thinking about the "angry demonstrators who had habitually confronted recent Presidents and Vice Presidents, furious over the Vietnam War and later the revelations of Watergate."

During his first hundred days, Carter did try to deliver on many of his promises. As he had proclaimed during his campaign, he refused to be boxed in by tradition. He ordered the U.S. Marines to stop playing "Hail to the Chief" whenever he walked into a room, and decided to sell the presidential yacht. All of this was symbolic, but initially Carter understood that symbols mattered to voters, especially in a period when so many Americans had become disillusioned with government.

With a Democratic president and Democratic majorities on Capitol Hill, many Americans were expecting big things. And in many respects the new president did not disappoint. On his first day in the White House, President Carter unconditionally pardoned tens of thousands of Americans who had failed to respond to their draft call during Vietnam. Former presidential candidate, Republican Senator Barry Goldwater, called this "the most disgraceful thing that a President has ever done."

A BOLD AGENDA

One of the first policy initiatives that Carter put forward was energy conservation. The gas lines of 1973 that resulted from the OPEC (Organization of the Petroleum Exporting Countries) embargo had made America's dependence on Middle Eastern oil a national issue. Although the sense of crisis abated when prices started to drop, policy makers understood that this was a long-term problem that needed to be resolved for the health of the national economy. Carter, wearing a cardigan sweater, delivered a televised address on April 18, 1977, when his approval ratings were skyrocketing at 75 percent, saying that the challenge to deal with energy was the "moral equivalent of war." He asked Americans to change their consumption habits and called for sweeping legislation (the National Energy Plan) that would cut certain regulations, encourage new energy sources, and promote conservation.

On foreign policy, Carter tried to respond to the ongoing trauma from the Vietnam War by offering a new ideological lodestar for foreign policy: human rights. "Our commitment to human rights must be absolute," Carter said in his inaugural address. Carter wanted the United States to show not just military strength, but also the moral strength to fight for social justice around the world. He took concrete steps to make this an integral part of American policy. The administration established the Bureau of Human Rights and Humanitarian Affairs within the State Department, and appointed Patricia Derinian, a veteran of the civil rights movement, to serve as assistant secretary of state for Human Rights and Humanitarian Affairs.

As an alternative to militarism, Carter moved forward with the SALT II Accord that entailed a second round of arms agreements with the Soviet Union (the first having been signed and ratified under Richard Nixon as part of his policy of détente). He knew the treaty faced stiff opposition in the Senate but didn't care. Carter's team also started to lay the groundwork for a peace initiative in the Middle East, centered on the possibility of brokering a treaty between Israel and Egypt. He wanted to make progress on a treaty with Panama that would return control over the Panama Canal, part of his effort to improve U.S. relations with Latin America.

Although few of these initiatives would come to fruition in the first months of his presidency, Carter set them into motion and was pushing for a bold agenda. He was not passive in any respect, and his team made an aggressive effort to build support for his ideas.

EARLY WARNING SIGNS

But during these months, Carter also started to reveal some of the fundamental weaknesses of his presidency, which would eventually become extremely debilitating as conservative opposition to his agenda mounted.

Carter's relations with Congress were never very strong. He didn't have much respect for the legislative branch, nor did he have a good sense of how much power Congress could wield. One of his earliest missteps took place in February when he announced that he would oppose nineteen water projects (out of three hundred) that had been included in President Gerald Ford's final budget. Carter characterized the projects as unnecessary waste. But legislators saw them in a different light. When Senators like Finance Committee Chairman Richard Long were slighted, they struck back. The funding was put back into the budget. There were other smaller mistakes that also triggered tensions, such as when a few legislators only learned the president was visiting their district by watching the news. "Carter has no feeling for institutional political necessity and little visible appreciation of the human, folksy, disorderly relationships that are an important feature of political life on the Potomac," wrote Meg Greenfield in *The Washington Post*.[2]

Nor did Carter do a very good job nurturing relations with the base of the Democratic Party. In 1977, the nation was going through a horrible economic period as Americans struggled with both inflation and high rates of unemployment (stagflation). There was strong pressure for a stimulus bill. Carter sent a proposal to Congress, although it was a pale version of what many party stalwarts preferred. Carter's stimulus revolved around tax cuts and a fifty-dollar rebate. Congressional Democrats, understanding that many of their constituents were not pleased with this meager proposal, especially because it lacked any substantial public works program, went out on a limb for the president and supported the bill. They pointed to the rebate as something that would help all wage earners.

However, when there were some signs of economic improvement, Carter bowed to pressure from fiscal conservatives and agreed to strip the rebate from the legislation, eliminating the one part of the measure that unions were happy about. "We do not need to proceed," the president said. Liberals were furious. The final legislation would pass in May, with tax cuts and financial assistance to the states. They also felt that the president wasn't giving any attention to the plight of the cities or to the needs of African Americans.

When Carter's first one hundred days ended, most commentators gave him strong marks. They noted that his approval ratings remained high, and he had taken a stand on a series of important issues. *Time* magazine concluded that, with approval ratings of 69 percent, "Carter has changed the tone for the better, he is making the presidency relate to the people."

But the weakness that had surfaced, particularly his lack of respect for Congress and the tensions that flared with liberal Democrats, would eventually catch up with Carter. By the end of his presidency, conservatives were gaining steam, and his failure to build strong relations with Congress, and healthy ties to the base of the party, proved costly. As conditions worsened, the political challenges grew. Carter faced stiff opposition for renomination from within his own ranks and was challenged in the 1980 primaries by Ted Kennedy. He would win that fight, but with much of his potential support dispirited, he could not win a second term.

◆　◆　◆　◆　◆

22. The First Hundred Days: Ronald Reagan

by Lou Cannon

The agenda of Ronald Reagan's "First Hundred Days" in office—indeed, in large measure, the agenda of the first year of his presidency—was defined by the promises of his 1980 election campaign. During that campaign, in which Reagan defeated incumbent President Jimmy Carter and independent candidate John Anderson, he repeatedly pledged to cut taxes, boost military spending, and balance the federal budget by reducing domestic spending. Anderson famously scoffed that these promises could be accomplished simultaneously only with "mirrors," but Reagan was serious about them. The clarity of Reagan's policy intentions and the electoral mandate he had received for them were decisive in giving the new administration a running start.

Reagan's transition teams had studied Carter's 1976 transition and learned from its mistakes. For instance, Carter had named separate campaign and transition staffs. The two staffs soon developed intense rivalries and competed for jobs and influence. In contrast, most of Reagan's pre-election planning was conducted by members of his top campaign hierarchy, and Reagan reached relatively quick decisions on the composition of his Cabinet and White House staff. Conflicts later developed between this staff and key members of the Cabinet—and within the staff itself—but their initial teamwork and focus on Reagan's well-defined objectives helped get the administration quickly off the mark.

Reagan's running start was aided by a compilation (later called "the Holy Scrolls"), directed by chief domestic adviser Martin Anderson, of every policy statement that Reagan had made during the campaign. New appointees were given copies of these statements and were told that they were the blueprints of administration policies. Also useful was the Initial Actions Project, a political guide to action prepared by pollster-strategist Richard D. Wirthlin, and his associate, the late Richard Beai, aided by David Gergen. This fifty-five-page report, known as the transition's "Black Book," was presented in draft form to Reagan a month before he took office. "How we begin will determine significantly how we govern," the report said.

INSPIRATIONAL LEADERSHIP

Taking his cue from his first political idol, Franklin D. Roosevelt, Reagan saw his own role as providing inspirational leadership to reverse what he believed was a crisis in public confidence. As a college student, Reagan had thrilled to the inaugural address delivered by FDR in 1933 during the depths of the Great Depression, and he memorized its stirring perorations. "My firm belief is that the only thing we have to fear is fear itself. . . ." Emulating FDR in manner, despite their considerable policy differences, Reagan displayed a sunny optimism in his meetings with congressional leaders and other Washington power brokers, and especially in television and radio speeches to the American people. Reagan's poll ratings rose notably between the time of his election and his inauguration. After Reagan delivered his economic message on February 18, 1981, a *Washington Post*-ABC News poll showed two-to-one support for the policies that would become known as Reaganomics.

It should be noted that Reagan did not regard all of his campaign promises as equal. During the transition and the first months of his presidency, he gave primacy to economic issues. Reagan had been advised to emphasize the economy and to put everything else on the back burner by former President Richard Nixon (in a memo disclosed in my book, *President Reagan: The Role of a Lifetime*), but it is likely that Reagan would have done so anyway. "If we get the economy in shape, we're going to be able to do a lot of things," Reagan confided to a friend soon after reading the Nixon memo. "If we don't, we're not going to be able to do anything."

This emphasis on the economy drove social issues such as abortion and school prayer, which were important to religious conservatives, off of the administration's political radar screen during Reagan's first months in office— and to some degree throughout his presidency. The administration's approach was summarized by James Baker, the practical White House Chief of Staff, who said, "We ought to have three goals, and all three of them are economic recovery."

TWO CAVEATS

Two caveats are necessary in any discussion of Reagan's beginnings as president. The first is that the administration was able to hew to its preferred emphasis on the economy because the fifty-two Americans who had been held hostage in Iran for 444 days were released in the first moments of Reagan's administration, as he was giving his inaugural address on the west front of the Capitol. (The details of this action do not concern us here; my research credits both the outgoing and incoming administrations, who sent a unified message to the Iranian regime, "Do not expect a better deal from Ronald Reagan.") Had the hostages remained in captivity, the American people would have demanded action, and the administration would have faced a difficult and sensitive foreign policy issue with the potential of becoming a crisis.

The second caveat is that Reagan's First Hundred Days in one sense lasted only seventy days—but in another lasted six months. On March 30, 1981, Reagan was shot and nearly killed in an assassination attempt. He was incapacitated for several weeks during which his aides of necessity did the day-to-day decision making. This probably reinforced Reagan's proclivity for excessive delegation, which later in the presidency had harmful consequences. But Reagan's courageous conduct in the face of death ("I hope you're all Republicans," he quipped to the doctors who were about to operate on him) made him a hero to the American people and yielded political dividends. Influential columnist David Broder wrote that the wit and grace displayed by Reagan after the assassination attempt elevated his "appealing human qualities to the level of legend." Baker and other White House aides took advantage of Reagan's mythic status to advance his tax and budget bills, as did the president in a memorable address to a joint session of Congress less than a month after he was wounded. Although the Democrats (led by House Speaker Thomas P. "Tip" O'Neill) put up a stiff fight, a coalition of united Republicans and conservative Democrats from the South and West won a series of legislative victories culminating in a seven-vote victory on a key budget bill on June 26, 1981.

This marked the real end of Reagan's Hundred Days.

◆ ◆ ◆ ◆ ◆

23. The First Hundred Days: George H.W. Bush

by John P. Burke

The George H.W. Bush transition to office in 1988 presents the only instance of an electoral transition within the same party since the passage from the Coolidge to the Hoover Presidency in 1929. Furthermore, it is the only electoral transition by a sitting vice president since Martin Van Buren took office in 1837. President Bush began a modest pre-election transition effort well before the November election. It was aimed almost exclusively at planning a personnel operation and was under the direction of longtime associate Chase Untermeyer. Bush had also given some personal thought to what his presidency might look like, and immediately after the election he not only set up a transition operation but also announced the appointment of James Baker as Secretary of State, Untermeyer as Director of White House Personnel, and another close aide, Boyden Gray, as his White House Legal Counsel. These latter appointments were especially useful in preparing for a personnel process that had become increasingly complex and time-consuming.

In filling both staff and other positions, Bush and his associates moved quickly for the most part and were able to draw upon a pool of talent that often had both close personal connections to George Bush and a variety of "inside the Beltway" experience. There was a bit of intramural politicking concerning John Sununu's role as Chief of Staff, especially whether a way could be devised to bring campaign strategist Robert Teeter on board. There were also delays in naming the White House economic and domestic advisers. Some of the organizational decisions made—particularly in downgrading White House units that would play a major role in "marketing and selling" policy proposals—would also have repercussions once the administration was in office.

But for the most part Bush had a well-organized and managed transition. It undoubtedly benefited from the good auspices of the Reagan Administration. Advice and information were quickly conveyed—both before and after the election—giving the Bush team an easy head start. Many of those tapped to serve could also draw on their own past experiences in Republican administrations. Moreover, a number of soon-to-be White House aides had not only served in the Reagan White House, but they also had easy access to the present occupants of the positions they would soon hold. It was not only a friendly takeover, it was a familiar takeover.

Throughout the transition, Bush played an active role, which was quite a change from Reagan's indifference to staff and organizational matters and President Carter's preference for letting his fellow Georgians work things out among themselves. Bush was directly involved, not just in selecting the Cabinet but also in choosing the key players on the White House staff, and he was attentive to the issues of organization, process, and management that are crucial to an effective staff and advisory system.

Yet neither during the campaign nor in the early months of his presidency did Bush present a bold new agenda to Congress and the nation, as Reagan had done eight years earlier. Representing a friendly takeover by a sitting vice president, Bush was perhaps hampered by a sense of continuity rather than radical change. As John Sununu told the press in late January 1989, "Everyone is looking for some drastic change or redirection [but] this is a conservative Republican president taking over from a conservative Republican."[1]

Nor had the election conveyed a mandate. Bush's margin of victory over Michael Dukakis was certainly respectable (53.3 percent to 45.6 percent), but it was well short of a landslide, and was accompanied by GOP losses in both the House and the Senate. Bush was only one of two postwar presidents elected to office (the other was Nixon) who had to contend with both houses of Congress being controlled by the other party. In fact, Bush faced a House with fewer Republican members than any newly elected Republican president in the 20th century.

President Bush sought to foster a cordial relationship with Congress, an effort that he even incorporated into his inaugural address. But his attempts were complicated in the Senate by his decision to pursue John Tower's increasingly troubled nomination as Secretary of Defense. In the House, Bush and the GOP continued to face partisan opposition under House Speaker Jim Wright, especially as Wright struggled with the ethics allegations that would lead to his resignation as Speaker in May. Within the ranks of House Republicans, comity was further attenuated by the increasingly partisan stance of Minority Whip Newt Gingrich and his followers.

The early days of the Bush Presidency, however, were not without their achievements. Especially in foreign policy, the team of Bush, Secretary of State James Baker, and National Security Council Adviser Brent Scowcroft developed a close working relationship that contrasted with the infighting of the Reagan years. During the transition period, Bush and his advisers successfully sought to defuse the contentious issue of aid to the Contras in Nicaragua (an issue that had bedeviled his predecessor) by crafting a bipartisan plan to extend humanitarian but not military aid. They also took steps to deal with mounting Latin American debt, which eventually became the Brady Plan, named after Treasury Secretary Nicholas Brady. Bush's late November meeting in Houston with Mexican President Carlos Salinas set the stage for what would become the North American Free Trade Agreement (NAFTA).

SAVINGS AND LOAN CRISIS

The transition period also saw a concerted effort to develop a plan to deal with the savings and loan crisis, which Bush presented to Congress on February 6 and was finally passed in early August. But like the Brady Plan, although it was an important policy achievement, the savings and loan plan did little to capture the public imagination. The kind of proactive effort on the domestic front that might have provided the "vision thing" that Bush appeared to lack, moreover, was handicapped by worsening deficit projections.

From December 1988 on, Richard Darman, the new Director of Office of Management and Budget, sought to craft a solution. Bush's hope, articulated during the campaign, of a "flexible freeze" (freezing total spending, adjusted for inflation, while flexibly increasing or decreasing particular programs) would not work in Darman's view. Instead, he developed a two-step approach: a first year budget that would avoid new tax increases and force Congress to make difficult cuts, with the issue of raising taxes postponed until the next year. With the "big fix" and the problem of dealing with Bush's "read my lips" election pledge to come later, it was a decision that led to the 1990 budget agreement and would have repercussions on Bush's chance for reelection. Given that the deficit issue and how to deal with it would loom large over this presidency, the administration's choices here raise some important "What if?" counterfactuals. Would Bush have been better off to bite the tax bullet early on, perhaps taking a political hit but striking an agreement with Congress during the more favorable "honeymoon" period, rather than on the eve of a midterm election? Or, conversely, should Bush have pushed harder on retaining a "flexible freeze" approach?

The early Bush Presidency was not bereft of domestic initiatives, but they often lacked fiscal commitments and suffered from poor marketing and selling. Media events were staged in the early weeks of the new administration to demonstrate Bush's commitment as the "Education President," the "Environment President," the "Anti-Drug President," and so on. Yet the administration's policy proposals in these areas emerged piecemeal in subsequent months, with little thematic continuity and waning media attention: a merit schools proposal (April 5), ethics-in-government legislation (April 12), expansion of Medicare (April 18), child-care legislation (May 9), a crime bill (May 15), and a major revision of the Clean Air Act (June 12).

MEDIA ACCESS

Interestingly, Bush was highly accessible to the press throughout his presidency. In his First Hundred Days as president, he held eleven press conferences, about one per week, and had nine additional question-and-answer sessions with groups of reporters. But these were often impromptu events, and informal as well: Bush preferred to brief reporters in the White House press room rather than stage the more formal events Reagan would hold in the East Room. It was a venue in which George Bush was more comfortable, but it did not result in a more favorable media. In one study of media coverage of the first sixty days of the new administration, Bush garnered only 505 references on the evening news broadcasts compared to 832 for Carter and 1,030 for Reagan.

Bush clearly wanted a different kind of presidency from that of his predecessor—less emphasis on pomp and public presentation, more on quiet achievement and in a lower key. Yet he and his advisers failed to lay the groundwork to ratchet down or otherwise alter public and press expectations. At least initially, the public appeared to like this president and his early performance in office: in June 1989 his approval rating stood at 70 percent, higher than Reagan's 58 percent rating eight years earlier and second only to Kennedy's in 1961. But Bush's standing in the polls might have fostered a false sense of security, as problems would mount and other perceptions would build later in his presidency

On March 7, 1989, six weeks into his presidency, Bush personally addressed the issue that his administration was adrift: "So I would simply resist the clamor that nothing seems to be bubbling around, nothing is happening." He told reporters, "A lot is happening, not all of it good, but a lot is happening." On March 16, he told the press that "more is going on than meets the eye or makes headlines." In late April, Bush's "Hundred Day" mark passed with less notice and media fanfare than had occurred in the Carter and Reagan Presidencies.

◆ ◆ ◆ ◆ ◆

24. The First Hundred Days: Bill Clinton

by Charles O. Jones

The success of a president's "First Hundred Days" is typically determined by how effectively he and his team have managed the transition from campaigning to governing. This view was well summarized by a senior aide to President Ronald Reagan: "In my view, [the transition is] hands-on management in operation. It's not so thematic and it's not so visionary except the crafting of the 100-day plan. . . . What was it you said during the campaign? And how does that fit with your 100-day plan?" The Reagan transition through to the "First Hundred Days" was, for the most part, linear. Benefiting from a clear agenda and substantial political advantages, Reagan advisers could and did proceed to organize effectively to "hit the ground running."

It would be hard to imagine a more stark contrast than that between the Reagan and Bill Clinton transitions. Pre-election transition planning for Reagan was integrated with the campaign organization; the two were separated for Clinton. Dismantling the campaign organization and creating the new presidency were separated for Reagan; they were integrated for Clinton. Principal White House staff appointments were made early for Reagan; they were made later for Clinton. Reagan's Chief of Staff was a Washington insider; Clinton's was a friend from Arkansas. The transition was not "hyped as a big separate thing" for Reagan (quoting a Reagan aide); it was in the news almost every day for Clinton. Reagan left for his ranch in California after the election, and aides announced his Cabinet appointments; Clinton continued to be involved daily in the transition—announcing appointments, conducting a conference on the economy, holding press conferences, giving speeches. The Reagan team managed expectations; the Clinton team raised expectations.

It is true that the Clinton campaign had been about "the economy, Stupid," James Carville's reminder to the campaign organization. But Carville had other advisories: "Change vs. more of the same" and "Don't forget health care." That the Clinton agenda was about more than the economy was evident from their book of promises, "Putting People First." It contained thirty-five proposals for the Clinton national economic strategy and 577 proposals for other crucial issues. Clinton was said to admire Reagan's concentration on a limited agenda, but his interest and involvement in this huge catalog of issues suggested a very different intention. Having an agenda with many items need not preclude setting priorities. Unfortunately, however, the Clinton Presidency began with more uncertainty than certainty in regard to priorities. A rereading of Bob Woodward's *The Agenda* and Elizabeth Drew's *On the Edge* provides the details.

An effort to focus on priorities by the new Clinton Presidency was made difficult early on by the president-elect having violated the rule against making policy pronouncements before taking office. At an early news conference Clinton discussed his intention, by executive order, to lift the ban on gays in the military. That issue then came to be more prominent than the new president would have preferred. Among other developments with the issue, President Clinton was unable to fulfill his commitment to act quickly by executive order. Rather, the matter extended well into the first year of his administration.

The president-elect had also announced that he would appoint a Cabinet that would represent the diversity of the nation. Although a laudable goal in many respects, it had the effect of encouraging the press and various groups to keep score and to rate selections as much by whom they represented as by their own talents. Such attention also sometimes distracted from the larger purposes of the new administration.

LIMITED POLITICAL CAPITAL

In fairness to Clinton and his team, they faced extraordinary pressures. Their political capital was limited (with a 43 percent win and reduced majorities in Congress), and yet expectations were high and cross-pressures abundant. This was the first all-Democratic government in twelve years. Liberals were expectant and centrists were eager (Clinton had chaired the centrist Democratic Leadership Council at one point). Further, he had been reassured by Democratic leaders in Congress that they could deliver on Clinton's program.

As it happened, those immediate actions that presidents take to demonstrate their "take charge" style were more likely to satisfy liberals than centrists in Clinton's case. Clinton signed executive orders regarding abortions performed in military hospitals, federal funding of fetal tissue research, and the importation of RU-486, the so-called abortion pill. As promised, he also signed the Family and Medical Leave Act, along with other legislation that President Bush had vetoed in the previous Congress. Clinton announced the formation of a health care task group to be headed by First Lady Hillary Clinton (suggesting that welfare reform lost out as an immediate priority). The promised middle-class tax cut was dropped.

These and other early actions strongly hinted that the Clinton Presidency would be more liberal and confrontational than might have been anticipated from the campaign and the election results. Accordingly, congressional Republicans found it easy to unite in opposition to a full menu of Clinton initiatives. Even the pacing of the economic proposals played into the hands of Republicans. An economic stimulus package was forwarded early. An effort by certain centrist Democratic senators to fashion a bipartisan compromise was turned down by the White House, and so the package was killed by a Republican filibuster. Republicans labeled it classic Democratic spending. The president's reaction to this defeat came at a news conference: "I just misgauged it and I hope I can learn something. I've just been here ninety days." Alas, those ninety days are important for any presidency in setting a style and tone.

I summarized the Clinton transition and First Hundred Days this way in my book *Clinton and Congress, 1993–1996: Risk, Restoration, and Reelection*[1]:

> First, expectations had been raised, not moderated, thus inviting accountability early and often. Second, postelection statements and priorities by the President and his staff, as well as initial actions once in office, were markedly more liberal than conservative or centrist in character. Third, congressional Republicans therefore had incentives to unify in opposition to the new administration on ideological and

procedural grounds. Fourth, it came to be impossible for the administration to meet its optimistic timetable in regard to health care, welfare reform, and the elimination of the ban on gays in the military, thereby permitting opposition to develop and the "L" word to be affixed to the President and his aides. (p. 77)

The Clinton experience offers lessons for future presidents during their First Hundred Days. First and foremost is the need to comprehend fully who you are, where you are, and how you got there. The "who" refers to your experience and that of your aides. The "where" refers to the fact that presidents enter a government already at work—in Congress, in the departments and agencies, throughout the nation and the world. The challenge is to fit you in effectively enough so as to lead. And the "how" refers to the political capital you have available to assist in convincing others that what you want is what they should want (a Richard E. Neustadt formulation). It is a fair judgment that Clinton and his team deserved the poor marks they received by these tests. They did, however, "learn something," as the president had hoped they would. It is preferable, nonetheless, to be educated in advance.

♦　♦　♦　♦　♦

25. The First Hundred Days: George W. Bush

by Peter Baker

For his belated victory speech in December 2000, George W. Bush chose to address the country from the chamber of the Texas House of Representatives, where he had struck repeated bipartisan deals with the majority Democrats during his tenure as governor. The choice was meant to send a bipartisan signal after the polarizing recount battle in Florida culminated in the intervention of the Supreme Court. "The spirit of cooperation I have seen in this hall," Bush told a national audience, "is what is needed in Washington, D.C. It is the challenge of our moment."

But if the head of the ticket was promising a spirit of cooperation, his number two had something else in mind. On the same day, the vice president-elect, Dick Cheney, met on Capitol Hill with several moderate Senate Republicans who had expected him to compromise on key issues only to find him adamantly opposed to any such preemptive concessions. "Our attitude was hell no," Cheney later recalled. "We got elected. You don't now go for half tax reform. We're not going to leave half the children behind. No, it's full speed ahead."[1]

The profound tension between those two instincts, between conciliation and confrontation, marked Bush's First Hundred Days and set the tone for the early period of his presidency. Bush arrived at the White House with a challenge unlike any of his modern predecessors. No elected president in more than a century had taken office after losing the popular vote, and none in that time had secured his office in the Electoral College after such a controversial, and still hotly disputed, legal battle. If that left Bush without the mandate he had sought, it also left him without much time to build his new administration. With just thirty-eight days between his victory and his inauguration, Bush had a shorter transition than any newly elected president in modern times, barely a quarter of the time Franklin D. Roosevelt had to prepare for his own hundred days back in the era when inaugurations were held in March rather than in January.

Bush genuinely wanted to set a cooperative tone to fulfill his vow to be a "uniter, not a divider." He bristled at the bombast and divisiveness of House Speaker Newt Gingrich, until then the dominant Republican on the national stage (and the conservative whose rebellion against his father's tax deal helped cost the elder George Bush a second term). But the new president also agreed with Cheney in rejecting the chattering class arguments that he should immediately scale back his ambitions. To do so would show weakness from the start, the two reasoned. They should proceed as if they had a mandate and force Washington to accept their legitimacy. Karl Rove, Bush's premier political adviser, noted that John F. Kennedy didn't trim his agenda just because he barely edged out Richard M. Nixon in their nail-biter showdown in 1960. But Kennedy had an advantage Bush did not. Since Nixon did not seek a recount, there was not the same sort of cloud hanging over Kennedy's election. And Kennedy came into office with his party in firm control of both houses of Congress, while Bush's Republicans held the Senate, deadlocked fifty to fifty, only through Cheney's tie-breaking vote as vice president.

THE DELEGATOR

Secluded at his Texas ranch through much of the transition, Bush also chose to do something no previous president had done—he essentially outsourced the construction of his new administration to his vice president. Even as the lawyers were haggling over hanging chads in Florida, Cheney set to work from the kitchen table at his home in McLean, Virginia, outside Washington, using an old Princess dial phone his wife had brought down from the attic for calls deemed too sensitive for a cell phone.

Bush had key people in mind for select positions—Colin Powell for secretary of state, Andy Card for chief of staff, and Condoleezza Rice for national security adviser—but he gave Cheney a remarkably free hand in filling out the cabinet and other top slots. Cheney tapped old colleagues from the Ford and first Bush Administrations, most notably his friend and mentor, Donald H. Rumsfeld, for a repeat tour as defense secretary.

Like others to follow FDR, Bush dismissed the First Hundred Days measurement as a "completely artificial date," as Rove put it. Nonetheless Bush understood, as others have since FDR, that momentum was important, and he thus set about advancing his agenda as fast as possible. From the start, he fulfilled campaign promises to conservatives by signing two executive orders: one limiting taxpayer money for organizations that promoted abortions overseas, and the other creating a White House office of faith-based initiatives.

And yet Bush was seized with the idea of duplicating the bipartisan success he had achieved in Austin working with Lieutenant Governor Bob Bullock, the state's dominant Democrat, and he set about searching for a new partner across the aisle. On his second full day in office, Bush invited Senator Edward M. Kennedy of Massachusetts, the nation's most prominent liberal, to the Oval Office to talk about education reform.

Kennedy, naturally wary of the cowboy from Texas, found himself surprised by Bush's understanding of the issue and commitment to reducing the achievement gap between white and minority students. Bush continued the courtship by renaming the Justice Department headquarters after Kennedy's brother, Robert, and by hosting the senator and his family for a White House screening of the Kevin Costner movie *Thirteen Days* about his other brother John's handling of the Cuban Missile Crisis.

The education reform package Bush and Kennedy ultimately assembled under the name "No Child Left Behind" would irritate stalwarts in both parties—it sought to impose accountability through more rigorous standardized testing to the aggravation of liberals, and it invested more federal money and increased the federal role in education policy to the consternation of conservatives. But Bush and Kennedy fended off the critics to forge one of the most important domestic legacies of his presidency.

PLAYING HARDBALL

For the most pressing priority of his First Hundred Days, however, Bush would have a harder time winning over the opposition—and he would play hardball. His model was Ronald Reagan, not Franklin Roosevelt, and so emulating his hero, Bush pushed for a $1.6 trillion, 10-year tax-cutting plan over the misgivings of even members of his own party who were concerned that he was squandering the budget surpluses he had inherited. He would win most of what he sought—eventually settling for giving taxpayers back $1.35 trillion—with bipartisan votes, but it came at a cost.

Senator James Jeffords, a mercurial moderate Republican from Vermont, insisted that Bush pare back the tax cuts and spend $200 billion on special education for children with disabilities. When Bush and Cheney refused, Jeffords bolted from the Republican Party, becoming an independent caucusing with the opposition and handing Democrats control of the closely divided Senate.

In other areas, at the urging of his vice president, Bush also sent signals of defiance to Democrats and even international allies. Although Bush had promised during the campaign to support a cap on carbon emissions by power plants to try to curb climate change, Cheney outmaneuvered his internal rivals, including Powell and Rice, and convinced the president to reverse his position, arguing that rolling blackouts in California made clear it was not the time to hinder the power industry. The president likewise renounced the Kyoto climate change treaty and the International Criminal Court, positions that were in keeping with Republican skepticism about subordinating national interests to foreign priorities, but handled with an indelicacy that even Bush came to regret as unnecessarily alienating. When critics tried to force Cheney to release information about his secret task force on energy, the president similarly backed his vice president's penchant for secrecy. "Stiff 'em," Bush told his staff.

Yet Bush also showed a more deft diplomatic touch at times. When a midair accident brought an American spy plane down on Chinese territory, Bush quietly negotiated to secure the release of the crew and, eventually, the plane with none of the bluster some had expected. Although conservatives were unhappy at what they considered a timid approach, Bush aides were so ecstatic about the outcome that they thought the new president had passed what they assumed would be the toughest foreign policy test of his first term.

Expecting to be a domestic policy president, Bush had relatively modest international ambitions for the opening of his administration. After promising a more "humble" foreign policy that would be less aggressive in the use of military force around the world, Bush's main national security priority was ramping up efforts to build ballistic missile defense. There was little urgency in formulating a new strategy to tackle a relatively obscure terrorist group known as al-Qaeda, but much talk about what to do about Saddam Hussein's Iraq.

Perhaps most important, Bush used his First Hundred Days to move beyond Florida and establish himself as a full-fledged president, not one with an asterisk next to his name. While many Democrats remained bitter about his contentious ascension to the Oval Office, Bush had impressed enough Americans with his performance that his approval rating at the hundred-day mark stood at 62 percent, higher than either Bill Clinton or his father had enjoyed at the same stage in their administrations.

If anything, he was successful enough that it was unclear what would come next. By the end of summer, he had passed the tax cuts and was well on the way to passing education reform. He whiled away much of August clearing brush at his Texas ranch while aides looking ahead to the fall worried that the administration had begun to drift. "There wasn't any galvanizing issue," Peter Wehner, one of his speechwriters, recalled.

At least not until a bright Tuesday morning in September changed everything, and it became clear that the First Hundred Days would not be his most consequential ones.

◆　◆　◆　◆　◆

26. The First Hundred Days: Barack Obama

by Jonathan Alter

An account of Barack Obama's first hundred days in office must begin with the dire economic conditions he faced upon assuming the presidency on January 20, 2009. During and after the 2008 presidential campaign, the U.S. economy fell off the cliff. It contracted by an astonishing 8.9 percent in the fourth quarter of 2008, more than twice as big a reduction in GDP as economists estimated at the time. Major banks began to melt down. This was the worst performing economic quarter since such statistics were first collected—worse than any single quarter in the early 1930s. In Obama's first month in office the economy lost more than 850,000 jobs. Had that level of job loss continued, the unemployment rate would have spiked to 25 percent by fall and the nation would have—without exaggeration—plunged into another Great Depression.

Instead, through a combination of efforts by the president, the Congress, and the Federal Reserve, unemployment peaked in late 2009 at 10.2 percent and the country experienced a great recession instead. While growth began again by mid-2009, signaling the formal end of the recession, the effects of the crisis Obama inherited have lingered for years and conditioned any assessment of his tenure.

Despite having no management experience or other preparation for confronting such a crisis, Obama handled his debut in office well. He enacted or set in motion major policy changes that put him in good historical company, behind only Franklin D. Roosevelt in 1933 and Lyndon B. Johnson in 1965 in the number and significance of bills signed into law during his first hundred days. And Obama managed to do it all with virtually no honeymoon.

Roosevelt and Johnson also had it easier than Obama politically. FDR took office as the economy touched bottom in early 1933 after three and a half years of decline; conditions were so grim that many prominent Americans wanted a dictator (a positive word then, used, for instance, by Studebaker as the name of a car) and majorities in both parties supported most of Roosevelt's early initiatives. Obama, by contrast, took the oath only a few months after the crisis began, which made most of its devastating consequences for the wider economy still an abstraction. It was easier for FDR to win support for addressing a depression than for Obama to convince Republicans to try to prevent one.

For his part, LBJ had mastered the Senate as majority leader in the 1950s. After he won a landslide presidential election in 1964, he enjoyed overwhelming Democratic majorities in Congress that helped him make 1965 the most successful legislative year on record. By contrast, Obama was a junior senator for only two years—2005 and 2006—before he began running for president, and during that time, he spent more time writing a book than cultivating colleagues. He was never a governor and thus lacked executive skills that might have helped him achieve more.

The political obstacles materialized immediately after Obama took the oath as the nation's first African American president. On the night of that historic inauguration, celebrated throughout the world, disciplined Republicans—meeting in secret at a restaurant on Capitol Hill—vowed to resist the olive branch of bipartisanship that the new president offered in his inaugural address. This stood in sharp contrast to Democratic offers to help Ronald Reagan when he took office in 1981 amid a less ominous economic crisis.

Even when Obama broke precedent and visited the House Republican caucus on Capitol Hill during his first week, House Minority Leader John Boehner and Senate Minority Leader Mitch McConnell refused to negotiate over the recovery plan. Two days after the inauguration, Republicans were already on television nitpicking details of the president's plan (e.g., Why re-seed the National Mall?) without offering any plan of their own for rescuing the economy beyond more tax cuts, a prescription that even conservative economists overwhelmingly rejected as insufficient. Politics preempted any patriotic rally behind the president in a time of national crisis, but Republican leaders succeeded in their goal of avoiding schisms in the GOP ranks and eventually reclaiming control of Congress.

In the meantime, Obama's first hundred days were chock-a-block with achievement. In his first week, he banned torture, restricted lobbyists, lifted the gag order on abortion counseling overseas, and signed the Lily Ledbetter Fair Pay Act.

In his first three months, Obama signed a mammoth stimulus package, stabilized the banking system, began withdrawing U.S. troops from Iraq, rescued the American auto industry, imposed tough new fuel economy standards, extended more health coverage to children, expanded AmeriCorps, and used his leverage to spread charter schools and establish the first national Common Core educational standards.

Within a year, many of the policy seeds planted during Obama's first hundred days bore fruit, as the president and Congress overhauled the U.S. health care system (a goal of progressives since the Bull Moose Party platform of 1912), reregulated Wall Street, and ended the discriminatory "Don't-Ask-Don't-Tell" policy on gays in the military, among other accomplishments.

"Every time I think he's gonna step on the brake, he hits the gas," Democratic Senator Mary Landrieu said in mid-2009.

CRISIS RESPONSE AND POLITICAL REACTION

Ironically, Obama was never a big believer in the "hundred days" concept. His longtime political adviser, David Axelrod, called it "a Hallmark holiday." But long before he was elected, Obama began planning his first months in office. The strategy was best summarized by his soon-to-be White House Chief of Staff, Rahm Emanuel, when he said, "You never want a serious crisis to go to waste." Although constantly trying (and failing) to tamp down expectations ("It is not going to be quick, it is not going to be easy," he said in his first postelection press conference), Obama knew he would be busy.

Some victories were distasteful, and the president later said he knew at the time that they were toxic politically. Shortly before the 2008 election, President George W. Bush won approval, after an initial rejection by fellow Republicans, for the $700 billion Troubled Asset Relief Program (TARP), a bank bailout so large that it was widely described as socialistic. But the bailout came in two stages, and it fell to President-elect Obama in the weeks before he took office to lobby through Congress the second $350 billion in aid for bankers.

After the inauguration, the first order of business was the $831 billion American Recovery and Reinvestment Act of 2009, better known as "the stimulus," which passed along partisan lines and which Obama signed less than a month after taking office. The stimulus was nearly six times as large as a $150 billion package rejected a year earlier by the Senate, but smaller than liberal economists recommended to meet the crisis. Those views were politically irrelevant. Emanuel was told on Capitol Hill that even Democrats wouldn't have voted for more.

Much maligned, the stimulus might have been better appreciated had it been broken up into component parts. It was actually five landmark pieces of legislation in one: the biggest tax cuts for the middle class since Reagan's a quarter century earlier; the biggest infrastructure bill since Dwight Eisenhower's Interstate Highway Act of the 1950s; the biggest education bill since Johnson's first federal aid to education in 1965; the biggest investment in scientific and medical research since the 1960s; and—with $150 billion for alternative energy—the greenest bill ever.

But Obama had played bad poker. In a failed bid for Republican support, he offered $300 billion in tax cuts up front. The GOP pocketed the tax cuts, which meant less money for liberal priorities. (Another $100 billion had to be spent just avoiding layoffs of thousands of teachers and first responders in the states that faced severe budget shortfalls.) Moreover, because "shovel-ready" infrastructure projects turned out to be largely a myth, Obama couldn't build projects like new schools, airports, and electric grids that might have given him more WPA-style permanent projects for his legacy.

Even so, the stimulus worked well as a tourniquet to help stop the bleeding. Despite efforts by critics and reporters to find waste and corruption, it proved to be predominantly scandal-free (much cleaner than New Deal programs). Even the Department of Energy loan program that funded lemons like Solyndra Corporation ended up turning a profit.

So did the bank bailouts. Early on, Paul Volcker, former Chairman of the Federal Reserve, told Obama that he had it worse than Roosevelt, whose "bank holiday" quickly restored confidence in the banks. Volcker said that today's depositors were sophisticated institutional investors who wouldn't assume that reopened financial institutions were safe. But midway through the first hundred days, Treasury Secretary Tim Geithner introduced "stress tests" to prove such safety. The plan worked, and by 2011, the banks paid back all of the $700 billion in TARP bailouts with interest.

Obama wasn't open enough to the advice of progressive economists, who were frozen out of deliberations in favor of more Wall Street–friendly figures like Geithner and Lawrence Summers, chairman of the National Economic Council. But those on the president's left who argued that ailing Citibank be taken over were mistaken. Obama's early decision not to assume control over banks (an echo of what FDR decided in 1933) saved hundreds of billions that would likely have been necessary to prop them up over time.

If the bank bailouts were savaged from the Left, the bailouts of General Motors and Chrysler came under fire from the Right, which seemed impervious to the cascading chaos that would have resulted from a GM liquidation. Like so much else in his first hundred days, here the president was forced to clean up his predecessor's mess—to manage "the shovel brigade," as Don Regan, Reagan's chief of staff, once called it. Obama later said that one of his biggest mistakes early on was failing to remind voters of Bush's legacy the way FDR trashed Herbert Hoover's stewardship and how Reagan pummeled Jimmy Carter's for years afterward.

The auto bailouts signaled a turning point in American politics. The White House assumed that voters who resented bailing out bankers would approve of saving the jobs of struggling autoworkers. But they didn't. The public despised the auto bailouts, too. Three years later, the decision to rescue automakers would help Obama get reelected, but at the time, he acted in defiance of public opinion.

Growing opposition to the stimulus and the bailouts—plus personal animus to the country's first black president—helped fuel what came to be known as the Tea Party. It began during Obama's first month when a CNBC reporter named Rick Santelli, a self-described "Ayn Rander," ranted on the floor of the Chicago Board of Trade against bailing out homeowners and promised a "Chicago tea party" to protest. The Tea Party, which grew into a mass movement almost overnight, made it harder for the Obama Administration to move aggressively in the early days to help homeowners left underwater by the subprime mortgage crisis. It took years to figure out how to do so without further inflaming the public.

A WIDER LENS

From the start, foreign policy was a further source of contention. While winding down the war in Iraq, Obama in February responded to the deteriorating security situation on the ground in Afghanistan by dispatching 17,000 additional troops. In the fall of 2009, he decided to send 30,000 more, before beginning a phased withdrawal in 2011 that was completed in 2014. During his first week in office, Obama signed an executive order to close the military prison at Guantanamo Bay within a year. But when four exonerated Muslim Uighur detainees were released (and eventually resettled in Bermuda), a firestorm erupted, and in May, the Senate voted 90–6 to prevent the transfer of any Guantanamo Bay prisoners to the United States. Obama's inability to convince Congress to help him close Guantanamo Bay—his only conspicuous failure during the first hundred days—was a harbinger of congressional trouble to come.

Throughout his early presidency, Obama insisted that terrorism, the economic crisis, and all the other daily challenges of the job would not derail his major domestic proposal—universal health care coverage and a reduction of runaway health care costs. In this he was virtually alone. Vice President Joe Biden told him that the American public would forgive him for setting aside health care while he focused on the economy. Emanuel told me later that he "begged the president not to do health care." Axelrod, who has a daughter with epilepsy and was passionately in favor of a bill, thought that politically it made more sense to tackle a big energy plan first. (This wouldn't have worked. While the House passed a cap-and-trade bill in 2009, it was dead-on-arrival in the Senate.)

When I asked the president why he went ahead with health care over the objections of his top advisers, he replied: "If we didn't get this done now, it was not going to be done." He was indisputably right about that.

In hindsight, Obama should have used his popularity during his first hundred days to push Senator Max Baucus, chairman of the Senate Finance Committee, to move the health care bill through faster. It didn't clear committee until the fall of 2009, and almost failed in early 2010 after Massachusetts Republican Scott Brown won a special election to the Senate, depriving the Democrats of the sixty votes needed to repass a final compromise version in the Senate.

As a consequence of the delay, the final bill that Obama signed in March of 2010 was the less progressive Senate version. Senator Charles Schumer has argued that the long debate on health care took Obama's eye off the economy. This analysis misreads the timing of legislative proposals in this period. Even if Obama had focused on the economy instead of health care, in truth there was zero appetite on the Hill for more stimulus funding in late 2009.

Obama's big first-term mistake on the economy came not in 2009, but rather in 2010. Immediately after signing the Affordable Care Act, widely known as "Obamacare," he should have pivoted to championing a jobs bill for the Democrats to run on in the 2010 midterms. Instead, he got bogged down dealing with the BP oil spill in the Gulf of Mexico and other matters, and the Republicans took control of the House in November 2010.

Remember the eighteen-and-a-half minute gap on Richard Nixon's Watergate tapes? Obama had an eighteen-and-a-half month gap, and it lay at the root of his early troubles. That was the length of time between the signing of Obamacare in the winter of 2010 and the president's futile introduction of the American Jobs Act in the fall of 2011, by which time Republicans, not Democrats, were driving American politics.

When Obama had first burst into the national spotlight at the 2004 Democratic Convention, he spoke eloquently about moving the country beyond an America of red and blue states. He urged the same spirit of bipartisanship in Grant Park on the night of his election, and in both of his inaugural addresses. In building a bipartisan political consensus he failed, although the blame lies mostly with obstructionists who have often bragged that they don't even believe in compromise, one of the great principles on which the American republic was founded.

But any student of the Obama years tempted to confuse failure to unify with failure to achieve need only look at the record of his early presidency. It is one of major progressive accomplishment. With the help of a Democratic Congress, Barack Obama put more legislative points on the board in two years than John F. Kennedy did in three, Jimmy Carter in four or Bill Clinton in eight. In retrospect, he should have done even more—pushing through comprehensive immigration reform, two free years of college, long-term infrastructure spending, and early childhood initiatives, to mention only a few of his deferred priorities—before the Republican takeover in the 2010 midterms dashed any hopes of further landmark legislative accomplishment. But neither critical conservatives nor disappointed liberals can contest the scorecard: President Obama quickly accomplished more than 90 percent of what Candidate Obama promised to do. Much of that was the legacy of his first one hundred days.

Presidential Domestic Milestones

27. Bigger Than the Pyramids: Public Works and the Interstate Highway System

by Geoffrey Perret

Dwight D. Eisenhower's first important achievement as president was to bring an end to the fighting in Korea. In June 1953, five months after his inauguration, he secured an armistice that remains in force to this day. Yet even as the armistice went into effect, he was worried about the economic implications of peace.

Eisenhower was deeply troubled that deficit financing on a prodigious scale was paying for the war, and he had pledged during the campaign that he would seek a balanced budget. If Eisenhower stuck rigidly to that goal however, the end of the Korean War would be followed by a severe and prolonged recession, something that every modern president has a duty to avoid.

Eisenhower's solution was entirely pragmatic. The budget remained in deficit in 1954 and the recession proved to be short lived and shallow. Meanwhile, Eisenhower looked for a public works project that would act as a counter to future recessions. Hastily improvised New Deal "work" projects like the Civilian Conservation Corps—"raking leaves," in his words—were not for him. What Eisenhower wanted was a wide range of public works projects that could be initiated when the economy was functioning successfully, and in peacetime when there was time to think carefully about national needs and devise programs that could be justified over the long term.

Eisenhower had in mind new highways, urban redevelopment, land reclamation, hospital construction, and water conservation. Such projects could move forward in low gear while the good times lasted, and when the economy turned down—most, if not all—could be rapidly accelerated and together might provide work for millions, if necessary.

COLD WAR CONSIDERATIONS

There was already a federal highway system, and most people considered it adequate for their needs, but Eisenhower was anticipating future demands, including those of national defense. This was, after all, the height of the Cold War. "If I had all the money I wanted right now," he told Senator Styles Bridges, "I wouldn't use it to keep men in the Army. I would much rather put that money into new highways and roads so we could get around this country in a hurry in case of attack."

He created a committee, chaired by an old friend and Army engineering officer, General Lucius D. Clay, to decide whether such a venture made economic sense. The committee's report, issued in January 1955, recommended 41,000 miles of divided highways, built over a period of ten years and costing as much as $101 billion.

The Democrats—and Lucius Clay—expected the federal government to finance the project. However, Eisenhower could not accept this and still achieve a balanced budget. He was also convinced that the states, as major beneficiaries, must bear part of the cost. Legislation was introduced in Congress in the spring of 1955 and passed the Senate but was rejected by the House—mainly because of disagreements over financing. Forced to think again, the White House reintroduced the measure in 1956, with a self-financing proposal: a tax on gasoline of four cents a gallon, and a small federal tax on new cars and trucks. The states would cover 10 percent of construction costs; the new taxes would allow the federal government to cover the remaining 90 percent.

As the legislation moved through Congress in 1956, the annual Governors' Conference met. The governors inevitably turned their attention to Eisenhower's highway project. A draft resolution was drawn up in which the governors commended the program as being "bold and imaginative" and proposed naming it in Eisenhower's honor. Governor Averell Harriman of New York, a highly partisan Democrat, got "bold and imaginative" struck out, along with the compliment to Eisenhower.

When this was drawn to his attention, Eisenhower laughed it off. "A project as good as this doesn't need to carry my name," he told his staff. It was enough for him that the Congress enacted his legislation.

The Federal Highway Act was an extraordinary achievement. The Democrats controlled both the Senate and the House and his own party—which contained a powerful and vociferous anti-New Deal element—hardly seemed to notice that Eisenhower's highway program amounted to the biggest public works project in American history. It was the biggest, some writers have even claimed, since the Pyramids.

The Federal Interstate and Defense Highway system came into being because Eisenhower was making an investment in the future of the country, rather than an investment in the next election; because his approach was nonpartisan yet persistent; because he had a clear idea of where he wanted to go and was flexible about how he got there; and because he did not seek to capitalize, either personally or as the leader of his party, on this legislative success. Nearly all the benefits, he knew, would accrue to the nation after he left the White House, not while he occupied it.

◆ ◆ ◆ ◆ ◆

28. Top Dollar: Building a Global Economy

by Katherine Theyson

In the summer of 1944, World War II was still in full swing, but the tide of the war had begun to turn. The Allies had, in early June, successfully landed on the German-held beaches of Normandy, and the July 1 correspondence between President Franklin Delano Roosevelt and British Prime Minister Winston Churchill was filled with discussions of the ongoing offensive: the Allied forces' liberation of the French city of Cherbourg and plans for an invasion of Southern France.[1] Conspicuously absent from the correspondence was mention of perhaps the most historically important event of the day: the opening of an international conference that would result in a new monetary order and, eventually, a governing body for world trade.

INTO BRETTON WOODS

On July 1, 1944, the Mount Washington Hotel in the tiny resort town of Bretton Woods, New Hampshire, began playing host to a three-week conference that would create a new worldwide monetary system. Despite the lack of a mention in his wartime correspondence, President Roosevelt had laid the groundwork for the conference and was clearly aware of its important implications.[2] Forty-four Allied nations had sent representatives to Bretton Woods, and Roosevelt had chosen his particularly well. The American delegation was led by the Secretary of the Treasury Henry Morgenthau, and Harry Dexter White, Morgenthau's right-hand man on monetary issues,[3] whom economic giant John Maynard Keynes praised as "one of the few constructive brains in the Treasury."[4]

Harry Dexter White was a dogged negotiator who managed to push back against the much more prominent Keynes and advanced the interests of the United States in the policies that emerged from the conference. White's life and his battle with Keynes have been documented extensively in an excellent book by Benn Steil, but our focus is what emerged from that policy battle-field. The Bretton Woods Agreement established an enduring international monetary system that was anchored by two institutions: the International Monetary Fund (IMF) and the International Bank for Reconstruction and Development (IBRD).

The IMF was the central institution for the functioning of the Bretton Woods system. Tasked with providing international financial stability, the IMF would provide loans that allowed countries to maintain relatively stable exchange rates in the face of trade imbalances and still utilize monetary policy for internal policy goals, such as maintaining or improving the standard of living.[5] Bretton Woods stipulated "pegged but adjustable" exchange rates, with each country pegging the value of its currency to the U.S. dollar and adjustments allowed only with IMF approval in situations of prolonged im-balances. The dollar provided the link between each of these currencies and gold, which was valued at a fixed $35 an ounce.[6] Furthermore, the United States agreed to buy and sell gold at this fixed value, reinforcing the idea that the U.S. dollar was "good as gold."

The United States was the only major developed nation in the world that had not been devastated by World War II. It was inevitable that the dollar would be an important currency after the war, as European nations sought U.S.-made goods in their rebuilding efforts. The use of the dollar as the "lynchpin" in the Bretton Woods Agreement, however, also gave the United States alone the power to determine its own monetary policy.[7] The agree-ment was the first step toward total dollar domination of international finan-cial markets.

There were several obstacles, however, that needed to be overcome on that path. One prominent issue was the decided lack of funds within European nations wishing to buy American goods. President Harry S. Truman was forced to rectify that situation. Truman became president in April of 1945 and in overseeing the end of the war in Europe made many important foreign policy decisions. In particular, his decision to support the Marshall Plan for the reconstruction of Europe had a significant impact on the prominent place of the United States and of the dollar in the interna-tional financial system.

As has been widely recognized, Truman's support for the Marshall Plan stemmed, in large part, from a fear that communism would spread from the Soviet Union and take hold in Europe.[8] In actual fact, Truman's decision cemented the role of the dollar as *the* international currency because the Marshall Plan (and its Japanese equivalent, the Dodge Plan) provided over $41 billion, over three-quarters of that in gifts, to allow the purchase of

U.S.-made goods to rebuild the war-ravaged nations.[9] This not only boosted growth in Europe, Japan, and the United States but secured the fragile Bretton Woods system, which would have surely collapsed had nations been forced to turn to barter.[10]

TOP DOLLAR

The efforts of Roosevelt and Truman placed the United States and its currency at the top of the post–World War II monetary order. Although the United States today does not wield such predominant economic power, its currency still dominates international trade and finance. More than $500 billion in currency is held outside the United States, representing more than half of all dollars in circulation.[11]

The use of the dollar in international markets confers substantial benefits on Americans in a number of ways. First, to obtain the dollars used internationally, foreign residents, companies, and governments must purchase those dollars. Thus, the United States has received more than $500 billion in real goods and services in exchange for allowing the international use of our currency. In addition, the internationalization of the dollar also reduces the cost of international trade and investment for U.S. companies. Because of the extensive use of the dollar, many international prices are denominated in dollars. This means U.S. companies doing business abroad can purchase and accept payment for goods in dollars, avoiding the costs associated with converting currency. The ability to avoid currency exchange also reduces the risk of doing business overseas because prices (and profits) will not be adversely affected by unexpected changes in exchange rates.

The international acceptability of the dollar also leads to higher demand for investments denominated in dollars, especially in times of economic trouble, when the dollar is seen as a refuge. This allows the United States to borrow money at very low interest rates, even in times of financial turmoil, reducing the cost of borrowing for both the government and the American consumer. The demand for such investments also finances the nearly perpetual U.S. trade deficit, allowing the nation to consume more goods than it produces each year.

There are also negative consequences of the dollar's dominance as well. In particular, the large international holdings of the dollar mean that a substantial share of the U.S. currency in circulation remains outside the control of the Federal Reserve. That makes it more difficult to implement independent monetary policy. Furthermore, the demand for dollars and dollar-denominated assets may have undesirable consequences on the value of the dollar in foreign exchange markets. For instance, during the 2008 financial crisis, a fall in the value of the dollar may have helped relieve the U.S. economic stagnation by making U.S.-made goods cheaper in foreign markets. But as the crisis unfolded, nervous investors fled to the safety of the dollar, keeping the dollar value relatively high and eliminating this naturally occurring relief for the economy. Policy is a double-edged sword, however, and the flood of funds into the U.S. market also allowed interest rates to remain historically low throughout the crisis.

THE GOLD STANDARD

The decision at Bretton Woods that the United States would buy and sell gold on demand at the fixed rate of $35 an ounce represented a calculated risk. The arrangement meant that the United States would need to maintain the value of the dollar relative to gold to avoid any runs on its gold reserves. Thus, the U.S. money supply would need to be constrained by its gold reserves, and the growth of those reserves was relatively slow. At the same time, the use of the dollar as an international currency meant that the United States needed to supply dollars internationally to lubricate the global economy and global trade, which were growing much more rapidly.

The conflict between these two requirements is called the Triffin Dilemma, after the economist who commented extensively on this problem. Triffin observed that if the United States failed to provide a sufficient number of dollars, then world economic growth would be adversely affected, but printing too much money would lead to a lack of global confidence in the commitment to buy and sell gold at a fixed price, leading to a demise of the gold–dollar linkage. At the time of the Bretton Woods Agreement, this problem was not an important concern, most likely because the United States held almost all of the world's gold reserves. However, by the 1960s, the value of U.S. dollars in circulation outside the United States exceeded the total U.S. gold reserves by as much as 250%[12] and the U.S. gold reserves were being rapidly depleted.

John F. Kennedy and Lyndon B. Johnson both attempted to save U.S. gold supplies by deterring foreign nations from converting their dollar holdings into gold through persuasion and through laws restricting international lending by U.S. banks. These measures might have proved fatal to the role of the dollar as the international currency were it not for the development of the Eurodollar market. Centered in London, the Eurodollar market was a market for borrowing and lending dollars outside of the United States. This market can be traced back to the Marshall Plan but was significantly reinforced when the Soviet Union decided to move its dollar deposits to London because of fears that the developing Cold War might induce Washington to freeze Soviet bank deposits in the United States. The Eurodollar market operated outside of U.S. control and provided liquidity in dollars, maintaining the dollar's grip on the world markets.

In the end, the Bretton Woods system went out with a whimper rather than a bang, so much so that it is difficult to determine when exactly the system ended. Certainly the end stemmed from the continuing pressure on U.S. gold reserves, which by 1968 had fallen by more than half from their peak.[13] Which of the subsequent developments spelled the actual end of Bretton Woods is unclear. In 1971, Richard Nixon, facing growing balance of payments deficits, rising inflation rates, and stagnating economic growth made the decision to end the convertibility of dollars to gold, effectively bringing an end to the Bretton Woods system as it was originally conceived. Despite this development, there were subsequent attempts to save the system by devaluing the dollar, appreciating foreign currencies, and allowing greater flexibility of exchange rates. The Smithsonian Agreement in late 1971 and the Jamaica Accords in 1976 formally ended the role of the dollar as the "lynchpin" in the global financial system. The remnants of that role remain to this day; however, as the dollar continues to dominate the worlds of trade and finance, the United States will reap both the benefits and costs.

GLOBAL TRADE AGREEMENTS

A longer run consequence of the Bretton Woods meetings was the trade agreement known as the Generalized Agreement on Tariffs and Trade (GATT). GATT was the predecessor to both the World Trade Organization (WTO) and the earlier, but ultimately failed, attempt at forming the International Trade Organization (ITO). The representatives at Bretton Woods determined that it was necessary to have an international trade organization that would act as the counterpart to the IMF. Thus, beginning in 1945 and concluding with the signing of the Havana Charter in 1948, the United States and its allied partners negotiated the terms for the International Trade Organization (ITO) and GATT.

The negotiations for these institutions were possible, at least in part, because of the executive power that President Roosevelt had secured from Congress in the form of the Reciprocal Trade Agreements Act (RTAA) of 1934. As noted by Toye (2012), the act ceded the power to alter tariff levels from Congress to the executive branch, allowing Roosevelt and subsequent presidents to negotiate reciprocal bilateral trade agreements. GATT itself was designed as a tariff bargaining forum that would form the foundation for the more comprehensive ITO. Truman failed to generate support for the ITO agreement in Congress, however, despite his own frequent assertions that to oppose trade liberalization was equivalent to voting against the "free world"[14] and strong public sentiment that such an organization was desirable.[15] The nature of this failure is much debated. Some insist that the Truman Administration failed to adequately promote the agreement, and others assert that the compromises that were necessary for agreement to be reached by the fifty-six countries at the final round of negotiations in Havana created a flawed and ultimately doomed document.

By 1950, the United States withdrew its support for the ITO and the failure was complete. It would be nearly half a century before a new international trade organization was instituted; in the meantime, the world only had GATT, a body that ran by consensus and lacked any serious enforcement mechanisms. Despite this obvious weakness, GATT was strongly supported by Truman and subsequent American presidents, including Eisenhower and Kennedy, and succeeded in reducing global trade barriers and increasing trade, stimulating economies throughout the world.

The GATT was not stagnant but evolved through eight rounds of negotiations, the full substance of which is beyond the scope of this essay. However in each round, the views of U.S. presidents played a major role in the evolution of the treaty. John F. Kennedy is credited with taking steps to lower U.S. tariffs and for pushing the same agenda with respect to the GATT.[16] This leadership brought about one of only two rounds of GATT negotiations named for an individual. The Kennedy Round, begun in 1962, resulted in significant reductions in tariff rates among developed countries and was declared by President Johnson to be the "most successful multilateral agreement on tariff reduction ever negotiated."[17]

The Reagan Administration proposed an agenda that opened what would be the final (and longest) round of negotiations. Reagan envisioned the Uruguay Round to focus on problems that had not previously been confronted, including trade in services, trade in high-technology industries, and counterfeit goods, as well as one long-standing issue: agricultural subsidies.[18] These issues may have come to President Reagan's attention during his time as the Governor of California because the state was a major player in many of the industries affected by these issues. Unfortunately, the controversial nature of agricultural subsides, particularly with European nations, resulted in a delay of several years before the official opening of negotiations.

The opening of the Uruguay Round in 1986 was set against the backdrop of rapidly growing U.S. trade deficits, which, although persistent since 1976, had more than doubled in a few short years.[19] Conventional wisdom asserted that this increase in the trade deficit was the result of unfair trade practices that reduced U.S. firms' access to foreign markets; thus, the United States pressed for, and got, both significant opening of markets and reductions in trade barriers. Although these policy changes did result in a reduction of U.S. trade deficits, such reductions proved short lived.

The Uruguay Round lasted for nearly a decade and the negotiations gave birth to the World Trade Organization in 1995. The United States was initially not receptive to the formation of the WTO because of congressional concerns about a loss of sovereignty, a desire to keep talks focused on the "substantive objectives for trade liberalization,"[20] and, perhaps also, a hope of gaining additional negotiating power. President Clinton did, in fact, have some difficulties getting Congress to pass the final WTO agreement. However, Clinton prevailed (with some concessions to Congress) and the United States joined the WTO, supported by large majorities in both the House and the Senate.

Although the WTO and its actions since its founding have been, at times, controversial, it has undoubtedly pushed the agenda of a new global system. One hundred and sixty nations are currently members of the WTO with another twenty-four acting as observer governments, representing well over two-thirds of global sovereign governments.

CONCLUSION

U.S. presidents played an important role in the formation of the Bretton Woods system, GATT, and the WTO. President Roosevelt, recognizing the role that economics played in the run up to World War II, took a leadership role that led to the formation of all of these organizations. Subsequently, Presidents Truman, Eisenhower, Kennedy, and Johnson continued to advance the cause of a global financial and trade system, enshrining these institutions and promoting the United States' role as a global leader. Nixon acted to preserve the integrity of the United States in a time when the strictures of the Bretton Woods system might have overwhelmed the nation. Reagan and Clinton presided over the movement toward and the final attainment of the long-planned WTO. In the pursuit of a global system, there were several moments of obvious failure, but overall these organizations are monuments to presidential success. They set the frame for world trade and finance in the modern era, bolstering the economic position of the United States and lending order to the international political economy.

BIBLIOGRAPHY

Allee, Todd. "The Role of the United States: A Multilevel Explanation for Decreased Support Over Time." In *The Oxford Handbook of the World Trade Organization*, M. Daunton, E. Narlikar, and R.M. Stern, Eds. New York: Oxford University Press, 2012.

Appleyard, Dennis, and Alfred Field. *International Economics.* New York: McGraw Hill, 2014.

Eckes, Alfred E. Jr. *A Search for Solvency: Bretton Woods and the International Monetary System, 1941–1971.* Austin: University of Texas Press, 1975.

Eckes, Alfred E. Jr. "US Trade History." In *US Trade Policy*, William A. Lovett, Alfred E. Eckes, Jr., and Richard L. Brinkman, Eds. Armonk, NY: M.E. Sharpe, 2004. 36–92.

Eichengreen, Barry. *Exorbitant Privilege: The Rise and Fall of the Dollar and the Future of the International Monetary System.* New York: Oxford University Press, 2011.

Goldstein, Judith. *Ideas, Institutions and Trade Policy.* Ithaca, NY: Cornell University Press, 1993.

Harry S. Truman Library and Museum. Biographical Sketch: Harry S. Truman, 33rd President of the United States. n.d. http://www.truman library.org/hst-bio.htm.

International Monetary Fund. *International Monetary Fund Factsheet.* 2014. https://www.imf.org/external/np/exr/facts/pdf/globstab.pdf.

Judson, Ruth. "Crisis and Calm: Demand for U.S. Currency at Home and Abroad from the Fall of the Berlin Wall to 2011." International Finance Discussion Paper 2012-1058. Washington, DC: Board of Governors of the Federal Reserve System, November 2012.

Kimball, Warren. *Churchill and Roosevelt, The Complete Correspondence, Volume II: Alliance Forged.* Princeton, NJ: Princeton University Press, 1984.

Kimball, Warren. *Churchill and Roosevelt, The Complete Correspondence, Volume III: Alliance Declining.* Princeton, NJ: Princeton University Press, 1984.

McKinnon, Ronald. *The Unloved Dollar Standard: From Bretton Woods to the Rise of China.* New York: Oxford University Press, 2013.

Preeg, Ernest. "The Uruguay Round Negotiations and the Creation of the WTO." In *The Oxford Handbook of the World Trade Organization*, M. Daunton, E. Narlikar, and R.M. Stern, Eds. New York: Oxford University Press, 2012.

Skidelsky, Robert. *John Maynard Keynes*, Volume 3: *Fighting for Freedom.* New York: Viking, 2001.

Steil, Benn. *The Battle of Bretton Woods: John Maynard Keynes, Harry Dexter White and the Making of a New World Order.* Princeton, NJ: Princeton University Press, 2013.

Toye, Richard. "The International Trade Organization." In *The Oxford Handbook of the World Trade Organization*, M. Daunton, E. Narlikar, and R.M. Stern, Eds. New York: Oxford University Press, 2012.

U.S. Census Bureau. *US Trade in Goods and Services—Balance of Payments (BOP) Basis.* 2015. https://www.census.gov/foreign-trade/statistics /historical/gands.pdf.

◆ ◆ ◆ ◆ ◆

29. Capitalism's Safety Net: Social Security, Medicare, and Medicaid

by Rudolph G. Penner

The main programs that constitute the social safety net are a dominant feature of American life. Increasingly, Social Security, Medicare, and Medicaid dominate our nation's budget, constituting 49 percent of total spending in 2014, up from 29 percent in 1980.[1] Although the growth in health cost has slowed dramatically in recent years, the Congressional Budget Office expects cost growth to accelerate once again unless these programs are reformed. The subsidies for buying health insurance in the exchanges created by the recent Affordable Care Act were a trivial portion of the total budget in 2014, but the subsidies are expected to grow rapidly as the new health plan matures. By 2024, they are expected to amount to 8 percent of total federal health spending.

This article focuses only on the history of the most important safety net programs. It does not consider smaller, but still significant programs, such as unemployment insurance, workman's compensation, or most welfare programs, such as food stamps.

SOCIAL SECURITY

Social Security,[2] created in 1935, is the government's largest single program. It was preceded by Civil War pensions that covered a remarkable portion of the population and came close to emulating today's Social Security system. The late 19th century also saw the beginnings of corporate retirement programs, but they were not widespread.

As the Civil War generation passed from the scene, more and more of the elderly had no pension support, and the Great Depression profoundly worsened the plight of the elderly. By 1930, more than half of men aged sixty-five and older were unemployed, at a time when the Depression also destroyed many corporate pension plans.

As the debate over helping the elderly evolved, states started creating old-age assistance plans for widows and men experiencing hardship. Such a plan was signed into law by Franklin Roosevelt when he was governor of New York. In 1934, Francis Townsend, a retired physician from California, created a plan for those unemployed and over age sixty. They would be paid $200 per month, but they had to spend it in thirty days, and the plan would be financed by a 2 percent tax on all transactions.

The Townsend Plan became popular and competed for public attention with the Social Security plan that eventually succeeded. President Roosevelt did not want a plan that was means tested in any way. He thus designed a plan financed by the "contributions" of workers who would eventually benefit, which was a stroke of political genius. Recipients did not feel as though they were on welfare. They really believed that they had paid for the benefits. However, until recently, most new beneficiaries had not. The system was progressive, but everyone—even the very rich—got some benefits, thus ensuring continued broad support for the program. The program also received strong backing from the children of the elderly who otherwise would have had to support their parents.

The Social Security system did not immediately alleviate the hardship created by the Great Depression. The first benefits were not even paid until 1942. Taxes were deposited into a trust fund that financed the payment of benefits. This added to the illusion that people paid for their own benefits.

There was an early debate over funding the program. That is to say, should enough be deposited in the trust fund to cover future liabilities? It was quickly apparent that funding the system in that way would require a large tax burden, and the idea was dropped in favor of a pay-as-you-go system. Current benefits would be financed by taxes paid by current workers.

A pay-as-you-go system can be likened to a social contract in which workers agree to turn over a certain share of their wages to the elderly in return for a promise that future generations will do the same for them. The financial health and the potential generosity of such a system are improved if the population of wage earners and their wage rates grow relatively rapidly, and the population of retirees grows relatively slowly. Then each generation of retirees can receive more than they gave their predecessors. The benefits going to retirees can be even more generous if the share of wages turned over to retirees grows over time, as it has with the Social Security system. But the pay-as-you-go system had no automatic mechanism for adjusting benefits to the revenue stream. Trouble comes if there are fewer workers or more retirees (or both) than expected.

In forecasting the health of the Social Security system early in its history, actuaries, led by the conservative Robert J. Myers, assumed that wages would remain constant. When wages actually grew, it provided politicians with the resources to increase benefits periodically. Nevertheless, benefits eroded in real terms during World War II, and the loss was not made up until a generous benefit increase in 1950.

Social Security coverage was expanded and a disability insurance program was created in 1957. An early retirement age of sixty-two was provided for women in 1956 and for men in 1962. This did not affect the long-run financial outlook for the system because benefits were reduced actuarially for early retirees.

The decade of the 1960s saw an unusually high rate of economic growth, which economists expected to continue, and this facilitated an increase in benefits of 15 percent in 1969, 10 percent in 1971, and 20 percent in 1972. The 20 percent increase was strongly opposed by President Nixon, but when the envelopes went out with the increased checks, they included a note from the president essentially claiming credit for the government's generosity.

Henceforth, the actuaries of the system would assume that future wages would grow. The assumption was more realistic than assuming constant wages, but it turned out to be too optimistic. That made benefit increases seem affordable with smaller increases in the wage base and tax rate than would eventually be required.

Indexing benefits to inflation was adopted in 1972, but the formula was seriously flawed and provided for very large increases in real benefits when inflation unexpectedly reached double digit levels. President Ford proposed a correction and most of his proposal was adopted by President Carter in 1977. The new formula indexed initial benefits to wages in order to keep initial benefits up with the standard of living of the rest of the population. After retirement, benefits were indexed to the price level. This kept benefits constant in real terms, but they were allowed to erode relative to workers' standard of living.

In the early 1970s, it was strongly believed that indexing would save money. It was assumed that when politicians passed discretionary increases, they could not resist being overly generous. Indexing would reduce the need for discretionary increases, thus giving politicians fewer opportunities to be extravagant.

In retrospect, it is less clear that indexing saved money. The large discretionary increases in benefits in the four years following 1968 were unusual. The ratio of average benefits to average wages was almost constant in the long period between 1950 and 1968. Rapid economic growth in the 1960s made it seem as though the nation could afford anything—guns, butter, and a happier elderly population. It is not at all clear that discretionary benefit increases would have been as generous as indexed increases when the nation's economy encountered stagflation in the 1970s.

In any case, slow growth during the 1970s and back-to-back recessions in 1980 and 1982 created severe financial pressures. The trust fund was being exhausted rapidly, and President Reagan created a commission chaired by Alan Greenspan to recommend solutions.[3]

The commission floundered but was saved by a subgroup led by Senators Robert Dole (R-Kansas) and Daniel Patrick Moynihan (D-New York). The subgroup convinced the whole commission to recommend increases in payroll taxes and cuts in benefits (including the taxation of benefits) that were roughly equal. The proposed reforms were expected to make the system financially whole for fifty years.

The reforms could have been scuttled by partisan demagoguery had not President Reagan and Speaker Tip O'Neill, D-Mass., agreed beforehand not to oppose any of the commission's recommendations.

During the House debate Rep. J.J. Pickle of Texas introduced a gradual increase in the retirement age for those reaching age sixty-two in 2000 and later. That was thought to make the system financially whole for the seventy-five-year time horizon traditionally used to judge the financial health of the system. Unfortunately, the economic and demographic assumptions used then proved to be too optimistic. The trustees of the system now believe that the OASI (Old-Age and Survivors Insurance) trust fund will be empty in 2034, and the Disabilities Insurance fund will empty in fiscal 2017. Unfortunately, Congress and various presidents have not been able to agree on reforms, even though it is apparent that necessary reforms will become more and more painful the longer we wait.

MEDICARE AND MEDICAID

Various plans to provide universal health insurance were debated throughout the 20th century. Between 1915 and 1919 several states attempted to enact plans, but they all failed.

The issue arose again as Social Security was debated in the years before 1935. But President Roosevelt strongly opposed the inclusion of health insurance in the legislation.[4] Given strong opposition from the American Medical Association (AMA) and business interests, he worried that adding health insurance would politically block his efforts to create old-age pensions.

Soon after World War II, President Truman pushed for national health insurance but again ran into furious opposition from the AMA and business interests. In 1951, there was an effort to create a health insurance program but only for the elderly already on Social Security.

The emphasis on the elderly was somewhat peculiar because no other nation has a health system solely for that segment of the population. But circumstances in the United States were unusual because large numbers of workers were covered by an employer-based system begun during World War II. Its spread was encouraged because the value of the insurance was not taxable.

President John F. Kennedy promised a Medicare plan for the elderly in his 1960 campaign, and in the emotional aftermath of his assassination, President Johnson was able to get a hospital insurance program passed by the Senate. Congressman Wilbur Mills (D-Arkansas), chairman of the Ways and Means Committee, resisted pushing the measure in the House. He did not want to try to pass something that would fail in the face of the continued opposition from the AMA, business interests, and conservative Republicans. He was also worried about costs. Action awaited a change in the political calculus, and the election of 1964, which greatly increased Democratic majorities in the House and Senate, provided it.

Throughout the bargaining process, President Lyndon Johnson worked hard to overcome the reluctance of Wilbur Mills, who was never enthusiastic about proceeding. Johnson promised Mills that he would be given full credit for any positive results. Because Johnson worked mainly behind the scenes, it remains somewhat unclear what role he played in crafting the eventual compromise.[5]

Democrats designed a Hospital Insurance program that followed some of the principles of social insurance. It was financed by a payroll tax and a trust fund was created. Chairman Mills then brought Republicans into the bargaining process. John Byrnes (R-Wisconsin), ranking member of the Committee, proposed a voluntary program for physicians' insurance financed by premiums and general revenues. It was accepted by Democrats. The poor were covered by a new Medicaid program based on federal cost sharing with the states. Somewhat more than 50 percent of the costs are covered by the federal government, and the states have considerable latitude in designing their programs. In the end, the plans for Medicare and Medicaid attracted considerable Republican support in the Senate, and in the House, more Republicans voted for than against final passage.

In 2003, insurance for prescription drugs was added to the program. It had originally been proposed by President Clinton and was passed with the support of President George W. Bush. This addition to Medicare was also passed on a bipartisan basis.

Paul Starr, a Pulitzer Prize–winning professor of sociology and public affairs at Princeton University, is scathing in his description of the passage of the original Medicare and Medicaid legislation. He notes that "So eager were Johnson and other Democratic leaders to placate health-care interest groups that the financing provisions, especially for Medicare, sharply inflated medical costs . . . and distorted the allocation of public spending for decades to come." There is much truth in Starr's analysis. Medicare has struggled to contain costs throughout its history. However, the program might not have been enacted were it not for the bipartisan compromise that facilitated its passage. Liberals were disappointed that the program was not structured in a way that would allow it to evolve into a universal health insurance system, but without the compromise, Republican opposition might have destroyed the deal altogether.

AFFORDABLE CARE ACT

Over the years there have been many attempts to significantly expand health insurance coverage. The Affordable Care Act (ACA) represents the latest effort in that long struggle.

The Obama Administration began the effort early in its first term. In the spring of 2009, there was a health summit at Blair House in which both parties put forth their ideas. But with sixty votes in the Senate—enough to prevent a Republican filibuster—Democrats decided to proceed on their own after Republicans balked at their suggested solutions. The contrast with the passage of Medicare and Medicaid could not be more striking. Although their congressional majority was larger in 1965 than in 2009, Great Society Democrats made a strong effort to compromise and gain Republican support. Whether stronger overtures to the opposition in 2009 would have won substantial Republican support for any national health measure remains an open question; the consequences of not doing so are clearer today.

The ACA passed the Senate in late December 2009 with sixty votes. However, the House objected to some features of the Senate bill. Then, in a stunning political upset, Scott Brown, a Republican, won a special election in Massachusetts to fill the Senate seat of the late Senator Kennedy. If the Senate compromised with the House and brought a new bill to the floor, they could no longer withstand a filibuster. Instead, they struck a deal in which the House agreed to pass the Senate bill if a subsequent bill making changes in the House's favor was put before the Congress. The Congress then used reconciliation procedures to pass the second bill. Reconciliation is part of the congressional budget process. It is meant to facilitate difficult budget decisions. Debate time is limited, and filibusters are not allowed. The Republicans felt doubly affronted. They had essentially no influence on the bill, and they believe that it was forced through arbitrarily.

The resulting policy has many components; only the main ones can be described here:

- Employers with fifty or more employees are mandated to provide health insurance to their employees.
- Individuals who do not get health insurance from employers or a public program are mandated to obtain insurance or else pay a fine.
- The mandated insurance has to meet certain standards, some of which, like the coverage of contraceptives, have proven extremely controversial. Insurance companies cannot consider medical preconditions.
- There are income-related subsidies to help individuals buy insurance. In 2013, the subsidies were available up to an income of $94,200 for a family of four.
- States are mandated to expand Medicaid to cover people up to 133 percent of the federal poverty line.[6] The federal government pays 100 percent of the additional initial cost, an amount eventually declining to 90 percent.
- The program is financed by a number of different taxes and by a cut in Medicare reimbursements. Subsidies for Medicare Part C are also reduced.
- The legislation included a number of provisions to control health costs, but the Congressional Budget Office decided that many were too uncertain to score.

The launch of the Affordable Care Act was a disaster. The website built to handle enrollments crashed in many states. The cancellation of many policies that did not meet the program's standards belied President Obama's promise that "If you like your health insurance, you can keep it."

The program was also relentlessly attacked by congressional Republicans and in the courts. The Supreme Court ruled that the individual mandate was constitutional but that states could not be ordered to expand Medicaid. A number of Republican-led states then refused to expand. Because there is no provision in the law to subsidize those who lack coverage because Medicaid is not expanded, coverage is not universal. Illegal immigrants are also not covered. In addition, some individuals will choose to pay fines rather than buy coverage. Nevertheless, medical coverage under the ACA has already expanded significantly compared with what existed before.

It is difficult to forecast how the full implementation of the law will evolve, but the experience so far indicates that any administration proposing a significant change in the policy would be well advised to work hard to obtain bipartisan support, even if it means adopting compromises that they find objectionable. That helped make Medicare and Medicaid politically sustainable. In present circumstances, however, Democrats will find it almost impossible to get Republican support even for technical changes meant to improve the law.

LESSONS LEARNED

As implied earlier, it was an act of political genius to have Social Security and Medicare support both the rich and the poor. When reforms have been discussed recently, it is often proposed that the biggest slowdowns in benefit growth or increases in taxes should fall on the rich. Social Security already has a progressive benefit formula, and recently, premiums for Parts B and D of Medicare have been linked to income. It is interesting to speculate whether these programs will retain their strong political support if they are increasingly perceived as welfare programs.

There is one certainty and many uncertainties as we look forward. The one certainty is that Social Security and Medicare are extremely popular politically. Adequately adjusting these programs to the demographic pressures created by the aging of baby boomers and continued increases in life expectancy will be difficult. Nor is it certain that recent reduction in the growth of health costs will continue. If rapid growth resumes, how will the programs be adjusted? Or will they?

Even if the growth of these programs does not accelerate, they are already large enough to make it difficult to pursue new federal initiatives, whether for infrastructure, education, child welfare, or anything else. This creates strong pressures to raise taxes. Thus, both the political left and right should have a strong incentive to favor reforms in these basic safety net programs. Let us hope that they recognize it.

BIBLIOGRAPHY

Blumenthal, David, and James A. Morone. *The Heart of Power: Health and Politics in the Oval Office.* Berkeley: University of California Press, 2009.

Penner, Rudolph G. "Myth and Reality of the Safety Net: The 1983 Social Security Reforms." In *Triumphs and Tragedies of the Modern Congress: Case Studies in Legislative Leadership*, Maxmillian Angerholzer III, James Kitfield, Christopher P. Lu, and Norman Ornstein, Eds. Center for the Study of the Presidency and the Congress. Santa Barbara, CA: Praeger, 2014.

Schieber, Sylvester J., and John B. Shoven. *The Real Deal*. New Haven, CT: Yale University Press, 1999.

Starr, Paul. "The Health-Care Legacy of the Great Society." In *Reshaping the Federal Government: The Policy and Management Legacies of the Johnson Years*, Norman J. Glickman et al., Eds. Available at: https://www.princeton.edu/~starr/articles/articles14/Starr_LBJ_HC _Legacy_1-2014.pdf.

Twight, Charlotte. "Medicare's Origins: The Economics and Politics of Dependency." *Cato Journal* 16, no. 3 (Winter 1997): 309–38.

◆ ◆ ◆ ◆ ◆

30. "We Shall Overcome": Presidential Leadership and Civil Rights

by Kareem U. Crayton

Washington, D.C., is the seat of the federal government and capital of the leading nation in the world community of democracies, but the scope and depth of this city's official power can be easily overstated. Before the power of the national government can affect fundamental change in society it must first be focused on a specific problem, and the political forces pressing for change on a given issue must become aligned in support of a policy response. This rarely happens. That's why there are few moments in U.S. history when the actions taken in Washington have had a truly immediate, transformative impact on the lives of most Americans.

Mobilizing the government to adopt a transformative policy, one that fundamentally reshapes society, is as uncommon as it is difficult, just as the Founders intended. Their design of a representative system based on organizational principles of federalism, a separation of powers, and governmental checks and balances reflects a grave distrust of concentrated power and its quick exercise.[1]

The presidency itself reflects this truism about political power in America. Although the office is the only repository of national power in the United States managed by a single person,[2] the chief executive nonetheless is constitutionally limited in his or her ability to impose policy outcomes unilaterally. There are other political actors with major influence whose roles are often indispensable.[3] As political scientists often point out, the president's ability to persuade other powerful actors—including the Congress, the electorate, and even members of his or her own administration—is often the key to success.[4] Put another way, the president only succeeds where he or she can bend other powerful players to his or her will or capitalize on the potential for momentary agreements. Doing either requires consummate skill to both cajole and threaten other actors in proper measure. That's why the great presidents are often masters of improvisation; they manage to respond and adjust to evolving political situations.

The civil rights movement amply illustrates both the possibilities and the perils associated with the exercise of strong presidential authority. The campaign to realize the promises in the Reconstruction Amendments stretched out over many decades but certain moments demonstrated the distinct ways that presidents can lead the country toward achieving important national goals and aspirations.

DEFINING THE CIVIL RIGHTS ERA

The civil rights movement typically refers to that era when the U.S. government made significant progress toward realizing the principles of equality and opportunity outlined in the Reconstruction Amendments.[5] Specifically, the key period in question is the decade starting in the mid-1950s with the U.S. Supreme Court's decision in *Brown v. Board of Education*, and reaching its zenith with the 1965 enactment of the Voting Rights Act.[6]

Although the movement reached its crescendo during this decade, one must also recall that the long march for racial justice is not neatly situated within these years alone. For example, *Brown* itself was the culmination of a series of lawsuits that incrementally attacked state segregation policies in higher education.[7] Furthermore, efforts such as the public lobbying to adopt antilynching legislation in Congress championed by the NAACP (founded in 1909) also trace back as far as the turn of the 20th century.[8] These campaigns were a reaction to the complicity of the federal government in racial segregation and to a political movement in the former states of the Confederacy to sustain the legalized subjugation of African American citizens.[9] After hastening the end of Reconstruction, these states dismantled laws and policies designed to ensure equal treatment for African Americans, replacing them with a system of legalized race segregation known as "Jim Crow."[10]

While *Brown* was a legal triumph in the campaign against Jim Crow, the citizen-organized opposition to segregation in the South started in 1955 with the Montgomery Bus Boycott.[11] This yearlong protest against segregated public facilities was prompted by the arrest of Rosa Parks, who refused to surrender her seat to a white passenger, but it was sustained by a variety of local and regional organizations, including the Southern Christian Leadership Conference. During the decade that followed, spinoffs of the movement emerged in communities throughout the South, drawing attention to local and state governments that had rejected the constitutional directive to provide equal access to citizens, regardless of race. Allied civil rights groups adopted a combination of mass protests, litigation, and lobbying to challenge every facet of the Jim Crow system.[12] Although these efforts were not uniformly successful, the campaign ultimately led to the formal demise of the practice as a matter of law.

Among the individuals who played important roles in shaping this movement, presidents stand out for their efforts to strike a balance among competing interests. As political leaders and government officials, presidents faced a difficult challenge. They had to negotiate with conservative white Southern Democrats (or "Dixiecrats"), whose states represented a large share of electoral votes, and who, by virtue of their seniority in Congress, wielded great legislative power. At the same time, growing constituencies of African American voters and politicians populated large cities such as Chicago, St. Louis, and New York—places that were also relevant in national contests. And as chief law enforcement officer, the president furthermore had the duty to maintain the safety in the locations where civil rights groups held their protests, even while enforcing the principle of free speech.

Not only did presidents in this era have to respond to lobbying from national civil rights organizations, they also had to consider the international ramifications of the civil rights movement. Displays in the press of overt hostility and violence toward African Americans under Jim Crow clashed with the U.S. government's own assertion during the Cold War that democracy excelled at protecting individual rights and freedoms. Altogether, presidents in this era juggled a dizzying array of considerations that affected virtually every aspect of their jobs and every decision they made with regard to civil rights.

The civil rights era is replete with cases in which the skill of the president and the power of the presidency were tested mightily. Three specific episodes during this period illustrate how presidents successfully used their powers to avert disaster and advance the cause of freedom. These highlighted episodes are the desegregation of public schools in Little Rock, Arkansas; the legislative management of the Civil Rights Act of 1964; and the introduction of the 1965 Voting Rights Act.

EPISODE ONE: SCHOOL DESEGREGATION

In 1954, the U.S. Supreme Court issued a unanimous ruling in *Brown v. Board of Education*, which signaled the end of racial segregation in public schools.[13] Speaking for a unanimous Supreme Court, Chief Justice Earl Warren announced that the 1896 holding in *Plessy v. Ferguson* (which had upheld segregation that allowed "separate but equal" accommodations) was unworkable and logically flawed in its very nature.[14] The Court reasoned that separating students based on race imposed a badge of inferiority on African American students, which fell short of the test of equal protection in the 14th Amendment. Thus, the Supreme Court invalidated state policies that maintained such divisions as a matter of law.

Of course, even the most celebrated Supreme Court rulings can only call for governmental action that will comply with the law. Judicial orders have impact only to the extent that government officials decide to respect their terms and ensure that the rulings are enforced; such compliance cannot be taken for granted.[15] For Dwight D. Eisenhower, the president and chief law enforcement officer, the challenge imposed by *Brown* came in two forms. On one hand, Eisenhower had no formal means to control the timing of the decisions taken by the Supreme Court. Eisenhower thus needed to improvise in reacting to the sweeping implications wrought by the Supreme Court's ruling.

Eisenhower also had to contend with the fact that the Supreme Court is an unelected institution whose rulings are not inherently sensitive to majority will or public opinion. Indeed, the federal judiciary is designed to be an anti-majoritarian institution.[16] Thus, there are no guarantees that either the timing or the substantive reasoning of a Supreme Court decision will show regard for the ever-present electoral pressures that federal and state political actors face. Presidents, especially those who choose to run for reelection, have to think carefully about the political ramifications and the public reactions to decisions taken by the Supreme Court.

That challenge certainly vexed Eisenhower, a Republican president who had ambitions to appeal to the South but who also had appointed Chief Justice Earl Warren to the Supreme Court. The events in Little Rock, Arkansas, in 1957 thus exposed the delicacy of his situation. Following the *Brown* decision, the NAACP pursued a strategy of enrolling African American children in previously all-white schools throughout the South. Nine students were thus slated to start the school year at Little Rock's Central High School, which drew objections from local white politicians. These groups were buoyed in part by Southern Democrats who publicly renounced their ties with the national party in the 1956 "Southern Manifesto." Although his third-party presidential campaign as a Dixiecrat failed, South Carolina Senator Strom Thurmond's advocacy of segregation was heartily joined by state politicians across the South.[17] Arkansas Governor Orval Faubus was among the more vocal defenders of Jim Crow, and he articulated the concerns of Southerners who resisted any effort to desegregate schools.

President Eisenhower therefore faced a pair of critical decisions. First, he had to decide whether to back a judicial order to implement a policy of desegregation that Governor Faubus adamantly opposed. Assuming that the Arkansas governor would resist the Supreme Court on the issue of desegregation, Eisenhower might need to activate the National Guard to protect the enrolling students. Importantly, the safe passage of the students was now a matter of federal law, thanks to a federal judge's order specifically endorsing their bid to attend Central High School.

Eisenhower's handling of the matter centered on a dual strategy of placing pressure on Governor Faubus behind the scenes, while providing limited (and sometimes cryptic) public statements about his intentions to take action. There were important factors that demanded a careful orchestration of each move. Had he refused outright to enforce a federal court order, Eisenhower would have raised serious problems for himself with several groups—not least of them, the civil rights community itself. While the timing of the *Brown* decision was beyond the president's power to direct, dealing with its implications was unavoidable. Eisenhower could not easily distance himself from his appointee's first ruling in a major case.

Governor Faubus proved a stubborn opponent in private negotiations. Despite the president's sustained efforts to convince Faubus to aid in the peaceful enrollment of the African American students, the governor made clear that he could not (indeed, would not) countenance any form of support for desegregation.[18] Yet the key to the entire enterprise was foreclosing the potential for a violent and embarrassing confrontation in Little Rock. Federal officials were well aware of several groups that threatened to protest and potentially block the students' attempt to enter school. Additionally, using the National Guard also posed challenges. The U.S. military had been desegregated under President Truman, and the presence of armed troops (some who were black) might deepen the already tense feelings of white Arkansans who vehemently opposed the *Brown* decision.

Eisenhower's solution to this impasse essentially split the difference. Governor Faubus was tacitly permitted to continue his vocal opposition in public to the court's desegregation order. Recognizing that Faubus represented a significant political base with similar hostile views about desegregation, Eisenhower understood the need to preserve space for Faubus to avoid public embarrassment.[19] Thus, Faubus could not be forced into embracing this policy.

At the same time, Eisenhower issued a carefully worded announcement that he would enforce the decision taken by *Brown*. The president's statement was careful to acknowledge the public concerns of the white citizens who opposed the ruling, but it also noted that he had an obligation as president to follow the law. Pursuant to a specific request from the mayor of Little Rock (which was itself quietly encouraged by the White House), the president therefore approved an order to mobilize the 101st Airborne Division to protect the enrollment efforts by the "Little Rock Nine." Importantly, officials orchestrated a timely reassignment of the African American troops who were part of this force to limit the chances of unrest in Little Rock.[20]

The president's strategy in Little Rock, although not completely defusing white outrage, effectively resolved the standoff and likely avoided a more widespread, violent result. The behind-the-scenes talks with Governor Faubus did not shift his position on desegregation, but Eisenhower did convince him to take a less confrontational posture and not to instigate violence by whites in Little Rock. This strategy was surely aided by the president's noncommittal tone in public statements leading to his decision to mobilize federal troops. Confronting a core part of the Jim Crow ideology ultimately meant superseding the governor, and yet the president worked to ensure compliance with the desegregation order without provoking widespread resistance. Thus, Eisenhower was able to balance his constitutional charge to enforce the law while also maintaining the peace, a power that might well have been tested further if the court order had been ignored or overtly undermined on the ground.

EPISODE TWO: THE CIVIL RIGHTS ACT

Few other pieces of legislation transformed the lives of a major segment of the American public as rapidly or profoundly as the 1964 Civil Rights Act. The law essentially superseded custom and practice in the South, insofar as it mandated the end to the Jim Crow practice of segregation in public accommodations. By orchestrating the legislative passage of the act, President Lyndon Johnson ensured equal access to restaurants, stores, hotels, and conveyances nationwide.[21] The episode highlights the success of the president in engaging the Congress, a coequal branch of government, and using both expected and unexpected events to his advantage.

Over the first half of the 20th century, efforts to adopt a meaningful civil rights bill had either been scuttled or severely undercut.[22] The concept had a deep well of support, but as with most legislative proposals, the gap between proposal and enactment in Congress was wide. As recently as 1960, a civil rights bill had been introduced with major provisions that armed federal lawyers with the authority and the resources to challenge unlawful provisions across the South. The proposal drew several unfriendly amendments, producing a severely watered-down measure that undermined many of its ambitious aims.[23] Very senior and powerful Dixiecrats in Congress managed to prevent the most meaningful parts of the proposal from ever reaching the president's desk. Faced with a choice between a weakened bill and nothing at all, pragmatists settled for incremental improvement.

Interestingly, one of the principal leaders involved in the Southern opposition to the bills was then-Senate Majority Leader Lyndon Johnson of Texas. As president, however, Johnson had promised to fulfill the legacy of the assassinated John F. Kennedy, and that charge included the issue of civil rights. Proclaimed the "Master of the Senate" during his service as a legislator, Johnson knew exactly where to apply pressure and persuasion in the appropriate doses in moving the bill through the legislative process.[24] In 1964, President Johnson functioned as the sponsor, shepherd, and floor manager at every stage of consideration of the Civil Rights Act. As a testament to his enduring influence, Johnson picked apart the once-impenetrable coalition of Southern Democrats to find individuals who were willing to join him in supporting the legislation.[25] Whether Johnson acted out of moral conviction or political expediency, the new legislative coalition he assembled symbolized a bipartisan rejection of Jim Crow. Johnson's achievement effectively spelled the end of the once mighty Dixiecrat bloc in Congress.

Despite the sustained opposition to the bill by Southern stalwarts who remained in legislative gatekeeping posts, there were two important factors that strengthened LBJ's hand in getting the civil rights bill enacted in 1964. One factor shaping the debate was entirely unpredictable, while the other, a cyclical event, was quite expected.

As mentioned earlier, President Johnson's ability to win members of his own party to the cause was greatly enhanced by the event that led Johnson to assume the presidency in the first place—the assassination of John F. Kennedy. The sudden and tragic national loss trained public attention on questions of Kennedy's legacy. From the moment he took the oath, President Johnson embraced the idea of completing Kennedy's unfinished term.[26] Accordingly, Johnson unreservedly announced that passing the Civil Rights Act (which had languished in Congress during much of Kennedy's term) was a hallmark of his predecessor's legislative agenda. Johnson's proposal thus served as a lasting testament to Kennedy's achievements. The move responded to the public's grief and succeeded in rallying the Democratic caucus in Congress. Even Southern Democrats were hesitant to register opposition to a bill dedicated to the memory of a beloved and deceased president. Regardless of their personal opposition to the bill, critics also could not heap vitriol onto legislation associated with a fallen president, especially not in the wake of such a horrific episode in American history.

Momentum for the bill was also spurred by the upcoming national elections in 1964. Just as adopting a civil rights bill represented a capstone to the Kennedy Administration, the bill equally represented a start to Johnson's own presidential campaign, one in which he would reposition himself as a national leader for racial fairness in his own right. The election would place Johnson at the head of the Democratic Party, articulating the cause for dozens of Democrats running for federal and state offices further down the ticket. In his quest to secure a national mandate for a reform agenda, Johnson framed his "Great Society" vision to include a moral call for respecting the rights of all citizens—regardless of race, religion, or station.[27] Thus, civil rights generally, and the Civil Rights Act in particular, became a defining issue of the 1964 election, all the more so because Republican presidential nominee Senator Barry Goldwater of Arizona joined the failed filibuster by Southern senators to derail the bill. With the partisan stakes in full view, Johnson was able to establish a working coalition for civil rights legislation that included liberal Democrats and moderate Republicans.

Johnson's strategy for winning over Congress rested on his near-encyclopedic knowledge of the members who wielded the most authority. Chief among his strategic aims, for instance, was securing an early endorsement of the bill by Republican Everett Dirksen of Illinois, a figure who could clear the way for bipartisan support of the law.[28] Enlisting Dirksen as a partner and sponsor involved a series of compromises. But practically speaking, the support of Republicans like Dirksen was necessary to offset the Southern Democrats who would almost surely oppose the legislation at every turn. By holding on to the liberal wing of the party and partnering with moderate Republicans who rejected racial segregation, Johnson crafted a new and effective legislative majority.

Still, final passage of the bill was not predetermined. Aside from the failed filibuster in the Senate, Southerners in leadership positions in the House attempted to kill the bill by adding various "poison pill" amendments. Regardless, the president's coalition not only held firm; it gained strength. An effort by Virginia Representative Howard W. Smith to derail the measure by extending its coverage to gender discrimination backfired because supporters agreed to press on with the bill by incorporating that change.[29] Thus, even in unexpected ways, Johnson's new coalition not only succeeded in passing this bill but shifted the balance of power within Congress in ways that led to the passage of a series of social programs that formed the core of his Great Society agenda.

EPISODE THREE: VOTING RIGHTS

The final episode of the civil rights movement that illustrates the key role of presidential power was the 1965 Voting Rights Act. For most of this decade, many civil rights workers were focused on voting rights and organizing to help qualify African Americans in the South to vote. The work involved steering intrepid members of the African American community through an often frustrating and complex registration process run by white officers who had little regard for the constitutional directive to register voters regardless of race.[30] The enfranchisement efforts typically were met with violent resistance in many locations—particularly in majority black counties (collectively called the Black Belt) where the realization of black political power threatened the political careers of some of the South's staunchest racists. Among the most infamous instances of violence occurred in Mississippi during the Freedom Summer in 1963, when three young men who were working to register black voters were abducted and brutally murdered.[31] Their deaths were a poignant reminder of the perils for civil rights groups challenging franchise restrictions in the South without meaningful governmental protections.

Having just won a full term of office in 1964, LBJ organized his Great Society agenda around policies to improve the economic situation of poor and working-class Americans. President Johnson saw his sweeping victory at the polls in 1964 as a chance to forge a new coalition in support of public action to confront systemic disadvantage and poverty. Johnson's electoral strategy meant to unite constituencies like the poor of Appalachia in common cause with the urban poor in Chicago.[32] While civil rights matters were not inherently inconsistent with this agenda, the White House reasoned that passing the 1964 Civil Rights Act had exhausted the well of support behind race-equality policies for the foreseeable future.[33] The president recognized voting rights as an important cause, but he viewed the other parts of the Great Society as a priority in his planning for congressional action.

Another issue that shaped Johnson's thinking was his increasing anxiety about the war in Vietnam, which accounted for a growing portion of the national budget. Committing additional troops and money to support military operations there threatened any commitment of funds for domestic development programs. Politically, the problem also placed pressure on the president to maintain a shaky alliance between the already unhappy Southerners and the recently expanded liberal wing of Congressional Democrats, many of whom had ridden into office on the president's coattails. Johnson understood that he might not be able to sustain another bill that further antagonized Southerners, whose support he needed to hold together a "guns and butter" agenda. Accordingly, he urged civil rights leaders to be patient with regard to their voting rights bill.[34]

Matters changed drastically because of events in Selma, Alabama, a major flashpoint in the effort to secure access to the ballot for African Americans. As in other counties in the Black Belt, African Americans represented a majority of the total population in Dallas County (and of the county seat Selma), but only a paltry share of those citizens were registered to vote. To draw public attention to the unlawful management of the registrar's office across the region, civil rights groups (including the Southern Christian Leadership Conference and the Student Nonviolent Coordinating Committee) staged a variety of public protests to press local government actors to register more voters.

That campaign came to a head on March 7, 1965, when nonviolent marchers were attacked by Alabama State Troopers on the Edmund Pettus Bridge. Like other confrontations during this era, the attacks were brutal and demonstrated the unflinching commitment of both state and local elected officials to defend the Jim Crow system, by violent force if necessary.[35] Unlike most of the other cases of state-sanctioned violence, however, this confrontation was broadcast on national television. Indeed, the stark images from the scene—including women and young children attacked with tear gas, police dogs, and swinging nightsticks—were broadcast into the living rooms of citizens across the country.

As with Eisenhower's experience with confronting school desegregation, the challenge facing President Johnson was not one of his own choosing. The conflict moved the public's attention away from the other matters on the White House agenda toward an issue on which the president would have to expend significant political capital, if he chose to act. And the choice of not taking action was all but foreclosed when the unprovoked and unwarranted use of force against peaceful marchers was broadcast nationwide. Still the agile politician, LBJ quickly adjusted to changing conditions and joined the cause of restoring order to the cause of advancing rights.

Days after the Selma incident, Johnson spoke before a joint session of Congress to announce his plan to guarantee the vote to African Americans. Pitching his speech in broad moral terms, Johnson reminded Americans of the horrific scenes on the Selma bridge, and linked that episode to the enduring struggle of African Americans to enjoy the full measure of American citizenship.[36] And perhaps to make clear that his demand for meaningful action from Congress was unequivocal, Johnson ended his speech by invoking the familiar phrase in the hymn often sung in the civil rights movement: "And we shall overcome."[37]

Johnson recognized an opportunity in this unexpected event, and he seized it. The brutal repression of the Selma protesters galvanized public support to address a persistent and complex problem that might have otherwise taken years to tackle. In tapping that potential, the president switched almost immediately from defense to offense and set about mobilizing the forces in Washington necessary to pass the Voting Rights Act. He deployed his Attorney General to begin drafting a proposal immediately, and summoned his legislative allies to commence the business of scheduling hearings. Even though the timing for introducing the bill was not of his choosing, Johnson was out in front of events to show the public and Congress that he was capable of leading the nation productively through the turmoil. Utilizing many of the same levers of persuasion that he had used the year before in passing the Civil Rights Act, Johnson moved the Voting Rights Act through Congress in near-record time.

In retrospect, the civil rights movement offers a telling illustration of how presidents can successfully advance major national policy by using events and deploying his powers of persuasion, pressure, and improvisation. A court order in Little Rock, the Kennedy assassination, the protest in Selma—none of this was under the president's control, but Eisenhower and Johnson orchestrated responses to each event to advance a transformative agenda. The powers of the office alone do not themselves force compliance; rather, the president must employ informal tools to convince others to cooperate. Sometimes the task demands striking a balance between competing interests, and at others, it involves political improvisation to account for changing circumstances. In all cases, though, the president must recognize that the path to achieving his aims is neither a simple nor unilateral one. Rather, the ability to enact enduring social change, as the civil rights episodes clearly demonstrate, relies on the unique ability of presidents to entice other political actors, as well as the public, to join their cause.

♦ ♦ ♦ ♦ ♦

31. A Giant Step for Mankind: The U.S. Space Program

by Jeff Foust

On May 25, 1961, President John F. Kennedy gave the most influential speech in the history of the American space program. In an address on "urgent national needs" before a joint session of Congress, Kennedy uttered one of the signature lines of his presidency: "I believe that this nation should commit itself to achieving the goal, before this decade is out, of landing a man on the Moon and returning him safely to the Earth."[1]

That single declarative statement launched the National Aeronautics and Space Administration (NASA)—established less than three years earlier—on a trajectory that would end eight years later with astronauts Neil Armstrong and Buzz Aldrin landing *Apollo 11*'s lunar module on the Sea of Tranquility. The accomplishment required the combined efforts of hundreds of thousands of people working at NASA and the private sector, as well as a massive infusion of federal funds to NASA.

Kennedy's speech also had long-term effects on NASA and space policy that went well beyond the Apollo program and continue to this day. It established a model of presidential leadership that begins with a bold call to action in space and the setting of an ambitious goal. Other presidents have emulated that model, although with far less success. Now, more than fifty years after Kennedy's speech, with the momentum of the early age of space exploration largely spent and the world a far different place than in 1961, it may be time for a different policy approach that focuses on a more sustainable space exploration program.

APOLLO TO THE SPACE SHUTTLE

The Kennedy model of presidential leadership in space policy took some time to evolve. After Kennedy's assassination in 1963, President Lyndon B. Johnson continued his effort to send men to the Moon. In some respects, the Apollo program became a memorial to Kennedy, and any early doubts about its feasibility and effectiveness were set aside.

Richard Nixon thus became the first president after Kennedy to have an opportunity to redirect civil space policy. Shortly after taking office, he chartered a committee called the Space Task Group, led by Vice President Spiro Agnew, to examine what NASA should do after the Apollo program. It came up with an ambitious plan that included continued missions to the Moon, construction of a space station, and human missions to Mars as early as 1981.

The price tag of that plan, though, was far more than Nixon, or Congress, was willing to pay. For a time, there was a debate within the Nixon White House about whether there should even be a human space program after Apollo. Nixon eventually decided to approve one aspect of the Space Task Group's recommendations: development of a reusable spacecraft called the Space Shuttle. That announcement, though, came in a simple statement from the president, not in a speech meant to rally the country to an ambitious program like Apollo.

Although low-key, that single decision to build the Space Shuttle was one of the most profound of the post-Apollo era for NASA, shaping its human spaceflight program for the next four decades. Neither Presidents Ford nor Carter did much to change those plans, for instance, or set new goals for the space agency during their administrations. The Space Shuttle, after years of development delays, finally flew in April 1981 on the first of what would be 135 missions spread out over thirty years.

As NASA transitioned the Space Shuttle into an "operational" vehicle, charged with launching satellites and performing scientific studies, the administration of President Ronald Reagan weighed what to do next in space. The Space Task Group report of 1969 and other studies provided various options for human spaceflight.

SPACE STATION AND BEYOND

Reagan announced his decision on space exploration, like Kennedy, before a joint session of Congress, this time as part of the annual State of the Union address in January 1984. "Tonight, I am directing NASA to develop a permanently manned space station and to do it within a decade," he told Congress. That started what became known as Space Station Freedom, initially a rival to the Soviet Union's Mir space station.

Both the Space Shuttle and the Space Station survived the *Challenger* accident in 1986, although a bold plan for future exploration developed by a presidential commission around the time of the accident was shelved. Exploration plans were reenergized when President George H.W. Bush took office in 1989. He revived the National Space Council, an oversight committee led by Vice President Dan Quayle that had been largely moribund since the Kennedy days, and asked it to examine future directions for human spaceflight.

Like Kennedy and Reagan, Bush announced his plans in a speech, this time on the steps of the National Air and Space Museum in Washington on

July 20, 1989—the twentieth anniversary of the *Apollo 11* plan. Bush pitched a three-stage proposal that started with completion of the space station, followed by a human return to the Moon and then human missions to Mars. Bush set an ambitious goal of a human landing on Mars by the fiftieth anniversary of *Apollo 11* in 2019.

The overarching plan, called the Space Exploration Initiative (SEI), had trouble getting off the launch pad. Internecine battles between the White House and NASA hindered its development and eventually led to the dismissal of the NASA administrator, former astronaut Richard Truly, at the time of the plan's rollout. An initial study of the plan by NASA suggested its overall cost could be as high as $500 billion, a price tag that scuttled SEI in Congress.

SEI had largely faded away by the time Bill Clinton became president. He made no overarching space policy pronouncements during his two terms in office, focusing instead on salvaging the space station program as it faced growing opposition in Congress because of its increasing cost and delayed schedule. The fall of the Soviet Union provided an opportunity to bring Russia into the program as a partner, leveraging its spaceflight experience and keeping Russian aerospace engineers employed in peaceful projects. The International Space Station, as it became known, thus found more support in Congress, even though issues of cost and schedule persisted with the program.

George W. Bush did not immediately alter those plans after taking office in 2001. His primary space policy concern early on was development of the space station, as cost and schedule problems continued. However, the loss in February 2003 of the space shuttle *Columbia*, which broke apart during reentry and killed its seven-person crew, triggered a reexamination of space policy by his administration.

In January 2004, following the model of his predecessors, Bush unveiled his plans in a speech at NASA Headquarters in Washington. His bold plan, called the Vision for Space Exploration, called for completing assembly of the space station by 2010, at which time the shuttle would be retired. NASA would then develop a new crewed spacecraft and launch vehicle capable of taking people beyond Earth's orbit, with a goal of returning humans to the Moon by 2020.

SPACE PROGRAM ADRIFT

Bush's plan won early support in Congress, but over the remaining years of the Bush Administration, the White House's budget requests for NASA failed to keep up with the plan Bush laid out in his 2004 speech, and Congress failed to supplement those requests. That funding gap caused delays in the development of the new spacecraft and launch vehicles—collectively called Constellation—as NASA focused on returning the shuttle to flight and launching the final elements of the space station.

When Barack Obama took office in 2009, he commissioned a blue-ribbon panel to examine the current state of NASA's human spaceflight plans. That panel, led by retired aerospace executive Norm Augustine, concluded that NASA required an additional $3 billion per year above its budget of $18 billion at the time to continue Constellation on a schedule anything close to its original plans.

Obama departed from the Kennedy template by announcing his plans not in a splashy speech but in his fiscal year 2011 budget proposal, released in February 2010. He proposed cancelling Constellation, replacing it with a mix of technology enhancement programs, and providing seed funds for the development of commercially operated vehicles to transport astronauts to and from the space station.

That proposal met with strong opposition from the handful of members of Congress who closely follow space issues (usually because of the presence of NASA centers or other space industry facilities in their states and districts). They were concerned not just with the impact the cancellation of Constellation would have on NASA, but also the lack of specific goals for human spaceflight beyond continued operation of the international space station.

In part to counter the sense of drift in U.S. space policy, Obama then returned to the old Kennedy model, giving a speech at NASA's Kennedy Space Center in Florida in April 2010. He offered some long-term goals for NASA's human spaceflight program: a mission to a near Earth asteroid by 2025, and a human mission to orbit Mars in the mid-2030s. "And a landing on Mars will follow," he added. "I expect to be around to see it."

The administration and members of Congress worked out a compromise incorporated into a NASA authorization bill passed later that year. One element of Constellation, the Orion crewed spacecraft, would survive, but its rockets would be replaced by a new vehicle, the Space Launch System, to be completed by 2017. The administration's technology development and commercial crew programs would survive, although at a lower funding level than originally proposed.

As of early 2015, that plan remains in place, but like the Bush Administration's Vision for Space Exploration, it has suffered delays and funding shortfalls. Now the Space Launch System is not scheduled to launch until sometime in 2018, and will not carry astronauts until its second launch in 2021. NASA's proposal for carrying out the goal of an asteroid mission by 2025, which involves shifting an asteroid as small as a few dozen feet into an orbit around the Moon, has faced skepticism both in Congress and among scientists.

BEYOND THE COLD WAR PARADIGM

So what will the next president do when he or she takes office in January 2017? If the past is any guide, the new president will be tempted to put his or her own stamp on the space program: a commission to review ongoing efforts, followed by a speech laying out an altered, if not wholly new, direction for NASA's human spaceflight programs. Then the agency will try to and implement that plan, likely with budgets that fall well short of projections.

The presidents who have adopted that approach have, deliberately or unwittingly, been following the model set by President Kennedy more than a half-century ago. Many in the space community, from industry executives to grassroots advocates, have longed for just such a "Kennedy moment" for NASA and human spaceflight. And yet, efforts to duplicate Kennedy's achievement and transplant its lessons to new eras have, by and large, failed.

"The fact is that we have been trying to relive Apollo for the last 40 years," said Lori Garver, deputy administrator of NASA for part of the Obama Administration, in a speech defending its plans in 2010. "We have not been able to recreate that since, and I am not even sure that we would want to, given even that did not provide us with a sustained presence in space."[2]

One of the reasons the Kennedy model no longer works is that the world is a very different place compared to 1961. At that time, the United States and the Soviet Union were intense adversaries in a Cold War, and space was a major area where they could peacefully compete for superiority. Moreover, space technologies often had military applications, and vice versa: the rockets that launched NASA's Mercury and Gemini spacecraft, for instance, were repurposed ICBMs (Intercontinental Ballistic Missiles).

That rivalry, strong enough to fuel a race to the Moon in the 1960s, no longer exists. Space activities are increasingly multinational, and rivalries multilateral. Although some have attempted to play up a new "space race" with China, given its growing space capabilities, no real competition has emerged. In part this is due to the gradual approach China has taken for its human spaceflight program, but it is also partly due to the complex relationship between China and the United States, which are both strategic competitors yet close trading partners. Even the United States and Russia continue to cooperate in space, despite the fact that their relations have soured because of the Ukraine crisis that began in 2014.

However, as the Obama Administration discovered, veering too sharply from the Kennedy template of bold goals can also generate a strong negative reaction. A future president who wants a less ambitious and costly space program—and space is typically a far lower priority than most other major foreign and domestic policy issues—is likely to see such proposals languish in favor of the status quo.

Meanwhile, the momentum established by Kennedy's speech is slowly grinding to a halt. The shuttle, which the Nixon Administration started to keep NASA's human spaceflight program going after Apollo, ended in 2011. NASA and its partners in the International Space Station have agreed to operate it to at least 2020 (although NASA is seeking to extend its life to at least 2024, and perhaps 2028.)

Whatever approach the next president chooses, it's clear that trying to follow the model of President Kennedy—a major speech, an audacious goal—won't work again barring an unforeseen change in the geostrategic landscape. Coming up with a compelling rationale, or rationales, for funding future human spaceflight may be the equal of any technical challenge. As a National Research Council study in 2014 concluded, "no single rationale alone seems to justify the costs and risks of pursuing human spaceflight."

That report didn't give up on human spaceflight, however: it argued that a mix of "practical" and "aspirational" rationales could support a sustainable human spaceflight program, with a series of stepping-stone missions to the Moon and asteroids before landing on Mars, sometime between the 2030s and 2050s. Even that plan will require significant additional funding, the report argued.

Winning, and sustaining, such funding will be a challenge not just for the 45th president but for each president who sits in the Oval Office in coming decades. That funding challenge recalls another important part of Kennedy's 1961 speech, one largely forgotten over the years. After calling for landing a man on the Moon by the end of the decade, he called on Congress to stand behind the program with adequate funding. "If we are to go only half way, or reduce our sights in the face of difficulty, in my judgment it would be better not to go at all," he said.

That advice is as true today as it was in 1961.

♦　♦　♦　♦　♦

32. A Tale of Two Presidents: Conservation and Environmental Protection

by William D. Ruckelshaus

In any survey of our great presidents, at the very top of the rankings are always the same three: George Washington, Abraham Lincoln, and Franklin D. Roosevelt. All three of those presidents were wartime leaders who were seen as strong, reassuring figures during a time of existential crisis. During each of their tenures we Americans had one overwhelming, unifying concern—national survival. Obviously, personal survival concentrates the mind and unifies a people behind a political leader.

On the issue of preserving America's natural wonders and protecting its environment, the public is much less united and motivated, making leadership more difficult. In fact, public enthusiasm for environmental protection is subject to wild swings. It's much higher in periods of relative prosperity and less so in times of economic stress or ideological resistance like today. The two great environmental presidents understood that tendency and used it to their advantage, the first acting out of conviction and the other from political calculation, one leading and inspiring the public and the other reacting to their concerns. Although they make strange presidential bookends, I would argue that the American people benefitted greatly from the environmental policies of both Theodore "Teddy" Roosevelt and Richard M. Nixon.

THE CONSERVATIONIST

Teddy Roosevelt constantly stirred up trouble for himself by taking on powerful moneyed interests in America and convincing the public they should share his outrage at the conduct of the big shots. He did this through his speeches, his personal magnetism, and his indefatigable energy. According to one of his biographers, Doris Kearns Goodwin, Roosevelt used prominent contemporary muckrakers like Ida Tarbell, Lincoln Steffens, and William Allan White to stoke the public's anger.

Roosevelt had an agenda that was broad, deep, and aimed at correcting the wrongs he saw in society. He was realistic in understanding the limits of his power but aggressive in attacking those he saw as wrongdoers. T.R. also thoroughly understood how to use what he called the "bully pulpit" of the presidency to generate public demand for his objectives. His rhetoric focused public attention on the abuses of monopolies and other powerful interests in order to build support for his preferred solution.

In terms of the environment, T.R. had a vision for America that incorporated immense respect for the land and the water, as well as for the wild things that share that land and water with us humans. He loved nature, the outdoors, and "the strenuous life" (one of his favorite phrases and the title of one of his many books). Even as a small boy, Roosevelt collected insects, birds, and other forms of wildlife. Yes, he was a hunter and a taxidermist, but as a youngster, he was stimulated by an intense curiosity about all life. And as he grew and matured, Roosevelt became committed to conserving and, later, preserving nature for generations yet unborn.

Roosevelt's vision and lifelong love affair with wild things and wild places guided his actions while president, to the delight of conservationists, hunters, fishermen, birders, and nature lovers, and to the dismay of those who would exploit nature for their own financial gain. His belief that the federal government had a major role to play in realizing his dream of permanent public access to vast reaches of unspoiled land placed him way out in front of conventional wisdom and the American people at the turn of the 19th century. He was a dedicated follower of Charles Darwin and embraced his belief that the way to study nature and evolution was by observation in the field and not in the laboratory or, even worse, from the pulpit. I believe he was ahead even of most Americans today in understanding the importance of protecting the environment and preserving unspoiled and often fragile ecosystems.

In every sense of the word, Roosevelt led public opinion toward his concept of the common good and the critical role that conservation played in it. Historian Douglas Brinkley's wonderful book *Wilderness Warrior* chronicles in exquisite detail T.R's environmental awakening, his early experimentation and ultimately his lifelong passion for conservation. T.R.'s unprecedented environmental record stemmed from more than his love of hunting and the outdoors. Yes, as president he championed the creation of innumerable parks, bird sanctuaries, national forests, monuments, and wildlife refuges. As Brinkley's book details, T.R. was the most active president ever in the designation of public land for noncommercial, human enjoyment. He made a key distinction between the use of land and natural resources for monetary return, which Roosevelt decried, and its use and preservation for the common good, which he fought for with passion.

Roosevelt was focused foremost on the preservation and conservation of natural spaces, but even on air and water pollution, he was far ahead of his time, believing that the United States and every other country should have strict laws controlling pollution. In 1907, in a speech to the National Editorial Association in Jamestown, Virginia, he thus assaulted factories "that polluted the air and turned rivers into cesspools."

His presidential record on the environment, like the man himself, has few peers. During his presidency, Teddy Roosevelt created or enlarged 150 National Forests, designated 51 National Bird Sanctuaries, 4 National Game Preserves, 6 National Parks and 18 National Monuments under the Antiquities Act. The Antiquities Act itself spoke to his keen instincts in wielding presidential power. It was passed in 1906 by large majorities in both Houses of Congress without lawmakers having a clue of its potential reach, or of what T.R. had in mind for its use. Under the Antiquities Act, Roosevelt was empowered to designate land as National Monuments by the simple unilateral presidential statement, "I so declare." That literally was all he had to say, and he said it a lot in part to show Congress who was boss. And by such presidential decrees were places such as the Grand Canyon, Mount Olympus in Washington State, and the petrified forests of Arizona preserved for the use of wild things, and for future generations of Americans.

Although Roosevelt's actions on behalf of nature were supported by many Americans, they were mightily resisted by some powerful interests. The timber barons and mining interests, in particular, objected to his Public Lands policies. They thought he was snatching public lands out of their reach, and in some cases they were right. The commercial interests were pursuing monetary gain, and he was pursuing the common good. He never tired of pointing out the discrepancy to the public, and they never tired of hearing it. T.R was a master of the bully pulpit.

Of course, T.R.'s land policies were treading on some of the most sacred principles that exist in the West—property rights and the use of natural resources for private profit. Recognizing the danger of taking on the small farmer or rancher in the West, T.R. trained his guns instead on the big moneyed interests who exploited nature for profit. That political posturing is called populism—the little guy against the big guy—and in Roosevelt's case, it was all the more effective because he really believed in what he was saying.

Of course, history is not black and white; it also involves many shades of subtlety. Teddy Roosevelt was certainly more nuanced in his policies than in his populist rhetoric. He led a coalition of both preservationists and conservationists, and they didn't always agree on policy. The former was primarily committed to wilderness preservation, and the latter was committed to the regulated use and planned economic development of federal lands. Gifford Pinchot, TR's point man on this issue and the Chief Forester, led the conservationist camp, and he repeatedly butted heads with preservationists. Both he and Roosevelt did oppose unregulated development, as already mentioned, but as stewards of federal lands, they also sought to find a balance that treated the various stakeholders fairly.

Nevertheless, during his tenure Roosevelt thus set aside 234 million acres of land for public use and the common good, or roughly one half the size of the Louisiana Purchase, which was the largest acquisition of land in the history of the United States. For him, this was a labor of love. There were some who wholeheartedly agreed with him, and others who did not, but Roosevelt convinced a majority of his countrymen that conservation and preservation of lands would enrich their lives and those of countless generations to follow.

AN UNLIKELY ENVIRONMENTALIST

Like Teddy Roosevelt, President Richard Nixon's environmental record is also extraordinary. During his five and a half years in office he introduced and signed sixteen major pieces of environmental legislation, more legislation on one issue than at any time since Franklin Roosevelt's New Deal. This included major laws on Clean Air, Clean Water, Safe Drinking Water, the Toxic Substances and Pesticides laws, and on and on. He signed the National Environmental Policy Act (NEPA) on January 1, 1970, and on that New Year's Day said from his vacation home in San Clemente, California, "The 1970's must absolutely be the year when America pays its debt to the past by reclaiming the purity of its waters and its living environment. It is literally now or never."[1]

In his State of the Union address three weeks later, Nixon proclaimed, "Making peace with nature is a cause beyond party or faction, it has become a common cause of all the people in the country." Imagine a conservative Republican saying that today? In the spring of 1970, however, the House of Representatives passed the modern Clean Air Act by a landslide, 374–1. Three months later, the Senate passed its version, 74–0. The public's will was reflected by their representatives.

That same year Nixon, with overwhelming congressional support, also massively reorganized the executive branch and created the Environmental Protection Agency (EPA). The reorganization took fifteen separate agencies and pieces of agencies and put them under a single umbrella.

Unlike Teddy Roosevelt, however, Nixon was responding to public opinion in 1970, not leading it. Rachel Carson's *Silent Spring* started the public outcry in 1962. Public concern continued to mount because of well-publicized examples of pollution, including flammable rivers in Cleveland, Ohio, and thick clouds of air pollution hanging over major cities around the country. Public awareness of pollution was also reinforced by color TV spreading into the living rooms across America in the mid-1960s. A yellow outflow of toxic pollution into a blue river, or brown smog outlined against a blue sky, is much more impactful when depicted in color as opposed to black and white. The American people could smell, touch, and feel pollution by the early 1970s—much like the Chinese people today—and they had had enough of it. And President Nixon and Congress responded to their outcry.

When the EPA was created and various environmental laws were passed at the time, no one had a clue about the significant economic effect of pollution reduction on our society. EPA was literally telling the automobile companies how to build engines. The catalytic converter controls carbon monoxide and hydrocarbon emissions from every car on the street today because EPA ordered it in 1972, over the expressed outrage of the automobile industry. EPA's regulatory reach touches virtually every aspect of American life, something that remains controversial to this day. Several current congressmen at the time of this writing were running on the promise to abolish EPA.

By the time the 1972 election neared, Nixon himself had become disillusioned with his own environmental initiatives. He felt that the actual environmental laws he was getting back from Congress were too extreme, putting him in the awkward position of vetoing his own initiatives. In October 1972, Nixon nevertheless pivoted, vetoing the Clean Water Act just three weeks before his reelection. Even though Nixon would defeat Senator George McGovern (D-South Dakota) in a landslide, the Congress voted overwhelmingly to override his veto and pass the Clean Water Act over his objections, with significant Republican support.

A couple of years ago, I was on a panel at the Nixon Library celebrating the 40th Anniversary of Earth Day. Also on the panel were John Whitaker, the head of Nixon's Domestic Council and his principle environmental advisor. Whitaker told me a wonderful story. He was with Nixon in his office in New York about a year before he died. Nixon was standing next to a large plate glass window staring down Park Avenue. He was reminiscing and he said, "Well, John, whatever they say about us, we did some great things in our administration." Whitaker, seeking to capture the moment, said, "Yes, Mr. President, and you will go down as one of the greatest environmental presidents of all time."

Whitaker said that Nixon turned and looked at him and said, "God, I hope not, John."

CONFRONTING CLIMATE CHANGE

So, we had two great environmental presidents, one who acted out of conviction and one from political calculation. In each case democracy worked, in Roosevelt's case when people responded to inspiring presidential leadership and vision, and in Nixon's case when a president responded to valid and growing public concerns. In my opinion, the environment and the American people benefitted greatly from the actions of both men, regardless of their personal motivations.

In considering that record, I find myself asking an important question: What would T.R. or Nixon have done about climate change? Climate change is a far more global threat than anything that Roosevelt or Nixon confronted. T.R. did want our example of preserving wild places to be adopted by other parts of the world, and he worked at that until the end of his life. However, T.R.'s foreign policy prescription of "walking softly and carrying a big stick" might not have sufficed for an issue as daunting as climate change.

Supposing we could say to Roosevelt or Nixon, "The science is clear that the earth is warming, and human activity is the most likely culprit. On the other hand, the science is not as clear on the pace warming is occurring or its full impact." President Roosevelt would likely have applied his tremendous persuasive powers and ability to tie science and public policy together to get the American people to recognize the threat and to act. Nixon might have waited until the public was so persuaded, but once the political winds had shifted, he was capable of bold policy action.

On issues like climate change, Americans today are said to be ideological liberals and operational conservatives. They are all for doing something in the abstract until it affects them adversely in some concrete way. That is the problem with climate change. Its solution will affect the way we generate energy, heat our homes, and drive our cars—in short, the way we live. It's not impossible to overcome that challenge, but it will certainly entail making some profound changes. Whether they will have to be led by a visionary leader like Teddy Roosevelt or to persuade a canny politician like Richard Nixon to act on their behalf, the solution is only likely to come when the American people demand it.

◆ ◆ ◆ ◆ ◆

33. Federal Power and States' Rights: Defining American Federalism

by Larry N. Gerston, Garrick L. Percival, and Mary Currin-Percival

The political relationship between the national government and the states, otherwise known as federalism, has changed dramatically with the passage of time. The expansion of national administrative capacities and the rise of a more powerful "modern presidency" have profoundly affected federal–state relations. But the transformation of American federalism has not been one-dimensional. The legacy of 240 years of political and constitutional develop-ment is subtle and complex.

The outlines of this story are familiar. Early in the 20th century, the U.S. economy shifted from an agricultural base to an industrial, technological base. The Constitution's 16th Amendment gave the federal government the ability to raise and spend vast sums of money. Congress has flexed its muscles vis-à-vis the states through a liberal interpretation of the "necessary and proper clause" tucked at the end of Article I, Section 8 of the Constitution. The federal gov-ernment gained the authority to shape policy in areas in which it once played a small role, including environmental protection, law enforcement, workplace safety rules and regulations, banking and finance, and civil rights enforcement. In recent decades, Washington has also witnessed a dramatic expansion in the number of nationally organized interest groups that constantly vie for law-makers' attention and influence. Likewise, the judiciary branch has become prominent through its self-declared ability to exercise judicial review over ac-tions undertaken by the other branches as well as by the states.

The states, however, have undergone substantial change in their own right. Social and economic forces have spawned huge urban centers that pres-ent new opportunities for state governance, but also myriad challenges. On the one hand, state governments have been compelled into action from a growing list of top-down initiatives, grants-in-aids, and regulatory mandates; on the other hand, they have responded to a growing (but varied) list of citi-zen demands. To help cope, states have developed more professionalized legislatures and larger and more numerous state bureaucracies. This has made them more equal partners with their federal counterparts. States actors have also formed new nationally organized professional associations that make new claims on policy and resources at the federal level.

It should be no surprise that presidents have played a starring role in this ongoing story. Through the force of their actions and an expansive reading of executive power, presidents have transformed the nature of federalism and, at the same time, found themselves challenged and constrained by it. Presidents looking to shape their policy agenda, and with that their historical legacy, must effectively maneuver through the complex and dynamic networks that constitute U.S. federalism today.

PRESIDENTIAL POWER AND THE STATES

The quiver of the modern presidency contains arrows that the Framers never imagined. Historians will no doubt quibble about exactly when the modern presidency began to reshape federalism from its original design of a much more balanced arrangement between the national and state governments. Was it with Southern reunification with the North after the Civil War and federal administration of reconstruction policies? Was it through trust busting Theodore Roosevelt, who described the president as the steward of all the people regardless of where they lived? Or was it with Franklin Roosevelt, whose New Deal policies during the Great Depression orchestrated a variety of nationally funded work-related programs under state administration? Or was it the way that Lyndon Johnson used his influence to push through landmark civil rights legislation and to bring voting rights and civil rights enforcement under the federal umbrella? Arguments can be made for these and other presidencies as providing crucial turning points in national–state relations.

In retrospect, it seems reasonable to conclude that the presidential role in the transformation of federalism evolved over time. It was likely the work of several presidents over several decades rather than the achievement of any one individual. The simple, inescapable fact is that collectively, for more than 150 years, presidents have used their influence and interpretations of constitutional authority in an effort to shift power in key areas of economic and social policy from the states to the national government. The effort has taken place with the deference of some in Congress and the general approval of the federal courts.

In the 21st century, the president certainly has a wide variety of tools at his disposal to influence the states, beginning with a swelled collection of advisers and specialists and extending to a massive bureaucracy of federal agencies. However, two long developing sources of power have been particularly helpful to reconstructing federalism—the executive order and use of the Office of Management and Budget. With these tools, the president has attempted to solidify the powers of his office, often in tandem with increased national authority.

Nowhere in the Constitution is there precise language, for instance, that even permits the president to write executive orders. Nevertheless, presidents have assumed the power to issue decrees with respect to implementation of existing laws. Through the use of this tool, presidents have added to the power of the national government at the expense of the states.

For the first 150 years or so of American history, executive orders tended to be rather narrow in scope, often providing technical instruction to federal agencies to carry out legislation. The concept was vindicated by the U.S. Supreme Court after President Harry Truman temporarily seized the nation's steel mills during the Korean War on the grounds that he was overtly legislating. Although the Court denied Truman's reach in that case, a majority agreed the president had the power to issue executive orders.

Through executive orders, presidents have profoundly affected the relationship between the national and state governments. In 1943, Franklin Roosevelt issued an executive order to create the Fair Employment Practices Commission to investigate complaints of racial discrimination in the workplace. During his presidency, John F. Kennedy issued a series of executive orders on housing, employment, and other issues related to civil rights, limiting state powers in the process. Likewise, Lyndon Johnson advanced the civil rights issue by establishing affirmative action through executive order. Recently, in 2014, President Barack Obama signed an executive order ensuring individuals public hospital visitation rights regardless of their sexual orientation, again limiting the scope of state powers.

Presidents have also influenced state economies through executive orders. Shortly after passage of the National Environmental Policy Act in 1969, President Richard Nixon signed an executive order creating the Environmental Protection Agency, thus centralizing federal administration of environmental issues. Presidential interventions in environmental policy have intruded on state privilege ever since. In 2014, again reaching back to the original 1969 legislation, President Barack Obama issued an executive order requiring power plants to curb pollutant emissions. President Obama advanced federal authority in 2014 with his executive order on immigration, which gave temporary residence to as many as 5 million undocumented immigrants.

Some executive orders have actually reversed course and deferred to state power. In 1987, President Ronald Reagan issued an order that deferred to the states interpretations of "national standards," whenever possible. In 1993, however, President Bill Clinton reversed Reagan's directive by ordering federal agencies to limit the policy-making capabilities of the states and local governments. Clearly, the president has a powerful instrument for shaping federalism in the executive order, but an order can be reversed by a successor or by Congress in the form of law. This back-and-forth in the use of executive order gives a uniquely modern cast to American federalism, introducing fluidity and contingency into a seemingly fixed constitutional relationship.

OFFICE OF MANAGEMENT AND BUDGET

One of the most significant executive orders signed by President Richard Nixon in 1970 created the Office of Management and Budget (OMB). The new agency was a reconstituted version of the Bureau of the Budget, initially created by Congress in 1921 as a rudimentary "numbers crunching" accounting and budget office. Under Nixon's reorganization, the OMB took on a more overtly political role, far from the agency's original conception as repository of neutral expertise. Through this newly expanded agency, all decisions regarding federal regulations had to pass the "smell test" at the White House. Ever since then, presidents have used the OMB as an extension of their political philosophies, particularly with respect to the division of responsibilities between the states and federal government.

Congress didn't take well to this new tool for presidential domination of policy. Thus, in 1974, legislators created the Congressional Budget Office as a means of countering presidential analysis of budget data and economic projections. In retrospect, it is difficult to ascertain the extent to which the new unit tempered presidential zeal. In the wake of Watergate, the Ford Administration was rather ginger in its use of the OMB, as was the Carter Administration. Post-Watergate hesitation toward presidential assertions of administrative power did not, however, last long.

The OMB became much more active and partisan under Ronald Reagan and George H.W. Bush when the White House demanded that federal policies pass cost–benefit tests and shifted the management of numerous policies back to the states. Reagan particularly used the budget office to deflect a rash of proposed federal regulations.

Bill Clinton reversed course and used the OMB to centralize policy making. But Clinton went a step beyond his predecessors by appointing OMB liaisons in key federal agencies, thereby ensuring a smooth chain of command and cooperation. George W. Bush followed Clinton's example by installing his own sub-OMB bureaucracy to mirror his political views. Concerned about business being stifled by excessive federal control, Bush consistently relied on the OMB to block federal regulations that might be harmful to state protections of commercial interests. Bush's zeal for decentralization led to key breakdowns in governance, however, especially with respect to the poor coordination between the OMB and Federal Emergency Management Agency in the wake of Hurricane Katrina.

Barack Obama has shifted the emphasis of the OMB yet again. In one of his first executive orders, Obama reversed the Bush OMB structure that reduced regulatory proposals from federal agencies. The idea was to make OMB actions more transparent while allowing agencies to do their work unencumbered by any resistance. Since then, a number of agencies have initiated regulatory efforts to set standards for living conditions and public safety, including the Environmental Protection Agency, the Occupational Safety and Health Administration, and the Bureau of Land Management. Each of these efforts has increased national power. Not only has the OMB become a powerful presidential tool, its back-and-forth approach to state discretion has made it a powerful regulator of federalism.

THE STATES PUSH BACK

Presidential scholar Richard Neustadt once observed that presidential power is "the power to persuade." There is no doubt that on day-to-day matters—even many pressing policy matters—the president must spend much of his political capital convincing others to follow through on his directives. After all, there is a world of difference between directing that a task or policy be carried out and confirming that the order has been executed as expected. Governing institutions push back against presidential direction, and they process presidential preferences in their own ways. Neustadt focused his analysis of resistance to the president from Congress, noting that its two chambers and decentralized committee system posed major obstacles for any president. Scholars of federalism recognize that the state governments pose a similar constraint. Despite presidential efforts to strengthen their influence over state government authority, presidents often find themselves frustrated, forced to deal with watered-down policy outcomes.

The reasons for this can be traced to the constitutional structure and the enduring influence of "states' rights" in American political culture (although specific state context plays a role as well). The debate over states' rights dates back to at least the Articles of Confederation. It continued well into the 19th century when South Carolina Representative John Calhoun advanced a theory of state nullification. State sovereignty is prominently featured in the country's constitutional DNA. The institutional capacity of presidents, let alone Congress, to compel states into action has limits. States have diverse populations with unique interests, making it hard for the federal government to justify, much less impose, "one-size-fits-all" policies.

States' different racial histories, financial resources, economies, and ideological orientations combine to produce an asymmetry in their receptiveness to presidential action and congressional mandates. President Obama's executive order on immigration, mentioned briefly earlier in the essay, was accepted by some states but met with legal actions initiated by the governors of seventeen states who alleged the mandate ignored states' rights. Federal environmental laws such as the Clean Air and Water Acts are also implemented in very different ways at the state level. States with a larger industrial base or a general antiregulatory tenor in their politics enforce these federal environmental laws with less vigor than those with a greater affinity toward environmental protection. In 2014, using his authority under the Clean Air Act, President Obama issued an executive order requiring power plants to curb carbon emissions. Officials from states with a larger share of coal-fired power plants were furious. If history is a reliable guide, this too will be carried out more stringently in some states than others.

The implementation of the Patient Protection and Affordable Care Act (the ACA, or "Obamacare"), arguably the greatest domestic policy achievement of President Obama's two terms in office, serves as a recent and highly salient example of state governments upsetting the presidential policy agenda. Democratic presidents dating back to Harry Truman have sought to build an American health care system with near universal coverage. When fully implemented, Obamacare promises to take a bigger step toward achieving this goal than any policy since the adoption of Medicare and Medicaid passed under President Lyndon Johnson. Health coverage under the ACA was expanded through two primary mechanisms. First, state governments could establish new health care "exchanges" where people could shop health insurance plans and sign up for new coverage. Second, the ACA expanded the eligibility for Medicaid to households earning up to 140% of the federal poverty level.

Republicans in Congress fiercely opposed the ACA. Once enacted, it met equally ferocious resistance in many Republican-controlled state legislatures. Many GOP-led states simply refused to establish new health insurance exchanges (instead, choosing to let the federal government's Department of Health and Human Services take the lead). After the Supreme Court ruled in 2012 that the federal government could not force states to expand Medicaid under the ACA, nearly two dozen Republican-leaning states also refused to expand their Medicaid rolls. Despite helping millions of people since its adoption in 2010, the expansion of coverage under the ACA has remained uneven across the states—a byproduct of state-level politics and ideological pushback.

State governments tasked with implementing top-down mandates have increasingly sought relief from federal regulations by applying for executive waivers. Executive waivers first became available in 1962 for programs authorized under the Social Security Act, and then for education programs in 1994. During the 1980s, a number of states received waivers from requirements under the nation's major welfare program, Aid to Families with Dependent Children (AFDC). This trend continued even after President Clinton pushed major welfare reform through Congress in 1996 with the passage of the new Temporary Assistance for Needy Families (TANF) program. States routinely received waivers from the Department of Health and Human Services, the agency charged with writing rules governing the implementation of TANF.

Under both AFDC and TANF, states were given more freedom to shape welfare requirements than originally envisioned under federal law. State governments had the ability to innovate and structure welfare policies that more closely matched their preferences. Greater state discretion in welfare provision, however, has also imposed costs on many of the most marginalized Americans—particularly poor blacks. States with a greater share of black residents were more likely to adopt stricter work requirements and to offer less generous welfare cash assistance.

During the 1990s and 2000s, state governors secured waivers for Medicaid, granting states more leeway in the delivery of health care. Not surprisingly, waivers have also played an important role in shaping the implementation of Obamacare. Several GOP-leaning states, including Arkansas and Tennessee, who otherwise opposed expanding Medicaid under the law, have nonetheless sought a middle ground by seeking waivers to expand Medicaid through privatized means. States' interests are often at odds with presidential plans. Given the delicate balance between executive power and state political preferences, presidents must sometimes make concessions on both implementation and policy grounds. As waivers become more prominent in the implementation of federal policy, federal–state relations are also drawn into a more continuous process of negotiation.

STATE LOBBYING

State and local governments have also become major lobbying forces in Washington, D.C. They have joined a crowded list of groups and organizations that place major policy demands on the White House. Indeed, as the federal government has encroached on matters traditionally reserved to the states, their stake in national politics has never been higher. Over time, the emergence of state or locally oriented lobbying organizations in Washington, D.C., has increased the influence of states and municipalities on the executive branch and Congress. Organizations such as the National Conference of State Legislatures, National Governors Association, the National League of Cities, the U.S. Conference of Mayors, the National Association of Counties, and the International City/County Management Association have increasingly influenced federal policy, especially on those issues where states have common interests. Efforts to limit federal mandates, increase federal funding for federal–state programs, or weaken federal statutes that limit state authority consistently rank at the top of states' policy agendas.

The rise of state lobbying organizations in Washington, D.C., does not necessarily translate into trouble for presidents' policy initiatives. If presidents are receptive to ideas originating from a variety of sources, or if they work to coordinate federal initiatives with state agencies and organizations, they can find ways to benefit from this dynamic tension. State governments act as what Supreme Court Justice Louis Brandeis aptly called "laboratories of democracy." They experiment with different policy ideas that match their ideological orientations; they test what works (and what does not) to help solve complex problems.

As one example, the design of Obamacare was heavily influenced by Massachusetts's own comprehensive health reforms adopted in 2006 under then-Governor Mitt Romney. More broadly, information and policy expertise flow from the "bottom up" in the federalist system just as much as they flow from the "top down." Successful policy creation and implementation involves a multitude of actors and institutions at all levels of government. Innovation should thus be the main theme of federalism today.

State agencies and public organizations that lobby Washington can serve as important partners for presidents who are serious about improving outcomes associated with complex federal programs. For instance, the National Governors Association worked closely with officials in the Department of Transportation to coordinate the outlay of state infrastructure projects funded under the American Recovery and Reinvestment Act of 2009. Similarly, liaison offices in the Department of Energy helped coordinate state and local governments' efforts to weatherize homes, purchase energy efficient vehicles, and deploy solar power technologies. The Office of Intergovernmental and External Affairs, housed within the Department of Health and Human Services, is charged with communicating federal initiatives and perspectives while engaging with state and local government stakeholders. In recent years the Council of State Governments, a nonprofit organization with a mission to help improve state policy performance, coordinated efforts to reform criminal sentencing and improve prisons with officials in the White House's Office of National Drug Control Policy, the National Institute of Corrections, and the National Institute of Justice.

The degree to which these types of institutions and partnerships lead to successful outcomes varies widely across presidential administrations and policy areas. Nonetheless, they remain crucial elements of any modern president's strategy to help cope with the challenges of governing in a complex federalist system.

◆ ◆ ◆ ◆ ◆

34. Leaving None Behind: The Odyssey of Education Reform

by Jesse H. Rhodes

For much of U.S. history, elementary and secondary education policy was left to the discretion of state and local governments. This reflected both Americans' preference for local control of schooling and the widespread belief that American schools were meeting the nation's needs. Beginning in the 1960s, however, growing public awareness of the educational challenges presented by racial and economic inequality led to new federal efforts to support schools, especially in disadvantaged areas, most notably President Lyndon Johnson's Elementary and Secondary Education Act (ESEA) of 1965.

The new millennium witnessed another pivotal moment highlighting presidential influence in developing federal education policy. Widespread concern among policy makers, education experts, and parents that elementary and secondary schools were failing to prepare students adequately for college and work spurred federal efforts to raise education standards and hold schools accountable for results. The much-heralded (and subsequently, much-maligned) No Child Left Behind Act (NCLB) of 2002, a measure spearheaded by President George W. Bush, was the most prominent result of this initiative.

Since that time, federal education policy has been suspended in a political tug-of-war between reformers, currently led by President Barack Obama, who hope to refine and extend federal involvement in schooling, and those who believe that control over education should be returned to state and local authorities. Many citizens hold conflicting views: although they support the broad principle of federal efforts to strengthen education, they often take issue with the consequences of specific federal reforms. Aware of the political perils associated with legislative initiatives, President Obama has made aggressive use of his regulatory authority to prod states to adopt further education reforms, with mixed success.

Over time, the tension between federal leadership and the desire for local control has fostered a cyclical pattern in education policymaking: new federal initiatives have fed demands for devolution of control, while dissatisfaction with the uneven pace of state and local reforms has sparked renewed interest in federal action. In 2014, the public mood favors the devolution of responsibility for education, but this suggests that renewed enthusiasm for federal involvement is just around the corner.

RUBE GOLDBERG REFORMS

Assessment of the possibilities and pitfalls of federal education policy begins with the Rube Goldberg–like structure of recent federal education reforms, and the political history underlying their development. Swept up in the spirit of the Great Society, reformers in the 1960s perceived education as a key pathway to economic prosperity and equality of opportunity, and President Johnson vowed to use the powers of the federal government to improve educational opportunities for disadvantaged children.

The ESEA, which was developed by the Johnson Administration and enjoyed the full backing of the president, established a new grant-in-aid program in which the federal government supplied funds for remedial education programs designed and implemented by state and, especially, local governments. Importantly, the ESEA was not intended to drive fundamental changes in school curricula, testing, or accountability; rather, it was supposed to provide targeted remedial assistance to vulnerable student groups, especially African Americans, Latinos, and students from impoverished families who had been disadvantaged by lack of economic opportunity. This emphasis reflected the view, widespread at the time, that most schools and students were performing adequately and that federal efforts should be focused on providing assistance to especially needy student groups.

In a politically astute move, the ESEA's architects designed the program to spread federal funds as widely as possible to ensure that it would enjoy a broad base of political support. In the end, virtually every school district received some federal funding as a result of the program.

In the ensuing decades, funding for the ESEA—and for related policies such as the Individuals with Disabilities Education Act, which served students suffering from a variety of cognitive and physical disabilities—became more lavish. The expansion of federal funding for remedial education programs was propelled by the advocacy of a powerful interest group constellation comprising state and local education administrators, civil rights and disability activists, teacher union groups, and parents of affected children—all of whom believed strongly in the policy and benefited from federal largesse.

Recognizing the electoral utility of increasing aid for programs that served almost every district in the country, presidents and members of Congress worked in a bipartisan fashion to renew and extend these measures. Consequently, federal education policy largely escaped the highly politicized struggles over racial, economic, and social justice that paralyzed policy making in many other areas during the Nixon, Ford, and Carter Presidencies. By the 1980s, the remedial education regime developed under the ESEA program was deeply entrenched in American education policy making, buttressed by interest group activism and broadly supported by Democrats and Republicans alike.

REAGAN WEIGHS IN

However, as the new decade dawned and President Ronald Reagan assumed office, the education agenda began to change. Rising global economic competition, coupled with growing evidence that many students were not meeting high academic standards, encouraged policy makers to shift the focus of education policy making from providing remedial services to vulnerable groups to ensuring quality education for all students. Interestingly, this agenda was embraced both by business leaders, who believed school improvements were essential to economic growth, and civil rights groups, who were increasingly doubtful of the adequacy of remedial policies to combat racial and economic inequality.

President Reagan fanned the flames of the "excellence in education" agenda by publicizing the findings of *A Nation at Risk* (1983), a government report that portrayed students' modest academic achievements as a fundamental threat to the nation. *A Nation at Risk* spurred a new wave of efforts to strengthen education.

Consistent with prevailing norms against federal control of education, school improvement efforts were initially concentrated at the state and local levels. During the 1980s, states experimented with a broad array of reforms to improve curricula, testing, accountability, teacher recruitment and training, and school organization. But frustration with the slow pace and modest results of state and local efforts led to growing calls for expanded federal involvement in bettering education.

Between 1989 and 2002, Presidents George H.W. Bush, Bill Clinton, and George W. Bush each increased federal involvement in the school reform agenda. Whereas the first Bush was content to exhort state and local officials and facilitate agreement on voluntary measures, Clinton and George W. Bush proposed a more rigorous and directive role for the federal government.

This change in the federal education agenda was accompanied by considerable continuity in institutional forms and funding arrangements. The political popularity and institutional entrenchment of the ESEA program made it the inevitable jumping-off point for subsequent education reforms. Cheered on by the same business leaders and civil rights activists who had previously supported state-level measures, both Clinton and George W. Bush sought to piggyback comprehensive education reforms on the ESEA's financial and administrative architecture. Essentially, both presidents offered state and local governments a new deal on old money: if they wanted to continue to enjoy access to federal education funds under the ESEA, they would have to adopt higher academic standards, institute tests assessing schools' progress toward the standards, and implement corrective actions against schools that failed to make yearly academic progress.

However, just as the original ESEA granted states and localities extensive leeway to design and implement compensatory education programs, the reforms envisioned by Clinton and Bush devolved responsibility for implementing standards, testing, and accountability policies to state and local governments. This ungainly system was first established with the Improving America's Schools Act of 1994 and dramatically expanded with the No Child Left Behind Act of 2002.

NO CHILD LEFT BEHIND

At the time it was enacted, NCLB was portrayed as combining the best aspects of federal leadership, on one hand, and state and local experimentation, on the other. In practice, however, NCLB institutionalized some of the worst pathologies associated with both approaches to policy making. The law mandated that states bring 100 percent of their students to academic "proficiency" by 2014 but gave states free rein to define what proficiency meant within their borders. These requirements had the perverse consequence of encouraging some states to set low academic standards so that they would appear to be making progress toward the federal government's stringent (and arguably unachievable) proficiency mandate. This behavior both undermined NCLB's central objective of spurring school improvement and generated considerable cynicism about the efficacy of federal involvement. Meanwhile, other states were prompted by the law's strict accountability requirements to institute corrective actions against schools that would have been rated as high-performing under voluntary standards, outraging parents, teachers, and students.

By the end of President Bush's second term in office, NCLB was wildly unpopular, especially among teachers and parents in schools labeled "failing" by the Act. Despite the intensity of the backlash, however, Bush and members of Congress failed to agree on a plan to revise the law. In truth, NCLB's unpopularity discouraged elected officials on both sides of the aisle from discussing the law in public, except to criticize its obvious flaws. At the same time, relatively few members of Congress were willing to dismantle the Act and thereby terminate federal involvement in school improvement efforts, and President Bush made clear any such proposal would be met with a presidential veto. NCLB thus lingered in political and legal limbo. Its provisions remained in force, but the Bush Administration used its waiver authority to give states much more flexibility in implementing them. Meanwhile, Congress periodically reauthorized federal funding for the ESEA's underlying programs, without making substantive changes to NCLB's requirements. The result was a growing gap between what NCLB said on its face and what states and localities were doing in practice.

OBAMA'S EDUCATION REFORMS

Gridlock over the renewal of NCLB encouraged President Barack Obama to try a different approach to reforming the nation's schools. Drawing on a discretionary pool of $4.35 billion in federal funds from the American Recovery and Reinvestment Act of 2009, Obama established the "Race to the Top" program, which infused participating states with federal funds in exchange for promises to institute specific reforms that the administration deemed especially effective. These included expanding charter schools, linking student test score data with teacher information, and enhancing the clarity and specificity of academic standards.

Notably, Race to the Top was a competitive program: states were required to apply for funds and could be denied access to resources if their applications did not conform to administration priorities. Despite this requirement, the governments of virtually every state—all of which were desperate for financial assistance in the wake of the Great Recession of 2008–2009—applied for, and eventually received, Race to the Top grants.

Despite its modest budget, Race to the Top promoted significant changes in state and local education policy making. This drew rave reviews from many education stakeholders in the short term, but eventually it became a source of considerable controversy. Notably, Race to the Top broached the delicate issue of teacher accountability. Because of legal restrictions or lack of administrative capacity, states have historically refrained from attempting to hold individual teachers responsible for their students' achievement. However, to gain access to "Race to the Top" funding, many states removed legal or administrative "firewalls" separating student achievement data from teacher evaluations. In principle, these changes could help states hold teachers accountable for student performance, but serious questions remain about both the technical feasibility and fairness of these efforts. Meanwhile, changes to teacher accountability policies engendered considerable anger and resistance from teachers and their unions, and eroded teachers' commitment to the Obama Administration's broader education agenda.

Obama's efforts to induce states to raise academic standards helped propel another important, albeit controversial, education project: the Common Core State Standards Initiative. The "Common Core" was conceived by the president, state elected officials, and local education leaders as a solution to the perverse consequences associated with NCLB's academic proficiency mandate. Under the Common Core, states voluntarily agreed to adopt a common set of educational standards in English language arts and mathematics for students in kindergarten through twelfth grade, and to participate in one of several consortia to develop new assessments aligned with the common standards. President Obama and many state leaders believed that this arrangement would encourage states to focus on strengthening academic standards and raising the quality of their assessments.

While the president and other "Common Core" supporters sought to distance the new initiative from the discredited NCLB brand, the plan nonetheless raised a clamor among both liberals and conservatives. Many liberal Democrats and activists argued that the Common Core reinforced NCLB's relentless emphasis on standardized testing at the expense of a deeper and more meaningful approach to educating students. At the same time, many conservative Republicans and activists charged that the Common Core was a way station on the road to a national curriculum and the consolidation of federal "control" of education. Critics on both sides of the aisle complained that the Common Core was designed and implemented with little input from teachers, parents, and students.

In some states, backlash against the Common Core was so severe that elected officials backed out of participating in the initiative. By 2014, only forty-three states were still actively involved in the Common Core, and there remained serious questions about the alignment of proposed tests with Common Core objectives.

EDUCATION REFORM STALLS

In the end, the political stalemate over NCLB has seriously hamstrung President Obama's efforts to influence the course of education reform. Because Obama has not been willing or able to achieve a comprehensive reform of NCLB, he has been forced to use much smaller pots of money to advance his objectives. Facing massive budget deficits and desirous of maintaining good relations with a new president, states initially went along with this agenda. However, as economic conditions improved and Obama's star fell, resistance mounted, especially among constituencies (teachers, public school parents, and civil rights activists) important to the president's coalition.

By all appearances, Obama's response to these developments has been to downplay controversy over education and refocus public attention on issues enjoying broader political support. As a result, education policy has fallen from the place of prominence on the public agenda that it enjoyed in the 1990s and 2000s.

The tangled history of federal education reform from 1965 to the present offers important lessons for presidential leadership in the area of education. First, the existing structure of federal education regulations and funding commitments imposes significant constraints on new presidential initiatives. Because existing policies institutionalize a division of labor between the federal government and the states, and draw support from a diverse constellation of powerful interest groups, presidents are usually required to work through existing channels to accomplish reform goals. This prompts presidents to layer new reforms atop old funding streams and administrative arrangements, with generally mixed results.

More broadly, the history of American education reform teaches us that the political half-life of presidential education reform initiatives is short. Proposals to renew the nation's schools are initially greeted with considerable enthusiasm, but cynicism and resistance quickly set in as the limitations of unwieldy federal reforms are revealed in due course. This reflects not only the inevitable disillusionment that attends the translation of abstract ideas during the course of implementation but also the essential ambivalence Americans feel about federal involvement in elementary and secondary schooling.

◆　◆　◆　◆　◆

35. Dawn of the Information Age: Presidents and the Internet

by Reed E. Hundt

In the winter of 1993–1994, the Clinton Administration recognized that the Internet could become the most important information platform in the world, and it used the considerable power of the White House and the executive branch to make that vision real. The White House wanted U.S. businesses, schools, libraries, and households to lead the world in adopting the new medium. If Internet access grew quickly in the United States, they reasoned that U.S. firms would have a jump start in creating value on the new platform. The winning firms and early users could also create an "Internet culture" that prized American values such as entrepreneurial competition,[1] democracy, and freedom of expression.[2]

The Clinton Administration had come into office seeking economic growth through increased competition both domestically and overseas. At the same time, Japan's economic success in the 1970s and 1980s—as illustrated by the tremendous gains made by Japanese firms against U.S. rivals in markets ranging from automobiles to electronics—suggested the power of activist government policies that anticipated business cycles and advances in technology. Meanwhile, the collapse of the Soviet Union and end of the Cold War offered new hope for global free trade not only in goods and services but also in information.

The Internet seemed the perfect medium for those times: it encouraged domestic investment, U.S. expansion into international markets, and a global competition in technology and ideas. The new medium would compete against both television and telephony. U.S. firms, even if initially only glimmers in venture capitalists' eyes, could beat Japanese firms to the punch. E-mail and websites might spread democracy and free speech in an era of global reach.

Of course, technological breakthroughs, especially in private and government research centers, created the opportunity the Clinton Administration embraced. But governments often burden with regulation, and, sometimes, outright ban breakthrough technologies—especially those likely to disrupt well-established market structures, and status quo politics and policies. Nevertheless, coming into office the administration sought a global strategy for prospering in the dawning Information Age, and by early 1994, it chose the Internet as the means for realizing those strategic goals. Vice President Al Gore asked me, as chair of the Federal Communications Commission from November 1993 to November 1997, to execute regulatory tactics in line with that strategy

AN INFORMATION REVOLUTION

The strategy worked, only faster than we expected. The rapid spread of the Internet ignited an economic and technology boom that stretched from 1994 to 2001. In those years, the private sector invested about $1 trillion to replace the old information platform (analog television, fixed-line telephones, voice) with the new medium (digital, computers, Internet, wireless telephones, data). Unemployment fell; real wages rose. Economists who told President-elect Clinton in 1992 that burgeoning federal deficits could doom his presidency were surprised when the technology boom eventually helped produce annual surpluses.[3]

In the newly digitized information and communications technology sector, ascendant U.S. firms (Microsoft, Intel, Cisco, Yahoo!, Qualcomm, and then in later stages, Google, Facebook, etc.) rose to achieve huge market capitalizations and great influence in business, society, and culture. They outpaced their rivals in Japan, Europe, and almost everywhere else except China, which by means of aggressive state action now hosts the only firms capable of challenging U.S. firms in the global digital economy.

Of course, the Internet did not just explode into a world-shaking commercial and social phenomenon totally unbidden or unaided. Two decades earlier computer pioneers had developed "packet-switching" technology that allowed computers to communicate with one another, but that communication had been limited to private and academic networks. The Clinton FCC, exercising powers conveyed by the 1934 Communications Act, and also in the course of implementing the 1996 Telecommunications Act, made the critical decision to allow the Internet to "borrow," at no charge, the physical infrastructure of the existing telephony network, which was the largest and most expensive unified machine ever built.

That single gift gave the Internet developers and providers the physical infrastructure—which had cost many hundreds of billions of dollars to create—that they needed to make the Internet a historic commercial and social phenomenon.

The gift was the federal government's to bestow because of a bit of trust busting dating back to 1983, when the Department of Justice broke AT&T into a long-distance company that connected to customers through local

Bell monopoly companies. The long-distance companies had to pay the local Bells for the right to connect to customers. When calls went across state lines, the FCC regulated the payments as access charges. The long-distance companies collected the money from customers, and paid it to the Bells. Access charges could amount to 30 to 60 percent of the price of a long-distance charge.

During the breakup, Congressman Ed Markey urged the FCC to exempt from access charges business connections used principally to transfer information. In decisions known as Computer I and Computer II, the FCC created this "enhanced service provider" exemption. In the 1990s, people connected to the Internet by disconnecting a phone line from a telephone and connecting it to a computer. Then the computer dialed a phone line that in turn connected to a network linked to other networks, and that network of networks constituted the Internet.

Obviously, the Internet crossed state lines, so the FCC exercised jurisdiction over the connections. But we used that jurisdiction to exempt Internet communication from access charges. As a result, Internet service providers did not have to pay local phone companies anything when they marketed access to the Internet.

ENABLING RAPID GROWTH

We took a variety of other measures to promote the rapid spread of the Internet. The FCC did not, for instance, require licenses from Internet Service Providers (ISPs). By contrast, telephone, cable, radio, broadcast TV, satellites and even ham radio operators all had to attain FCC licenses. As a result of that exemption, thousands of companies sprung up to offer Internet access. America Online, or AOL, became the biggest, but growth was expedited by the massive competitive entrepreneurship.

The FCC also required the telephone companies to give telephone lines to access providers at low, rate-regulated prices, and in the volumes demanded. The ISPs used the lines to connect users to the backbone of the Internet, which was a competitive market. If the telephone companies had been able to limit the supply or charge more for those connections, they could have gained market power over the Internet.

Pursuant to the 1996 Telecommunications Act, we also ordered the Bell companies to lease portions of their network to firms that offered high-speed Internet access,[4] especially to businesses that launched new content on the platform, such as e-Bay, Amazon, and Google.[5] These pro-Internet, anti-Bell measures were later labeled by Vice President Gore as "regulatory jiu-jitsu."

He nailed the metaphor perfectly. The vast extent and smooth workings of the existing phone network made it the perfect medium for the rapid spread of the Internet, even though that new form of communication would usurp the importance of the phone network in American society and business. We let the ISPs use the phone network against the industry that owned it in the name of increased competition.

AN INTERNET CHAMPION

The principal who set the strategic goal—the big picture—was Vice President Gore.

Gore brought to the vice presidency an intellectual's curiosity and creativity and a venerable politician's knowledge of how to manipulate the levers of power. He knew something Clinton learned later: to get things done in Washington, D.C., relentless focus matters, and political capital has to be spent wisely. Vice presidents typically had few meaningful responsibilities up until that time, but President Clinton empowered Gore by giving him unusual authorities. Gore had the power of the pen, for instance, giving him the authority to have the last word in signing off on all issues relating to communications and the environment. Everyone in the White House reported to Gore on those two topics. In practice, President Clinton refused to hear appeals about Gore's decisions.

Bill Clinton's willingness to delegate was a hallmark of his presidential leadership.[6] Similar examples were his trust in the Russia policy designed chiefly by Strobe Talbott, deputy Secretary of State; his willingness to let the Food and Drug Administration try to regulate tobacco more stringently; and the freedom given to Treasury to rescue Mexico from its financial crisis.

Empowered by the president, Gore spent months in 1993 summoning a large team for biweekly meetings to plan the administration's strategy for the information and communications technology sector. Participants included economist Joe Stiglitz, later a Nobel Prize winner, but then on the Council of Economic Advisers; Anne Bingaman, head of the DOJ Antitrust Division; Greg Simon, a key Gore aide; Larry Irving, who was running the National Telecommunications Information Agency; Mike Nelson, a physicist in the Office of Science and Technology Policy; myself; and up to a half-dozen others.

Developing a technology strategy at all broke with tradition. At least since Jimmy Carter's election in 1976, virtually all Republicans and many Democrats had championed deregulation and private sector ingenuity, while explicitly or implicitly communicating that government ought to have only a small role in regulatory oversight. True, the federal government was instrumental in building the social safety net. And, obviously, the government had exercised substantial control over the entire economy in order to fight World War II. But after the stagflation of the 1970s, the primary narrative in Washington held that strict monetary policy, budget cuts, and deregulation would boost the private sector and increase the country's standard of living.

According to this widely held view, an intrusive federal government that attempted to maximize technological and business opportunities in the name of the public interest was a throwback to the failed policies of the old Democratic Party.[7] Getting out of the way was now supposed to be the job of government.[8] In this view, the United States had a clockwork economy that ticked perfectly well as long as government did not meddle with its gears.[9]

In the late 1980s and early 1990s, however, Al Gore had a different view, drawn from new growth economics. As explained by economist Paul Romer in a 1990 *Journal of Political Economy* article,[10] the more information available on easily accessed networks, the more wealth would be created. By contrast, traditional economics assumed that such "returns to scale" decreased. In that view, unless firms could achieve productivity gains—making more for less—entropy prevailed and growth would tend to decline.

By contrast, Gore's vision promoted more information for everyone. An early example had come in 1992 in the CERN laboratory in Switzerland, which gave away for free the software invented by Tim Berners-Lee (such as HTML and HTTP-IP). That software in turn created ways to format, display, and transmit digital content, creating the World Wide Web. That, of course, was the application that would make the Internet the dominant communications medium—as soon as creating and visiting websites was made easy for everyone. This last necessary and inevitable software invention came in late 1993 from Marc Andreessen, age twenty-two, and colleagues at the supercomputer laboratory at the University of Illinois. Gore spotted their Mosaic browser soon after its creation.[11]

THE MISSING PIECE

By that time virtually the only missing piece was the network itself. From his election to Congress in 1976 and the Senate in 1984, Gore had articulated a vision of global connectivity. He had often expressed a desire to have the "schoolgirl in Carthage, Tennessee, go to the Library of Congress without buying a bus ticket."[12]

Time Warner and others had proposed building the networks for Gore's vision and for delivering TV in lieu of Blockbuster or satellite service. But the Time Warner plan would have cost up to $5,000 per household, or about $500 billion for all Americans. The private sector would not finance it. The Clinton Administration, bent on balancing the budget, was unwilling to build a new network for the Internet with taxpayer funds.

The only viable answer was the telephone network, which already reached nearly 100% of all households in the United States. The FCC's "gift" of the phone network to the Internet service providers stemmed directly from the administration's strategy and vision. Without the White House's support, the agency could never have taken such a dramatic step.

Some may question whether the federal government should embrace any particular technological vision, even when no company was selected as a special favorite or a guaranteed winner. But throughout its history, the FCC has repeatedly promoted new technologies that promised to increase the public's access to news, entertainment, and communications, to include radio, telephony, broadcast television, cable TV, satellites, and wireless. The FCC has also fostered, or at least tolerated, oligopoly and even monopoly as the initial market structures for the latest medium.

Indeed, when the Roosevelt Administration sponsored the Communications Act of 1934 creating the FCC, the commission was given the mission of promoting the AT&T monopoly in order to provide low-priced phone service to low-income Americans in rural areas. (In this respect the FCC resembled the Tennessee Valley Authority, which was given the task of providing low-cost electricity to rural homes in that region.)[13] According to the theory behind Roosevelt's first "New Deal," multifirm competition in new technological mediums wasted resources that were better spent building networks to all businesses and homes. In exchange for running a monopoly, the firm had to accept FCC regulation.[14] The same view of allowing monopolies prevailed when it came to the franchising of cable systems in the 1970s and 1980s to achieve widespread multichannel video distribution.

By the 1990s, however, Congress and the administration had come to support competition as the best means for delivering innovation and rapid growth. That had been the approach favored by most economists since the 1970s. By opening the telephone network to the ISPs, the FCC enabled thousands of private firms to compete in building the Internet. In that respect, we departed from common FCC practice. But in desiring a robust common medium that reached everyone, the Clinton-era FCC was part of a long-standing tradition of government support for new information platforms that traced back to Roosevelt.

PROMOTING THE INTERNET

Gore championed the Internet in the United States and around the world. Ultimately, the administration's ideas coalesced into a set of proposals called the National Information Infrastructure initiative, or NII. Its global counterpart, the Global Information Infrastructure (GII), represented the foreign policy of the Internet. Its creation resulted from negotiations held between 1994 and 1997 and led by Trade Ambassador Charlene Barshefsky, who reached an agreement by which sixty-nine countries accepted various rule-based principles that promoted Internet connectivity.

In a noteworthy speech to the International Telecommunications Union in Buenos Aires in March 1994, Gore laid out a paradigm of open access, universal service, and free speech on a new global information platform. A year later, in May 1995, Clinton, Gore, and other members of the cabinet fanned out across California to "pull wire"—drag phone lines—into classrooms to demonstrate how Internet access for students and teachers would transform education. Previously, technology companies engaged with the federal government primarily as suppliers meeting government procurement requests. Now the CEOs of Microsoft, Intel, Yahoo, and other tech companies began to discuss public policy issues with the president and vice president.

By stoking enthusiastic public support for the Internet, the administration encouraged investors to back companies that exploited the new platform. Early in 1994, I had dinner at Eric Schmidt's house—yes, the host was the future CEO of Google—to discuss the Internet with John Doerr, the most important venture capitalist in Silicon Valley, and the extremely young Marc Andreessen, who had invented Mosaic, as well as a number of other technology leaders. Speaking for the administration, I told them to go for it: build the Internet as fast as possible. President Clinton and Vice President Gore sent the same message on numerous occasions.

Gore's team outlined legislation in line with what was already being negotiated in the House and Senate. The Gore outline authorized the FCC to issue dozens of rules promoting competition in all markets, while including various public interest mandates such as connecting all classrooms and libraries to the Internet. The outline also included a provision carving out the Internet for special favor.

Congressman Edward Markey, D-Mass., and Senator Earnest "Fritz" Hollings, D-South Carolina, drafted the Telecommunications Act of 1994, which passed the House by a huge bipartisan majority. Senator Dole blocked it in the Senate, in anticipation of a Republican takeover of Congress in the elections that November. The Republican dominated Senate eventually passed a bill that was very similar to the Telecommunications Act, however, and it passed with bipartisan majorities in both Houses. President Clinton signed the bill into law in the Library of Congress in February 1996.

That bill delegated to the FCC immense regulatory powers over the Internet. The FCC was authorized to raise and spend money, for instance, to connect every classroom, library, and rural health care facility to the Internet. It issued rules for rivals to lease parts of the telephone network and otherwise connect to that network. These rules, along with the authority granted by the 1934 Act, permitted the FCC to allow Internet developers and providers to "borrow" the telephone network, as described earlier.

LEGACY COMPANIES SURPRISED

The early entrepreneurs of the Internet benefitted from the relative indifference of the broadcast and telephone industry lobbyists to the new medium. The broadcasters primarily wanted Congress to grant each local television station a second channel for free, in order to build a digital television station to replace analog broadcasting. They also wanted many years in which to make the transition from analog to digital.

The local phone companies attached the greatest importance to extending the local voice business into long distance, to compete with AT&T and MCI. Previously the Department of Justice had obtained a court order barring local Bells from leveraging their monopoly into long distance, as part of the break-up of AT&T. Under the Telecommunications Act of 1996, the court order was lifted.

However, by early 1997 the Bells realized they had missed the significance of the Internet. Only about 3 percent of Americans were connected to the Internet in 1993, but four years later the number had ballooned to 15 percent.[15] The new medium had already captured the imagination of the public; investors were pouring money into any company that seemed to use or benefit from the Web, however that might be defined.[16]

In early 1997, the Bells tried to put the genie back in the bottle. They challenged the FCC's notion that the Bells could not charge anything extra if the customer connected the line to a computer instead of a phone. The Bell lobbyists persuaded the leading voice in the Republican Senate on this topic, Senator Ted Stevens of Alaska, that every e-mail should incur a charge of three or four cents, like a stamp on a letter, with the ISP paying the local Bells for sending the message on locals lines and paying the long-distance company for carrying it between cities.

Stevens thus argued that an e-mail should be treated like a long-distance phone call, with ATT and the local phone company splitting the revenues. If you don't do that, he told me, the economics of the phone system will collapse. You will have ruined the communications industry, he warned, when your job is to preserve it.

At the time, firms such as AOL charged much less for unlimited Internet access plus e-mail than the Bells charged for local phone service. Given that Internet users might spend hours a day browsing websites or sending e-mails, the Stevens position, supported by the incumbent phone companies, would have raised the cost of the Internet to prohibitive levels. It would have crushed all the ISPs and also stifled the growth of the Internet. Even if the new medium survived, the telephone industry would control it under Stevens's proposal. Disruptive competition and innovation would be dashed; some other country's entrepreneurs would create the Web.

AOL was then the leading e-mail provider and Internet service provider. I called the CEO, Steve Case, to the FCC for a meeting. In my office I explained that Senator Stevens was the most powerful person in the Republican Party as far as the FCC was concerned and that the Republicans controlled both Houses of Congress and hence my budget. Stevens's views would be the end of the Internet's already explosive growth, I argued.

Case needed no persuading that Stevens's proposal would stifle the Internet's growth and cause AOL's stock to crash. Steve Case reached out to his customers, causing more than 400,000 e-mails to be sent to Senator Stevens. At that time, members of Congress heard from the public primarily by means of letters, phone calls, and personal visits. The new medium of the Internet increased input by orders of magnitude: a development that was not necessarily welcomed by elected representatives but was certainly noted. That was the first online political campaign in history.

As a result, Senator Stevens and the Bells did not block our designation of the Internet as "enhanced service provision"—a category that exempted ISPs and Web users from paying tolls to the phone companies.

CREATIVE DESTRUCTION

The Senator was not wrong in arguing that the Internet would destroy the economic model of the existing telephone industry. In fact, AT&T and MCI did not survive the disruption; early in the 2000s, Bell companies bought these long-distance firms for a fraction of what they were worth at the time of my meeting in Senator Stevens's office. Nor did Case's firm, AOL, go on to enduring success. At the height of the dot.com market bubble, AOL and Time-Warner merged in a transaction that has justly been regarded as mutually disastrous. AOL is now a shadow of the firm that, celebrated in movies like "You've Got Mail," seemed to define the Internet in the late 1990s. Time-Warner as a cable firm is seeking governmental approval to be divided between Comcast and Charter, cable firms that were its poor cousins in the previous century.

But our strategy was not to promote a single firm; it was the medium we wanted to succeed. The narrowband era of telephone line connections to the Internet led to rapid growth of the new medium. As users and websites proliferated, however, both consumers and content creators demanded higher speeds of connectivity. The cable network seized the opportunity and became the dominant provider of high-speed access—now called "broadband"—in most markets.

Cable had invested in creating large hybrid fiber-coaxial networks to carry hundreds of TV channels. That investment of about $100 billion in the 1990s was in large part a response to the FCC's implementation of the Program Access requirements of the 1992 Cable Act. The FCC had enabled the direct-to-home satellite industry, with its massive capacity to carry channels, to get access to cable-owned content. It also stated that cable companies could increase their retail prices to consumers if they increased the number of channels they offered. These pro-competitive and pro-consumer rules contributed to the industry's decision to build bigger capacity "pipes" to homes. Fortunately from the industry's perspective, the larger pipes were more suitable to carrying larger volumes of Internet traffic than were the comparatively narrow "pipes" of the copper telephone networks. Thus, cable could, and did, become the dominant physical medium for broadband Internet access.

Meanwhile, the Bells, having lost the opportunity to be the nation's leading Internet providers on fixed wires, decided to become primarily wireless, rather than wired, firms. After more than a decade of mergers, two of the regional Bells, Verizon (renamed after Nynex executed a string of mergers) and SBC (renamed AT&T after it bought the formerly dominant long-distance firm in 2004) emerged as the two inheritors of the Bell legacy. They have also become the primary providers of mobile, or wireless, access to the Internet.

These exact outcomes were only dimly imagined in the early 1990s. The Clinton Administration and its FCC had a strategy that focused on one main goal: making sure that the Internet would grow faster than any communications medium in history as a consequence of low prices and great ease of connection. What companies benefitted the most from that revolution was not our concern, and picking such "winners and losers" would have been outside the proper role of government.

Technological advances create forks in the road of history. At such points, government can choose whether to act for the public interest or whether to cede decision making to the most powerful actors in the private sector. In many cases, the latter is wise. But private firms will act in the best interest of their shareholders, and that is not always identical to the long-range best interest of the country as a whole or of the world.

Even when the government wants to advance the public interest by favoring a particular communication medium—or, as is currently necessary, favoring certain types of energy over others—the choices are not easy. Even though the Clinton Administration saw the Internet as the most desirable platform for information exchange, other contestants had cases to make, including digital over-the-air broadcast, cable television, and cellular telephony. Each of these mediums have played a continuing and important role, but all are now part of the larger, more robust and diversified structure of the Internet. That was not obvious two decades ago.

Nor has the Internet proven ideal in all aspects. Its development has raised a number of critical issues, including invasion of privacy and increased vulnerability to serious security breaches. The creative destruction left in its path has rocked many industries. But by choosing to embrace the Internet, the United States chose to move boldly into the future.

If we had not intervened, the astounding story of the Internet might have unfolded more slowly, with much reduced economic benefits. And perhaps some other country's firms and people—with different value systems—might have led in the creation of the Internet economy. I am proud that we chose instead to act in the public interest and to do what we thought was right for the future of the country.

◆ ◆ ◆ ◆ ◆

36. Boom and Busts: Presidents and the Politics of Energy

by Guy Caruso

In the United States the politics of energy are distinctly different from energy policy. The two are aligned at times but not always, as good policies are not always good for politics. In fact, there is often an inherent conflict between good energy policy and the politics of getting elected. Good energy policy requires long-term planning to influence the long lead times needed for effective investments in energy technology and supply. The election cycle is much shorter, and events are seldom cooperative.

A case in point is President Obama's decision to reject approval of a pipeline project carrying Canadian oil to the United States—the Keystone XL pipeline—because it has become a hot-button issue for his constituents in the environmental movement, who have used it as a proxy for the climate change debate. From a strict policy perspective, facilitating more Canadian oil production should have been a no brainer. But politics has interfered in this energy issue—and not just the typical party politics either. Labor unions that typically support Democratic candidates remain strongly supportive of the Keystone project, for instance, but the strong opposition from environmental groups made the president's decision a tough call.

When evaluating energy issues, presidents must consider national security and foreign policy, and the economy, as well as environmental concerns. Prioritizing any of those areas involves making real trade-offs. So far, economic and security concerns have generally trumped environmental objectives, but environmental issues have made the politics of energy increasingly tough going back to the early 1990s when the Rio Convention placed the issue of climate change on President Clinton's desk. Striking the right balance between all of the competing interests is the inherent challenge behind U.S. energy policy.

A GEOPOLITICAL ISSUE

In earlier days, the politics of energy pitted pro-development forces against conservationists. The extraction of fossil fuels such as coal, oil, and natural gas usually won the political battles as states such as Texas, Oklahoma, Louisiana, Pennsylvania, Ohio, and West Virginia successfully opposed federal regulation. President T.R. "Teddy" Roosevelt was the first chief executive to have some success in championing natural resource conservation.

After his election in 1904, Roosevelt also took on big-business interests when he ordered the Department of Justice to investigate the Standard Oil Trust. The investigation led to a successful antitrust suit against the company, which was dissolved in 1911. The Standard Oil case embellished Teddy's reputation as a trustbuster, and represented an early-20th-century version of "Main Street versus Wall Street."

Oil developments during World War II and its aftermath raised energy politics to the geopolitical level. President Franklin D. Roosevelt, wary of a potential shortfall in petroleum supplies to support the war effort, sided with Secretary of the Interior Harold Ickes,[1] giving the Department of the Interior the authority to intervene in the global oil markets through direct purchases of oil, domestic price controls, supply rationing, and domestic production allocation. The role of the U.S. government in energy markets was thereafter primarily linked to interventions in the name of national security.

President Harry S. Truman also could not escape the conundrum of energy politics. In the early 1950s, Iranian oil supplies were disrupted by labor unrest, prompting the Interior Department to form an oil industry advisory group—the Foreign Petroleum Supply Committee (FPSC)—to advise the U.S. government on actions to compensate for the Iranian supply problem. The Committee's advice led to global supply allocations, higher prices, and higher profits for the companies represented on the committee. Under strong congressional pressure, the Federal Trade Commission investigated the actions of the FPSC and recommended that criminal charges be pursued against the companies represented on the committee. President Truman recognized the political sensitivity of his own Department of Interior being involved in the FPSC's actions and chose not to pursue a criminal case. The relationship between the petroleum industry and the U.S. government has required a delicate balancing act ever since, especially during supply disruptions caused by geopolitical developments and/or natural disasters.

For instance, national security concerns related to the fast growth of oil imports led to the establishment of oil import quotas in the mid-1950s. President Eisenhower first tried a voluntary program, but the economics of the global oil markets were too tempting for companies to ignore. At the time Middle East crude oil was selling at under $2 per barrel compared with domestic crude at $3 per barrel, creating a significant arbitrage opportunity. In 1959, President Eisenhower responded with a presidential proclamation establishing mandatory oil import quotas. The decision to impose trade restrictions on oil was a classic political tradeoff between national security and economic efficiency. U.S. consumers paid the higher domestic oil price for fourteen years. The quotas remained in effect until abolished by President Nixon in April 1973 as part of an effort to combat inflation.

SCARCE SUPPLY, HIGH DEMAND

During the past forty years, energy policy has been heavily influenced by three major trends and assumptions: scarce energy supply (forecasts of natural gas supply shortages in the 1970s, for instance, led to legislation banning the use of gas under boilers); steadily rising energy demand, especially oil in the transportation sector as U.S. consumers drove more miles per household and shifted their preferences to larger, more powerful vehicles; and rising dependency on oil imports, often from unstable (and unsavory) areas of the world. Every U.S. president since Richard Nixon, with the possible exception of Ronald Reagan, has shaped his energy policy based on these drivers. Nixon took a strong interest in energy and sent several messages to Congress beginning in 1971 proposing numerous policy initiatives to balance energy security, economic efficiency, and the environment. Nixon's message to Congress was simple: "For most of our history a plentiful supply of energy is something the American people have taken very much for granted."[2] He concluded "we cannot take our energy supply for granted any longer." But Nixon lacked the political power to pass his proposed legislation, and his words proved prophetic when the United States faced an energy crisis in 1973.

The so-called Yom Kippur War between Israel and several Arab neighbors broke out on October 6, 1973. In response to U.S. supply of military equipment to Israel, the Organization of Arab Petroleum Exporting Countries (OAPEC) imposed an oil embargo on the United States, Canada, and the Netherlands, and also reduced overall oil output. Oil prices rose sharply, threatening global economic growth and complicating U.S. energy politics.

In November 1973, President Nixon was already under intense political pressure from the Watergate scandal, and he now faced the prospect of gasoline shortages and an economy headed for recession. In a national address on November 7, 1973, Nixon announced emergency measures and a new initiative designed to mitigate the effects of the embargo. "Let us unite in committing the resources of this nation to a major new endeavor, an endeavor that in this bicentennial era we can appropriately call 'Project Independence.' Let us set as our national goal in the spirit of Apollo, with the determination of the Manhattan Project, that by the end of this decade we will have developed the potential to meet our own energy needs without depending on any foreign energy sources."[3] Nixon's speech gave rise to the political slogan "energy independence," a mantra that would be adopted by every president from Gerald Ford to Barack Obama.

Aware of the political impacts of higher gasoline prices, President Nixon also imposed broad price controls in 1971 as part of an anti-inflation program. Price controls were not fully removed until President Ronald Reagan did so early in 1981. Gasoline price controls were a major contributing factor to the poor allocation of petroleum products during the first energy crisis in 1973–74, and in the aftermath of the Iranian oil disruption in 1979–80. Market solutions to supply disruptions were stymied by energy politics.

Nixon did receive some short-term emergency authority to deal with the shortages, but in his weakened political state no major energy initiatives were passed before his resignation in August 1974. One notable success, however, was passage of legislation authorizing the construction of the Trans-Alaska

Pipeline System. The final vote was so close that the pipeline required a tie-break by then–Vice President Spiro Agnew.

ENERGY CRISIS MENTALITY

President Ford carried on the policy which held that government instruments were the best solution to energy scarcity. In fact, market-based solutions were conspicuously absent from either the Nixon or Ford energy proposals. Ford proposed much bolder government initiatives than Nixon, potentially impacting energy production, consumption, technology, and strategic reserves. Those initiatives were all designed to end by 1985 U.S. vulnerability to economic disruption as a result of dependence on foreign oil.

Facing a difficult election in 1976, however, Ford lacked the political clout to implement all of those initiatives, and he eventually had to settle for much tamer legislation, the Energy Policy and Conservation Act (EPCA), which Ford signed in December 1975. EPCA included authorization for a strategic petroleum reserve, fuel efficiency standards for automobiles, federal assistance to state conservation programs, U.S. participation in the International Energy Agency (IEA), and a broad energy research and development program.[4]

That energy crisis mentality and penchant for strong government intervention continued with Jimmy Carter's administration. He was given authority in 1977 to establish the Department of Energy (DOE), comprising thirty-seven federal entities including the nuclear weapons program and the national laboratory system. President Carter appointed James R. Schlesinger as the first Secretary of Energy. Carter also approved the first National Energy Plan, which "contained a sweeping combination of tax incentives and federal subsidies for preferred fuels and technologies: more coal, less natural gas and oil, more ethanol and solar power. It proposed regulations to mandate energy conservation in automobiles, commercial buildings and homes."[5]

Congress passed legislation giving Carter much of what he requested. The most heated battles were fought over the extension of energy price controls that Carter supported. This issue offered a good example of regional politics versus party politics. Lawmakers from consuming states, regardless of party affiliation, were strongly in favor of continued oil and gas price controls during this period of rampant inflation. The consumers prevailed and price controls remained, although Carter did begin to phase out petroleum price controls before he left office.

After some success in the energy politics wars, Carter was thrust into crisis management during the United States' second energy crisis. Labor unrest in Iran's oilfields during 1978 led to a large production decline from the world's second largest oil exporter (Saudi Arabia was first), and sharp crude oil and gasoline price increases. The Shah of Iran was deposed in February 1979, leading to further foreign policy difficulties for the Carter Administration. The Iranian crisis of 1979–80 was not managed well from a domestic or an international standpoint. The U.S. strategic petroleum reserve was just in its early days of development, and the amount in storage was insufficient and therefore would not be able to bring prices down. The IEA was unable to orchestrate an effective coordinated response, and many members chose to pursue "beggar-thy-neighbor" policies by purchasing crude oil on the spot market, driving the price of crude oil up from $11 per barrel to more than $40 per barrel. This was not good news for a Carter Administration actively trying to combat soaring inflation.

Once again the ability to efficiently manage distribution of gasoline and other petroleum products was hampered by price controls. The Iranian hostage crisis further damaged the Carter Administration's political prospects, and the American public rejected Carter's reelection bid in 1980.

SHIFT TO MARKET SOLUTIONS

President Ronald Reagan brought a clear shift in energy policy in his movement away from government intervention in the marketplace. In a largely symbolic move, Reagan issued an executive order right after his inauguration, fully decontrolling oil prices. Carter had already started a process that would have removed price controls by September 1980. Nevertheless Reagan's quick action sent a clear signal that market solutions were now favored in energy policy.

Reagan's attention on energy policy shifted away from the domestic front to geopolitical concerns over the Soviet Union's sales of natural gas to Europe. Reagan was concerned about our European allies' dependence on Soviet gas for two reasons: Europe's heavy dependence on the Soviets would weaken the transatlantic alliance, and earn much needed foreign exchange revenue that the Soviets could spend on their vast military arsenal. Reagan achieved some success under the auspices of the IEA when he convinced European members to limit their dependence on Soviet gas to 30 percent of their total supplies.

George H.W. Bush continued to support policies that favored market solutions, but discovered that they also came with a downside, especially when it came to geopolitical events. The third energy crisis in seventeen years was kicked off by Saddam Hussein's invasion of Kuwait in early August 1990, with Iraqi forces quickly taking control of Kuwait's oilfields. Bush quickly marshalled a coalition under United Nations auspices and successfully prevented Iraqi forces from entering Saudi Arabia and disrupting a much larger share of world oil exports. The blockage of Iraqi and Kuwaiti oil exports to the world oil market sent prices soaring once again, however, contributing to higher inflation and a subsequent U.S. recession.

President Bush initially made the policy decision in September 1990 not to draw oil from the Strategic Petroleum Reserve (SPR) as recommended by Secretary of Energy James Watkins. Bush's economic advisers at Treasury, Office of Management and Budget, and the Council of Economic Advisors all insisted that letting prices rise demonstrated that markets were working smoothly and that releasing the SPR would amount to an unwarranted government intervention in the market.[6] Ultimately Bush agreed to an IEA decision to release strategic oil stocks in coordination with coalition airstrikes on Iraqi forces in mid-January 1991. Iraq's quick capitulation and inability to threaten further oil supplies led to oil prices plummeting immediately. Nevertheless, the economic damage to the U.S. economy was done. A weak economy in 1991 and a slow recovery in 1992 were important factors in Bush's 1992 election loss to Bill Clinton. One of Clinton's most effective campaign sound bites was "It's the economy, Stupid."

President Clinton came to office with an activist policy agenda, and, along with Vice President Al Gore, he was closely aligned with the environmental community. Early in 1993, the Clinton Administration supported a proposal for a broad based energy tax designed both to discourage fossil fuel use and to limit greenhouse gas emissions as recommended by the Rio Summit of 1990. Clinton sorely underestimated the bipartisan aversion to taxes, however, and he quickly realized this was a political fight he could not win. The energy tax proposal was dropped. Clinton generally benefitted from a period of relatively low oil prices during his two terms in office, however, which enabled him to put energy issues on the back burner.

George W. Bush brought to the presidency a firsthand knowledge of the energy industry from his father's business endeavors and from governing Texas, the largest oil-producing state. Vice President Dick Cheney took the lead in developing a comprehensive National Energy Plan, released in May 2001. The plan contained dozens of comprehensive energy policy recommendations, many of which required legislative action. Unfortunately energy policy was pushed aside by the terrorist attacks of September 11, 2001.

CRISIS MANAGEMENT AGAIN

Energy policy was dominated by crisis management in Bush 43's first term. Venezuelan oil supplies were severely disrupted beginning in December 2002 as oil workers protested against Socialist President Hugo Chavez. President Bush chose not to utilize the SPR, leaning instead toward markets and suppliers such as Saudi Arabia to fill in the shortfall. Oil prices rose steadily throughout 2003, especially after the U.S. invasion of Iraq in 2003 shut down that country's considerable oil exports.

A good example of the complexity of balancing energy, environmental, macroeconomic, and national security policies and goals is the biofuels mandate. Bush 43 supported expanded use of ethanol as a component of the gasoline supply as a way to mitigate the country's growing dependence on energy imports. Congress passed strong legislation in 2005 and again in 2007 supporting ethanol produced mainly from corn. The legislation had little impact on domestic fuel prices, however, and by the summer of 2008, crude oil and gasoline prices were at historically peak levels. The strong demand for corn also had the unintended consequence of raising food prices.

President Barack Obama's campaign in 2008 carried a strong energy message based on the prospect of scarce supplies of oil and natural gas and high energy prices. Obama proposed an ambitious transformation away from fossil fuels toward alternative energy supplies such as renewable energy (wind, solar, biomass, etc.). He also strongly emphasized energy efficiency and sharp reductions in greenhouse gas emissions as a way to address climate change concerns. By Election Day, however, the Great Recession had reduced energy demand and exerted strong downward pressure on energy prices. Once again, energy policy was thrown onto the back burner.

A sudden reversal of U.S. energy fortunes—declining demand and growing U.S. production—prompted a reevaluation of venerable energy policies in Obama's second term. Obama's dilemma on energy policy has thus been unique among presidents. The reality of energy scarcity, steadily rising demand, and increasing energy import dependence has been turned on its head, and energy prices have fallen considerably as a result.

So, why is President Obama not smiling? Because U.S. energy resurgence has created a policy dilemma. Obama has struggled to realize the energy and environment goals he laid out in the 2008 campaign. U.S. fossil fuel technology innovations such as hydraulic fracturing have postponed the hoped for transition to alternative fuels. As a result, Obama's climate change goals and those of the environment community will be more difficult to achieve. Obama has tried to balance the good news of more abundant U.S. sources of fossil fuel energy with his vision for the environment. He, like most presidents before him, has struggled to balance the politics of energy and sound energy policy. At times it has left him, like so many of his presidential predecessors, straddling the fence.

BIBLIOGRAPHY

Goodwin, Craufurd D. *Energy Policy in Perspective: Today's Problems, Yesterday's Solutions.* Washington, DC: Brookings Institution, 1981.

Stagliano, Vito A. *A Policy of Discontent: The Making of a National Energy Strategy.* Tulsa: PennWell, 2001.

Yergin, Daniel. *The Prize: The Epic Quest for Oil, Money & Power.* New York: Simon & Schuster, 1991.

◆ ◆ ◆ ◆ ◆

37. Depression's Shadow: Managing the Great Recession

by Edwin M. Truman

The Great Recession and global financial crisis posed the largest test of presidential economic leadership since the Great Depression of the 1930s. In fact, only determined policy action prevented a repeat. Future historians gleaning lessons from the recent Great Recession will undoubtedly note the impressive policy continuity of the George W. Bush and Barack H. Obama Administrations and the political protection they offered to those implementing controversial and imaginative policies; the degree to which both White Houses became deeply enmeshed in financial system issues; and the U.S.-led global crisis responses that had a lasting impact on the international financial architecture.

SEEDS OF DISRUPTION

The origins of the recession and financial crisis can be traced in part to the U.S. housing and housing finance markets. U.S. residential construction peaked in the third quarter of 2005, but its tapering off after that year was not enough to explain the economic downturn that later followed. Henry M. "Hank" Paulson, Jr. was sworn in as the 74th U.S. Secretary of the Treasury on July 10, 2006. Paulson quickly told Bush and his other economic advisers in August 2006 that the administration's main economic goal should be "crisis prevention." He "was convinced we were due for another disruption."[1]

The subprime mortgage market experienced increased turbulence in early 2007, but the Treasury and the Federal Reserve said that the situation was "largely contained." The first major event signaling a broader financial crisis occurred in Europe, not in the United States. On August 9, the French bank BNP Paribas suspended withdrawals from three investment funds holding U.S. subprime-backed securities. The Federal Reserve, under Chairman Ben Bernanke, and in concert with the central banks of other advanced economies, took the lead in responding through conventional monetary policy measures such as reducing interest rates and liberalizing access to central bank liquidity.

By the end of 2007, the full fury of the brewing crisis was still obscure. The National Bureau of Economic Research (NBER) would eventually establish that the recession started in December 2007, and lasted eighteen months, longer than any since the Great Depression.[2]

In early 2008, the Bush White House saw a need for fiscal stimulus even though the Council of Economic Advisors (CEA) was not forecasting a recession.[3] The Bush legislative package included tax cuts and rebates and assistance for the housing market. Then in March, the investment bank Bear Stearns was rescued via a sale to JP Morgan Chase, with extraordinary assistance from the Federal Reserve. Despite the White House's visceral aversion to financial bailouts, the administration backed the plan.

Financial markets and the economy continued to deteriorate during the spring and summer of 2008. Concerns focused on the viability of the Federal National Mortgage Association (Fannie Mae) and the Federal Home Loan Mortgage Corporation (Freddie Mac). After a protracted internal debate, the administration proposed, and Congress passed, the Housing and Economic Recovery Act (HERA). On signing the bill, Bush noted that he did so only on the Treasury Secretary's strong recommendation. HERA authorized the Treasury to advance funds to Fannie and/or Freddie. On September 6, less than six weeks later, it did so. The mounting concerns of other countries clearly affected Treasury Secretary Paulson's aggressive actions.

Lehman Brothers was the next shoe to drop, just as political opposition to government bailouts was rising. Josh Bolten, Bush's chief of staff, had informed Paulson that he had presidential approval to "wind-down" Lehman without using federal resources. If government resources were needed, Paulson was told he would have to come back to the president for approval. Lehman could not find a domestic or foreign buyer, the already-reeling banking community could not come to its rescue, and the U.S. government (Treasury and Federal Reserve) concluded that they did not have the legal authority to act to save Lehman Brothers. No one foresaw, however, the full impact Lehman's failure would have on the domestic and global financial systems.

GLOBAL PANIC

The panic was on. The failure of Lehman ignited a firestorm of negative reaction. International and domestic markets were in turmoil. Within forty-eight hours, the Federal Reserve decided it had to rescue the global insurance giant American International Group (AIG) and its subsidiary AIG Financial Products. Bush chaired a meeting of the President's Working Group on Financial Markets (PWG) that discussed the AIG situation on the day it was rescued.[4] By that time, Bush had told Paulson to do whatever was necessary.

Two days later, at Bernanke's strong personal urging, Bush chaired another White House meeting at which it was decided that the U.S. government needed more resources to deal with the rapidly escalating crisis. The administration asked Congress for the legislation that evolved into the $700 billion Troubled Asset Relief Program (TARP), formally called the Emergency Economic Stabilization Act. It was originally designed primarily to purchase illiquid mortgage-backed securities, but was later transformed into a program to give capital support to financial institutions and other programs.

The potential collapse of the financial system had by then overridden Bush's reluctance to intervene. "If we are in the midst of a financial meltdown, all I'm asking is whether it will work," said Bush, who added, "We don't have time to worry about politics." The administration needed to figure out what was the right thing to do, Bush told Paulson, and let the Congress know that it needed to act.

On September 24, 2008, Bush delivered a presidential address to the nation from the White House laying out the origins of the crisis and the need for the TARP legislation. During this fraught period when Congress debated passage of the TARP legislation, presidential candidate Barack Obama embraced the administration-backed measure and lobbied his Senate colleagues for their support. The Republican ticket of Senator John McCain and Alaskan Governor Sarah Palin equivocated. The TARP legislation passed Congress on October 3 on its second try. TARP was used to inject capital into major financial institutions, and Bush also blessed the Federal Deposit Insurance Corporation's use of its power under exceptional circumstances to guarantee the new debt of banks and bank holding companies.

Meanwhile, the financial crisis was sweeping through world financial markets like a flash fire. Because the network of normal international funding relationships was paralyzed, government bailouts were necessary, and associated moral hazard concerns about distorting future behavior were, for the moment, set aside. On October 10, the Group of Seven (G7) finance ministers and central bank governors met in Washington and issued a short statement. The first point was agreement to "take decisive action and use all available tools to support systemically important financial institutions and prevent their failure."[5]

On November 14–15, after the U.S. election, Bush hosted the first Group of Twenty (G20) leaders' summit in Washington. He had brushed aside proposals for an earlier meeting and also for a meeting that would be restricted to the leaders of the G7 major industrialized countries and a few ad hoc invited leaders. Instead, he chose to build on the existing G20 structure of meetings of finance ministers and central bank governors. The G20 summit attendees agreed on a shared commitment to economic and financial stabilization, the avoidance of protectionist measures, a strengthening of official international financial institutions, and a thorough agenda of financial reform.

OBAMA'S TURN

President-elect Obama put in an appearance at the G20 summit, but he limited direct public engagement with the Bush Administration's ongoing crisis management team. However, Josh Bolten and Rahm Emanuel, the outgoing and incoming chiefs of staff, were in frequent contact. Bush told Obama that he would not dump the problem of the failing automakers on him, and the Obama team implicitly endorsed the eventual use of the TARP to support the industry. Incoming Director of the National Economic Council Lawrence "Larry" Summers wrote to President Bush and asked him to seek congressional approval to release the second, $350 billion tranche of the TARP, which was received on January 15, 2009.[6]

Lee Sachs headed the Obama transition team's liaison with the Treasury Department. During the transition, the Treasury acted further to stabilize Citigroup and AIG, and Bank of America's purchase of Merrill Lynch was completed. On November 25, the Federal Open Market Committee announced it would begin the first of what in the end were three rounds of large-scale asset purchases (popularly known as quantitative easing).

Obama and Summers, his principal economic adviser, assembled an experienced staff that included David Lipton, Diana Farrell, and Mary Goodman, and they worked closely on financial system issues with Lee Sachs at Treasury. Christina Romer became Chair of the Council of Economic Advisers, and Austan Goolsbee, a long-time economic advisor to Obama, was a member. Paul A. Volcker was recruited to head the Economic Recovery Advisory Board. Treasury Secretary Timothy Geithner provided continuity, having previously served as president of the Federal Reserve Bank of New York. He was the only Senate-confirmed official at the U.S. Treasury for months, and thus had to rely on appointed counselors and a few holdovers from the Paulson Treasury.

The Obama Administration embraced the view that to fix the broader economy, the financial system first had to be fixed. Obama came into office in the depths of the recession, but its scale was still largely unknown at the time.

The administration's first legislative priority was economic recovery and passage of the American Recovery and Reinvestment Act (ARRA). The challenge was to propose a sufficiently large package of economic stimulus measures to do the job and that a balky Congress would pass. Romer wanted a much bigger package than the $800 billion that was finally settled on. The ARRA passed the House with no Republican support. Even after the legislation was scaled back and recalibrated, only three Republican senators supported it. Today, many say they regret that the stimulus package was too small and too back-loaded, but it was the most ambitious package that could get passed at the time.

The U.S. financial system competed with the needs of the overall economy for White House attention. The willingness to try new approaches was strong within the Obama Administration, but the only available tools were those left by the Bush Administration, principally the TARP and Federal Reserve powers.

THE OBAMA PLAN

On February 10, 2009, Secretary Geithner unveiled the administration's Financial Stability Plan. In his words, the Plan involved "fundamentally reshaping the government's program to repair the financial system." He pledged "to prevent the catastrophic failure of [U.S.] financial institutions that would damage the broader economy." The plan had four components. The first was comprehensive stress tests to determine the needs of major U.S. financial institutions for additional capital to meet the risks on their balance sheets under three downside scenarios. If they could not raise the needed capital on the market, the Treasury would supply it via the TARP.

Second, a Public-Private Investment Program (PPIP) was designed to remove troubled legacy assets from bank balance sheets. Third, the Term Asset-Backed-Securities Loan Facility (TALF) was expanded to include consumer and business lending. The framework for this program involved equity provided by the TARP and liquidity provided by the Federal Reserve. It was announced in November 2008 but was not fully operational until March 2009. Finally, a comprehensive housing program was promised, although there would be many such programs during Obama's tenure with limited overall impact.

The results of the stress tests (technically the Supervisory Capital Assessment Program, or SCAP) of nineteen major banking organizations were not available until May 7, 2009, which seemed an eternity to the political staff. While the stress tests were underway, the policy focus shifted to how to manage the institutions that might be found to have capital shortfalls and whether those decisions should be taken before the stress-test results were available. Some officials, including Summers, argued for establishing a bright line for dealing with institutions with insufficient capital, such as prospectively Citigroup. His view was that the government should intervene and wind down such banks and financial institutions, even though the government lacked a mechanism for doing so. Winding down a large international financial institution also risked the type of catastrophic failure the administration had pledged to avoid and could consume a significant amount of TARP funds. Geithner and others argued for staying the course and seeing what the stress tests revealed before making any binding decisions that might leave the government as a majority owner of some banks. President Obama supported the Geithner view. Thus, the results of the stress test would dictate how best to use the limited funds remaining in the TARP.[7]

The stress tests revealed a need to raise more capital than the banks as a group had assembled in the run-up to the crisis. However, the visibility the stress tests provided about the banks' reasonably sound underlying financial condition allowed most of them to raise sufficient capital in the market, and only a few of them required further TARP funds.

A popular perception grew that TARP and other actions were designed to "save Wall Street," the alleged perpetrators of the financial crisis, while ignoring Main Street, the victims of the resulting economic meltdown. That prevailing populism was aggravated when the rescued institutions continued to pay large bonuses to their top people. Both the Bush and Obama Administrations, however, saw stabilizing the financial system as a key ingredient for restoring growth to the Main Street economy, even though both administrations failed to convince a skeptical public. The *Economic Report of the President*, prepared under the direction of Romer, devoted two pages to the links between the Wall Street and Main Street economies, with little apparent influence on the public debate. Geithner lamented this failure when he wrote in his memoir: "We did save the economy, but we lost the country doing it."

GLOBAL FINANCIAL SYSTEM

The new Obama Administration did not concentrate exclusively on the U.S. domestic economy and financial system. They also designed and then pressed for the adoption of concrete initiatives at the second G20 economic summit in London on April 2, 2009, Obama's first foray into international diplomacy.

The London meeting produced a joint pledge to use fiscal and monetary policies to revive the global economy. Financial support for the global economic revival was to be provided through a commitment of $1.1 trillion in additional resources for international financial institutions and in support of global trade. A framework for strengthening the supervision and regulation of the global financial system was also agreed upon. Membership in the Financial Stability Forum was expanded to include all the G20 countries and was rechristened the Financial Stability Board (FSB), which had a broader set of responsibilities. A commitment was also made to reforming the governance of the International Monetary Fund (IMF) and the World Bank and to adding to the resources of those organizations and the other multilateral development banks.

The Obama Administration supported the decisions made in London by obtaining congressional approval for an enlarged U.S. commitment to the New Arrangements to Borrow (NAB) by July 2009.[8] The administration also agreed to host the third G20 summit within twelve months in Pittsburgh in September 2009, and at that meeting to advance IMF governance reform by increasing the voices and votes of dynamic emerging-market and developing countries. The Pittsburgh meeting also cemented the status of G20 summits by designating "the G20 to be the premier forum for our international economic cooperation" and by laying out a framework to achieve strong, sustainable, and balanced growth in the world economy.

U.S. financial markets bottomed out in early March 2009, and the U.S. recession ended in June 2009. By the end of 2013, the various financial rescue programs of the U.S. government, including the Federal Reserve and the FDIC, were estimated to have actually turned a modest profit of $166 billion, although that was obviously not their primary purpose.

Perhaps the economy would have recovered faster if the U.S. government had been more ambitious in its bailouts and rescue programs. Were the U.S. government's interventions in the economy and financial system too massive, contributing to future inflation and an increase in moral hazard risks, or insufficient, contributing to a lackluster recovery? Historians and economists will debate the issue for decades.

GREAT DEPRESSION AVOIDED

While history's judgment of the Bush and Obama Administrations' response to the Great Recession waits, the immediate record shows that a repeat of the

Great Depression was averted. Recognizing the tremendous scope of the threat to the economy and the financial system writ large, both presidents reached deep into the fiscal toolbox and used extraordinary measures, to include a massive fiscal stimulus from the American Recovery and Reinvestment Act; both conventional and unconventional monetary policy actions by the Federal Reserve; a commitment to avoid failure of any systemic financial institution after the Lehman bankruptcy; the Federal Deposit Insurance Corporation's use of its power to guarantee the new debt of banks and bank holding companies; the stress tests of major U.S. financial institutions; a Financial Stability Plan that included an expanded Term Asset-Backed-Securities Loan Facility; and U.S. designed and supported initiatives to revive the global economy.

Despite differences in emphasis, organization, and style, the Bush and Obama White Houses and the Paulson and Geithner Treasuries displayed a remarkable degree of continuity in their approaches and policies. Both presidents not only deferred to their expert advisers—led by Hank Paulson under Bush, and Tim Geithner and Larry Summers, under Obama—but also provided them with substantial political protection.

Both White Houses also became deeply engaged in the rescue not only of the U.S. economy but also of the U.S. financial system, including through the support of individual markets and financial institutions. The policies of both administrations also transformed the international financial architecture, including through the establishment of the Financial Stability Board; increasing the seats around consultative tables such as the G20; and expanded global financial cooperation. Only history can judge whether those steps are sufficient to avoid a future Great Recession, but they clearly prevented the 2008 financial crisis from collapsing into a Great Depression, and for that both George W. Bush and Barack Obama deserve credit.

BIBLIOGRAPHY

Bush, George W. *Decision Points.* New York: Crown Publishers, 2010.

Economic Report of the President (ERP). Washington, DC: U.S. Government Printing Office, 2010.

Geithner, Timothy F. *Stress Test: Reflections on Financial Crises.* New York: Crown Publishers, 2014.

Geithner, Timothy F. Financial Stability Plan. Remarks prepared for delivery, February 10, 2009. Available at http://money.cnn.com /2009/02/10/news/economy/geithner_remarks/?postversion =200902011.

Paulson, Henry M. Jr. *On the Brink: The Race to Stop the Collapse of the Global Financial System*. New York: Business Plus, 2010.

◆ ◆ ◆ ◆ ◆

38. Green Eye Shades in the Oval Office: Presidents and Budgets

by Stanley E. Collender

The president has a surprisingly limited formal role in developing the federal budget each year. First, he or she is legally[1] required to formulate a budget that is supposed to be submitted to Congress between the first Monday in January and the first Monday in February. The president's budget is not, however, binding in any way, and Congress is free to accept or (and far more likely in recent years) reject it in whole or in part.

Second, with limited exceptions,[2] the U.S. Constitution requires the president either to sign or veto the spending and taxing legislation that implements the budget Congress adopts.

Everything that happens inbetween the submission of the president's budget and the passage of the spending and revenue changes assumed in a congressional budget is legally Congress's responsibility.

In practice, however, the president's role in federal budgeting is far larger than just initiating and ending the process. Even in years when Congress doesn't carry out its responsibilities by adopting a budget resolution and there is little implementation legislation to be signed or vetoed (as has largely been the case over the past decade), the president typically plays a far greater informal role in virtually every aspect of spending and revenue policy making than the laws specify.

The White House is heavily involved in detailed discussions with lawmakers, for instance, on all spending, revenues, and debt-related legislation considered in the House and Senate. In one way or another, the president thus plays a much larger day-to-day role in federal budgeting than is apparent in a simple reading of the budget laws.

THE PRESIDENT'S ROLE IN BUDGETING

The word "budget" doesn't appear in the U.S. Constitution. Neither is there any mention of the process the president and Congress must follow to put a budget together. The Constitution does state[3] that only appropriations "made by law" may be drawn from the U.S. Treasury and that a regular statement and account of the receipts and expenditures of all public money must be published from time to time. It also gives Congress the power to determine "taxes, duties, imposts and excises and to pay the government's debts," as well as the authority "to borrow money on the credit of the United States."[4]

But the Constitution doesn't require the president or Congress to produce an annual budget and no procedure is specified by which a budget is to be formulated or considered. Instead, budgets and budgetary procedures are required by statute.

There actually was no requirement for an annual presidential budget until President Warren Harding signed the General Accounting Act (more commonly called the Budget and Accounting Act) into law in 1921.[5] Among many other things, including the creation of the Bureau of the Budget[6] and the General Accounting Office (GAO),[7] that law required the White House to compile the spending requests from the various federal departments and agencies (which until that time had sent their proposals directly to Capitol Hill), establish priorities, and send everything to Congress to consider. This was the first time all federal spending and revenues were available for all to see, and the procedure gave the White House enormous visibility and influence over budget matters.

Congress wasn't required[8] to develop its own annual budget until the Congressional Budget and Impoundment Control Act was enacted in 1974.[9]

The president was preeminent in federal budgeting in the fifty-five years between when these two laws went into effect: he proposed a budget and got a great deal of (usually positive) attention for doing so. The president's budget typically was the lead story on the evening news and the country's major newspapers all devoted multipage spreads to it the day after it was released.

In addition, until 1976[10] there was no congressional budget to compete with what the president proposed, so the White House's seemingly coordinated and harmonized plan was front and center. Congress never voted on total spending and revenues and never had to go on record approving or disapproving the deficit or surplus. Indeed, Congress had no procedure for determining fiscal policy and thus had to wait for an executive branch agency or department—usually either the Office of Management and Budget or the U.S. Treasury—to provide it with estimates, projections, and results.

The percentage of the budget Congress actually had to vote on and approve each year kept shrinking during this fifty-five-year period. An increasing percentage of federal spending was enacted as "mandatory"[11] and didn't require annual appropriations, and only the proposed or expiring changes to the tax code had to be reapproved. That meant that Congress focused on a declining percentage of the federal budget pie and received far less attention when it did so.

The president's preeminence in federal budgeting began to erode with the Congressional Budget and Impoundment Control Act. The law, which was enacted in 1974 but was under consideration for the two years before, was prompted in large part by President Richard Nixon's heavy-handed treatment of Congress on budget matters. It created a requirement for an annual congressional budget, established the Congressional Budget Office as the legislative branch's analog to the Office of Management and Budget, and created the House and Senate Budget Committees to develop the budget resolution that included all federal spending and revenues and an estimate of the deficit (or surplus) and debt.

The act also created a process with multiple highly visible steps through which the House and Senate were supposed to develop and adopt a congressional budget. There was to be a "concurrent resolution," a form of legislation that does not become law, does not have to be signed by the president to go into effect and, therefore, cannot be vetoed.[12]

That meant that Congress finally had a way to develop its own budget. The budget resolution was supposed to be the congressional equivalent of the presidential budget, although it was far less detailed[13] than what the White House submitted earlier in the year.[14]

Not only did this give Congress a prominent role in federal budgeting that it didn't have before, it also weakened the importance of what the president submitted. The fight over the congressional budget resolution often took center stage in the years that followed the enactment of the Congressional Budget and Impoundment Control Act. In many years, the president's budget was even dismissed out of hand and declared "dead on arrival" in Congress.[15]

NEVER DEAD ON ARRIVAL

Regardless of the rhetoric or the passion with which members of Congress and talk-show radio hosts speak the words, for several reasons the president's budget is never really dead on arrival. To the contrary, it's as important as ever.

First, Congress simply doesn't have the staff or time needed to review every line item in the president's budget in detail. As a result, Congress eventually accepts what the president proposes without much change.

Second, much of what the president proposes involves agency operations that are largely noncontroversial. These "nuts and bolts" decisions are seldom worth criticizing by a member of Congress because there is little media or voter interest in them. As a result, they get little attention.

Third, Social Security, Medicare, Medicaid, and other mandatory programs, as well as interest on the national debt and most of the tax code, don't require an annual review. The president's budget calculates the spending and revenue for these programs based on existing law and economic forecasts, plus any changes the White House is then proposing. Congress then most often focuses just on the recommended changes. About 70 percent of the federal budget now falls into this mandatory category, meaning that, with relatively small variations, the president's budget effectively determines how much gets spent and taxed on what.

This continued presidential preeminence on the federal budget doesn't even take into account many of the informal ways the executive branch influences congressional spending and taxing decisions. For example, Congress relies heavily on the executive branch agencies and departments to send details each year when the president's budget is released. These documents, which are often referred to as "justification books," are the in-the-weeds minutiae that congressional committees depend on to draft their bills. This gives the White House enormous influence on agency budgets that is largely hidden from view.

Cabinet and subcabinet officials also frequently testify before Congress each year on what the president is requesting. Although the appearances often are not always pleasant for the officials who are testifying, being able to deliver the administration's messages on the budget request represents a significant advantage for the president.

Cabinet and subcabinet officials ultimately have the responsibility of implementing the budget legislation that is enacted. They will, therefore, have a significant impact on how the money is actually spent and the revenue collected. This provides additional incentives for Congress to work with the executive branch on all budgeting questions. That's especially the case when, as often happens, the directives that come from the House and Senate about how appropriations are to be spent vary.

PRESIDENTIAL BUDGETARY CLOUT

While it's certainly true that Congress has taken a more aggressive stance in recent years and has the ability to deny resources to the White House, in reality nothing much has changed. Unless there is a two-thirds majority in both the House and Senate willing to override a veto or the president is unwilling to use the veto power given to him by the U.S. Constitution, little happens on budget issues without the president's direct and indirect involvement and agreement. The president's legally required involvement at the start and end, plus the ability to participate at all other stages, makes him or her by far the most significant player in the budget process.

In some ways the president's significance to the federal budgeting process actually has grown in recent years. For example, the government shutdown in 2013 revealed once again that it is the president rather than Congress that determines which federal agencies and departments, or parts of federal agencies and departments, are "essential" and will continue to operate even when there is no appropriation. During the shutdowns of 1995–96 and 2013, it was the president who made changes to this list when the White House determined it was necessary.[16]

And it's the president's Office of Management and Budget that makes the official determination on how a provision Congress has adopted will be "scored," that is, how much it will cost or save or how much revenue will be increased or lost. That means it is the president and Office of Management and Budget rather than the Congressional Budget Office that determines whether spending caps and other budget process requirements have been met.

One of the most influential presidential powers on spending and taxing continues to be the ability to garner public support for his or her position. Not all presidents use this power well, and some fail to use it at all. But Congress can seldom compete when a president effectively uses her or his capacity to persuade on budget issues.[17]

A SHIFTING BALANCE

The future could bring a substantial change in the relative positions of Congress and the president on the budget. A two-thirds majority in both houses willing to override a veto will immediately enhance Congress's power on all spending and taxing issues. That change would only continue as long as the supermajority existed, but it would be dramatic while it lasted.

A similar change could occur if a new law were passed that reduced or eliminated much of the president's involvement in the budget. It could, for example, do away with the requirement that the president submit an annual budget, assuming that Congress would override the almost inevitable veto, and that too would also dramatically alter the federal budget landscape.

But absent that significant a change, the current presidential preeminence on virtually everything having to do with the federal budget will continue.

◆ ◆ ◆ ◆ ◆

39. Waging Financial Warfare: Economic Sanctions That Work

by Juan C. Zarate

Since September 11, 2001, the United States has waged a new brand of financial warfare, unprecedented in its reach and effectiveness.[1] This "hidden war" has often been underestimated or misunderstood, but it is no longer secret and has since become central to America's national security doctrine under Presidents George W. Bush and Barack Obama. In a series of campaigns of financial pressure, the United States has economically squeezed and isolated its principal adversaries of this period—al-Qaeda, North Korea, Iran, Iraq, Syria, and Russia. Far from relying solely on the classic sanctions or trade embargoes of old, these campaigns have consisted of a novel set of strategies that harness international financial and commercial systems to ostracize rogue actors and constrict their funding flows, inflicting real pain. America's enemies have realized they have been hit with a new breed of economic power. And they have felt the painful effects.

Al-Qaeda has found it harder, costlier, and riskier to raise and move money around the world, for instance, and it has been forced to find new ways to raise capital for its movement. The documents found in Osama bin Laden's compound in Abbottabad, Pakistan, reflect a terrorist leader and movement in search of new sources of money. Nor was this money squeeze a new development—from 9/11 on, the movement struggled to maintain its core financing. In statement after statement—intended for donors and sometimes only for internal consumption—al-Qaeda admitted that it has been choked financially. In a letter dated July 9, 2005, to Abu Musab al-Zarqawi, leader of al-Qaeda in Iraq, Ayman al-Zawahiri, then al-Qaeda's number two, asked for money, noting that "many of the lines [of financial assistance] have been cutoff."[2]

The campaign against North Korea also had a direct and immediate impact. In the wake of financial pressure unlike any the regime had seen during decades under international sanctions, North Korea found its bank accounts and illicit financial activity in jeopardy. A North Korean deputy negotiator at the time quietly admitted to a senior White House official, "You finally found a way to hurt us."[3]

The Iranians, too, have suffered the economic effects of a targeted financial assault. On September 14, 2010, former Iranian President Akbar Hashemi Rafsanjani urged the Iranian Assembly of Experts to take seriously the painful sanctions and financial pressure being imposed by the United States and the international community. "Throughout the revolution," he said, "we never had so many sanctions [imposed on Iran] and I am calling on you and all officials to take the sanctions seriously and not as jokes. . . . Over the past 30 years we had a war and military threats, but never have we seen such arrogance to plan a calculated assault against us."[4]

The journalist Moisés Naím has opined that the financial pressures on Iran "are biting, the sanctions are very, very powerful. They are the most sophisticated economic and financial sanctions imposed on a country ever."[5]

BLUEPRINT FOR FINANCIAL WARFARE

All of these assaults against America's enemies derive from a blueprint for financial warfare developed by the United States in the wake of the September 11, 2001, terrorist attacks. This is warfare defined by the use of financial tools, pressure, and market forces to leverage the banking sector, private-sector interests, and foreign partners to isolate rogue actors from international financial and commercial systems and eliminate their funding sources. It redefined the very nature of financial warfare.

These capabilities—which fall somewhere between coercive diplomacy and kinetic warfare—would increasingly become the tools of choice for the most difficult international security issues facing the United States. Now the United States can call on these techniques to confront its most critical national security threats, from terrorist groups and international criminals to rogue states such as North Korea and Iran.

After September 11, 2001, the U.S. Treasury Department waged an all-out offensive, using every tool in its toolbox to disrupt, dismantle, and deter the flows of illicit financing around the world. The "smart" sanctions of the late 1990s that had targeted rogue leaders and the entities they controlled were now put on steroids to target the al-Qaeda and Taliban networks and anyone providing financial support to any part of those networks.

Three primary themes defined this post-9/11 campaign: the expansion of the international anti–money-laundering regime; the development of unique financial and intelligence gathering tools geared specifically to dealing with broad national security issues; and the growth of strategies based on a new understanding of the centrality of both the international financial system and the private sector in terms of financing transnational threats. This campaign of financial pressure reshaped the ways in which key actors—namely, the banks—operated in the post-9/11 world.

Reliance on the anti–money-laundering regime permitted an all-out campaign to ensure that funds intended for terrorist groups such as al-Qaeda were not coursing through the veins of the international financial system. This focus reshaped the international financial landscape forever, presenting a new paradigm that governments could use to attack terrorists, criminals, and rogue states. It was a paradigm rooted in denying rogue financial actors access to the international financial system by leveraging the private sector's aversion to doing business with terrorists.

In this context, governments implemented and expanded global anti–money-laundering regulations and practices based on principles of financial transparency, information sharing, and due diligence. They applied new reporting and information-sharing principles to new sectors of the domestic and international financial community, to include insurance companies, dealers and brokers in precious metals and stones, money-service businesses, and *hawaladars* (*hawala* is a trust-based money transfer mechanism often used by terrorist organizations).

This approach worked by focusing squarely on the behavior of financial institutions rather than on the classical framework of past sanctions. It recognizes that the policy decisions of governments are not nearly as persuasive as the risk-based calculus of financial institutions. For banks, wire services, and insurance companies, the rewards of facilitating illicit transactions were suddenly outweighed by the risks—reputational and regulatory—that such illegal actions would be uncovered.

Because of these new strategies, the chance of exposure grew dramatically for rogue actors who try to use the financial system to launder money, finance terrorism, underwrite proliferation networks, or evade sanctions. They could be denied access by the financial community itself. And the sanctions are based on the conduct of the rogues themselves, rather than on the political decisions of governments. It is the illicit or suspicious behavior of the actors themselves as they try to access the international financial system that triggers their isolation.

Such an approach was only possible because of the unique international environment that existed after September 11, 2001. The international landscape after the terrorist attacks allowed for amplified and accelerated use of financial tools, suasion, and warfare to attack asymmetric and transnational threats.

A GLOBAL FINANCIAL SYSTEM

The 21st-century economy is defined by globalization and the deep interconnectedness of the financial system—as seen in the contagion of financial crises like the Great Recession of 2008. The United States has remained the world's primary financial hub, with inherent value embedded in the simple access to the American financial system. In that system, the dollar serves as the global reserve currency and the currency of choice for international trade, and New York has remained a core financial capital and hub for dollar-clearing transactions. With this concentration of financial and commercial power comes the ability to use access to American markets, American banks, and American dollars as a financial weapon. The tools the United States applied to tracking and disrupting illicit financial flows—in particular, terrorist financing—were given greater muscle and reach after 9/11. The more aggressive and directed use of these tools amplified their impact and served to shape and condition the international financial environment, making it riskier and riskier for financial actors to do business with suspect customers.

That campaign focused on ferreting out illicit financial flows and using that information to our enemies' disadvantage. The military and intelligence communities contributed by focusing their attention and collection efforts on sources of enemy funding and support networks. The Treasury Department then used targeted sanctions, regulatory pressure, and financial suasion globally to isolate newly exposed rogue financial actors. For their part, law enforcement agencies and regulators hammered banks and institutions for failing to identify or capture illicit financial activity and for failing to institute effective anti-money-laundering systems. The United States leveraged the entire toolkit and exploited the aversion of the legitimate international banking system and commercial environment to illicit capital, to craft a new way of waging financial warfare.

This new approach puts a premium on targeting rogues based on their own illicit conduct. Interestingly, under the right conditions, the model creates a virtuous cycle of self-isolation by financial scofflaws. The more isolated the rogue actors become, the more likely they are to engage in even more evasive and suspicious financial activities to avoid scrutiny, and the more they find themselves excluded from financial networks.

But perhaps the most important insight enabling Treasury's campaign was its focus on the financial sector's omnipresence in the international economic system. Financial activity—the use of bank accounts, wire transfers, letters of credit—is the lifeblood of international commerce and financial relationships. The banks are the arteries of the international system.

The U.S. Treasury Department realized that these private-sector actors—most importantly, the banks—could drive the isolation of rogue entities much more effectively than governments. That power is based principally on their own interests and the desire to avoid unnecessary business and reputational risk. Indeed, the international banking community has grown acutely sensitive to the business risks attached to illicit financial activity and has taken significant steps to bar it from their institutions. As the primary gatekeepers to all international commerce and capital, banks in turn have motivated legitimate private-sector actors to steer clear of suspect business relationships. When governments call for isolating rogue financial actors, the banks fall into line because it is in their interest to do so. Reputation and perceived institutional integrity became prized commodities in the private sector's calculus after 9/11. Our campaigns simply leveraged the power of reputational risk.

SYNCHRONIZING FINANCIAL PRESSURE

In such an environment, the U.S. Treasury Department, foreign finance ministries and central banks, and financial regulators around the world all used their unconventional tools and influence for broader national security purposes. The old orthodoxy of unilateral versus multilateral sanctions became irrelevant—the strategic question was instead how to amplify or synchronize the effects of financial pressure with other international actors, including states, international institutions, banks, and other commercial actors.

Like it or not, transnational nonstate actors and rogue regimes are tied to the global financial order regardless of location or reclusiveness. Dirty money eventually flows across borders. Moreover, in this environment, the banks, as the central arteries of the international financial system, control the financial ecosystem, with established regulatory expectations, routine gatekeeping practices, and penalties. Such a self-policing, risk adverse system makes America's enemies vulnerable.

This new brand of financial coercion was spawned by both design and necessity. We recognized the possibilities this new environment presented for reshaping the way the United States used its financial influence to strengthen its national security. The strategies that resulted focused squarely on protecting the broader international financial system and using financial tools to put pressure on legitimate financial institutions to reject dealings with rogue and illicit financial actors.

These tools and this approach are no longer new. Economic sanctions and financial pressure are now the national security tools of choice for presidents when either diplomacy or military force is deemed undesirable or ineffective. This tool of statecraft has become extremely important in coercing and constraining the behavior of both nonstate networks and recalcitrant, rogue regimes, which often appear beyond the reach of more traditional government power.

But these rogue actors are already adapting. It is only a matter of time until U.S. competitors use the lessons of the past decade to wage financial battles of their own—especially against the United States.

More worrisome, these powers of financial coercion could diminish as the economic landscape changes. The potency of this presidential tool of coercion, and Treasury's influence, ultimately stem from the ability of the United States to leverage its financial power globally. This ability, in turn, derives from the centrality and stability of New York as a global financial center, the importance of the dollar as a global reserve currency, and the amplification effect of any U.S. step, regulatory or otherwise, on the broader international system. If the U.S. economy loses its predominance or the dollar sufficiently weakens, our ability to wage financial warfare could wane. It is thus vital that policy makers and ordinary Americans understand what is at stake and how this new brand of financial warfare works. In the meantime, presidents will continue to rely on the newly sharpened tool of economic coercion, one that leverages the centrality of American financial power and influence and aligns with the realities of an interconnected era of globalization. That has been Treasury's war.

National Security and Foreign Affairs

40. Atlas Ascendant: Building the "American Century"

by James Kitfield

For a public reared on the mother's milk of "American exceptionalism," it may seem that the nation has always cast an oversized shadow over world affairs. It's easy to forget just how recently the country was fit for its super-power suit of armor, at least by historical measures. As recently as the late 19th century, for instance, the United States was still focused on internal development and bringing order to the western frontier.

Some might argue that Theodore "Teddy" Roosevelt ushered in the American Century as the nation's youngest president in 1901, promptly rallying the country to his unique brand of foreign affairs activism. In short order, the former Rough Rider and hero of the Spanish-American War put down insurrection in the Philippines, abetted a revolution in Panama that led to U.S. acquisition of the Panama Canal, and won the Nobel Peace Prize for mediating a quarrel between Russia and Japan. In 1907, Roosevelt dispatched the Great White Fleet on a cruise around the world. An America in the "prime of our lusty youth," Roosevelt proclaimed, would "speak softly and carry a big stick" in world affairs.

And yet those were only the early indicators of the potential for global power. Throughout the latter half of the 19th century and the first half of the 20th, the United States was largely a strategic ward of the British Empire on which the sun famously never set. Only at the end of World War II in 1945, with Europe in ruins and Great Britain exhausted by two world wars, did the United States truly assume the mantle of Western leadership.

For really the first time, U.S. presidents were forced to consider a grand strategy that would order the world to America's advantage, contain the spread of Communism, and hopefully avoid the kinds of cataclysms that made the first half of the 20th century the most blood-soaked epoch in human history. With the recent advent of nuclear weapons and the U.S. bombings of Hiroshima and Nagasaki near the end of World War II, there were no guarantees that mankind would even witness a 21st century.

A STRATEGIC GRAND SLAM

At important moments in their ascent all great powers are blessed with visionary leadership. In the United States' case, this was supplied in that critical period of the 1940s by Presidents Franklin Roosevelt and Harry Truman, and the handpicked and seasoned team of subordinates who became known as the "Wise Men." Plucked primarily from the worlds of finance, banking, statecraft, and the military, that group included the likes of Dean Acheson, George Kennan, Paul Nitze, and George Marshall. Under strong presidential guidance, they responded to a post–World War II period of epic crisis with the strategic equivalent of a grand slam.

President Truman's administration oversaw the establishment of the United Nations in hopes of avoiding future world wars, the World Bank to fund postwar reconstruction, and the International Monetary Fund to promote free trade. By reaching out with the Marshall Plan to help rebuild Western Europe, as well as to defeated foes Germany and Japan, the United States avoided the mistakes of the interwar years of the 1920s and 1930, when ostracizing the defeated Weimar Republic after World War I led to the resurgence of a belligerent Germany. The article that George Kennan published anonymously under the name "X" in a 1947 issue of the magazine *Foreign Affairs*—together with Paul Nitze's National Security Council Directive 68 and the establishment of the NATO alliance under Secretary of State Acheson—laid the foundation for the strategy of containment that not only deterred World War III but ultimately won the Cold War.

As a framework for that containment, the United States constructed and maintained a ring of U.S. military commands and bases on the periphery of the Soviet Union and Warsaw Pact, bracketing the Eurasian continent from Europe to the Pacific. In the 1970s, the ring was extended south to the Middle East after President Jimmy Carter, in response to the 1970s energy crisis and Soviet invasion of Afghanistan, pronounced a doctrine that any attack on the vital oil supplies of the West would be considered an attack on the United States.

Much as the British had in the 19th century, the United States in the second half of the 20th century thus engaged in a sort of imperial policing of those regions because it reaped the greatest rewards from their stability. This was a "soft empire" of ideals. It was premised on the spread of a liberal international order, fueled by free trade and capitalism that played to the strengths of open and democratic societies. In his book *The Liberal Leviathan: The Origins, Crisis, and Transformation of the American World Order*, political scientist G. John Ikenberry of Princeton University argues that in this period "the United States engaged in the most ambitious and far-reaching liberal-order building the world had yet seen."[1]

WEIGHTY PRESIDENTIAL BURDENS

And yet victory in the Cold War and success in building a liberal order were never foreordained, and coupled with the imperative to avoid a potentially devastating World War III, the effort weighed heavily on every commander-in-chief of the post–World War II and Cold War eras. Nearly all of them would send troops into harm's way only to have some return in flag-draped coffins, and each man emerged from his tenure in the White House prematurely aged. Such are the burdens of global leadership.

Truman would turn back communist aggression with a "police action" that cost the lives of more than 36,000 U.S. service members in the Korean War. Dwight Eisenhower managed to avoid a hot war only with risky gambles and threats to "go nuclear" against the Soviet Union and an emerging Communist China. John F. Kennedy took the world to the brink of nuclear Armageddon to block Soviet missiles from the Western Hemisphere during the Cuban Missile Crisis.

Lyndon Johnson felt he had to take a stand against Communist aggression in Vietnam and was undone as president by a Vietnam War that would claim the lives of more than 58,000 U.S. service members. Despite promises of a "secret plan" to end the war, Richard Nixon was unable to bring Vietnam to an honorable conclusion during his first term and was widely criticized when it was revealed he had ordered a secret bombing campaign in Cambodia. After the Communist Khmer Rouge government in Cambodia seized the crew of the U.S. merchant *Mayaguez*, Gerald R. Ford lost forty-one U.S. Marines trying to rescue the crew. Jimmy Carter lost eight U.S. service members in the unsuccessful operation to rescue U.S. hostages held in Iran and was blindsided by the Soviet invasion of Afghanistan. Ronald Reagan's decision to deploy U.S. "peacekeepers" to Lebanon ended after 241 were killed in a suicide bombing of their barracks. George H.W. Bush, the last Cold War president, would launch an invasion of Panama, the Persian Gulf War to turn back an Iraqi invasion of Kuwait, and a humanitarian mission in Somalia that would later go south. All three operations resulted in U.S. casualties.

When victory in the Cold War came in 1989 with the toppling of the Berlin Wall and subsequent dissolution of the Soviet Union, the United States was suddenly left with a globe-spanning superpower military and no superpower rival. American ideals of free markets and democracy spread throughout the world, including in Eastern Europe, Asia, and Latin America.

NEW WORLD ORDER

With the end of the Cold War and collapse of the Soviet Union, the United States' leaders might have reasonably pocketed a massive "peace dividend" and contented themselves to letting the country become just one among a number of competing major powers in an anticipated benign era of democratic expansion. After all, bringing the troops home after war and disbanding wartime alliances was an American tradition and in keeping with the avoidance of "entangling alliances" about which Founding Fathers George Washington and Thomas Jefferson had warned.

At another seminal moment in its history, the United States benefitted from the foresight of leaders who had come of age during World War II and the Cold War. After Ronald Reagan abandoned détente and pressed the Soviet Union toward collapse with the largest peacetime defense buildup in U.S. history, George H.W. Bush helped engineer a soft landing, promoting good relations with Russia and a peaceful reunification of Germany. The NATO alliance was not only maintained but eventually expanded eastward to provide a protective umbrella for the new democracies of the former Warsaw Pact.

In his book *The Grand Chessboard: American Primacy and Its Geostrategic Imperatives,*[2] former national security adviser Zbigniew Brzezinski described the country at the dawn of the post–Cold War era as the rarest of historical anomalies: "America is the first, the only, and the last superpower in the history of international relations."

According to one of the chief architects of the post–Cold War order, George H.W. Bush never seriously considered that the United States would go out of the superpower business with the collapse of the Soviet Union. Once Russia had voted to approve a UN Resolution that Bush sought to legitimize military force against Iraq, Bush 41 and his National Security Adviser Brent Scowcroft began talking about a "New World Order" in which the 20th-century scourge of state-on-state aggression was banished. It would require continued heavy U.S. engagement and leadership.

"If after the Cold War the United States had just pulled out of Europe, or Asia or the Middle East, things would have gone to hell in a hurry," Scowcroft told the author. "Japan would have doubled its defense budget and probably gone nuclear, upsetting the balance in Asia. Israel would have soon been fighting the Palestinians and might have faced a united Arab coalition once again. In Bosnia and Kosovo, Europe would soon prove that it was not ready to tackle really tough problems without U.S. leadership. So the United States still had to shoulder those burdens, because we had a better chance to construct a world representative of our core values than in any other time in a rather bloody century."

THE INDISPENSABLE NATION

As the first president from the baby boom generation, Bill Clinton inherited a country hailed as a lone superpower in a unipolar world, deciding that its role in the post–Cold War era would be as the "indispensable nation." Even as America stood at the height of its power and international influence, however, rumblings of a backlash against U.S. predominance and the phenomenon of "globalization" that helped fuel it began sounding, both at home and abroad.

After the United States' successful 1991 war with Iraq, for instance, failed states replaced state-on-state aggression as the primary source of global instability. Crises followed in rapid succession in Somalia, Haiti, the Balkans, and Rwanda, as civil wars of nationalism, tribalism, and self-determination that were held in check during the bipolar Cold War standoff erupted with increased frequency during the 1990s. The Clinton Administration sent military forces to try and quell the crises (declining to do so only to stop genocide in Rwanda, which Clinton later rued as one of his greatest regrets). Clearly, being the "indispensable nation" did not relieve commanders in chief of the burdens of the office that had weighed so heavily on presidents during the "American century."

Soon enough the tide of democratic liberalization and free market capitalism that swept across the world at the end of the Cold War would begin to sputter and in some cases recede as Russia and countries in Eastern Europe, Asia, and Latin America struggled with democratic transitions and attempted to weather major disruptions in world financial markets. The same dynamic forces that sped the movement of capital, goods, and people around the world also spread the technological and material ingredients of doomsday weapons. Islamist extremism and its attendant terror grew throughout the decade, as parts of the Muslim world in particular pushed back fiercely against the encroachment of modernity and what they viewed as the imposition of a corrupt Western culture and values. That was the whirlwind that President George W. Bush reaped on September 11, 2001, in his first year in the Oval Office, when the country learned conclusively that being the "lone superpower in a unipolar world" put an outsized target on America's back.

GLOBAL INSTABILITY

As the end of President Barack Obama's second term looms, each day seems to bring a new affront on the foreign policy stage. A newly aggressive Russia continues to dismember its neighbor Ukraine, having already chewed off pieces of Moldova and Georgia. A rapidly ascendant China bullies its neighbors in the

South and East China Seas. Iran and North Korea spew anti-Western rhetoric and pursue nuclear weapons programs (suspected in the case of Iran, confirmed with North Korea). Taking advantage of failed states and civil wars in the Middle East, the terrorists of the Islamic State of Iraq and the Levant (ISIL) continue to expand territory under their control and assault the sensibilities of the civilized world with mass executions, beheadings, and sexual slavery.

Republicans lay the blame for those international woes squarely on President Obama's doorstep. They object to his supposed squishy multilateralism, his willingness to engage odious adversaries in diplomacy, his apologies for past American mistakes, and his reluctance to use U.S. military force even when crises seem to demand it. They doubt Obama's conviction that America remains a "shining city on a hill" and the indispensable beacon to all free peoples. They blame him for a too-early exit of U.S. forces from Iraq and insufficient attention to a costly war in Afghanistan that is dragging on toward an unsatisfactory conclusion.

Just a few years ago, however, Obama and the Democrats blamed President George W. Bush for an unsettled global strategic landscape. They blamed him for failing to check China and deter Iran. They objected to Bush's swashbuckling unilateralism, his decision to ignore diplomacy with disagreeable countries, and his "with-us-or-against-us" triumphalism that tended to alienate even close allies. They charged that he had tarnished the beacon of America's promise by endorsing torture and confusing the spread of democracy with the kind of regime change at the point of a gun that Bush blundered into in Iraq. They questioned his one-sided fealty to Israel and blamed him for wars in Iraq and Afghanistan that were dragging on toward unsatisfactory conclusions.

The fact that two presidents with such different foreign policy and national security instincts have both run up against—and in many cases been stymied by—the same international challenges suggests that the geostrategic landscape has shifted fundamentally. In his article "George W. Bush, Barack Obama, and the Future of U.S. Global Leadership,"[3] James Lindsay of the Council on Foreign Relations wrote that U.S. presidents in the current era, despite their styles and instincts, must manage friends and foes who feel increasingly empowered to ignore or contest American dominance. The unipolar moment of the immediate post–Cold War, in other words, has passed. "Americans have this ingrained notion that U.S. leadership and predominance is the natural state of world affairs, with Democrats thus concluding that gentle engagement will automatically cause countries to rally to our banner, and Republicans believing that firmness and consistency will have the same impact," Lindsay told the author. "They are both fundamentally misreading the geostrategic environment."

That landscape and America's place in it have been fundamentally altered by two costly U.S. wars, a Great Recession, and political dysfunction in Washington that blocks solutions to long-standing and debilitating problems such as a long-term U.S. debt crisis and that foils bipartisan foreign-policy consensus that used to be expressed in the adage that "politics stops at the water's edge." More broadly, in the era of globalization, power is increasingly diffuse, and challenges are complex and transnational, whether the issue is Islamist extremist terrorism, the spread of pandemics like Ebola, a proliferation of failed states and weapons of mass destruction, or climate change. All of those pressing issues defy the efforts of any one nation. "If a unipolar moment ever really existed, it's not just passed—it's gone permanently,"[4] said Richard Haass, president of the Council of Foreign Relations and a former top State Department official.

Sustaining U.S. leadership in such an era will mean making tough strategic choices. The next president, whether a Republican or a Democrat, will have to rank core U.S. interests in order of priority; determine an affordable size for hard- and soft-power instruments (the armed forces, the diplomatic corps, foreign aid); rethink the forward presence of U.S. forces and a current alliance structure that dates back to World War II; and more carefully weigh the risks of action versus inaction in response to an endless list of global crises.

The original architects of the American Century had a grand strategy and a goal: a world in which nations were so heavily invested in the liberal international order that the system would eventually police itself and the American Atlas could lay down the burden. But unlike America and Great Britain in the 1930s and 1940s, there is no liberal power waiting patiently in the wings to claim the mantle of global leadership, even if the American public has wearied of the burdens of indispensability. In fact, perhaps the chief lesson of the American Century is that leadership is not claimed but bestowed by others. And that, when the world comes knocking, it's in America's nature to answer the call.

"We're still the only country that can mobilize collective international action to confront the big global problems like terrorism, proliferation, climate change, and access to energy," said former national security adviser Brent Scowcroft, speaking to the author a few years ago. "But it will require a change of character in U.S. leadership. We'll have to lead more by persuasion than coercion or dominance. That's an art, and I hope our strategic culture is still capable of it."

♦ ♦ ♦ ♦ ♦

41. The 3 AM Phone Call: Presidential Crisis Management

by Michael K. Bohn

"This is a national disgrace," former California governor Ronald Reagan said of President Jimmy Carter's handling of the Iran hostage crisis.[1] The actor turned GOP presidential hopeful frequently castigated Carter during March and April 1980. The presidential primary election season that spring yielded plenty of potshots aimed at the president, especially from Republicans exploiting the stalemated crisis in Tehran. At that time, fifty-three people from the U.S. embassy remained in captivity.

When Iranian students overran the embassy the previous November, many Americans expected President Carter to take immediate and decisive action to free the hostages. Yet by March, Carter had yet to find a forceful solution to the crisis, at least one that didn't endanger the hostages' lives. To that point, he had opted for diplomacy and negotiation, a strategy that did not satisfy expectations for forceful presidential action. That gave Reagan the political advantage, as he likely spoke for the majority of the American public.

"I'm not a jingo thinking about pushing the war button when it wouldn't do any good," Reagan said to the media regarding the hostage situation. "But this administration has dillied and dallied for five months now." On March 27, Reagan urged Carter to block the shipment of food and oil to Iran and use the U.S. Navy to blockade Iranian ports. Had he been president, Reagan said that he would have given Iran a private ultimatum to free the Americans by a set deadline. If Iran failed to meet the deadline, he would have threatened "very unpleasant action."[2]

Fast-forward to June 1985. Iranian-backed Hezbollah terrorists hijacked an American airliner over Europe, TWA Flight 847. The hijackers demanded that Israel release hundreds of Palestinian prisoners and then killed a passenger, a U.S. Navy sailor, to add urgency to their demands. With no vigorous options available to free the hostages, President Reagan found himself standing in Carter's shoes, and the irony was pinching from heel to toe.

Reagan ultimately made a "no-deal deal" with the Israelis to release their prisoners, and he promised Syria's leader Hafez al-Assad that the United States would not retaliate against Hezbollah targets in Lebanon. That led to the TWA passengers' release. Reagan didn't play a Hollywood action figure in this drama but rather a cautious negotiator. That approach, although sensible and successful, once again failed to meet expectations of the public and the media. The headline for a *Washington Post* op-ed piece by *Post* reporter Lou Cannon read, "What Happened to Reagan the Gunslinger?" The *Wall Street Journal* editorial page called the president "Jimmy Reagan."[3]

HIGH EXPECTATIONS, LIMITED OPTIONS

President Reagan learned what candidate Reagan did not yet understand: there's a gap between public expectations for presidential action during an international crisis and what the commander in chief can realistically accomplish. As all newly elected U.S. presidents have learned in the past sixty-five years, Reagan discovered that handling the 3:00 AM phone call is a daunting challenge. And no experience could have prepared him for White House crisis decision making. Nothing said as a candidate or as a sideline critic will work in the Situation Room. Talk is cheap when one does not have any skin in the game. All of the no-fly zones that look so easy to implement from the campaign trail become deadly battle spaces after enforcing a presidential order.

Given the difficulties facing a president during an emergency, immediate and conclusive action only happens in the fairy tale model of crisis management espoused by opposing politicians and pundits. *New York Times* columnist David Brooks has recognized a president's dilemma in confronting an unanticipated incident. "Everybody wants to be a striding titan," Brooks wrote in 2009. "Almost all alpha leaders want to be the brilliant visionary in a time of crisis—the one who sees the situation clearly, makes bold plans and delivers the faithful to the other side." He noted that it almost never happens that way: "In real crises, the successful leaders are usually the ones who cope best with ignorance and error."[4]

Public expectations for bold presidential action in a crisis arise from cultural touchstones. The 1776 Revolution was certainly bold, as were the frontiersmen who tamed the West and the rugged individuals prized in American history. Folks remember Washington, Lincoln, Wilson, and the two Roosevelts for their transformative actions. Another source of high expectations is the public's "collective memory," according to Denise Bostdorff, Wooster College professor of political rhetoric. She points to celebrations of "the good war," World War II—Tom Brokaw's books on the greatest generation and dramatizations such as *Saving Private Ryan* and *Band of Brothers*— as reinforcing examples of a collective memory that feeds public expectations in a crisis.

Today's mass media create some of the public expectations for presidential action, according to Dr. Mark Rozell, a presidential scholar at George Mason

University. "The pictures in our heads come from journalistic perceptions of 'strong' leadership, entertainment media portrayals of heroic leaders and popular biographies of 'great' presidents," Rozell told me. "On the latter, those always seem to be the figures that come across as larger-than-life personalities, who did big, transformative things in office."[5]

Another well-regarded student of the presidency, James David Barber of Duke University, examined types of expectations that the public thrusts up to the presidency. Barber grouped them into reassurance in the face of fear, legitimacy that holds a president above politics, and the action of a take-charge doer. Barber also noted that expectations change in cycles. For example, when a president overdoes action to the point that his policies become too political, public expectations shift to legitimacy and reassurance.

Political analyst Charlie Cook has elaborated on the cycles of expectations. "After President Nixon's fall in the Watergate scandal, we opted for former Georgia governor Jimmy Carter, who exuded honesty and promised that he would never lie to us. After the Iranian hostage crisis, when Carter seemed weak and indecisive, we elected Ronald Reagan, the closest we could come to John Wayne."[6] Additionally, Cook noted, after George H.W. Bush (Bush 41) focused on foreign policy, Clinton ran on the theme, "It's the economy, Stupid." And you do not need an expert to understand that Americans voted in Barack Obama when they tired of George W. Bush's wars.

CRISIS RHETORIC

Presidential rhetoric also shapes public expectations in times of crisis and public danger. One theme often articulated is that a dangerous and evil man/ country/terrorist organization is threatening the United States and other peace-loving countries. John Kennedy accused the deceitful Soviets of deploying nuclear ballistic missiles to Cuba and described the action as a "clandestine, reckless, and provocative threat to world peace."[7] During the 1990–91 Persian Gulf War, Bush 41 characterized Iraq's Saddam Hussein as the new Hitler, who sanctioned rape and pillaging.

Furthermore, a president separates a dangerous international development from the usual tensions by how he describes it. Political rhetoric expert Theodore Windt described the birth of a crisis: "Situations do not create crises. Rather, the president's perception of the situation and the rhetoric he uses to describe it mark an event as a crisis."[8] Although some incidents need no characterization—the 9/11 terrorist attacks—the public usually must look to the president for an incident's significance. For example, when a Soviet fighter jet shot down a Korean Airlines 747 in September 1983,

President Reagan called it a "wanton misdeed" and lamented the horrible loss of life.[9] On the other hand, in June 1985, he seemingly inflated the hijacking of TWA Flight 847 by calling it an "attack on all citizens of the world" and a "dangerous and volatile situation."[10]

When Bush 41 demonized Saddam Hussein, his rhetoric became a double-edged sword. After Bush unilaterally called a ceasefire after only 100 hours of ground combat, the mismatch of words and deeds sowed confusion. The allegedly evil Saddam Hussein was left in power and with much of his military intact. Lawrence Freedman and Efraim Karsh, in their book *The Gulf Conflict, 1990–1991*, noted how the second edge of Bush's sword undercut the characterization he had created of Saddam Hussein. "Perhaps if, in President Bush's rhetoric, [Saddam Hussein] had not been built up into such a monster, all this would have sufficed," they wrote of the foreshortened war. "But for a monster it was not good enough."[11]

Multiple factors contribute to the gap between presidential rhetoric and the expectations it creates and the actions presidents can pursue without exacerbating the crisis, unnecessarily endangering lives or contributing to a potential debacle. Foremost is the "fog of war," the blanket that obscures desperately needed information about what happened. Faulty intelligence, or worse, faulty interpretation of intelligence, adds to the cloud cover shrouding the crisis landscape. Bickering and turf wars between senior advisers get in the way of bold action. Worse, cabinet secretaries and military leaders who ignore presidential orders or secretly conspire with the president's political opponents sometimes hinder forthright crisis resolution. Any incident involving Israel will unleash a storm of political pressure in America and can severely limit action alternatives. A White House sex scandal can undercut bold action if the public perceives the president is mainly trying to change the subject. A reelection campaign can get in the way because doing the right thing in a crisis isn't always synonymous with raising money and winning a second term. And during much of the time since 1950 there was a far more robust reason for caution—the risk of a nuclear holocaust.

LIMITED LEVERAGE

Lack of U.S. leverage in an incident is another common brake on bold action. Can the president decisively affect a crisis outcome? If not, he may push aside blunt military options and sticks in favor of diplomacy and perhaps economic sanctions. During the 1956 Suez crisis involving Great Britain, France, Israel, and Egypt, for example, the Soviets invaded Hungary to reestablish a Communist regime. Eisenhower knew that he had no leverage short of all-out war, so he retreated to rhetoric. In 2008, Russia intervened in Georgia to support pro-Russian separatists, and Bush 43 didn't have risk-free means to bolster democracy in the country. Obama didn't want war with Russia over Ukraine in the spring and summer of 2014, so economic sanctions on Russia were his preferred option. On the other hand, Reagan had leverage in a backyard mini-crisis in the Caribbean nation of Grenada in 1983, and so did Bush 41 in his 1989 military intervention in Panama.

Kennedy acknowledged the frequent scarcity of American clout in international situations in an interview two months after the 1962 Cuban Missile Crisis. "Well, I think in the first place the problems are more difficult than I had imagined they were," he explained. "Secondly, there is a limitation upon the ability of the United States to solve these problems."[12]

As a president looks for action options in a crisis that won't blow up in his face, his deliberations may draw accusations of wavering and weakness. Critics who shout, "Do something!" usually haven't a clue that every bold action in a crisis can have untoward consequences and trigger blowback reactions. Hedging bets and keeping the powder dry while seeking the right time to act often represents the best option. For example, in the bloody early stages of the Arab Spring in Libya during February 2011, President Obama appeared to be doing little. One op-ed writer blamed him for "fiddling while Libya burns."[13] But administration officials talked little about Muammar Qadhafi's ruthlessness so as to minimize retaliation aimed at Americans in the country. The president didn't want another hostage crisis on top of violent demonstrations, and he suffered the heat in silence until Americans had been evacuated.

But Obama, and President Kennedy before him, erred early in crises by attempting to get ahead of expectations by drawing a red line that would trigger a forceful U.S. response to a crisis. The idea of an ultimatum has come up frequently in White House crisis meetings since 1950, but the dangers of an unfulfilled threat or unwelcome, unintended consequences usually quieted that impulse. However, Kennedy and Obama made unscripted remarks about red lines in election years—during the 1962 Cuban Missile crisis and in 2012 regarding Syrian chemical weapons use. Each admitted after the crisis that the line drawing had limited his options once push came to shove. Mark Rozell has offered one explanation for their behavior: "The unwillingness to somehow look weak or irresolute sometimes drives presidents to follow a poorly conceived course of action."[14]

One final note about the public's expectations for presidential crisis management: domestic political issues, whether they spring from election pressures or special interest groups, are always present in the White House during international crises. While the public wants, as Barber described, "a man who will rise above politics, a man of all the people," that man is rarely available.[15] Every president from Truman through Obama has felt domestic political pressure during international crises. A few—Nixon, Carter, and Clinton— even attempted to use a crisis to distract the public from their domestic problems or gain traction in an election campaign.

♦ ♦ ♦ ♦ ♦

42. Harry Truman: Cold War Architect

by Elizabeth Edwards Spalding

The political history of the 20th century would have been far different, we often hear, without Adolf Hitler, Josef Stalin, Winston Churchill, or Franklin Roosevelt. To think of Hitler and Nazi Germany determining the shape of the 20th century and beyond, or to think of Stalin and the Soviet Union defining the future, or to think of the two of them resuming their Nazi–Soviet Pact and directing all of world politics, seems inconceivable today. To raise the possibility of these alternative geopolitical outcomes, however, highlights just how different the world might look today were it not for the emergence of the United States as a global superpower.

Both FDR and Churchill played critical roles in that story, of course, but a surprisingly important protagonist was Harry Truman, an accidental president, who is often considered a lesser statesman. And yet it was Truman who oversaw the conclusion of World War II and made the tough decision to drop atomic bombs on Japan to hasten an end to the war. It was also Truman who grasped early on the nature of the Cold War, and thus initiated and presided over the strategy of containment that eventually brought victory over the Soviet Union. It was Truman who understood that an enduring liberal world order required the global leadership of a free, strong, and prosperous United States. In the end, there would have been no "American Century" without President Harry Truman.

Central to the growth of the United States as a superpower was Truman's appraisal of the East–West conflict. Also essential were the institutions and initiatives of American global leadership that Truman created and supported and that formed the bedrock of the foreign policy of containment: the Truman Doctrine, the Marshall Plan, and the North Atlantic Treaty. In these unprecedented programs, which were established in three short years, Truman created the architecture that allowed the United States to lead the democracies during the Cold War. They were the essential high ground from which the United States defended and promoted freedom in the noncommunist world, and held out hope for a better future to those behind the Iron Curtain. As the United States grew as a superpower, it became the acknowledged standard bearer for the free world.

THE TRUMAN DOCTRINE

As a foreign policy, the Truman Doctrine was unprecedented on several levels. At the time, it was a unique commitment on the part of the United States. Truman thus knew that his argument in support of the doctrine had to be carefully and convincingly framed. The United States intended to pledge itself politically, financially, and strategically to two European countries threatened by the encroaching shadow of Soviet communism. Truman also knew that the borders of Greece and Turkey would be where containment began, not where it ended. "I am fully aware of the broad implications involved if the United States extends assistance to Greece and Turkey," he explained in his speech on March 12, 1947, "and I shall discuss these implications with you at this time."[1] To his cabinet members a week before the speech, he conveyed that he was "faced with a decision more serious than had ever confronted any President."[2]

As president, Truman already had experience with containment in northern Iran, where U.S. and United Nations troop resolve had forced the Soviets to withdraw in 1946. From his lifelong study of the Bible and world history, he also viewed Greece and Turkey as the gateway between West and East, thus connecting the two countries to Europe and to America's strategic interests. If the United States failed to aid Greece and Turkey "in this fateful hour," the last obstacles to Soviet domination of the Balkans and the eastern Mediterranean would be removed, not only threatening these regions, but also the Middle East, the Suez Canal, and Western Europe.[3] For Truman, both strategic and civilizational factors dictated action.

Although the Truman Doctrine was first applied to Greece and Turkey, Truman stressed that the new international position of the United States was as a bulwark against totalitarianism. In the absence of an effective United Nations, America was the one nation capable of defending freedom and establishing peace.

"This is no more than a frank recognition that totalitarian regimes imposed upon free peoples, by direct or indirect aggression, undermine the foundations of international peace and hence the security of the United States," said Truman. He underscored that a primary objective of Cold War policy was to create conditions in which the United States and other nations worked out "a way of life free from coercion." Although no government was perfect, he added, one of the chief virtues of a democracy is that "its defects are always visible and under democratic processes can be pointed out and corrected."[4] The Truman Doctrine—and containment generally—would promote democracy by defending the conditions necessary for freedom.

The speed with which the administration formulated and implemented the Truman Doctrine was impressive. The degree of bipartisan agreement and cooperation also set a standard for postwar U.S. foreign policy. The White House used the same impressive powers of persuasion with Congress to pass the Marshall Plan and the North Atlantic Treaty. Senator Arthur Vandenberg (R-Mich.), who was chairman of the Senate Foreign Relations Committee, was indispensable and guided the Truman Doctrine through the Senate in April 1947.

Indeed, the period 1947–48 was the high-water mark of executive-legislative cooperation and bipartisanship in the modern era, with passage of the Truman Doctrine, the Marshall Plan, and the Vandenberg Resolution, which paved the way for establishment of the North Atlantic Treaty Organization (NATO), the bedrock Western security alliance. The amount of U.S. treasure initially devoted to the Cold War enterprise was also unprecedented. For instance, the Truman Doctrine required a $400 million outlay to just two countries: Greece ($300 million) and Turkey ($100 million). Greek–Turkish aid was explicitly earmarked for political and military purposes.

The Truman Doctrine outlays were easily eclipsed, however, by the more than $13 billion committed to the Marshall Plan, a program to help seventeen western and southern European countries rebuild after the devastation of World War II. Truman was already committed during World War II to the idea of what became the European Recovery Program, and he knew that the Truman Doctrine would be insufficient by itself to stop the encroachment of communism. France and Italy were facing real communist threats, for instance, and Europe was still in desperate need of recovery. With hard work, Truman thus won congressional support for the Marshall Plan. The fact that it would draw western European democracies into the U.S. sphere of influence was not lost on Moscow, which did not allow any Eastern European countries to participate. President Truman thus saw the Truman Doctrine and the Marshall Plan as complementary pillars of U.S. leadership.

A SUPERPOWER FOUNDATION

The next important foundation stone put into place was the North Atlantic Treaty, which was started in July 1948, signed by its member countries' foreign ministers in April 1949, and ratified by the U.S. Senate in late July 1949. The United States was already bound to the Truman Doctrine and the Marshall Plan, but Truman realized that Western Europe's defense remained shaky. In addition to ongoing communist pressure on Western Europe, the loss of Czechoslovakia to the Soviet sphere and the start of the Soviet block-ade of Berlin, both in 1948, were felt keenly. In key ways, the political, mili-tary, and strategic imperatives that informed the Truman Doctrine and Marshall Plan were folded into the alliance structure of NATO.

Because of their Cold War significance, Greece and Turkey held associate status from the beginning and became full NATO members in 1952. Truman saw collective defense as a new way to institutionalize security in a critical region, and, in a confidential discussion with the NATO foreign ministers in April 1949, he disclosed "our best estimate is that we have several years in which we can count on a breathing spell" before the Soviets acquired atomic weapons. Even NATO would not be enough to stop the expansion of Soviet communism, Truman argued, "and the only way to defeat it eventually is not merely to contain it but to carry the ideological war to the Soviet sphere it-self."[5] Immediately after Senate ratification of the North Atlantic Treaty, Truman asked Congress for approval of a $1.4 billion military assistance pro-gram for, among others, the NATO countries Greece and Turkey, as well as for the Philippines.

Truman was acutely aware that he also needed institutions and structures on the home front to support his bedrock foreign policies and facilitate his general strategy of Soviet containment. Truman recognized that the Office of Strategic Services had been vital in terms of intelligence collection and analy-sis during the Second World War, for instance, and he reasoned that a follow-on agency would be needed to successfully prosecute the Cold War.

Toward the end of his presidency, Truman told a room full of government officials, "Only two people around the White House really knew what was going on in the military affairs department [in April 1945], and they were Admiral [William] Leahy and Admiral [William] Brown. I would talk to them every morning and try to get all the information I could." Recalling that it took a disproportionate amount of his time to read all the reports from vari-ous sources, Truman said, "And finally one morning I had a conversation with Admiral Leahy, and suggested to him that there should be a Central Intelligence Agency, for the benefit of the whole government as well as for the benefit of the President, so he could be informed."[6] Truman would go on to approve the beginning of covert operations by the newly established CIA, and he deeply appreciated the centrality of its information and intelligence gathering.

What Truman expressed about the CIA reflected his general thinking on the need to transform the instruments of U.S. foreign policy and national security for the looming Cold War. His vision was expressed in the sweeping National Security Act of 1947, which provided the essential architectural blueprint for the national security superstructure needed to contain Soviet expansionism. The act created the National Security Council (NSC) and NSC staff to allow the White House to coordinate the government's vast foreign policy and national security apparatus; formally established a permanent CIA as the successor to the wartime OSS; established a separate Air Force service branch and Department of the Air Force; and merged the War Department and Navy Department into a Defense Department headed by a secretary of Defense.

The National Security Act derived from the broad concept of national security that Truman put forth in his strategy of containment. The NSC would be the president's highest advisory council, but as the famous sign read on the president's desk: "The buck stops here." The NSC was to advise the president "with respect to the integration of domestic, foreign, and military policies relating to the national security so as to enable the military services and the other departments and agencies of the government to cooperate more effectively in matters involving national security." When pertaining specifically to military matters, it was intended to "assess and appraise the objectives, commitments, and risks of the United States in relation to our actual and potential military power, for the purpose of making recommendations to the President in connection therewith."[7]

Truman was aware that some of his NSA reforms were controversial. In a confidential memorandum in February 1947, Secretary of State George C. Marshall boldly stated that the NSC "by statute would dissipate the constitutional responsibility of the President for the conduct of foreign affairs" and that "the Secretary of State would become the automaton of the Council."[8] Even after changes in the legislation removed the NSC's proposed statutory powers and responsibilities, Truman rejected the idea that the NSC would somehow supplant the commander-in-chief or marginalize the Secretary of State. As he put it in the fall 1947, the NSC was "*his* council and . . . he expected everyone to work harmoniously without any manifestations of prima-donna qualities."[9] Nothing could or should supplant the relationship between the president and his secretary of state.

CRISIS MANAGEMENT

Truman used the NSC for its express purpose of coordinating advice to help him make critical decisions as president. While administration and congressional debate was taking place over the National Security Act, the president was busy pressing for the Truman Doctrine. When the NSA was enacted, Truman was occupied in promoting congressional approval of the Marshall Plan. In June 1948, he made his decision that United States military forces would stay in Berlin despite the Soviet blockade; he then presided over NSC meetings from July to September 1948 to organize specifics of the Berlin airlift.

After deciding that U.S. military forces would defend South Korea in 1950, Truman regularly attended NSC meetings for recommendations about coordinating military, diplomatic, and intelligence policies. In April 1949, Truman said that NSC and CIA reports had "proved to be one of the best means available to the President for obtaining coordinated advice as a basis of reaching decisions."[10] In this vein, the most famous Truman document out of the National Security Council was NSC 68 of 1950, which detailed the president's architecture of American leadership in the Cold War and put forth a comprehensive explanation of the containment strategy.

Truman's NSC was never as formal or large an institution as councils under subsequent presidents. What some might see as bureaucratic immaturity ended up working for Truman, who welcomed useful input from the NSC but still relied on valued insights and policy support from a circle of smart, trusted advisors. The NSC could never replace Dean Acheson's political acumen, Robert Lovett's dedication or personal contacts with Republicans on the Hill, or George Marshall's stature and experience. Sometimes this dependence on key advisors meant that Truman could not point to a formal paper chain in the formulation of policy, but he succeeded on the most pressing Cold War issues.

As an example of where this process produced flawed policy, China comes to mind. Truman very much admired and trusted Marshall, as did Acheson. Both Truman and Acheson thus followed the lead of Marshall, who detested Chiang Kai-shek and his Nationalists and thought them more corrupt than the communists. In following Marshall's advice, Truman did not push back as hard as he might against communism in China. Although he spoke often during the Korean War against communism in the new People's Republic of China, his China policy fell short of his usual standards in promoting freedom and opposing communism. Truman and Acheson knew more about Europe, and Truman knew more about the Middle and Near East. In those regions, the president generally judged and chose well.

If America was the arsenal of democracy during World War II, it became the global leader of free peoples and free governments during the Cold War. Some strongly criticize Truman for building the national security state in the process. But if one sees the Cold War as Truman did—as a conflict between good and evil, between freedom and tyranny, between liberal democracy and totalitarianism, between capitalism and communism—then the United States had to be more than a powerful bystander. America had to be the global leader in defending and promoting freedom where it existed, preserving it where it was threatened, and holding out hope for freedom where it was denied. That was Harry Truman's vision, and realizing it meant that the United States would have to embrace prudent yet unprecedented leadership in the world throughout the "American Century."

◆ ◆ ◆ ◆ ◆

43. Dwight D. Eisenhower: The War Hero

by Evan Thomas

The Great Man Theory of history has long been criticized. For more than a century, academic historians have argued that history is shaped by broad social forces, not by "great men." While popular historians (like me) still churn out biographies, most scholars disdain the study of "Dead White Males," as they say in the academy, and focus on economic data and the stories of the broad mass of people and of social movements.

I am persuaded that history was not made exclusively, or perhaps even primarily, by presidents and generals. But I want to make the case for one general who was also president of the United States, Dwight Eisenhower. I would argue that he kept the peace at a very dangerous time—the dawn of the nuclear weapons era. You can argue that he—and we—were lucky, and it's true that vast social and economic forces were at play in the 1950s. It is also true that the Eisenhower presidency was not just one man; "the administration" was a collective enterprise that drew forward policy from the past. It had a coherent foreign policy—a grand strategy, if you will—which advanced and refined the containment doctrine first conceived by diplomatist George Kennan, working for the Truman Administration in 1947. Broadly speaking, the policy was successful.

But I would argue that this policy worked during the eight years of the Eisenhower Administration (1953–61) largely because of Eisenhower's particular character, experience, and style of leadership. He was, I believe, uniquely the right man for his time. The policy worked because he—and only he—was suited to carry it out. Eisenhower effectively bluffed with nuclear weapons. No other chief executive was credible enough to pull that off.

Ike is remembered, a little dimly, as a hero of World War II, the command-ing general at D-Day and through to the defeat of Nazi Germany. He had a winning smile, and he played well the role of victorious general. But he was hardly Napoleon. He is not regarded by military historians as a particularly brilliant campaigner, but rather as a deft soldier-politician able to manage the clashing egos atop the Allied forces. Ike also had flaws. He had a huge tem-per, which he mostly disguised, except from his immediate subordinates. But he had a kind of confidence, humility, and courage that proved essential for his time.

A DANGEROUS TIME

Make no mistake, his time was indeed a dangerous one. The nuclear age had arrived with the dropping of the atom bomb in 1945, but the era had become infinitely more fraught just as Eisenhower was elected in 1952. While golfing after the election, Ike was informed that America had just blown up an atoll in the South Pacific with a bomb—the "Super," or hydrogen bomb, that was 200 times more powerful than the bombs dropped on Hiroshima and Nagasaki. Alarmingly, the Russians, who had exploded their own atom bomb in 1949, would develop a crude hydrogen bomb within a year. More menac-ingly, the Russians' captured Nazi scientists were at work on long-range mis-siles that, by the end of the decade if not before, would have the capacity to deliver nuclear bombs to the United States within a matter of minutes.

At the same time, Soviet communism was expansionist and on the move. Stalin's Russia had absorbed Eastern Europe in one gulp at the end of World War II, and global communism appeared to be on the march in newly Red China and all through decolonizing Asia, Africa, and Latin America—what became known as "the developing world." Upon assuming office in January 1953, Eisenhower also inherited a hot regional war in Korea, where Chinese and Soviet-backed communist troops from the north had invaded the south in June 1950. The political pressure was intense to build up U.S. military forces to oppose the communists wherever they encroached, especially in a Western Europe still ravaged by World War II. Cold warriors in the outgoing Truman Administration were pushing a document called NSC 68, which called for massive increases in defense spending.

Eisenhower did not want to do that. He feared the rise of the National Security State, both because of the risk to civil liberties and human freedom (the memory of fascism was still fresh) and because heavy spending on the military threatened to throw the economy out of whack, certainly over the long term.

Eisenhower believed that true national security started with a sound economy, and he was determined not to overspend and overtax. It is a little known fact that during his eight years as president, Eisenhower trimmed defense spending by about 20 percent—mostly by cutting back his beloved Army (while expanding the Air Force as a strategic deterrent).

Eisenhower's immediate challenge on taking office was to end the Korean War. This he did by threatening to use nuclear weapons. He discreetly hinted through diplomatic channels that unless North Korea came to the peace table, the United States might drop atom bombs on communist territory.

The Korean War, which had been stalemated, ended within six months. Scholars still debate whether the armistice was brought about by Ike's nuclear threat or by Stalin's death in March 1953 and a general war-weariness in Moscow, Beijing, and Pyongyang. Regardless, Eisenhower had come up with a strategy that would drive his foreign policy for the rest of his presidency. That policy was called "Massive Retaliation." In 1954, Eisenhower's secretary of State, John Foster Dulles, announced that any communist incursion anywhere in the world would be met by massive retaliation—meaning nuclear attack—by the United States.

"Massive Retaliation" was immediately questioned—by allies, by the press, and by Eisenhower's own advisers. Were we really to believe that the United States would use nuclear weapons to stop a communist incursion anywhere in the world? European capitals were doubtful that the United States would risk a global nuclear war to stop an invasion—that Washington would "trade Boston for Bonn," as the saying went. In the United States, military thinkers like General Maxwell Taylor, chief of staff of the Army (which stood to lose the most resources from Ike's strategy) began pushing for a policy of "flexible response," the capacity and intention to fight small wars with conventional forces.

AVOIDING SMALL WARS

But Ike didn't want to fight small or "limited" wars. He knew from his own experience as a wartime commander, as well as from his nuanced reading of military history and especially von Clausewitz's *On War*, that small wars had a way of becoming big wars, of getting out of control. For Ike, it was all or nothing. Go big or don't go. He did not want the United States to get sucked into "brush fire" wars that could spread into great conflagrations.

Ike's determination to avoid small wars was tested when the French military collapsed in Vietnam in 1954. There were strong calls for U.S. intervention, but Ike resisted. He did not want to fight a ground war in Asia. Vietnam was split in two, and the United States felt compelled to give guarantees to come to the aid of South Vietnam (promises that in later administrations would become problematic).

At least in his time, Eisenhower finessed Vietnam. But the threats kept coming. In China, Mao Tse-tung began shelling offshore islands occupied by the Nationalist Chinese, who had been driven from the mainland to their island redoubt of Taiwan in 1949. The United States was pledged to protect the Nationalist Chinese from Red China. Twice, in 1955 and again in 1958, Eisenhower threatened to use nuclear weapons (comparing them to "bullets") if the Red Chinese did not back off. Both times, Chairman Mao did.

The gravest risk came from Berlin. In November 1958, the bellicose Soviet leader, Nikita Khrushchev, delivered an ultimatum: the West had to be out of Berlin in six months, or else. The former German capital, still free even though it was isolated a hundred miles inside communist East Germany, was set to become the flash point of the first U.S.–Soviet confrontation.

In Washington, Eisenhower's advisers called on him to deploy more conventional forces to resist a Russian takeover. Ike said no. It would be all or nothing—the Americans had to be willing to go nuclear. That January, Ike, who had been such a good poker player in the Army that he had to quit playing (he was winning so much money that other officers resented him), used a poker analogy with the National Security Council. The note taker recorded the president saying, "In order to avoid beginning with the white chips and working up to the blue, we should place them [the Soviets] on notice that our whole stack is in play." He meant no escalation from white chips—conventional forces—to blue chips—nuclear bombs. Rather, the Americans would "hit the Russians as hard as we could." The Russians "will have started the war, and we will finish it. That is all the policy I have," said the president. Ike added, "This is not going to be some nice, sweet, World War II kind of war."

Eisenhower had great interpersonal skills. He usually refused to use the phone because he liked to meet people face to face. He wanted to meet with Khrushchev to take his measure and to make the Kremlin boss his partner in avoiding world war. The issue, he wrote in a smart letter to a friend in 1956, "is not merely man against man or nation against nation. It is man against war."

In the summer of 1959, Ike invited Khrushchev to the United States and brought him to Camp David. An inveterate blusterer, Khrushchev ranted and threatened that the tanks would roll in Berlin. By lunchtime, the talks seemed at an impasse.

But Ike took a nap and had an idea. Ike's Gettysburg farm was close by. He called his daughter-in-law, Barbara, and told her to have her kids all spruced up and on the porch of the farmhouse in 30 minutes. He brought Khrushchev to meet them.

Ike knew that Khrushchev was not suicidal. Indeed, he was a survivor. He had survived Hitler and Stalin. The Kremlin leaders, Ike said, were not "early Christian martyrs." They wanted to live, too.

Khrushchev was charmed and warmed by Ike's grandchildren. He, too, had grandchildren. The next day, after some more dickering, he lifted his ultimatum on Berlin. The crisis passed, at least for a time.

A COLDER WAR

Of course, it was not the end of crises or the end of the Cold War. After a U-2 spy plane was shot down by the Russians on the eve of a summit meeting in May 1960, the Cold War entered a new and more dangerous phase. It did not ease until the superpowers went to the very brink of nuclear Armageddon during the Cuban Missile Crisis in October 1962.

But Eisenhower succeeded in avoiding nuclear confrontation during his crucial years in office, when both sides were developing their nuclear arsenals and it was unclear what might provoke an attack. It is noteworthy that once Ike got America out of Korea in 1953, he never again committed U.S. troops to combat. No other modern president has been so successful at staying out of war.

Ike's record is not flawless by any means. To avoid using conventional troops, Eisenhower relied too much on covert action by the CIA. After some early coups in Iran and Guatemala (which hardly look like successes in hindsight), the CIA blundered and left a trail of ill will and suspicion of American meddling in much of the world. But, in his time, Eisenhower was able to largely avoid armed conflict. He even virtually ordered the British, French, and Israelis to cease their invasion of Egypt during the 1956 Suez Crisis.

And he did so discreetly. Ike was never a showoff. (He had learned how *not* to behave by studying the vainglorious General Douglas MacArthur, his boss in the 1930s.) Ike exuded confidence, but also moderation and humility.

But his strategy—to play brinksmanship—was something that only he could have pulled off. We can never know whether Ike actually would have used nuclear weapons. He made a point of telling no one, not even his closest aides, and may not have known himself.

Such weighty responsibility was not unfamiliar. As Supreme Allied Commander, Ike had given the order to "go" on D-Day. In August 1944, his air force commander, General Carl "Tooey" Spaatz, came to him with a dilemma. The Americans were bombing military targets by day. The British were bombing civilian targets by night. The British wanted the Americans to join them on massive city bombing. Spaatz didn't want to—he did not wish, he wrote Ike, to later face recriminations as a "war criminal" for bombing civilians. Eisenhower asked simply, "Will it end the war sooner?" The answer was yes, and American bombers joined in the raids on German cities.

No civilian presidential candidates have carried such awful burdens. Ike's stomach was a mess, and he was smoking too much by the end of World War II, but he had learned to handle the loneliness of command in a way few others could match. It is fortunate that he answered the call to duty (both political parties wanted him) in 1952, just at the time when the American president became the first human in history to have the power to save civilization—or end it.

I am not saying that only military commanders with war experience are suited to being president in dangerous times—far from it; most military commanders are not suited for civilian politics. Ike's brinksmanship would be too risky in less sure hands. But Ike was up to the challenge, fortunately. He was a unique figure and a godsend at a particularly tense juncture in the nation's history.

♦ ♦ ♦ ♦ ♦

44. John F. Kennedy: Bearing Liberty's Burden

by Larry J. Sabato

Despite serving a tragically shortened term, John F. Kennedy had a major impact on America's position as a global superpower.[1] JFK's time in the White House came during a peak of the Cold War, shaping his view of the world as essentially bipolar—communism versus capitalism, the Soviet Union (and China) versus the United States. The significant foreign policy crises and accomplishments of 1961–63 were all tied to this worldview and chilly strategic landscape: the Bay of Pigs disaster, the building of the Berlin Wall, the Cuban Missile Crisis, growing involvement in the Vietnam conflict, and the attempt to reduce tensions with the first successful negotiation with the Soviet Union on arms control, resulting in a partial Nuclear Test Ban Treaty.

America's deep-seated fear of communism and the specter of nuclear war had spurred JFK to campaign in 1960 on a "missile gap" that allegedly existed between the United States and the Soviet Union. After Election Day, Kennedy accepted that the gap was nonexistent and let that rhetoric die, yet he continued to reflect the Cold War tenor of the time. In a memorable inaugural address that still rates as one of history's best, President Kennedy spoke of the "long twilight struggle" against tyranny, proclaiming, "[W]e shall pay any price, bear any burden, meet any hardship, support any friend, oppose any foe, in order to assure the survival and the success of liberty."

Despite the tough rhetoric, however, Kennedy's first actions included peaceful initiatives to strengthen the American image abroad. Two of Kennedy's early programs, the Peace Corps and the Alliance for Progress, were designed to lessen the influence the Soviets and the Chinese wielded in developing nations. On March 1, 1961, he established the Peace Corps through an executive order, and, more than a half-century later, it remains one of JFK's most vital legacies, a popular avenue for public service, especially among young Americans. Kennedy unveiled his Alliance for Progress program—a Latin American version of the Marshall Plan—during a March 13, 1961, ceremony at the White House. Congress appropriated an initial $500 million for the program, and the following year allocated more than $1 billion more to Latin America.

Of course, Kennedy understood that programs like the Peace Corps and Alliance for Progress—which would be characterized as "soft power" initiatives today—could not stop the spread of communism by themselves. He had served in the Pacific Theater during World War II as a Navy patrol boat commander, and had been wounded in combat. Kennedy also lost his older brother Joseph "Joe" Kennedy, Jr., a naval aviator who was killed in the war. He thus knew from experience that force and sacrifice were sometimes necessary to protect national interests and freedom itself. Unfortunately for an untested commander in chief only months on the job, Kennedy's initial use of force went terribly wrong.

BAY OF PIGS FIASCO

In April 1961, in what turned out to be perhaps the worst decision of his presidency, Kennedy allowed a CIA-trained paramilitary force of some 1,400 men to launch an ill-fated invasion of Cuba at the Bay of Pigs.

Since the day after his election, JFK had been urged to confront Premier Fidel Castro. JFK's transitional "Committee on National Security Policy" warned that a lack of "firm action" in Cuba would allow the country's communists to consolidate power.

In late January, CIA officials ratcheted up the pressure by urging the president to launch an attack before Castro could fully align himself with the

Soviet bloc and spread communism throughout the Western Hemisphere. The attack, advocates claimed, would spark a homegrown uprising against Castro's government. Allen Dulles, director of the CIA, and Richard Bissell, deputy director of planning, assured the president that the invasion would be short and decisive. Yet the scheme was so harebrained that some observers later wondered whether top CIA and military officials pushed it on Kennedy to embarrass him or force him to commit fully to overthrowing Castro once the poorly planned assault inevitably collapsed.

Most of Kennedy's military advisers ultimately supported the invasion. Just as important, the president thought that the operation had already received the scrutiny and blessing of his predecessor, former general and hero of the D-Day invasion Dwight D. Eisenhower. In reality, Eisenhower had only approved the *training* of Cuban paramilitaries and had not given the green light for a specific attack plan.

Despite multiple warning signs, Kennedy went ahead with the operation. On April 15, eight aging B-26 bombers painted with Cuban Air Force insignia dropped bombs on three of Castro's air bases. Some Cuban T-33 jets survived, however, and they later helped repel the U.S.-backed paramilitary force.

Worried that the American role was about to be revealed to the world, Kennedy cancelled a second airstrike scheduled for April 17, even though CIA officials insisted it was essential to the success of the invasion. JFK also ordered the USS *Essex*—on patrol in the West Indies—to steer clear of the fighting. Without American military support, the invading brigade didn't stand a chance. Castro's T-33s destroyed six of the B-26s and two ships. One hundred fourteen exiles were cut down on the beach; 1,189 others were captured and thrown in jail to await possible execution.

A few days later, Kennedy called Eisenhower and asked the former president to meet him at Camp David to discuss the crisis. "I believe there is only one thing to do when you go into this kind of thing," Ike replied matter-of-factly, "It must be a success." He asked why Kennedy hadn't provided air cover for the rebels. JFK answered that he had been worried about the Soviet response in Berlin. Eisenhower assured the president that the communists only attacked when they detected weakness. "The failure of the Bay of Pigs will embolden the Soviets to do something that they would not otherwise do," he warned.

"Well," said Kennedy, "my advice was that we must try to keep our hands from showing in the affair." Eisenhower was stunned. "Mr. President, how could you expect the world to believe that we had nothing to do with it? Where did these people get the ships to go from Central America to Cuba? Where did they get the weapons?"

The sad truth was that the inexperienced Kennedy had not paid enough attention to the details of the plan. He was also overly deferential to some military and civilian advisers and failed to fully think through the consequences of his actions. Kennedy loyalists tried to pin the blame for the defeat on everyone but the president. Even Eisenhower served as a convenient scapegoat for a brief time.

To his credit, JFK accepted full responsibility for the fiasco in short order. "There's an old saying," he told the press, "that victory has a hundred fathers and defeat is an orphan . . . I am the responsible officer of the government and that is quite obvious."

The American people appreciated the young president's candor, and they rallied behind their leader at a time of crisis. By the end of April, Kennedy's approval ratings had soared above 80 percent. Behind the scenes, JFK internalized the lessons of the Bay of Pigs fiasco. He learned the hard way that each crisis and international situation had to be evaluated from the unique perspective of the commander in chief in the Oval Office, and from no one else's point of view—a lonely realization that all his successors have come to terms with as well.

There is no steeper learning curve than for presidents new on the job, however, and the Bay of Pigs crisis not only strengthened ties between Havana and Moscow but also caused considerable damage to America's reputation abroad. Almost immediately, Castro issued an official declaration that Cuba was a Marxist-Leninist country. The following year, of course, Castro would allow the USSR to put nuclear missiles in Cuba, a decision that triggered the most serious crisis of the Cold War. By that time, however, John F. Kennedy would prove a more seasoned and steadfast leader.

A CRISIS IN BERLIN

In the interim, JFK sought to make peace, not wage war. On June 3, 1961, Kennedy shook hands with Khrushchev on the steps of the American embassy in Vienna. When Kennedy suggested that the two leaders work together to maintain the geopolitical status quo, Khrushchev lectured the young president on the inevitable triumph of communism. "Ideas have never been destroyed and this is proven in the whole course of human development," Khrushchev railed. "The Soviet Union supports its ideas and holds them in high esteem. It cannot guarantee that these ideas will stop at its borders."

When Kennedy warned about the dangers of miscalculation and war, Khrushchev told a story about a man who kept trying to control his son after he'd already grown up. One day the son simply refused to take any more instructions from his aging father. The parallels were obvious. "We have grown up," said the Soviet chairman. "You're an old country. We're a young country." At the end of the day, JFK hung his head in dismay. "He treated me like a little boy," the president complained.

The sparring match between the leaders of East and West continued the next day. Talk turned to Berlin, and the Soviet chairman grew visibly agitated, describing the West's part of the city as "the bone in the Soviet throat." Kennedy would have none of it, insisting that the United States would defend West Berlin at all costs. Khrushchev bellowed, "If the U.S. wants to start a war over Germany, let it be so." The Soviet Union would sign a peace treaty with East Germany by the end of the year, starting the process of West Berlin's absorption, and it was up to the United States to decide whether that meant war. Kennedy didn't flinch: "Then, Mr. Chairman, there will be war. It will be a cold winter." The Berlin crisis had begun.

The crisis that grew out of a divided German city became one of the most dangerous moments of the Cold War. A single misstep on either side could have plunged the earth into nuclear winter, and that thought weighed heavily on Kennedy. According to the journalist James Reston, the president appeared "shaken and angry" after his summit with Khrushchev.

Bobby Kennedy thought that there was a "one-in-five chance of war" during this period. Dean Acheson, former secretary of state, advised the president to draw a line in the sand for the Russians. "Until this conflict of wills is resolved," he wrote in a top-secret memo, "an attempt to solve the Berlin issue by negotiation is worse than a waste of time and energy. It is dangerous."

Kennedy settled on an aggressive approach, and in a nationally televised address on July 25, he asked Congress for an extra $3.2 billion, enough additional soldiers, sailors, and airmen to require a massive expansion of the draft, and authority to activate the reserves.

And yet JFK still hoped to avoid a fight. What he had intentionally left out of the speech was just as important as what he had included. When the Warsaw Pact Council convened in early August 1961, East German communist leader Walter Ulbricht pointed out that Kennedy had limited his comments to the defense of West Berlin's rights. Thus, Ulbricht proposed closing the border between East and West Berlin, a plan known as "Operation Chinese Wall" that had been tossed around in communist circles for several years. Khrushchev approved the scheme, and in the early hours of August 13, East German troops began building the infamous, 103-mile-long Berlin Wall, running through the center of the city and dividing the eastern and western sectors. West Germans were shocked and demanded a forceful response, but Kennedy declined lest military escalation on both sides gather momentum and prove irreversible.

At the same time Kennedy reassured West Germany of America's commitment to its security. He dispatched about 1,500 troops to drive down the autobahn through East Germany to West Berlin; they received a warm welcome as they rolled through the city's shopping district. Kennedy also sent General Lucius Clay—the hero of the 1948 Berlin airlift—and Vice President Johnson to meet with Mayor Willy Brandt and boost Berlin's spirits. Tensions over Berlin gradually eased. In June of 1963, Kennedy himself would travel to Berlin, where his famous "Ich bin ein Berliner" ("I am a Berliner") speech served as a milestone signaling U.S. commitment to the Western alliance.

However, it was partly to create a bargaining chip for Berlin that Khrushchev deployed nuclear missiles to Cuba the following year. The end of one crisis thus planted the seeds for the next, far worse one.

THE CUBAN MISSILE CRISIS

On the morning of Tuesday, October 16, 1962, JFK was still in bed reading newspapers when his national security adviser, McGeorge Bundy, arrived with urgent news: a U-2 spy plane flying over Cuba two days earlier had detected Soviet medium-range missiles that could be fitted with nuclear warheads and fired on U.S. cities.

The president was genuinely stunned—were the Russians trying to start a nuclear war? None of his Kremlinologists had anticipated the move, and in September JFK had made it clear that if Khrushchev tried to supply Cuba with offensive (rather than just defensive) weapons, the "gravest issues would arise." How could the Soviet leader engineer a provocation so threatening it was certain to invite the most serious possible response from the United States?

Days of tense meetings with the president's top intelligence, military, and foreign policy advisers followed, hidden from view while an image of normality was projected to the nation. The information at Kennedy's disposal was uncertain, and his advisers differed widely in their preferred approaches. No one even knew for sure whether any missiles were operational, or if there were other missile sites on Cuba that might be more advanced.

Khrushchev's full game plan also remained opaque. The Soviets might be trying to compensate for a perceived American advantage in the nuclear balance of terror. Short-range missiles in Cuba were a cheap, effective way to deliver a heavy payload against U.S. targets. In addition, Khrushchev might be trying to use Cuba as a bargaining chip for Berlin. If the United States launched a preemptive strike against Castro, the Soviet leader would have an excuse to send tanks into West Berlin.

The debate among JFK's team was intense, with some favoring military options such as air strikes on the Soviet missile sites and a full-scale invasion of Cuba, which very possibly could have led to an exchange of nuclear weapons between the two superpowers. The president made clear he wanted to take some decisive action but nothing that would lead to nuclear war, which he described as "the final failure." Kennedy decided on a naval blockade of Cuba to turn around Russian ships bringing missiles to the island.

It was finally time to go public. On the evening of Monday, October 22, 1962, Americans huddled around television sets and radios. Kennedy began, "This government, as promised, has maintained the closest surveillance of the Soviet military buildup on the island of Cuba. Within the past week, unmistakable evidence has established the fact that a series of offensive missile sites is now in preparation on that imprisoned island. The purpose of these bases can be none other than to provide a nuclear strike capability against the Western Hemisphere." Therefore, the United States would begin a "quarantine" of Cuba; the word "blockade" was not employed because it had graver diplomatic implications.

Kennedy called on Khrushchev "to halt and eliminate this clandestine, reckless, and provocative threat to world peace and to stable relations." The United States would regard a nuclear attack from Cuban territory on any country in the Western Hemisphere as an attack by Russia itself, Kennedy said, which would trigger "a full retaliatory response upon the Soviet Union."

THE SOVIETS BLINK

The quarantine went into effect at 10:00 AM on Wednesday, October 24, 1962. By then, sixty-three ships, including a number of Latin American vessels, were patrolling the waters around Cuba. Scores of other ships, airplanes, and troops were on standby, awaiting orders from the president to attack. At 10:25 AM Kennedy received a report that several of the inbound Soviets vessels had stopped short of the quarantine line. Word came a few minutes later that other ships were returning to Russia.

"We're eyeball to eyeball and I think the other fellow just blinked," whispered Secretary of State Dean Rusk. Actually, unbeknownst to the White House, Khrushchev had ordered his vessels to turn back more than a full day earlier, and they were farther from the quarantine line than U.S. reports suggested. Still, Rusk was right, and for the first time since the crisis began, events were moving away from war.

The crisis was far from over, however, and could not end while Soviet missiles remained in Cuba. On Friday, October 26, the State Department received a letter from Khrushchev addressed to the president. Worried about the prospect of a nuclear war, Khrushchev offered to withdraw the missiles in exchange for a U.S. pledge not to invade Cuba.

Kennedy remained appropriately skeptical, given the earlier duplicity by the Soviet regime. His suspicions hardened the next day when the Soviets released a second statement, adding a new condition for peace: the withdrawal of American missiles stationed in Turkey. As a reply, Robert Kennedy suggested that they simply ignore the second statement and respond to Khrushchev's original letter. JFK liked the idea. He also dispatched his brother to meet with Anatoly Dobrynin, the Soviet ambassador to the United States.

At the same time, Kennedy was coming under increased pressure from his military advisers to launch an attack. At 4 PM he learned that a Soviet surface-to-air missile had killed a U-2 pilot, Major Rudolf Anderson, overflying Cuba earlier that day. The Joint Chiefs demanded an "eye for an eye" response, but the president refused. Khrushchev needed time to mull over his proposal, and a military response of any kind might short-circuit the only real chance to avert nuclear war. Moreover, the Bay of Pigs crisis had taught Kennedy that his generals could be very wrong.

At 7:45 PM, Robert Kennedy received Ambassador Dobrynin in his office at the Justice Department. "I want to lay out the current alarming situation the way the president sees it," the attorney general explained. The downing of the U-2 plane meant that there was "now strong pressure on the president to give an order to respond with fire if fired upon" that could easily spark a "chain reaction."

RFK then summarized the main points of the president's response to Khrushchev's October 26 letter: if the Soviets dismantled their missiles, the United States would lift its embargo and promise not to invade Cuba. When Dobrynin asked about the missiles in Turkey, RFK assured him that the issue was negotiable, although the president could not publicly announce any such deal for fear of undermining the NATO alliance. Instead, President Kennedy would order the dismantling of the missiles in a few months, after the crisis had passed.

When Khrushchev learned about the meeting, he wasted no time in accepting Kennedy's terms. The Soviet leader further ordered an immediate radio broadcast of his decision so the news would be received and confirmed by Washington before events could spiral further out of control on either side. JFK was inclined to believe the crisis was over but some of his military advisers disagreed. They were convinced that the Soviets were employing a clever delaying tactic and urged the president to attack.

Yet after the Bay of Pigs, Kennedy was a different leader. He had learned the value of caution—that discretion truly was the better part of valor. In a nod to their concerns, however, the president promised he would maintain the Cuban quarantine until all of the missiles were removed.

KENNEDY'S FINEST MOMENT

Although decades have elapsed since the Cuban Missile Crisis, it continues to fascinate as well as haunt us. Without question, it was the most perilous moment of the Cold War and, one could argue further, one of the most dangerous moments in the history of mankind. A nuclear exchange with Russia would have made the carnage of Hiroshima and Nagasaki seem minor.

The lessons we can draw from the crisis still apply, even in a messier world that has long since ceased to be bipolar. Perhaps above all, governments should remember that peace can be achieved even under the most difficult circumstances. Shrewd leaders must understand, as Kennedy did, how to combine the threat of military force with face-saving diplomatic options that rational regimes (where they exist) will normally prefer to their own destruction. Military options are often enticing because they offer the promise of quick and total victory, yet the promise usually turns out to be an illusion.

In the case of Cuba, the president's generals would have preferred to destroy the missile sites, solving the immediate threat while very possibly creating a far greater one—all-out war. President Kennedy's intelligence, patience, and probing questions during the crisis validated the wisdom of the Founders' decision to put military leaders under civilian control.

A less thoughtful or guarded commander in chief might have given in to his generals' pleadings. Kennedy's wisdom and sober judgment in October 1962 have justifiably been praised by historians, and this was probably his finest moment as president. The costly lessons learned at the Bay of Pigs paid off for the president and the world.

Not incidentally, the harrowing events of "the missiles of October" prodded President Kennedy to reevaluate his policies. Could some longer-term good come from this near-death experience? Was a search for common ground between East and West more promising than he had yet conceded? Might the United States and the Soviet Union work together to limit the proliferation of nuclear weapons? Kennedy would emphasize these themes in his final year in the White House.

BANNING NUCLEAR TESTS

During the summer of 1963, the president began to rethink America's Cold War objectives. The Cuban Missile Crisis gave him a greater appreciation for the precariousness of life in the nuclear age. He wanted to reduce tensions between the superpowers before it was too late. In June, on the day before a nationally televised civil rights address, Kennedy outlined his new vision for "world peace" in a graduation speech at American University in Washington.

"What kind of peace do we seek?" he asked. "Not a Pax Americana enforced on the world by American weapons of war. Not the peace of the grave or the security of the slave. I am talking about genuine peace, the kind of peace that makes life on earth worth living, the kind that enables men and nations to grow and to hope and to build a better life for their children—not merely peace for Americans but peace for all men and women—not merely peace in our time but peace for all time."

After reminding his listeners of the futility of "total war" in the nuclear age, JFK challenged Americans to examine their own prejudices and assumptions. "First: let us examine our attitude toward peace itself," he said. "Too many of us think it is impossible. Too many think it unreal. But that is a dangerous, defeatist belief. It leads to the conclusion that war is inevitable—that mankind is doomed—that we are gripped by forces we cannot control."

Instead, JFK wanted Americans to feel hopeful about the future. Moreover, as a World War II veteran, he knew the enormous human costs of conflict. Since war was a "manmade" problem, he said, it could be eliminated by men, for "no problem of human destiny is beyond human beings." (Barack Obama chose these words to be stitched into his presidential carpet in the Oval Office.) Although JFK acknowledged that there were enormous differences between the United States and the USSR, he believed that the two nations could work together to find common ground. "And if we cannot end now our differences, at least we can help make the world safe for diversity. For, in the final analysis, our most basic common link is that we all inhabit this small planet. We all breathe the same air. We all cherish our children's future. And we are all mortal."

Nikita Khrushchev called it "the greatest speech by any American president since Roosevelt." The frigid relationship between Moscow and Washington began to thaw. A nuclear test ban treaty, which had been discussed off and on for years, now seemed a possibility, and Soviet and American diplomats hammered out the details of the treaty in the summer. In early August 1963, diplomats from the United States, the USSR, and the United Kingdom signed a treaty banning all nuclear weapons testing in the atmosphere, under water, and in outer space (although not underground). The

U.S. Senate ratified it overwhelmingly, and President Kennedy signed it on October 7, 1963—his last major accomplishment and, according to his brother Robert, the one of which he was proudest.

Most other countries became signatories as well, although significantly, not China, France, or North Korea. It is often said that a crisis should never go to waste, and in this sense, the Cuban Missile Crisis led to a diplomatic breakthrough that was a precedent for even more sweeping arms control agreements of the 1970s and 1980s.

THE VIETNAM "TAR PIT"

In the Cold War crises that came to define the early 1960s, the seeds were also sown for what was arguably America's most misguided and damaging international intervention of the post–World War II era—at least until the Iraq War in the 21st century.

The record is clear that President Kennedy escalated the conflict in Vietnam. When he took office, 800 American military personnel were stationed in South Vietnam; he increased the number to 16,000 in two years. President Eisenhower had been wary of American involvement in Vietnam, having watched the French get bogged down in Southeast Asia, ending in a humiliating withdrawal in 1954. In his own view, Kennedy chose a middle path. He refused a 1961 Pentagon recommendation to commit 200,000 U.S. troops to Vietnam, but he dreaded seeing any country fall to communism on his watch and eventually committed American prestige in Southeast Asia.

Gradually, U.S. troop "advisers" were drawn surreptitiously into direct fighting. Kennedy ordered Green Berets to use counterinsurgency tactics against communist guerrillas; he approved the use of napalm—a jellied gasoline that sticks to the skin as it burns—as well as Agent Orange, a defoliant that was later discovered to cause birth defects; and he provided Ngo Dinh Diem, the authoritarian ruler of South Vietnam, with guns and money.

But by the autumn of 1963, Kennedy appeared to realize his Vietnam strategy was failing. The previous December, Democrat Mike Mansfield, the Senate majority leader, returned from Indochina with a gloomy report—the United States was getting sucked into a tar pit, just as the French had a decade earlier. The brutal execution of Diem on November 2, 1963, in which the United States had played a considerable role, caused JFK to intensify his reassessment of U.S. involvement in Vietnam.

In public, President Kennedy had been consistent and resolute, for the most part, about the U.S. role in Vietnam. In private, at least as his closest associates told it later, he remained skeptical about deeper intervention in the region. "They keep telling me to send combat units over there," he said with regard to his generals' demands for additional troops. "That means sending draftees, along with regular Army advisers, into Vietnam. I'll never send draftees over there to fight."[2]

However, JFK never publicly made his doubts clear, nor precisely outlined his intentions and goals in Vietnam. That left his successor Lyndon Johnson room to define his own policy on Vietnam, while claiming it was Kennedy's.

Undeniably, there were also contradictions in JFK's Vietnam policy; he said one thing but did another. In October 1963, President Kennedy announced that the United States would withdraw 1,000 military personnel by the end of the year. At first glance, this decision seems to indicate that Kennedy was ready to wind down operations in Vietnam. On November 21, 1963, the day he departed for Texas, he told an aide to put together "an in-depth study of every possible option we've got in Vietnam, including how to get out of there." He wanted to review the "whole thing from the bottom to the top."

Yet the address Kennedy was supposed to deliver at the Dallas Trade Mart on the day he was assassinated contained a firm message: "Our security and strength, in the last analysis, directly depend on the security and strength of others, and that is why our military and economic assistance plays such a key role in enabling those who live on the periphery of the communist world to maintain their independence of choice. Our assistance to these nations can be painful, risky and costly, as is true in Southeast Asia today. But we dare not weary of the task."

A CONSEQUENTIAL LEGACY

As with almost all presidents, the Kennedy legacy in foreign and national security affairs is mixed. JFK was in the mainstream of his party and country during a period of global war both hot and cold, and as a result he was both anticommunist and pro-defense. Yet he also evolved into a wary executive, one determined to critically examine the recommendations of his subordinates from the unique perspective of the highest office.

President Kennedy also displayed the kind of flexibility and pragmatism that defines a successful White House tenure. He was not pigeonholed or constrained by ideology, and he was resolute—in an age when Armageddon always loomed just around the corner—in preferring peace to war, and negotiation to confrontation.

The bellicose Kennedy of the inauguration eventually gave way to a leader in search of peace and common ground with the communist world. Some say that Kennedy's failures at the Bay of Pigs and in early negotiations with the Soviet Union contributed to the nearly disastrous superpower encounter over Cuba in 1962. However, as Ted Sorensen insisted to me just days before his death in 2011, "Every generation needs to know that without JFK the world might no longer exist as a result of a nuclear holocaust stemming from the Cuban Missile Crisis."

Staring into that abyss turned Kennedy, as well as the Russians, away from a sole reliance on combative rhetoric and military might and toward treaties, détente, and a lessening of international conflict where it was possible. That alone is a considerable legacy, arguably one of the most consequential during the nation's long march from strategic free rider on the British before World War II to the colossus that would win the Cold War and put its indelible imprint on the "American Century." At a moment of maximum peril in that journey, the nation very nearly veered down a dead end toward nuclear annihilation. John F. Kennedy steered America back on course.

♦ ♦ ♦ ♦ ♦

45. Lyndon B. Johnson: Committed Warrior Undone by Vietnam

by Marvin Kalb

"Let us continue."

Thus spoke Lyndon Baines Johnson on November 24, 1963, two days after he had been propelled into the presidency by the assassination of John F. Kennedy. LBJ, as he was soon to be called, wanted to assure the American people (and an anxious world) that he would continue JFK's policies at home and abroad—there would be no surprises, no abrupt changes.

Shortly after taking the oath of office in the unlikely setting of Air Force One in Dallas, Texas, Johnson immediately set course for Washington, DC. As his sleek jet streaked through the blue skies, the new president considered his awesome responsibilities, pausing long enough to make a "private vow" to himself. "I [will] devote every hour of every day during the remainder of John Kennedy's unfulfilled term," he recalled in his memoirs, "to achieving the goals he had set."[1]

On the domestic side, these included such stalwarts as economic progress and greater racial justice, and, on the foreign side, continuing to serve as the standard bearer of the Western alliance, a responsibility that traced back to U.S. victory in World War II in 1945 and the subsequent policies of Harry Truman aimed at maintaining a global U.S. military presence.

At the time, however, no goal seemed more pressing and, in a way, more frustrating than managing the war in South Vietnam—or "the mess," as Defense Secretary Robert McNamara often referred to it. Although he tried, early in his administration, to project an image of the tough Texan standing tall at the Alamo with a no-nonsense approach to the war, Johnson was actually haunted by a split vision of the conflict: on one level, he harbored the deepest doubts about the ability and willingness of the South Vietnamese to fight their own war; and yet, on another level, he was fiercely determined to uphold the "national commitment" of former presidents to stop the spread of communism in Southeast Asia, even if this meant employing American military power.

Not for the first time, a president would soon commit American troops to a war that deep down, he doubted could be won. And once a president committed the United States to a course of action, as Presidents Truman, Eisenhower, and Kennedy had done in the case of Vietnam, Johnson found that it became near impossible for their successor to abandon it. Despite his doubts, into this problematic war he plunged, explaining his actions as honoring a national "commitment" pledged by former presidents.

AMERICAN ARCHETYPE

Johnson was an old-fashioned patriot, a Texan of modest means yet unbounded ambition. He had served as an officer in the U.S. Navy during World War II and, in a career dedicated to public service, as a congressman (for twelve years), a senator (also for twelve years), and a vice president.

He was of that special generation that experienced the Great Depression; the Munich appeasement of Hitler in 1938; the hot, global war against fascism and imperialism; and then the Cold War against Stalin and communism. He emerged from this cauldron of conflict and challenges as a successful politician and a cautious cold warrior. Johnson believed, to the very depths of his soul, that the U.S. had a "commitment," a concept he embraced with an almost religious fervor, to protect America and its friends and allies from communist aggression anywhere in the world. The West had failed at Munich to stop Hitler and thus head off a catastrophic world war, and Johnson believed history had in his time provided the United States with another opportunity to do the right thing in South Vietnam—and stop communism in its tracks.

The phrase was not in common usage in the early 1960s, but Johnson truly considered the United States to be the "indispensable nation," the one nation the world could depend on to do its job in a dangerous time. As his Secretary of State, Dean Rusk, once explained to skeptical reporters, thumping his right thumb on a coffee table to make his point, "When the United States applies pressure on something, that something gives." He meant that if the United States had a job to do, it did it, no questions asked.

Like Rusk, Johnson simply could not imagine a situation in which the United States, once committed to a task, would be unable to complete it, whether in Europe or Asia. This was less a matter of hubris than it was a deep faith, an unshakable confidence, in America's will and capacity, born of the seminal experiences of the Great Depression and World War II.

A WORLD OF DANGERS

Johnson's "first important decision," as he put it, came on November 26, 1963, four days into his presidency, when he signed National Security Action Memorandum 273 (NSAM 273), which reaffirmed American policy in South Vietnam—"to assist the People and Government of that country to win their contest against the externally directed and supported communist conspiracy." The NSAM was Johnson's way of informing department heads that the Kennedy policy on Vietnam would now be his policy too. There were to be many NSAMs on Vietnam as the war expanded and America's involvement deepened.

The following day, in his first address as president to a joint session of Congress, Johnson pledged: "This nation will keep its commitments from South Vietnam to West Berlin." By unfortunate circumstance—an assassination—the United States had to have a new president, but Johnson was making clear that the policy direction would stay constant.

Johnson was thrust into the presidency at the height of the Cold War. Dangers were plentiful. Just one year earlier, President Kennedy had successfully maneuvered Soviet leader Nikita Khrushchev into removing his nuclear-tipped missiles from Cuba, for instance, thus ending a crisis that had propelled the world's two superpowers to the edge of nuclear Armageddon. Fortunately for the world, Kennedy and Khrushchev both had the wit and guile to accept concessions that diffused the crisis. Six months later, having stared into the nuclear abyss and pulled back in horror, they searched for solutions to other deadlocked problems and found one in atmospheric nuclear testing. Such testing by both countries had been poisoning the atmosphere, endangering people's health as well as national agricultural output. Soon thereafter, the two superpowers signed an agreement imposing specific constraints on nuclear testing in the atmosphere.

Although Johnson was to face many national security challenges, it quickly became clear to him that one towered over the others—U.S. relations with the Soviet Union. That relationship defined the Cold War. If there had ever been any doubt, the Cuban missile crisis erased it. Whether the issue was missiles in Cuba, or a divided Berlin, or conflict in Vietnam or the Middle East, the first question on Johnson's mind was always: was the Soviet Union involved? How? And why?

Johnson's chronic anxiety about Soviet strategy did not actually begin on January 6, 1961, early in the Kennedy Administration, but on that day it deepened considerably. The reason was a chilling speech by Soviet leader Nikita Khrushchev on what he called "wars of national liberation." The Soviet leader also spoke about Cuba and Berlin, two traditional trouble spots, but his focus now was on "guerrilla wars," which he said the Kremlin supported "wholeheartedly and without reservation." Where might such "guerrilla wars" erupt? In Cuba, Algeria, and Vietnam, he warned. If "world wars" had now become too dangerous for the nuclear-armed superpowers ("the living would envy the dead," he once said), then "uprisings of colonial peoples against their oppressors" would become, for Moscow, the preferred form of warfare, one communists could rally behind not only with enthusiasm but also with the conviction that they were "in the vanguard of the peoples fighting for liberation." Such support for "wars of national liberation" might have been ideologically appealing for Khrushchev, but Kennedy and Johnson saw them as warning signals of communist expansion and aggression.

THE FIRST DOMINO

Vietnam was considered the most probable battlefield between West and East, and had been since the Eisenhower Administration. General Dwight Eisenhower, the hero of World War II, had as president espoused the theory that if one U.S. ally in Indochina fell to the communists, then its neighbors in the region were also likely to quickly capitulate in a "falling domino" effect.

A few years earlier, while pressing for passage of the Southeast Asia Treaty Organization, Secretary of State John Foster Dulles told the Senate Foreign Relations Committee that a "novel feature" of the communist challenge in Southeast Asia was "subversion . . . a very difficult thing to combat." Subversion? Senators wanted to know what he meant by that. Dulles explained, mincing no words: "It is virulent. It is well organized. It is effectively prosecuted by trained persons . . . and [it] will tax our resources and ingenuity to the utmost." Dulles's prescient testimony about "subversion" foreshadowed the guerrilla war Johnson faced in South Vietnam.

By the spring of 1965, that challenge had become stark and real. South Vietnam was collapsing under sustained communist assault and subversion. What Johnson had feared all along was unfolding before his eyes. What to do? His choice, as he later put it in Texas shorthand, was "gettin' in or gettin' out." "Out" was unacceptable to Johnson—the United States, on his watch, would not "cut and run." And "in," he suspected, would only open the door to a thousand different headaches.

More than anything else, Johnson, at that time, wanted to launch his Great Society program at home, not another bloody war in Asia. And yet, relentlessly, Vietnam tugged at his sense of national responsibility. He decided, after much agonizing deliberation, that he had to go with the "gettin' in" option—he ordered U.S. combat troops to deploy to Vietnam, even though he continued to doubt the wisdom of an American military engagement in the war.

One of his speechwriters, Douglass Cater, remembered Johnson saying, "I don't know what to do. If I send more boys in, there's going to be killin'. If I take them out, there's going to be more killin'. Anything I do, there's going to be more killin'."

On one issue only was there absolute clarity in his thinking: Johnson wanted, and got, congressional approval for any military action in Southeast Asia that he would take. By an overwhelming vote (416–0 in the House, 88–2 in the Senate), Congress, in August 1964, passed the Tonkin Gulf resolution. Although only a congressional resolution, and not a declaration of war, as required in such circumstance by the U.S. Constitution, it nevertheless authorized Johnson "to take all necessary measures to repel any armed attack against the forces of the United States and to prevent further aggression." He later explained to reporters, "If the president is going in . . ., he wants the Congress to go in right by the side of him." (Johnson had always criticized Harry Truman for not getting congressional authorization for American military action against North Korea.)

Prompting the resolution was an attack on the U.S. destroyer USS *Maddox*, which was on an intelligence-gathering mission in the Gulf of Tonkin, by North Vietnamese patrol boats. Johnson was furious at the August 2, 1964, attack, but in the midst of a presidential campaign in which he had projected himself as a "man of peace," he decided not to retaliate. His opponent, Republican Senator Barry Goldwater of Arizona, on the other hand, was a noted hawk. Two days later, in this hothouse political environment, reports surfaced of another North Vietnamese attack. This time, Johnson decided to retaliate, else he would be open to GOP criticism that he was weak. Johnson ordered air attacks against North Vietnam, opening a new phase in the war.

But there was a problem. The reports of a second North Vietnamese attack were fallacious. There had been no attack—there was only a "confusion of radar signals." In other words, when Johnson ordered air strikes against North Vietnam, he already knew there had been no communist attack to justify his retaliation. He later explained to the State Department's resident dove, George Ball, "I just think those dumb sailors were shooting at flying fish. I don't think there was any, any attack."

A SLIPPERY SLOPE

Once Johnson decided, however reluctantly, that "gettin' in" was preferable to "gettin' out," he suddenly found himself on a slippery slope in South Vietnam. On April 1, he dispatched 20,000 U.S. Army troops, plus two Marine combat battalions, but he made no public announcement of this expansion of the American military presence in South Vietnam. On April 13, he ordered the 173rd Airborne Brigade to South Vietnam. Again, no announcement. No "premature publicity," as he cautioned an aide.

On April 27, a reporter asked the president if he could imagine "circumstances" in which American troops would be "fighting" rather than just "advising" the South Vietnamese. Johnson's curt and deceptive answer was that "our purpose in Vietnam is to advise and assist those people." He was, with deliberately vague statements of that sort, beginning to open an embarrassing "credibility gap" between what he said was happening and what in fact was happening, a gap that was, in a few years, going to yawn so wide that it would cripple his ability to govern.

In June 1965, General William Westmoreland, the new U.S. commander in Vietnam, requested an additional 175,000 troops. By year's end, there were 184,000 American troops in South Vietnam. Major battles were already being fought between the American and North Vietnamese armies. By December 1966, one year later, there were 385,000 troops in theater, an increase of 200,000. By the end of 1967, the number of U.S. troops in South Vietnam had risen to 548,000.

With this massive increase in troop strength, fighting, and casualties, was the United States any closer to victory or to an honorable exit? Congress wanted to know. General Westmoreland, for the record, responded positively, speaking of "light at the end of the tunnel." However, Johnson privately told Lady Bird, his wife, that "Vietnam is getting worse every day," and he confided to his former colleague, Democratic Senator Richard Russell of Georgia, that "a man can fight if he can see daylight down the road somewhere, but there ain't no daylight in Vietnam."

MIDDLE EAST CRISIS

As he presided over a deepening American involvement in the Vietnam War and guided his Great Society legislation through Congress, Johnson also found himself absorbed in a potentially dangerous confrontation in the Middle East. He could see it coming in 1966 when Israel fought skirmishes with Egypt, Syria, and the Palestinians, shells exchanged in an atmosphere of rising tensions and heated rhetoric. The Soviet Union, eager to elbow its way into a leadership role in the region, began shipping arms, tanks, and planes to Egypt and Syria, its clients. The United States was already supplying weapons to Israel and to a group of pro-Western Arab states.

On May 16, Egypt's fiery leader, Gamal Abdul Nasser, took the first of a number of steps leading to a new war in the Middle East. He sent a 160,000-man army into the Sinai, supported by almost a thousand Soviet-made tanks. Three days later, he unceremoniously expelled United Nations peacekeepers from Gaza and Sharm al-Sheikh, in direct violation of 1957 UN agreements. Nasser explained his aims in no uncertain terms—"the destruction of Israel." "The Arab people," he added, with feigned casualness, "want to fight."

Israel warned Nasser that he was on a collision course. War was on the near horizon. Nasser, with a wave of his hand, not only dismissed Israel's warnings, but also took another step toward war by arbitrarily closing the Straits of Tiran to Israeli shipping. For Israel, this was an unmistakable casus belli for action.

Prime Minister Levi Eshkol's military advisers leaped immediately into preparations for a preemptive strike against Egypt. Eshkol himself was hesitant. He wanted a superpower ally: Egypt had the Soviet Union; he wanted the United States. And this alliance had precedent. In 1957, Eisenhower had given Israel assurances, first, that it had a "right" to free passage in the Gulf, and, second, that if free passage were denied, Israel could, under Article 51 of the UN Charter, fight for that right. Eshkol wanted to know whether Johnson agreed with Eisenhower—and, if so, what would the United States do now to help Israel?

Johnson had always been sympathetic to Israel's plight. Harry MacPherson, a speechwriter, once joked that there must be "a great many Jewish corpuscles" in LBJ's blood. "He really reminds me of a six-foot-three-inch slightly corny Texas version of a rabbi or a diamond merchant on 44th Street."

Johnson threw himself into the crisis, hoping he could both head off a war between Israel and Egypt and block any further Soviet advances in the Middle East. He met with Israeli and Egyptian diplomats, hoping to buy time. He went to the United Nations, where advisers pushed his idea of organizing an international armada to open the Gulf. Johnson felt he needed UN backing, even though Israel did not trust the world body.

Johnson also consulted with senators and congressmen in an effort to win their support in the event the United States, already bogged down in Vietnam, suddenly found itself having to take military action in the Middle East. On Capitol Hill, one war was controversial; two wars, unacceptable.

The Israelis, feeling their backs up against the wall, decided that they would give Johnson ten more days, two weeks at the most, to open the Gulf to Israeli shipping, or else they would launch a preemptive strike against Egypt. Eshkol wanted to trust Johnson, but, in the final analysis, he could not. The Israelis felt they had a clear presidential commitment of American support from Eisenhower. Yet Johnson, trapped by the war in Vietnam, was wary of providing that support without first getting UN and then congressional backing. Israel felt betrayed. War now was unavoidable.

On June 5, 1967, Israel opened the "Six Day War" with a stunningly successful preemptive attack against Egypt. On the first day, Israeli warplanes effectively destroyed the Egyptian air force, and then, on successive days, Israel quickly captured the Golan Heights from Syria and the West Bank and all of Jerusalem from Jordan. Not only had the Arabs lost; the Soviets had been humiliated.

One evening during the war, while doing a TV report from the White House, I spotted Johnson walking his dog. When he paused for a moment, I approached and asked how he thought Israel was doing. He clearly did not want to do a formal interview, but he smiled, and, with a vigorous nod, replied, "Feisty. A very feisty country." I had the impression he used the word in a very complimentary way. Israel had won, and, as its chief backer, so had the United States.

THE TET OFFENSIVE

The story was very different in Southeast Asia, where the Vietnam War shifted into a new phase. The decisive battle took place in late January 1968, when the North Vietnamese opened a major offensive up and down the spine of South Vietnam, catching American troops totally off guard. The infamous "Tet Offensive" had begun.

Viet Cong insurgents allied with North Vietnam actually breached the defensive perimeter of the U.S. Embassy in Saigon but were eventually repulsed. In fact, American and South Vietnamese troops regrouped and counterattacked, killing tens of thousands of Viet Cong guerillas and North Vietnamese troops. From a strictly military point of view, the communists lost the battle, but, from a psychological point of view, the Tet Offensive was a strategic victory.

Proof came on March 31, 1968, the year of another presidential campaign, when Johnson told the American people that he would not run for president again. For almost a year Johnson had toyed with the idea of pulling out. Family pressures and medical problems were accumulating, but, more than anything, the war was robbing him of energy, decisiveness, vision—the qualities he needed to lead a country at war. "Fire in the belly," the essential ingredient in a driven candidate, was no longer there.

Vietnam had claimed yet another victim, only this time it was the man in the Oval Office. There would be others.

Richard Nixon succeeded Johnson. Even before he took office, he told one of his advisers, "There is no way to win this war, but we can't say that, of course. In fact, we have to seem to say just the opposite."

♦ ♦ ♦ ♦ ♦

46. Richard Nixon: Deeply Flawed Visionary

by John Aloysius Farrell

As presidential events go, it seemed most forgettable: a meet and greet with Midwestern media executives at a Holiday Inn in Kansas City. Richard Nixon would offer his analysis of domestic issues, the press was told.

The date was July 6, 1971, and Nixon's mind was elsewhere. He left cattle and commodity prices behind and went winging into geopolitics. The postwar era was coming to an end, he told the journalists. No longer would the peace of the planet turn on the relationship between two great blocs of East and West, communists and capitalists.

Nixon sketched a new, multipolar world, in which the resurgent nations of Western Europe and Japan would join the United States and the Soviet Union as centers of power and stability. And China, too, would play a role, Nixon said. "Instead of there being just two superpowers," he said, there would be "five great power centers," with the Chinese among them.

"The goal of U.S. policy must be, in the long term, ending the isolation of mainland China and a normalization of our relations," Nixon said. "The United States, as compared with that position we found ourselves in immediately after World War II, has a challenge such as we did not even dream of."

The notion, to the news executives at least, seemed far-fetched. Yes, the Chinese had just hosted a U.S. ping pong team that spring. But for twenty years, Americans had been warned about monolithic communism. The fear of a Red tide, knocking over nations like dominoes, was why families had sent their sons to fight and die in Korea and Vietnam. China was a huge, terrifying enigma—still in the throes of a cultural revolution that, in its grim purges, had slaughtered thousands of its own people. The U.S. ties to Taiwan were tended by a fierce anti-China lobby.[1]

And so his countrymen missed the import of Nixon's spontaneous riff on world affairs. Henry Kissinger missed his boss' press briefing as well— although he, at least, had a good excuse. As Nixon spoke, Kissinger was on a secret mission to Beijing, to explore a rapprochement between the United States and China.

Arriving in the Chinese capital, Kissinger was thus baffled when the Chinese premier, Zhou En Lai, referred to Nixon's Kansas City remarks. Helpfully, Zhou supplied his own copy to Kissinger, who saw that it was underlined and annotated. If Americans missed the import of Nixon's comments, Zhou had not.

China and the Soviet Union, driven apart by ideological and cultural differences, had their hands around each other's throat, with dozens of armored divisions poised on both sides of their long, desolate border. Nixon and Kissinger saw an opportunity to exploit those tensions, to play one Red giant against the other, and so restrain them both.

"What Nixon sought . . . was to seize the opportunity presented by a particular confluence of forces in the world that might not be repeated—and to use this opportunity to create a new structure that could maintain peace," wrote speechwriter Ray Price. "The keys to this were provided by the tensions between Moscow and Peking."

Eight months later, Nixon was himself in Beijing, stepping down from Air Force One, offering a warm handshake to Zhou, playing "the China card." Four decades have passed, but that February, 1972 visit to China still lives up to what he called it then: "the week that changed the world."[2] It was, in its marriage of vision and expediency, a distinctively Nixonian endeavor.

A STRATEGIC VISION

"In his complicated personality," Kissinger recalled, Nixon's "high motives constantly warred with less lofty considerations."

There is no doubt that Nixon had lofty dreams: to replace the crumbling Cold War paradigm with a new, sturdy balance of power, and thus secure a generation-spanning peace. It might last, he believed, for twenty or even fifty years. He called it "a system of stability."

Yet Nixon was nothing if not a realist. He had hope, but took what he could get: mistrusting his foes, always mindful of reelection, never forgetting the insistent political need to bring the war in Vietnam to an end. It was, Kissinger recalled, an "amalgam of high national purpose and political and personal calculation."

There is no single reason why Nixon was so mesmerized by foreign affairs; it was a coincident of heredity and environment. He grew up in rural California, longing to escape, hoping to become a train engineer, an adventurer, or a political leader who "will do good for the people." His Quaker mother, to whom he was devoted, was an admirer of Woodrow Wilson, the idealistic peacemaker. And Nixon witnessed, firsthand, the waste of war when serving in the South Pacific during World War II.

"He seemed to be dreaming about some new order which would make wars impossible," said Gretchen King, who knew Dick Nixon and his wife Pat in those days after the war. "He impressed us in those days as an idealistic dreamer."[3]

On his climb to power, as a candidate for the House and Senate, Nixon could be ruthless: slandering his Democratic opponents as communist dupes and questioning their patriotism. The cartoonist Herblock portrayed him as an ill-shaven spidery creature, creeping from the sewers with a bucket of tar. But once in office, Nixon spoke and voted as a centrist: a defender of American internationalism, the Marshall Plan, and the bipartisan U.S. policy of containment. He helped Dwight Eisenhower defeat Republican isolationists in the 1952 presidential race and, as his reward, was selected as Ike's running mate. He was then just thirty-nine.

As vice president, Nixon traveled the world on good will tours for the aging Eisenhower. He confronted Nikita Khrushchev in Moscow, welcomed Fidel Castro and Winston Churchill to Washington, and narrowly escaped injury when his motorcade was attacked by anti-American mobs in Caracas, Venezuela. He forged friendships with foreign leaders and their deputies, which he carefully maintained during his years in political exile, after losing the 1960 presidential race to John F. Kennedy.

Americans embraced this latest iteration of "new Nixon"—the seasoned realist—when electing him president in 1968. He promised to free America from its Vietnam quagmire, without a humiliating surrender. "Peace with honor," he called it. It got him just enough votes—43 percent in a three-way race with Democrat Hubert Humphrey and independent George Wallace—to be elected. He took office as the first U.S. president since before the Civil War to enter office with a Congress controlled by the opposition. It is a testament to his political savvy that, under those conditions, he got anything done at all.

Nixon did so by going it alone. He cut himself off from Congress and the State Department and used secret, back-channel diplomacy to negotiate with the Soviets, Chinese, and North Vietnamese. This stimulated the bureaucracy's willingness to leak, which spurred Nixon into a self-defeating spiral of wiretapping aides and news reporters, and using illegal means like burglary in pursuit of leakers. Those same tactics, when employed against his Democratic opponents, ultimately led to the Watergate scandal and his resignation from office in August 1974.

Nixon was a Cold Warrior and inclined to see regional conflicts in Southeast and Southwest Asia, the Middle East, or Latin America through the prism of the U.S.–Soviet rivalry. At times, as during the India–Pakistan conflict of 1971, Nixon's myopic insistence on seeing every regional crisis as a great power confrontation brought the world to the lip of nuclear war. A particularly chilling White House tape captured the president and Kissinger as they discussed how the conflict could escalate into a nuclear exchange if China—at Nixon's urging—attacked India on behalf of Pakistan; the Soviet Union came to the defense of India by invading China, and the United States went to war to defend the Chinese.

But Nixon and others also believed that someday—although they could not say when—the standoff between East and West would come to an end. America's most influential Cold War theologian—George Kennan—had foreseen a day when the differing interests of the communist nations would tug them apart, Japan and Western Europe would rebound, and the resultant balance of power would create a moment for peace. There were also theorists—Nixon and Kissinger among them—who suggested during the 1960s that the United States should try to pierce China's isolation, if only, as Nixon liked to say, because 800 million people cannot be ignored.

Nixon should be credited for seizing this opportunity—but not creating it. A Chinese–American rapprochement "was inherent in the world environment" in the early 1970s, Kissinger recalled. Yet "the character of leaders is tested by their willingness to persevere in the face of uncertainty and to build for a future they can neither demonstrate nor fully discern." In Nixon's case, he recognized an opportunity in the armed clash between Soviet and Chinese border guards along the Amur and Ussuri Rivers in 1969 that led to months of military maneuvering, gunfire and tension between the two communist powers. And he seized it.

"The reason China and the United States finally got together is not because we or they finally reached the conclusion that we had been mistaken" about the other side, or its political system, Nixon told his cabinet on June 16, 1972. "Nations are motivated by self interest, not by love and understanding."

"This does not mean that understanding is not good," Nixon said, but warm feelings and fellowship "won't change the Mexican position on salinity of the Colorado River."[4] Only a cool, clear appraisal of national interest would.

Playing the China card put pressure on the Soviets. From their first back-channel talks with Nixon and Kissinger, the Russian representatives conveyed alarm about a Sino–American alliance. They pushed for their own summit meeting, in the spring of 1972, at which two historic arms control agreements were signed.

The Anti-Ballistic Missile and Strategic Arms Limitation treaties were also products of Nixonian expediency. Given his druthers, Nixon would have outspent and outbuilt the Soviet military machine—but the times were not ripe. A dovish Congress wearied by the long years of the Vietnam War was not about to fund massive new nuclear weapons systems. Leonid Brezhnev was willing to bargain, and Nixon and Kissinger cut the best deal they could, persuading Congress to fund an antiballistic missile system that they then used as a bargaining chip.

THE LIMITS OF REALISM

Nixonian realism had its limits. Expediency was the guiding value in late summer, 1971, when Nixon gathered his advisers at Camp David and came up with a plan to revamp the international economic order. The United States dropped the gold standard, moved toward floating currency rates, and embraced wage and price controls. The combination got him re-elected, but helped fuel the stagflation—stagnant growth rates coupled with high inflation—that crippled Nixon's second term and those of his immediate successors.

And while the atmospherics of the Soviet and Chinese summits provided great theater, the two powers, engaged in their rivalry for leadership of the Communist bloc, never applied the level of pressure that Nixon hoped they would on their North Vietnamese clients. In the end, it was the concessions Nixon made in negotiations, his 1972 reelection landslide, and his demonstrated willingness to "bomb the bejesus" out of North Vietnam that brought about the 1973 ceasefire and the end of American involvement in the war.

As in the India–Pakistan war, Nixon's unwillingness to intercede in a deteriorating situation until it was too late and to view the subsequent hostilities through the prism of Soviet–American competition, allowed the Middle East to get out of hand, resulting in the 1973 Yom Kippur war. The United States was compelled to rescue Israel and fend off Soviet intervention. In a bold display of shuttle diplomacy, Kissinger then exploited the good graces and shrewd thinking of Anwar Sadat (who had recognized that Arab self-confidence was an essential ingredient to a lasting peace) to broker an end to the war and lay a foundation for peaceful relations between Egypt and Israel.

AN UNFINISHED LEGACY

Many of Nixon's strategic plans hinged on a successful second term, and so were ruined by the Watergate scandals and his eventual resignation. Nixon hoped to keep North Vietnam at bay with the threat or use of American air power; instead, after an indecently short interval, Congress withdrew support from the South Vietnamese Army, and South Vietnam fell to the communists in 1975. The Nixon-Kissinger détente with the USSR came under fire from both Right and Left during the 1976 presidential election. After the Soviets invaded Afghanistan in 1979, the superpowers launched a new nuclear arms race.

Like the other Cold War presidents, Nixon gets credit for keeping the pressure on until communist tyranny collapsed on itself. That challenge, and their ultimate success, is today underappreciated. It was a delicate, dodgy game of bluff and bravado and bravery to resist totalitarianism without bringing on the century's third devastating—and this time nuclear—world war. As the United States inevitably slipped from its gloriously preeminent postwar perch, Nixon helped Americans understand the reasons and the factors at work, voiced hope and optimism, and supplied his countrymen and women with the vision of a new international order that could bring both peace and honor.

Nixon also bears responsibility, however, along with his predecessors and successors, for the sins of the imperial presidency—the assaults on civil liberties and the resort to political demagoguery and polarization at home, and the murderous and often-bungled covert acts abroad.

The great triumph of Nixon's foreign policy remains the opening to China—memorialized in opera and film ("Only Nixon could go to China," Mr. Spock tells Captain Kirk in *Star Trek VI: The Undiscovered Country*) and looking more brilliant with each passing year, as China has made a peaceful and orderly transition to economic superpower. History will always remember that Nixon was the president who resigned, but it will mark as well the historic meeting between Richard Nixon and Mao Tse-tung.

During his secret journey to China in that summer of 1971, Kissinger noted that Zhou and other Chinese officials seemed torn and conflicted by their new accommodation with the capitalist West. But not Mao. Not for a moment. Mao was as happy to cut deals with the Right as with the Left, he told Nixon. In fact, he preferred it. And Nixon assured Mao that men of the Right could make deals out of reach for liberals and leftists.

In the end it was true: only Nixon could go to China. And only Mao, whose dictatorial powers and revolutionary status were unchallengeable, could have hosted him. They were much alike: two visionaries guided by expediency, realists chasing dreams.

◆ ◆ ◆ ◆ ◆

47. Gerald Ford: The Healer

by James Kitfield

When he took the oath of office in a hastily arranged ceremony in the East Room of the White House at noon on August 9, 1974, Gerald R. Ford inherited one of the most devastating domestic and international landscapes any U.S. president has confronted. Just twenty-five minutes earlier, Richard Nixon's letter of resignation had been tendered in order that the thirty-seventh president not face certain impeachment for the Watergate cover-up. Coming at the end of a long and deeply unpopular war in Vietnam that cost the lives of more than 58,000 U.S. service members and represented the first American defeat in war, Watergate shredded the public's remaining faith in its institutions and government.

Political partisanship was at a modern-day high, the economy was rattled, and an acute energy shortage was worsening. Overseas, the withdrawal of U.S. troops from South Vietnam the year before had caused allies to question American leadership and commitment and was viewed by communist adversaries as an opportunity to be exploited. At home and abroad, the fundamental trustworthiness of the United States was being questioned.

Ford would later describe the moment: "It was an hour in our history that troubled our minds and tore at our hearts. Anger and hatred had risen to dangerous levels, dividing friends and families. The polarization of our political order had aroused unworthy passions of reprisal and revenge. Our government system was closer to stalemate than at any time since Abraham Lincoln took that same oath of office."

The man chosen to lead the country out of the morass was in many aspects the *anti*-Nixon: Ford was instinctively honest and straightforward. He was a politician with Midwestern values of hard work, common sense, and unimpeachable integrity. Whereas President Nixon famously kept an extensive "enemies list," Ford, even after twenty-five years in Congress, had no political enemies. Upon first hearing that Nixon kept an enemies list, Ford, then the Republican minority leader in Congress, reportedly remarked to an aide, "Anybody who can't keep his enemies in his head has too many enemies."

The manner of Ford's ascent to the highest office in the land attests to the nearly unprecedented tenor of the times. Ford became the first vice president to be appointed under the 25th Amendment to the Constitution when Nixon's first vice president, Spiro Agnew, resigned after pleading no contest to tax evasion. When Nixon later resigned rather than face impeachment, Ford thus became the first president in the nation's history that had not been elected president or vice president.

In his televised address to the nation upon taking office, Ford asked the public to help him "bind up the internal wounds of Watergate," adding, "My fellow Americans, our long national nightmare is over. Our Constitution works. Our great republic is a government of laws and not of men. Here, the people rule."

AN ABBREVIATED PRESIDENCY

Gerald Ford would serve only 896 days in the White House, and his most momentous decision as president came in his first month in office, all but guaranteeing that Ford would not be elected to the presidency when he ran for the office he already held in 1976. Shortly after returning from church on September 8, 1974, Ford went on national television to inform the nation that he was giving Richard Nixon a full pardon. The idea that Nixon would face no formal judicial retribution upset much of the country and was deeply unpopular. Ford would later admit that the widespread public anger over the pardon "was far worse than I anticipated."

Inundated with scathing editorial reactions and angry telegrams to the White House over the decision, Ford's own White House press secretary and friend, J.F. "Jerry" terHorst, resigned rather than try to publicly defend the Nixon pardon. But Ford himself was unrepentant. As the *New York Times* reported in its 2006 obituary, Ford believed that critics of the pardon hadn't thought through just how searing and disruptive a drawn out Nixon trial would have proven for an already traumatized country. In his 1979 biography, *A Time to Heal*, Ford noted that if Nixon had been required to face indictment and trial over many months, "all of the healing process that I thought was so essential would have been much more difficult to achieve."

With the advantage of hindsight, even some of the most vocal critics of the Nixon pardon came to view it as wise and selfless on Ford's part. In May 2001, the John F. Kennedy Library honored Ford with a "Profile in Courage" Award for his decision to pardon Nixon and decisively bring the desultory Watergate chapter in U.S. politics to a close. At the awards ceremony in Boston, Senator Edward Kennedy admitted that he had originally opposed the Nixon pardon. "But time has a way of clarifying past events," Kennedy said, "And now we see that President Ford was right."

Although his tenure in the Oval Office was abbreviated, Ford faced a tumultuous global landscape, and made a number of critical decisions in the realms of foreign affairs and national security. He brought to those decisions, in his own words, the worldview of "a moderate in domestic affairs, a conservative in fiscal affairs, and a dyed-in-the-wool internationalist in foreign affairs." That worldview was informed by Ford's service in the Navy during World War II, during which he won ten battle stars for participating in the Pacific campaign and the battles at Okinawa, Wake, the Philippines, and the Gilbert Islands. The experience, Ford would later say, changed him "from a passive isolationist to an ardent internationalist."

As part of that internationalism, Ford sought to continue Nixon's policy of détente with the Soviet Union as a way to ease Cold War tensions and outreach to China to divide great power adversaries. He traveled to the Soviet Union in November 1974 and met with Soviet leader Leonid Brezhnev, where the leaders signed a communiqué committing them to the Strategic Arms Limitation Treaty (SALT) negotiated by the Nixon Administration. The next year the United States and USSR would also enter into the Helsinki Accords, which pledged the thirty-five signatory nations to respect human rights and fundamental freedoms. Although the accords were nonbinding, they gave the United States, its Western allies, and nongovernmental human rights agencies a useful forum for criticizing Soviet crackdowns on internal dissent in the late 1970s and early 1980s. In 1975, Ford also travelled to China to continue Nixon's strategic outreach to Beijing.

MANAGING INTERNATIONAL CRISES

All presidents confront international crises not of their choosing, and despite serving less than a full term, Ford faced many, a number of them associated with the troubled end of the Vietnam War and perception of a U.S. retreat from Asia. Just months after he assumed office, for instance, North Vietnamese forces crossed into South Vietnam, revealing that Hanoi had no intention of honoring the Paris Peace Accords signed by the Nixon Administration in

1973, ostensibly ending the war. Ford proposed $972 million in emergency military aid for South Vietnam, but a war weary Congress overwhelmingly rejected the request. In April 1975, Ford thus gave a speech stating unequivocally that "as far as America is concerned," the Vietnam War was over. Days later, U.S. helicopters were lifting thousands of U.S. citizens and Vietnamese allies off the roof of the U.S. embassy in Saigon and evacuating them to U.S. Navy ships, just in front of advancing North Vietnamese forces. The Vietnam War was indeed over, and the United States and its South Vietnamese allies had lost. Ford would later pave the way for the immigration of 130,000 South Vietnamese refugees to the United States.

Just a month after the fall of Saigon and with the United States seemingly in full retreat in Asia, the Ford Administration was tested again. Recently victorious communist Khmer Rouge forces in Cambodia seized an American merchant ship, the *Mayaguez*, in international waters off its coast. Ford responded quickly and forcefully, immediately dispatching U.S. Marines to rescue the crew. In the ensuing chaos, during which the *Mayaguez* crew was released—unknown to the Marines—and the U.S. force was met with heavy resistance by Khmer Rouge fighters, forty-one U.S. servicemen were killed and fifty wounded. The strong response was generally supported by the American public, however, which gave Ford a significant boost in public opinion polls.

"We had just pulled out of Vietnam, out of Cambodia," Ford was quoted in the *New York Times*, explaining his first decision to send troops into harm's way. "And here the United States was being challenged by a group of leaders who were bandits and outlaws, in my opinion, and I think their subsequent record has pretty well proved it. And it was an emotional decision to tell the Defense Department we had to go in there and do something."

The challenges didn't stop with *Mayaguez*. Hopeful that the United States could also be induced to withdraw its troops and abandon South Korea, North Korean forces in August 1976 killed two U.S. officers and wounded South Korean guards who were part of a tree-trimming team in the Demilitarized Zone (DMZ). In internal deliberations, Secretary of State Henry Kissinger argued that a weak response would convince Pyongyang that the United States was the "paper tiger of Saigon." Ford agreed, and responded with a major show of force, deploying ground forces to the DMZ to cut down the tree in question, supported by B-52 bombers flying overhead. The North Koreans backed down.

Back home, Ford also showed he could make tough personnel decisions when national security issues were at stake. Although he admitted it went against his grain and genial instincts, Ford dismissed Secretary of Defense

James Schlesinger. A bookish and occasionally prickly intellectual, Schlesinger had no major disagreements with his commander in chief in terms of policy, but his personality and style rubbed Ford the wrong way.

"There was a tension. There was a personality problem," Ford acknowledged later, according to the *New York Times*. Schlesinger was "an honorable, decent person, but our chemistry doesn't fit."

In the final analysis, Ford lived up to his own description as a "dyed-in-the-wool" internationalist in world affairs. His was essentially a caretaker administration, but in the immediate post-Vietnam, post-Watergate era, there was much in America that needed taking care of, and plenty that needed healing. "He assumed power in a period of great division and turmoil," President George W. Bush said in 2006, after receiving word of Ford's death. "For a nation that needed healing, and for an office that needed a calm and steady hand, Gerald Ford came along when we needed him most. During his time in office, the American people came to know President Ford as a man of complete integrity who led our country with common sense and kind instincts."

◆ ◆ ◆ ◆ ◆

48. Jimmy Carter: The Troubled Peacemaker

by William B. Quandt

When Jimmy Carter left the White House in January 1981, many commentators were quick to label his presidency a failure. With the advantage of hindsight, it is now possible to gain greater perspective, especially on a foreign policy and national security legacy that includes both significant achievements and notable failures. Major milestones of Carter's tenure include the negotiations between Egypt and Israel that resulted in the Camp David Accords of 1978, and the subsequent peace treaty between these two belligerents; the Iranian revolution of 1978–79 and the ensuing hostage crisis; the American response to the Soviet invasion of Afghanistan at the end of 1979; and in particular the decision to build stronger defense capabilities in the Persian Gulf region, generally referred to as the "Carter Doctrine."

That Jimmy Carter led the nation during such a tumultuous period is in itself notable, especially given that he was an improbable candidate for the presidency when he began to signal his interest in 1975. Carter had served only one term as governor of Georgia and had earned a well-deserved reputation for being a progressive southerner on the sensitive matter of race. If he had views on foreign policy, they were hardly known outside his small circle of aides and advisers in Georgia.

When Carter faced unfamiliar issues, he became a diligent student, reading widely, tapping into the expertise of his circle of advisers, and traveling overseas. By the time he ran for president, Carter had thus begun developing ideas that would guide his initial foreign-policy agenda. In part, he was contesting the legacy of Richard Nixon and his influential Secretary of State Henry Kissinger. They were generally portrayed as having been too secretive and duplicitous, too slow to get out of Vietnam, and too prone to see the world through a Cold War lens. By contrast, Carter promised to be more open with the American public, more inclined toward diplomacy than force, and more intent on solving conflicts rather than merely managing them. Some detected a streak of idealism in his views, as well as self-confidence bordering on hubris.

Shortly after his election in November 1976, Carter announced his choice of Cyrus Vance for Secretary of State and Zbigniew Brzezinski for National Security Adviser. Both were well-known figures with long governmental and academic experience, respectively. Neither was far from mainstream views on the central issues of dealing with the Soviet Union and managing the NATO alliance. But many questions remained as to what policies Carter and his advisers would pursue in sensitive regions like the Middle East.[1]

MIDDLE EAST PEACEMAKING

Foreign policy priorities are often driven by crises and unforeseen events, and this was certainly the case with the Middle East in 1977. Carter and all of his advisers had a clear memory of the October 1973 Arab–Israeli war, which triggered an oil crisis, led to an emergency airlift of U.S. arms to Israel, and ended with a near confrontation between the United States and the Soviet Union. Afterward, Kissinger launched an impressive diplomatic effort that resulted in three partial agreements between Israel and its Arab neighbors. That process had come to an end by 1976, however, and there was a strong sense that a new initiative was needed to prevent a new outbreak of violence.

There were sound strategic reasons for Carter to prioritize Arab–Israeli peacemaking in early 1977, but there was also a personal dimension to his commitment. Carter was a sincere Christian and a student of the Bible. For him, the idea of bringing peace to the Holy Land was more than just a diplomatic challenge. When the task seemed hopeless, as if often did, he would simply redouble his commitment.

Carter was an engineer by training, and he brought a rather methodical manner to formulating his foreign affairs agenda. He would study a problem, discuss it with his advisers, try to frame a comprehensive approach, and then announce his project to the public. He was very ambitious, at one time pursuing at least twenty foreign policy initiatives at the same time. However, he had a hard time setting priorities and limiting his focus to the several issues that required immediate presidential attention. Once he had focused on a problem, Carter wanted to be personally involved in solving it.

As a politician, Carter often seemed to think that good ideas would automatically win support. He was not inclined to do much lobbying or arm twisting, especially with Congress. As for American public opinion, he was inclined to say what he thought and hope that people understood why he was right.

Arab–Israeli issues were politically sensitive in the American public arena, however, and it didn't take long before Carter's direct approach began ruffling feathers in the pro-Israeli community. Carter's initial idea was to try to develop parameters for a comprehensive peace settlement that would focus on borders, security, mutual recognition, meaningful steps toward peaceful relations, and some form of resolution of the Palestinian issue. Kissinger's cautious step-by-step approach no longer seemed to have much appeal, least of all to Carter.

During his first six months in office, Carter met with the leaders of Israel, Egypt, Jordan, Saudi Arabia, and Syria. He also went public in March with his initial views on borders, peace, and a Palestinian homeland. By putting his own ideas and parameters out in front, Carter shook up the stodgy folkways of Middle East diplomacy, setting off alarm bells among domestic advisers who worried about his apparent disregard for domestic politics. In fact, the important pro-Israel constituency in the Democratic Party was reacting with concern to all of Carter's ambitious plans.[2]

The first indication that Carter would have to recalibrate his Middle East peacemaking agenda came in May 1977 when Menachem Begin, leader of Israel's right-wing Likud Party, defeated Labor Party leader Shimon Peres. Ever since Israel's founding, the United States had dealt with more dovish Labor Party leaders. Now Carter would be forced to negotiate with an Israeli leader who took a tough line on all of the issues that Carter had been promoting—especially withdrawal from territories occupied by Israel since the 1967 Arab–Israeli War and recognition of Palestinian rights. The only issue on which Begin and Carter agreed was the ultimate goal of Middle East diplomacy: formal and binding peace treaties between Israel and the Arab states, as opposed to incremental steps or temporary truces.

It took Carter some time to take the measure of Begin, and the two leaders never developed a particularly close relationship, unlike Carter's friendship with Egyptian president Anwar Sadat. Carter did not readily give up on his idea of a comprehensive peace, but when Sadat made a historic trip to Jerusalem in November 1977, it became clear that the best chance for U.S.-led diplomacy was to focus on Egyptian-Israeli peace. Carter still hoped that something could also be achieved on the Palestinian issue, but Begin's intransigence made that doubtful. How then to proceed?

By mid-1978, Carter concluded that the only way to make headway toward Middle East peace was to convene a summit meeting with the leaders of Israel and Egypt. This was a big gamble, because if it failed, there was no "Plan B." Still, Carter was determined to push ahead with it, and in September 1978 the two leaders joined Carter at Camp David for what turned out to be thirteen days of nonstop negotiations.[3]

The summit resulted in a two-part document spelling out a detailed framework for Egyptian–Israeli peace and a much looser set of principles that might guide an Israeli–Palestinian negotiation. Carter deserves a great deal of the credit for getting an agreement and for seeing it through to a peace treaty between Egypt and Israel in March 1979. The agreement was not perfect, but it fundamentally changed the dynamics of the Arab–Israeli conflict and set the stage for a long-standing strategic relationship between Egypt and the United States. And although the peace between Israel and Egypt was never as warm as some had hoped, there has been no return to hostilities by these former enemies who had fought four wars against each other. Most analysts today give Carter high marks for his role in brokering the peace between Begin and Sadat. But Carter was already beginning to lose support in American public opinion by this time, and his signal success did little to reverse that trend.

THE IRAN HOSTAGE CRISIS

If Camp David was Carter's most obvious foreign-policy success, then Iran was the issue that caused him the most damage in terms of public opinion, as well as great personal anguish during the prolonged hostage affair. Carter's initial view of Iran and the Shah was no doubt colored by his open support for human rights, an issue where the Shah was subject to considerable criticism. But Carter had a realist streak as well as humanitarian ideals, and on New Year's Eve, December 31, 1977, he visited the Shah in Tehran and memorably stated: "Iran, because of the great leadership of the Shah, is an island of stability in one of the more troubled areas of the world."

Hardly had Carter uttered these words than the uprisings which later came to be known as the Iranian Revolution began to unfold. It took Americans some time to understand what was happening to this supposed "island of stability." The Shah himself was dismissive of the rioters and seemed to have no clear idea of how to respond. He wavered between threatening to crack down with an iron fist and a temptation to try to appease some of his adversaries. He received little good advice from his American friends, in part because Carter was unsure of what to suggest. Carter was also deeply engaged with his Arab–Israeli peacemaking at the time.

Even the American ambassador in Iran did not see the extent of the danger to the Shah until November 1978, and by then it was probably too late to save his throne. Carter's primary advisers, Brzezinski and Vance, were also divided on the issue. Brzezinski felt that only a unified Iranian military could stand up to the forces unleashed by the stern figure of Ayatollah Khomeini; Vance, by contrast, thought that the United States should stand back and let history take its course. Carter vacillated, finally siding with Brzezinski in trying to promote a military coup, but by then it was too late; the Iranian military was too divided.[4]

Even from the distance of thirty-five years, most analysts agree there were few if any good options for the United States in a struggle between a genuinely popular uprising and the autocratic Shah. Still, at the time many felt that Carter bore some blame for what had happened. And things were soon to get worse. In October 1979, Carter, under considerable political pressure, agreed to allow the exiled Shah into the United States for medical treatment. Shortly thereafter, Iranian radicals took over the American embassy in Tehran and within days Khomeini gave the seizure his blessing. The long hostage crisis, which paralyzed the remainder of Carter's presidency, had begun.

Carter and his advisers tried many avenues to win the release of the hostages. But as Carter entered his fourth year, there was no end in sight to the crisis. In desperation, he decided to launch a rescue mission. Operation Eagle Claw ended disastrously in the Iranian desert, with the loss of eight U.S. servicemen. Afterward, the Carter Administration returned to negotiations, which ultimately succeeded, but not in time to save Carter's battered presidency. In fact, it was not until Ronald Reagan was sworn in as president on January 20, 1981, that Khomeini finally allowed the hostages to leave Iran.

SOVIET INVASION OF AFGHANISTAN

As if Egyptian–Israeli peace and the Iranian revolution were not enough to preoccupy Jimmy Carter in 1979, at the end of the year, the Soviet Union invaded Afghanistan. The background to the invasion was complex, having much to do with factional rivalries within Afghanistan itself, as well as Soviet determination to show its strength in a strategically important region. The United States was in no position to check Soviet forces on the ground, but Carter was nonetheless criticized for showing a weak hand. Indeed, it was at this time that a revival of harsh Cold War rhetoric was common among Carter's critics, and some of his own comments implied that he had been quite naive about Soviet intentions.

Most of the ensuing Afghan story unfolded during the Reagan Administration, but Carter and his aides put two important pieces of an eventual strategy in place before they left office. Brzezinski became the outspoken advocate of arming the Islamist opponents of the pro-Soviet regime in Afghanistan. Over time, this had consequences not only for politics in Afghanistan, but also for Pakistan and Islamist movements in the area. Eventually the Soviets did withdraw their forces, and it is widely believed that their Afghan adventure contributed to the downfall of the Soviet Union. But all of that manifested long after Carter had left office.

The one other piece of strategy that was put in place by the Carter team became known as the Carter Doctrine. The core tenet of the doctrine was a warning to the Soviets not to think of intervening in the oil-rich Persian Gulf region. Any threat of that sort would be met by force, Carter warned.

The challenge was to back the doctrine up with more than just words. In early 1980 Carter sent his Secretary of Defense, Harold Brown, to the Gulf region to lay the foundation for a U.S. military force that could rapidly deploy halfway around the world. This required staging areas, overflight agreements, pre-positioning of heavy military equipment, training with friendly forces, intelligence sharing, and access to bases. Much of this work was completed by the Reagan Administration, but the basic outline and the first steps were taken by Carter. In August 1990, when Saddam Hussein invaded Kuwait, the United States thus had in place much of what was needed to deploy a large multinational force to expel Saddam's army from Kuwait in short order. The credit went to the George H.W. Bush Administration, but the origins of the strategy that made Desert Storm possible can be traced back to Carter, Brzezinski, and Brown a decade earlier.

A MIXED LEGACY

A fair evaluation has to take into account the breadth of Carter's foreign policy legacy, looking beyond the Middle East crises.[5] Perhaps most important, Carter pursued the full normalization of relations with China; negotiated a major strategic arms agreement with the Soviets (SALT-II); and reached an agreement to turn over control of the Panama Canal to Panama, a controversial measure at the time but one that looks inevitable and sound in hindsight. When added to the Camp David success and the Carter Doctrine, these achievements constitute the positive side of the ledger for Carter's foreign policy.

Iran and the hostage crisis will always lead the list of failures for Carter. Exactly what he could have done to avoid the disaster is less clear, but there is no denying that the Iranian Revolution cast a long and ominous shadow over American interests in the Middle East. The price of oil also shot up dramatically during the Iranian Revolution with negative global-economic consequences, setting off a round of inflation in the United States that was partly responsible for voters denying Carter a second term.

Carter also had to compromise on many of his early initiatives. Human rights were not as central to his foreign policy as Carter initially hoped. His support for a Palestinian "homeland" was well intentioned and in many ways prescient, but he had no strategy for overcoming the obduracy of Menachem Begin. Carter also failed to adequately explain his foreign policy to the American public, and he spent too little time building consensus with Congress. All of this weakened his hand at home, which had the effect of weakening him abroad. The fact that Khomeini would not release the hostages until Ronald Reagan had been sworn in was a sign of the low regard in which Carter was held by the Shah's successors.

In retrospect, if there were few dramatic successes in Carter's foreign policy, there were also no disasters comparable to Vietnam or the ill-considered Iraq War of 2003. Carter was disinclined to use force, which some saw as weakness at the time. But from the perspective of 2014, one can appreciate his preference for diplomacy in defending American national interests. And Carter showed that diplomacy could work when strong presidential leadership was provided. Unfortunately for him, he was unable to persuade the American public to give him a second term, so we will never know what he might have done with the challenges that faced the United States in the early 1980s.

◆　◆　◆　◆　◆

49. Ronald Reagan: The Overachiever

by Lou Cannon

Viewed through the prism of politics, Ronald Reagan seems the unlikeliest president in the history of the United States. His unique path to the White

House included careers as a radio broadcaster, movie actor, union president, television host, and salesman for General Electric. None of those occupations had ever groomed a U.S. president.

Reagan was fifty-four years old in 1964 and on no one's list as a potential presidential candidate save his own. He had a smart and attractive wife, Nancy, who believed in him, but no national following or political base. If people thought about Reagan at all, it was as an amiable actor, who had, as Garry Wills would put it, mostly played the heartwarming role of himself in some fifty Hollywood films.

But Reagan had moved on from the movies. Hired by General Electric in 1954 as the host of the popular television program *General Electric Theater*, Reagan's contract called on him to travel by train for ten weeks a year, talking to GE employees at 140 plants scattered across the nation. He became an effective public speaker who celebrated America and free enterprise in talks sprinkled with anecdotes and oddball stories clipped from local newspapers at train stops.

Reagan had been a lifelong Democrat, grateful to President Franklin D. Roosevelt for government jobs the New Deal had provided his father and brother during the Great Depression. But Reagan was hit hard by taxes on his film income at a time when individuals were not allowed to average their earnings. Increasingly, Reagan saw the government as a stifling force and the Democratic Party as its champion. In 1962, Reagan changed his party registration to Republican, and in 1964 he supported Senator Barry Goldwater of Arizona for president.

Goldwater had delighted conservatives by besting moderate Nelson Rockefeller to win the GOP nomination that year. But portrayals of Goldwater as an "extremist," first by Rockefeller and then by President Lyndon B. Johnson, took a heavy political toll. With Goldwater's campaign faltering and nearly broke, a Southern California businessman suggested to the senator's aides that a speech by Reagan ending in a fundraising appeal could replenish depleted campaign coffers. The aides were skeptical, but Reagan personally called Goldwater, who agreed to the nationally televised speech.

The speech came too late for Goldwater, who was routed the following week. But it was a milestone for Reagan, who was not on national political radar before he gave it and rarely off it after the address. *Washington Post* columnist David S. Broder described the speech as "the most successful political debut since Williams Jennings Bryan electrified the 1896 Democratic convention with his 'Cross of Gold' speech." The address raised $1 million, $7.63 million in 2014 dollars. Reagan was suddenly in demand. Two years later, he won the California governorship, and he was reelected in 1970. He nearly captured the GOP presidential nomination from a sitting president in 1976 and went on to win the nomination and the presidency in 1980 and to win reelection in a landslide in 1984.

AN ICONIC LEADER

Two decades after he vanished into the mists of Alzheimer's and more than a decade after his death, Reagan remains an iconic figure and part of the national political conversation. He is lionized by Republicans, some of whom conveniently forget that the GOP Establishment personified by George H.W. Bush, Howard Baker, and Bob Dole did their best in 1980 to prevent Reagan from ever becoming president. Nor do conservatives tend to recall that they denounced Reagan's accommodations with Soviet leader Mikhail Gorbachev, in George Will's words, as "moral disarmament." The American people, who liked Reagan then and now, have been more consistent. Respondents to Gallup's annual poll regularly rank Reagan among the three best presidents, the others being the martyred Abraham Lincoln and John F. Kennedy.

A major reason that the Reagan presidency still holds allure is the personal charm of the 40th president. Americans of his generation fondly remember his optimism, his sense of humor, and his resolute patriotism. Another reason is that Reagan's transformational presidency had a profound impact that lasted well beyond his eight years in the White House. Reagan played a decisive role in ending the Cold War, which was followed by the collapse of the Soviet Union. His economic policies led after a brief recession to ninety consecutive months of economic growth and a low-inflation mind-set that persisted into the 21st century.

There were also other achievements. Reagan named a commission headed by Alan Greenspan, which proposed a bipartisan reform that kept Social Security solvent. When Reagan signed the Social Security legislation, Democrat and House Speaker Thomas P. (Tip) O'Neill called it "a great day for America." With bipartisan backing, Reagan overhauled the nation's tax system and exempted 7 million low-income Americans from paying income taxes. There has been no Social Security or major tax reform since. Reagan also advocated for and signed the Immigration Reform and Control Act of 1986, which made 3 million immigrants legal residents of the United States.

On the debit side, Reagan authorized a deployment of U.S. Marines in Lebanon that ended in calamity when 241 of them were killed in a terrorist bombing. He also bears responsibility for the secret sale of U.S. weapons to Iran that embarrassed the United States with its allies and was the crux of the Iran-Contra scandal.

As a journalist and biographer, I observed Reagan at close range from 1965 until 1990, a year after he left the White House. In the process of writing five books and hundreds of articles, I often delved into his earlier careers for clues to his character and behavior as president. Reagan did not define his life by politics. Time and time again he drew on his earlier experiences, particularly in Hollywood, when making a presidential decision.

A COMMON TOUCH

Reagan was the mirror to an imagined America, but one that resonated with average voters. He identified with ordinary people because in his heart he was one of them. Stuart K. Spencer, his canny political adviser, said Reagan instinctively understood what "Joe Sixpack" was thinking. One of the things he understood was that Americans didn't much care for politicians—or anyone, really—who thought too well of themselves. Reagan didn't. His lack of vanity was an asset, all the more so because it often led his adversaries to underestimate him.

That underestimation began in the 1966 campaign when Governor Pat Brown insisted he had been doing great things for California while Reagan was being upstaged by a chimpanzee in the 1951 film *Bedtime for Bonzo*. Reagan defeated Brown by nearly a million votes, but the notion that "actor" somehow equated to "airhead" stuck. Reagan encouraged the underestimation. Asked what kind of governor he would be, he quipped, "I don't know. I've never played a governor."

Reagan had learned to poke fun at himself in Hollywood, where celebrity "roasting" was routine. No president since Lincoln was as self-effacing, and no president as effective at self-ridicule. Reagan regularly joked about his age, his work habits, his movies, his ideology, his vanities, his memory lapses, and his supposed domination by his wife. In the 1980 primaries, when his opponents suggested he was too old to be president, Reagan, then sixty-nine, turned the issue to his advantage with jokes about his birthday, which he called the "30th anniversary of his 39th birthday." In one debate Reagan said that wage and price controls had failed since being tried by the Roman emperor Diocletian, adding: "I'm one of the few persons old enough to remember that."

The underestimation of Reagan, coupled with his practicality, led him to success in Sacramento and Washington. He also proved an adaptive politician. As a candidate for governor of California, for instance, Reagan had promised to "squeeze, cut, and trim" the costs of government. Once in office, however, he soon realized that all the cuts in the world couldn't overcome the huge deficit he had inherited or help him balance the budget as required by law in California. Without qualms, Reagan signed off on a $1 billion tax increase, then the largest in the history of any state.

Reagan was similarly helped by Tip O'Neill's underestimation of him. In the first months of his presidency in 1981, Reagan proposed reducing the income tax, as promised in his campaign. On the face of it, the legislation to accomplish this goal faced an uphill battle in a House of Representatives controlled by Democrats, who were a majority in the House throughout the Reagan presidency. But Reagan realized that O'Neill's majority was less monolithic than it seemed, for it depended on southern Democrats, known as Boll Weevils, whose districts Reagan had carried in the 1980 election. The Boll Weevils feared they would lose their seats in 1982 if Reagan campaigned for their opponents. At the suggestion of his astute chief of staff James A. Baker, Reagan promised he would not oppose any member who voted for his tax and budget bills. The support of the Boll Weevils brought Reagan victory.

HOLLYWOOD AND ARMS CONTROL

Hollywood in the 1940s was beset by political conflicts and strikes involving the film industry's craft unions. The tiny but persistent Communist Party was also active, triggering investigations by the Red-hunting House Committee on Un-American Activities that led to the notorious Hollywood blacklist. I have examined Reagan's role in these conflicts in my book, *Governor Reagan: His Rise to Power*. Suffice it to say here that Reagan emerged from his Hollywood experiences as a staunch anticommunist committed to opposing the Soviet Union.

But Reagan learned more than anticommunism in Hollywood. He served eight years as president of the Screen Actors Guild (SAG), leading the union in a successful strike against the major movie producers. Reagan was proud of this advocacy. Soon after he returned from his first meeting with Gorbachev, I asked Reagan what was the most neglected aspect of his biography. Reagan said it was his negotiations as president of SAG. What had he learned from these negotiations? "That the purpose of a negotiation is to get an agreement," Reagan replied.

Even before he became president, Reagan anticipated reaching agreement with the country he would describe as an "evil empire." In June 1980, he came to a luncheon at the *Washington Post* where an editor suggested that if the United States increased military spending, as Reagan advocated, it would intensify the nuclear arms race. Somewhat to our surprise, Reagan agreed but added that the Soviets would not be able to compete economically in a stepped-up arms race and therefore would come to the negotiating table. He was telling us that he saw the arms race as a means toward an end.

So Reagan had a plan. He engaged, as Secretary of State George P. Shultz put it, in "strategic thinking," which to Reagan meant not only improving U.S. military capability, but also restoring an economy that was riven by high inflation and unemployment when he came into office. Only an economically secure United States, he reasoned, could bargain from a position of strength.

Even so, Reagan reached out to the Soviets from the beginning. While recuperating from the wounds he'd received in an assassination attempt, Reagan, over the objections of his first secretary of state, Alexander M. Haig, sent Soviet leader Leonid Brezhnev a handwritten note proposing a "meaningful and constructive dialogue which will assist us in fulfilling our joint obligation to find lasting peace." This was on April 24, 1981. The same day and also over Haig's objection, Reagan lifted the grain embargo against the Soviet Union that President Jimmy Carter had imposed in 1979 after the Soviet invasion of Afghanistan.

Reagan saw nothing inconsistent in reaching out to the Soviets even while denouncing their system. He had been conducting a similar balancing act in his mind ever since his Hollywood days, when Reagan's antagonism toward communism was matched by a fear that nuclear war might destroy civilization. This concern arose after the atomic bombings of Hiroshima and Nagasaki in 1945 and had prompted Reagan in 1946 to join the United World Federalists, a utopian group that advocated world government. Around this time Reagan became fascinated with science fiction, a genre in which a favorite theme was an invasion from outer space that prompted earthlings to unite in common defense. At his first meeting with Gorbachev in 1985, Reagan departed from the script and told the Soviet leader that his country and the United States would cooperate if Earth was invaded from outer space. Gorbachev didn't know what to make of this comment. Colin Powell, who would labor to keep interplanetary references out of Reagan's speeches, was convinced that the overture to Gorbachev was based on the 1951 science fiction film *The Day the Earth Stood Still*, which contained a message of world peace.

An end to civilization in nuclear annihilation was certainly on Reagan's mind at 1:30 AM on August 19, 1976, at Kemper Arena in Kansas City, Missouri, where President Gerald Ford has just been nominated over Reagan at the Republican National Convention. Seeking to unite a divided party, Ford invited Reagan to the podium. But it was the fate of the world, not party unity, which preoccupied Reagan. Speaking without notes, he declared: "We live in a world in which the great powers have poised and aimed at each other horrible missiles of destruction that can, in a matter of minutes arrive in each other's country and destroy virtually the world we live in."

Reagan's speech that night presaged his policy as president of rejecting the doctrine of "mutual assured destruction" (MAD) that was the central premise of nuclear deterrence. Calling this a "truly mad policy," Reagan said it was immoral to base U.S. nuclear policy on the murder of millions of civilians. This view prompted him to propose the Strategic Defense Initiative (SDI), a missile-defense shield that Reagan hoped (to the horror of the U.S. national security community) to share with the Soviets. Scientists dismissed SDI as unfeasible and critics derided it as "Star Wars," but it helped bring the Soviets to the bargaining table.

The scholarship on Reagan has struggled with the seeming cognitive dissonance between his anticommunism and his opposition to nuclear weapons. But this dissonance was reconciled by Reagan and Gorbachev, who also worried that a policy of keeping the peace through a threat of mutual annihilation was destined to fail, with potentially catastrophic consequences. As Alexander Bessmertnykh, the deputy Soviet foreign minister during the Reagan–Gorbachev summits, put it: "The experts didn't believe, but the leaders did."

MIDDLE EAST MISSTEPS

Reagan had no similar over-arching vision for the Middle East, and no alarm bells went off in his head in the summer of 1982 when Israel invaded Lebanon in an effort to expel the Palestinian Liberation Organization (PLO) from Beirut. Later that summer, Reagan, at the advice of Secretary of State George Shultz, who had replaced Haig, sent 800 U.S. Marines to join French and Italian military units in overseeing the evacuation of PLO forces from Lebanon.

Defense Secretary Caspar Weinberger feared that the Marines would soon become targets and urged Reagan to withdraw them to nearby ships, which the president did as soon as the PLO evacuation was completed. Four days later, on September 14, 1982, Christian leader Bashir Gemayel was killed during a speech by a powerful bomb nine days before he was to become president of Lebanon. Israeli troops stood by as Gemayel's militia entered Palestinian refugee camps at Sabra and Shatila and massacred more than 700 people, many of them women and children.

Reagan was sickened by the televised reports of these atrocities. Over the objections of Weinberger and John Vessey, chairman of the Joint Chiefs, who said Lebanon was "the wrong place" for U.S. troops, Reagan sent the Marines back into Lebanon as part of a new multinational force with the ambitious mission of restoring a strong central government. There they stayed for more than a year as the Lebanese government disintegrated and Hezbollah, the radical Shia terrorist group that was suspected of killing Gemayel, plotted to drive the United States from Lebanon.

Hezbollah made its presence known on April 18, 1983, when a delivery van filled with explosives destroyed the U.S. embassy in Beirut, killing sixty-three people including seventeen Americans. This should have led to withdrawal of the Marines, but Reagan, with Shultz and Weinberger still at odds, kept them in place as Israeli forces that had occupied most of Lebanon withdrew south. On October 23, 1983, a smiling young man drove a Mercedes truck through the parking lot of the four-story headquarters building where members of the 1st Battalion, 8th Marine Regiment were sleeping. The truck penetrated the lobby of the building and detonated while the occupants slept. Of the 350 servicemen in the building, most of them Marines, 346 were casualties of the attack. The death toll, including those who later died, was 241. Soon afterward, another bomb exploded in west Beirut, bringing down a nine-story building and killing fifty-eight French paratroopers.

Years later Reagan would remember the bombing of the Marine headquarters as the "saddest day of my presidency, perhaps the saddest day of my life." Reagan told me in 1990 that he blamed himself, saying, "Part of it was my idea—a good part of it." Shultz, a Marine combat veteran of World War II, was similarly shaken. At a meeting of the National Security Council after the Beirut bombing, he said, "If I ever say send in the Marines again, somebody shoot me."

Still, it was months before the Marines were withdrawn. Armed with the report of an investigative commission and with sentiment for withdrawal growing in Congress, Defense Secretary Weinberger seized his chance on February 7, 1984. While Reagan was speaking in Las Vegas and Shultz was out of the country, Weinberger made the case for a pullout to a National Security Planning Group (NSPG) meeting presided over by Vice President George H.W. Bush. Speaking to the president over a secure line in Las Vegas, Bush told him the NSPG had agreed the Marines should be "redeployed." Reagan reluctantly assented. He would never use the word "withdrawal," but he also would never again after pulling out the Marines put U.S. ground troops in harm's way.

Reagan relied more on his heart than his head in Lebanon. He was also poorly served by the persistent disagreement between Shultz and Weinberger and the resultant dysfunction between the State and Defense Departments. These two quarrelling cabinet members were also at odds on Soviet policy. When it came to the Soviet Union, however, Reagan had a strategic vision of what he wanted to accomplish and acted decisively. Both vision and decisiveness were lacking in Lebanon.

Ironically, as Weinberger ruefully noted, Reagan went most astray in his second term on one of the rare occasions when Weinberger and Shultz agreed. The issue was the sale of arms to Iran, which was then engaged in a protracted war with Iraq. U.S. policy makers feared that an Iranian victory would interrupt the flow of oil from the Persian Gulf and urged other nations not to sell weapons to either combatant—a boon to Iraq, which possessed ample Soviet weapons.

CIA Director William P. Casey was worried about the fate of William Buckley, the CIA station chief in Beirut and one of seven Americans kidnapped and held captive in Lebanon. Casey rightly suspected that Buckley was being tortured to reveal the names of other CIA agents. He encouraged National Security Advisor Robert McFarlane to explore a plan suggested by the Israelis to supply U.S. weapons clandestinely to a shadowy group of supposed Iranian "moderates" who might help secure release of the hostages.

Shultz and Weinberger urged Reagan to reject this half-baked idea. Shultz said the proposal would "negate the whole policy" of not making deals with terrorists. But Reagan—once more ruled by heart instead of head—empathized with the plight of Buckley and the other hostages. On January 17, 1986, he approved the covert initiative, writing in his diary that he had agreed to sell antitank weapons to Iran.

McFarlane's successor as national security adviser, John Poindexter, turned over operational details to Oliver North, a swashbuckling Marine officer who served on the National Security Council staff. On May 25, 1986, McFarlane, North, and a CIA official flew to Tehran from Tel Aviv in an unmarked Israeli plane loaded with anti-aircraft spare parts. They had expected to meet a high-ranking official but spent four days in Tehran without seeing anyone of importance. The "moderate Iranians" were a fiction; the operation was orchestrated by the Iranian government.

Reagan was briefly heartened on July 26 when an American hostage was released. But as Shultz had foreseen, the covert arms sale provided incentives for kidnapping additional hostages. Three Americans were kidnapped in Lebanon in September and October. After 500 antitank weapons were delivered to Iran at the end of October, three more hostages were freed—and three other Americans kidnapped in January 1987. A year after Reagan approved the arms deal, seven hostages were held in Lebanon. Two of the original seven had died, Buckley from medical neglect.

The scandal widened. On November 21, 1986, an assistant attorney general who was searching North's office came upon a document that revealed a plan to divert $12 million from the Iran arms sales to the contras, the irregular forces opposing the Sandinista government of Nicaragua. The plan was the brainchild of North and former Air Force officer Richard D. Secord, who pocketed a chunk of the proceeds.

Reagan ardently supported the contras but claimed to have no prior knowledge about the diversion to them of any arms sales proceeds. Independent counsel Lawrence Walsh, after an intensive investigation, eventually concluded that there "was no credible evidence that the president authorized or was aware of diversion of the profits from the Iran arms sales to assist the contras." Walsh, however, didn't make this finding until August 3, 1993, when Bill Clinton was in the White House and Reagan was long out of office and lost to Alzheimer's disease.

But while Reagan took no responsibility for the diversion, he did, at the prodding of First Lady Nancy Reagan, apologize for authorizing the sales of arms to Iran. On March 4, 1987, he said in a nationally televised speech: "A few months ago, I told the American people I did not trade arms for hostages. My heart and my best intentions still tell me that is true, but the facts and the evidence tell me it is not."

This roundabout apology reflected Reagan's state of mind and enabled him to recover politically. Reagan had a store of goodwill among the American people, most of whom deplored the Iran arms sales but realized he was motivated by a desire to free the hostages. As Walsh later told me, Reagan had done many things wrong, but he wasn't "dirty."

(For a more detailed explanation, see "Iran-Contra: Saving Reagan's Presidency," Chapter 55 in Section V of this volume.)

COLD WAR VICTORY

Reagan's bounce back in approval ratings following his apology restored his optimism and rescued his presidency. Although he was rarely guided by polls, Reagan needed the trust of the American people to function effectively. Putting Iran-Contra behind him freed Reagan to turn his attention to the Cold War to complete the great mission of his presidency.

By that time in his second term, the U.S. military buildup was in the rearview mirror. A sequence of geriatric Soviet leaders—Leonid Brezhnev, Yuri Andropov, and Konstantin Chernenko—had struggled with the faltering Soviet economy as relations with the United States soured. Reagan complained that the Soviet leaders kept dying on him, as indeed all of them did.

The Cold War took a different turn, however, after Gorbachev came to power in 1985. British Prime Minister Margaret Thatcher, Reagan's staunch ally, had met with Gorbachev a few months earlier and delivered an assessment to which Reagan paid attention: "I like Mr. Gorbachev," she said. "We can do business together."

Reagan and Gorbachev held four summit meetings: first in Geneva, then in Reykjavik, then in Washington, and finally in Moscow. The Reykjavik summit led to the Intermediate Nuclear Forces (INF) treaty that Reagan and Soviet President Mikhail Gorbachev signed in Washington on December 8, 1987. It was the first treaty to reduce U.S. and Soviet nuclear arsenals instead of merely stabilizing them at higher levels and was the cornerstone of future agreements that made deep reductions in nuclear arsenals and established a once-unthinkable process of mutual inspection.

Even today, when U.S.–Russian relations are at the lowest level since the Cold War, inspectors from the two countries routinely examine nuclear facilities on each other country's soil. Under the New START treaty, signed by President Barack Obama and Vladimir Putin, they will do so at least until 2021.

The world is safer today because of what Reagan and Gorbachev wrought. They did not do it alone. John Lewis Gaddis, the preeminent Cold War historian, credits Reagan for being a "saboteur of the status quo," who upended previous notions of what was possible and puts three other "saboteurs" on his list with the U.S. president and Gorbachev: Thatcher, Polish leader Lech Walesa, and Pope John Paul II.

The profound consequences of what these unconventional but productive leaders accomplished became clear on November 9, 1989, when the Berlin Wall came down after Gorbachev told the East German government it was no longer permissible to shoot people who were fleeing communism. The following February, in my last interview with Reagan, I asked him if he had ever expected this to happen. "Someday," he replied. As usual, he was content to let others take the credit.

Although the Cold War did not formally end on Reagan's watch, the nation's unlikeliest president had done the heaviest lifting.

◆ ◆ ◆ ◆ ◆

50. George H.W. Bush: Crafting a New World Order

by James Kitfield

President George H.W. Bush and his friend and National Security Adviser Brent Scowcroft were alone on the president's speedboat *Fidelity* off the coast of Kennebunkport, Maine, when they first imagined a "New World Order" for the post–Cold War era. It was the fall of 1990, and the Berlin Wall had come down just the year before. The Soviet empire was rapidly disintegrating, and the Bush Administration had just won unanimous UN Security Council backing for a U.S.-led military operation to reverse Iraq's recent invasion of Kuwait. For the first time the Cold War nemesis in Moscow had voted with the other permanent members of the Security Council to back U.S. action.

Although they were fishing in calm waters, both Bush and Scowcroft understood that they were in fact navigating through one of the most tumultuous and profoundly transformative periods of the past century. In a stretch of about three years after the breakup of the Soviet Union, they witnessed the subsequent liberation of Eastern Europe, realized an end to the decades-long Cold War, and beheld the unification of Germany. Added to all this was the Tiananmen Square massacre in Beijing as Communist China pushed back against the wave of democratization; a U.S. military intervention to reverse an antidemocratic military coup in Panama; and now a looming war in the Middle East that would constitute the largest U.S. military operation since the Vietnam War.

Scowcroft, an experienced former protégé of Henry Kissinger and a retired Air Force lieutenant general, remembered the moment when the vision of a New World Order came into view. "We were out on the water for about four hours without even a nibble, and it gave us a rare chance to talk philosophically about the state of the world, and where we were heading as a nation," Scowcroft told the author in an interview. "And it occurred to President Bush and me that a new vista was opening in terms of countering nation-state aggression against other states, one of the great scourges of mankind throughout history. That was the first time we used the phrase 'New World Order.'"

The American political dynamic often centers on the superficial, highlighting whether a politician has personal charisma or is capable of giving a rousing speech. Both are important attributes for a politician and a president, of course, and in each case George H.W. Bush suffered in comparison to his predecessor Ronald Reagan, the former Hollywood actor and "Great Communicator," whom Bush served loyally as vice president for eight years. While Bush himself once confessed that he was not good at "the vision thing," Reagan's vision of abandoning détente with the Soviet Union for a more confrontational approach had arguably hastened victory in the Cold War. For all of those reasons, Bush was viewed in many quarters as a second fiddle and a caretaker president who was figuratively completing Reagan's third term.

What too often gets lost in the focus on campaigns and the selling of presidential personality is the need to govern once a president and commander in chief actually enters the Oval Office. And in terms of having the experience, background, and temperament to govern in critical times, George H.W. Bush brought to the office a résumé that was arguably the equal of any in American history. He was the patrician son of a U.S. senator, and himself both a Yale graduate and a champion sportsman. Also a decorated war hero, he flew fifty-eight combat missions as the youngest aviator in the U.S. Navy during World War II, on one of which he was shot down and later rescued at sea. As a businessman and oil man, Bush became a millionaire by the age of forty. He went on to serve as a member of Congress, chairman of the Republican National Committee, the U.S. ambassador to the United Nations and to China, and director of the Central Intelligence Agency. During his eight years as vice president, Bush traveled the world, often representing the United States at state funerals, and he used the experience to forge close personal ties with many current and future heads of state.

The breadth of that background made Bush comfortable in the corridors of powers, fluent in the ways of both Washington and the wider world, and confident in his own judgment. He was also a shrewd judge of character. After being elected president in 1988, Bush assembled a national security and foreign policy team that reflected his own quiet competence and expertise, including Secretary of State James Baker; Secretary of Defense Dick Cheney; Chairman of the Joint Chiefs Colin Powell; and, of course, National Security Adviser Brent Scowcroft. In the tumultuous days ahead, the Bush national security team would prove one of the best since the Harry Truman Administration.

BERLIN WALL COLLAPSES

During the first six months of his presidency, Bush pushed his staff for initiatives to maintain positive momentum in U.S.–Soviet relations that had been gained by successful arms control negotiations, including limits on intermediate and short-range nuclear forces in Europe and a Conventional Forces Europe Treaty. Characteristically, Bush had established a friendly relationship with Soviet leader Mikhail Gorbachev, and he was determined to test the Soviet leader's professed appetite for liberalizing reforms. In this, Bush broke with the advice of Scowcroft, who worried that Gorbachev was duping the West in a calculated charm offensive. Intelligence suggested that Gorbachev's reforms were bitterly opposed by hardliners in the Politburo and in the Soviet military, however, and Bush was determined to try and support Gorbachev against his internal enemies and keep him on the reform path.

By the summer of 1989, it was clear not only that Gorbachev was sincere, but also that he was unleashing forces that were propelling events faster than U.S. policy could pace. In a speech at the United Nations, for instance, the Soviet leader proclaimed that the satellite nations of Eastern Europe could go their own way without the threat of another Berlin blockade or a repeat of Prague 1968, when Soviet military forces brutally crushed a nascent democracy movement. "Freedom of choice is a universal principle," Gorbachev proclaimed, and Hungary and Poland quickly tested his sincerity, with Czechoslovakia and East Germany quick to follow. Bush decided that the best the United States could do was to try and encourage and help guide the transformative change underway.

No one knew whether the massive Soviet military would step in and violently halt the disintegration of the empire that it had so brutally kept in line for an era; after all, throughout history empires had traditionally collapsed as the result of a big bang rather than a whimper, and such a crisis could quickly escalate into a confrontation between the nuclear armed Cold War superpowers.

Events came to a head on November 9, 1989, after East German leader Egon Krenz announced that he was opening the border, and East Berliners began flocking to the border crossing points by the thousands. If there were a moment when the hundreds of thousands of Soviet troops garrisoned in East Berlin and East Germany would step in and violently halt the march toward democracy, it was on November 9. Certainly no icon of Soviet communism was more pregnant with symbolism than the Berlin Wall. That evening, word came to the White House that the East Berlin border police had let the gates to the West swing free and that Soviet forces in East Berlin were staying in their garrisons. For all intents and purposes, the Soviet grip on Eastern Europe was broken.

At that moment the temptation for triumphalism was practically irresistible, given the decades of blood and treasure the United States had expended during the Cold War. Only Bush was having none of it. Understanding that Gorbachev would face withering criticism—and perhaps much worse—from hardliners at home, Bush was determined to do nothing that might seem as if the United States were rubbing his nose in a Western "victory."

In the film *41 on 41*, the George Bush Presidential Library and Museum chronicled Bush's time as the forty-first president by asking forty-one world leaders, politicians, and administration officials about their personnel recollections of those events. Condoleezza Rice, then a National Security Council official and a future Secretary of State, recalled the moment clearly. "The day the Berlin Wall came down is one that's indelibly etched in my memory. We quickly got ourselves together and we went over to the Oval Office and talked the president through what was happening there. So we said to him, 'Mr. President, you have to go to Berlin, you have to go for Kennedy, you have to go for Truman, you have to go for Reagan, all of whom were associated with monumental events in Berlin's history.' And [President Bush] very quietly just said, 'What would I do if I went to Berlin, dance on the wall? This is a German moment, not an American moment. And we need to make it so.'"

Bush's innate humility and caution proved infectious, and the entire Bush team adopted a restrained tone in commenting to the press about the world-shattering events taking place in Europe. Shortly after the fall of the Berlin Wall, Bush traveled to the Mediterranean island of Malta to meet with Gorbachev and send a reassuring message to the world about their close partnership. When asked about those discussions and the two nations' vast nuclear weapons arsenals at a press conference on Malta, Gorbachev said, "I assured the President of the United States that the Soviet Union would never start a hot war against the United States of America. And we would like our relations to develop in such a way that they would open greater possibilities for cooperation."

The following year Bush traveled to Moscow to join Gorbachev in signing the Strategic Arms Reduction Treaty (START 1), signaling the reduction of each nation's nuclear arsenal by more than one-third. Later in 1991, the Soviet Union dissolved, and Bush and Gorbachev declared a "U.S.–Russian strategic partnership," thus officially marking the end of the Cold War.

John Sununu, Bush's chief of staff, believes his boss's deft handling of the often fraught relationship with Gorbachev was one of his greatest achievements, and essential to managing a soft-landing to the collapse of the Soviet empire. "[President Bush] understood the pressures on Mikhail Gorbachev . . . from members of his party and government . . . and that he had to work as president of the United States to allow these changes to take place in a way that did not make Gorbachev feel like he was losing," Sununu said in *41 on 41*. "I think that's one of the great talents and arts that George Bush displayed as president of the United States."

GERMAN REUNIFICATION

Bush's close relationships with other world leaders also paid major dividends in helping to manage the tricky reunification of Germany, a policy that was initially opposed by the leaders of close allies France and Great Britain. As explained in *A World Transformed*, coauthored by Bush and Scowcroft, Bush 41's close relationship with Germany Chancellor Helmut Kohl made him "comfortable" with the idea of a reunified Germany at the epicenter of Europe and the NATO alliance, a comfort level not shared by other European leaders.

If not handled with deft diplomacy, German reunification had the potential to drive a wedge through the NATO alliance. After initially protesting reunification, Britain's Margaret Thatcher and France's François Mitterrand eventually fell into line behind a policy that was driven by Bush, Kohl, and Gorbachev.

The issue of German reunification was closely tied, however, to the future of the NATO alliance, the cornerstone of collective Western security. In exchange for removing 380,000 Soviet troops from East Germany, Gorbachev asked for and received assurances from Kohl that NATO forces would never be deployed to East Germany, which would have a "special military status." The German leader also suggested that the NATO alliance would not expand eastward, an idea that U.S. Secretary of State James Baker also floated when he spoke with Gorbachev.

However, Kohl was empowered only to speak for West Germany on the broader issue of NATO expansion, and the Bush White House never formally agreed to the limits; therefore, a ban on NATO expansion eastward was never codified in an official treaty. Gorbachev thought he had a "gentlemen's agreement," however, and when NATO later did expand eastward to include many nations of the former Soviet-dominated Warsaw Pact, Gorbachev and succeeding Russian leaders felt betrayed by the West.

The Treaty on the Final Settlement with Respect to Germany was signed in Moscow on September 12, 1990. It marked a major steppingstone toward a "Europe whole and free," a dream of U.S. diplomats dating back before World War II. The Bush Administration hardly had time to celebrate the achievement, however, as six weeks earlier Iraqi leader Saddam Hussein had invaded Kuwait, raising the specter that the new, post–Cold War order would be haunted by the same scourge that had made the pre–Cold War order the bloodiest in human history—state-on-state aggression.

THE PERSIAN GULF WAR

Inside the main lodge of the Camp David presidential retreat, President Bush huddled with his inner council of advisers on August 4, 1990, trying to determine what to do about Iraq's invasion and occupation of Kuwait two days earlier. Those present included Scowcroft, Baker, Defense Secretary Dick Cheney, Joint Chiefs of Staff Chairman Powell, Vice President Dan Quayle, White House Chief of Staff Sununu, CIA Director William Webster, and

General Norman Schwarzkopf, head of U.S. Central Command with responsibility for the Middle East.

Of all those present the official who had argued for the strongest response was Scowcroft. Left unanswered, he believed Saddam Hussein's aggression would undermine the hopeful New World Order that was then emerging, one in which the chief protagonists of the Cold War could for the first time work together to help ensure global stability and consign state-on-state aggression to the ash heap of history. As a combat veteran wounded in Vietnam, General Powell was perhaps the most cautious in the inner Bush circle about the use of U.S. military force to liberate Kuwait, with the other officials falling somewhere in between.

President Bush listened to his advisers, just as he had listened to "Iron Lady" Margaret Thatcher's entreaty that "this was no time to go wobbly, George." That prospect didn't seem likely. As he later wrote in *A World Transformed*, Bush had always felt the United States had a "disproportionate responsibility" to use its power "in pursuit of a common good." Now, Iraq had challenged what he viewed as the common good. Multiple participants at that critical Camp David meeting recalled that Bush was very clear that the Iraqi aggression could not go unchallenged. The next day at a press briefing Bush made it explicit: "This will not stand," he told the assembled journalists. "This will not stand, this aggression against Kuwait."

Once again turning to his unmatched rolodex of world leaders, Bush personally began reaching out to form an anti-Hussein coalition that would eventually account for more than thirty countries, importantly with many Arab participants including the key regional powers Saudi Arabia and Egypt. In a deft bit of arm-twisting that later was termed "checkbook diplomacy," the Bush Administration also convinced Japan and Germany to foot much of the bill for assembling a coalition army of more than 600,000 troops.

On November 29, 1990, the Bush Administration also won passage of UN Security Resolution 678, stating that Iraqi troops had until January 15, 1991, to withdraw from Kuwait, or else member states were authorized to use "all necessary means" to force them to do so. The UN backing was critical to winning the support of many European allies, and it bolstered the role of the United Nations as the accepted arbiter able to bestow legitimacy on the use of military force by one nation against another.

Winning congressional support for Operation Desert Storm was another matter. The last time Congress had debated an authorization for the use of military force was during the 1964 Gulf of Tonkin Resolution, when President Lyndon Johnson pocketed as a "blank check" to escalate the war in Vietnam, with disastrous results. The long shadow of the debacle in Vietnam hung over the debate over a brewing war in the Persian Gulf. Senator Sam Nunn (D-Georgia), the powerful chairman of the Senate Armed Services Committee, led opposition to the war and conducted a series of hearings in which many experts predicted a military catastrophe.

Not wanting to inject politics into the congressional debate, Bush waited until after the midterm election in November 1990 to request congressional backing. By the time of the actual vote in January 2001, the United States had already deployed hundreds of thousands of troops to the Middle East. Scowcroft in particular thought asking for Congress's backing at that late date was too risky, but he was overridden by Bush. In the end, the Democratic-controlled Congress passed the Iraq War resolution by a razor-thin margin in the Senate, 52–47, and by 250–183 votes in the House. At that point, the Bush Administration had done everything diplomatically and militarily possible to shape the battlefield to the United States' advantage.

Operation Desert Storm began on January 16, 1991, and quickly became one of the most lopsided military victories in U.S. history. After a massive air campaign that lasted five weeks, the U.S.-led ground attack quickly turned into a rout, with the Iraqi Republican Guard fleeing Kuwait and being decimated by superior U.S. firepower on its retreat back to Iraq.

With the road to Baghdad open and the aggressor Saddam Hussein still entrenched in power at the end of it, some Bush Administration hawks argued that the U.S. military should finish the job. Once again George H.W. Bush provided a steady, and yes, prudent hand at a critical juncture. Both he and Scowcroft never seriously considered a drive to Baghdad. The move would have fractured a carefully crafted U.S.-led coalition that included numerous Arab nations and left the U.S. military as occupiers in an Arab country of more than 25 million people.

"For a bunch of years, a lot of people who should know better have said that we had an alternative," then Chairman of the Joint Chiefs Colin Powell later told journalist Jeffrey Goldberg about the decision not to topple the Saddam Hussein regime. "We didn't. The simple reason is we were operating under a UN mandate that did not provide for any such thing. We put together a strong coalition of Gulf States, and Egypt and Syria, and they signed up for a very specific issue—expelling Iraq from Kuwait. Nor did President Bush ever consider it."

Tragically, the myriad risks entailed in the U.S. military invading and occupying Iraq in order to topple the regime would later be revealed when George W. Bush launched Operation Iraqi Freedom in 2003. Many national security experts consider the decision to invade Iraq while military operations in Afghanistan were ongoing as one of the worst strategic blunders in modern U.S. military history. Later, the nation would pay dearly for it in blood, treasure, and diminished international prestige; but that decision was on the son, not the father.

When facing his own moment of truth, Bush the elder's innate caution and grasp of how the world viewed American power led him to stop at the culminating moment of victory, with Kuwait liberated, the Iraqi Republican Guard decimated, and U.S. power and international prestige unmatched. In assessing the New World Order that the Bush Administration was crafting at the end of the Cold War, national security experts began talking about a rare historical epoch in which the United States would stand as the lone super-power in a unipolar world.

NEW WORLD DISORDER

With victory in the Persian Gulf War having raised U.S. influence in the Arab world, the Bush Administration moved quickly to capitalize by launching an intensive diplomatic campaign to end the Arab–Israeli conflict. That effort culminated in the Madrid Peace Conference of 1991, during which all of the parties to the Arab–Israeli conflict held direct negotiations for the first time. The conference was cochaired by Bush and Soviet President Gorbachev. Although it failed to achieve its lofty goal of ending the Arab–Israeli conflict, the Madrid Conference laid the groundwork for the Israeli–Palestinian peace process known as the 1993 Oslo Accords, which held out the hope of a two-state solution to that conflict, and for the Israeli–Jordanian peace treaty signed in 1994.

The benign New World Order imagined by Bush and Scowcroft, however, never fully materialized. Nationalistic, ethnic, and tribal conflicts frozen during the bipolar period of the Cold War began heating up as that global order melted away. Failed states began replacing state-on-state aggression as the scourge of the post–Cold War era, empowering destabilizing nonstate actors such as warlords, insurgents, and terrorist groups.

The Bush Administration's attempt to check mass starvation in Somalia by sending U.S. troops on a humanitarian relief mission in 1992 eventually led to a confrontation with local warlords, the death of eighteen U.S. troops in the "Black Hawk Down" battle, and, under the Clinton Administration, an ignoble retreat. Sectarian civil war soon broke out in the Balkans with the disintegration of Yugoslavia, eventually leading to the worst mass killings and atrocities in Europe since World War II.

The rumblings of discord and dissonance were heard on the home front as well. One year after George H.W. Bush was lauded as a hero of the Persian

Gulf War, he was defeated in the presidential election of 1992 by Democrat Bill Clinton, whose campaign mantra was "It's the economy, Stupid" and whose administration promised a peace dividend. The American people wanted respite from the burdens of a Cold War that left them saddled with a sluggish economy and a massive debt that had quadrupled during the Reagan–Bush years.

And yet, at important points in their ascent, all great powers are blessed with strong and visionary leadership, and in the United States' case it was supplied in the critical and potentially perilous period at the end of the Cold War by President George H.W. Bush and his foreign policy and national security team. In the broad sweep of what came to be known as the "American Century," they left the country on a higher ground and arguably at the pinnacle of its power and prestige.

"What I like to remind people is that there is no precedent in history for the collapse of a great empire without a major war," said Robert Gates, Bush's former CIA director (and a former Defense Secretary for Bush 43), speaking in *41 on 41*. "And the period 1989 to 1991 was one of the most momentous historically, I think, since World War II. Someday George H.W. Bush will get the credit he deserves for having managed that."

◆ ◆ ◆ ◆ ◆

51. Bill Clinton: A Baby Boomer Takes Charge

by Carl Cannon

On the awful day Muslim terrorists used hijacked passenger planes to topple the Twin Towers and inflict death and destruction at the Pentagon, Bill Clinton had been out of office for eight months. Enjoying the perks of private life, he was traveling in Australia making paid speeches. On September 11, 2001, as it happened, Clinton was addressing a business group in Melbourne when asked about Osama bin Laden.

"I could have killed him," Clinton said. "But I would have had to destroy a little town called Kandahar in Afghanistan and kill 300 innocent women and children, and then I would have been no better than him. So I didn't do it."

According to the 9/11 Commission, the intelligence on bin Laden was never airtight enough to present the commander in chief with precisely that stark a moral choice; in any event, Clinton's Australia remarks didn't surface until the Obama presidency. But if Clinton can be faulted—as he was in some quarters—for bequeathing a lethal and festering terrorism problem to his successor, this is also true: as evening fell on the day of the 9/11 attacks, 10,000 ethnic Albanians in Kosovo, almost all of whom were Muslim, marched in solemn solicitude for the United States. The demonstrators in the city of Pristina carried candles, American flags, and signs with messages such as this one: "America, we still share your sorrow." This pro-American sentiment was also part of Bill Clinton's legacy, thanks to a challenge he did not shirk: ethnic cleansing in Kosovo.

This juxtaposition points to a two-term presidency that was full of soaring achievements and disastrous stumbles during a tumultuous time—the transition between the Cold War and post–Cold War eras, and between a generation of presidents who came of age during World War II to the first baby boom generation commander in chief. In that sense, Bill Clinton's legacy was complex and full of contradictions, which befits the man at the center of the story.

TUMULTUOUS TIMES

Certainly all modern presidencies are eventful, but William Jefferson Clinton's was exceptionally so. Partly this is because he was an activist president who seemed to enjoy every part of governing and campaigning right up until the day he left office—and beyond. Partly it's because of events and forces that were roiling the world order and transforming domestic politics, some of which were only dimly understood while he was in office.

About once every century the United States is attacked militarily on American soil. Also, about once in a century a president is impeached. And every one hundred years or so an American president is inaugurated who actually received fewer votes than his opponent. Yet in a three-year period at the end of the Clinton presidency and the beginning of George W. Bush's White House tenure, all those things happened—and Bill Clinton was in the middle of it all.

Scholars or commentators looking for triumphs and tragedies will find plenty from each category in Clinton's two terms. Those looking for an overarching theme will have to look a little deeper and consider what occurred *after* the Clinton presidency as well as during it.

The Internet as a transformative technology evolved while Clinton was in office; so did the related dot.com boom and subsequent crash (see Chapter 35, "Dawn of the Information Age," this volume). The seeds of the housing bubble were planted in Clinton's tenure, even if the bursting of the bubble came later. The same might be said of al-Qaeda, which proved to be a ticking time bomb. Indeed, the technology and political ideology that in the new millennium would produce the dispiriting specter of Islamic extremists trolling online for volunteers—in the suburbs of Denver and Minneapolis, as well as elsewhere around the world—were incubating while Bill Clinton was president.

The man who foretold the disruptive possibilities of such an interconnected world was the forty-second president of the United States himself. "There is no longer a clear division," Clinton proclaimed in his first inaugural address, "between what is foreign and domestic." As examples, Clinton cited the global economy, the worldwide AIDS crisis, the international arms race, and the earth's environment. "They affect us all," he said.

Clinton would go on to give a second inaugural address, serve eight years in the White House, and withstand a Senate impeachment trial, all while presiding over a domestic economy that produced more than 23 million new jobs. Despite the sex and political fundraising scandals that tarnished his second term, he left office more popular than when he arrived, and he continued an active role on the world and American stages after departing the Oval Office. Due to his relentless ambition and gregarious temperament—not to mention his wife's own political career—Bill Clinton never really left the stage. He remains a significant power broker within the Democratic Party.

To his admirers, the forty-second president has matured into a world statesman with few peers. His many critics are more likely to be put in mind of the Dan Hicks country song, "How Can I Miss You If You Won't Go Away?"

Either way, President Clinton's January 20, 1993, rhetorical construct—that the lines have blurred between foreign and domestic policy—is a useful template in assessing his time in the White House. Was the North American Free Trade Agreement a foreign or domestic achievement? The answer is both, but what made this international accord possible was Bill Clinton's gift for domestic politics. If Clinton was prescient about how small and interdependent the world was becoming during the last decade of the old millennium, he wasn't always as insightful when assessing his own role in that dynamic. This is a normal human failing, but Clinton's handicap could be idiosyncratic: while in office, he often boasted an inverse relationship to his actual achievement.

FAMILY LEAVE AND IRISH PEACE

For years when listing his accomplishments, Clinton would cite his signing of the Family and Medical Leave Act. But that was a minor piece of legislation, and he had little to do with it. Passed by Congress in a bipartisan vote before

Clinton took office, all he had to do was sign it into law. He was happy to do so, of course, but the bill was largely symbolic. It guaranteed parents twelve weeks of parental leave upon the arrival of a child, either by birth or adoption, but the leave was unpaid and by 1993, most states (although not Arkansas, where Clinton had been governor for years) already had similar policies—as did most major U.S employers. The law had been passed previously and vetoed by George H.W. Bush for reasons that perplexed even his fellow Republicans. So this was an easy "win" for Clinton.

At the same time he was touting this marginal legislative achievement, a major drama was unfolding—the beginning of the end to "The Troubles" in Northern Ireland that had claimed so many lives—and in that Clinton's role was central. His involvement had a political genesis: during the 1992 primary season, Clinton had yet to lock up the Democratic presidential nomination when he narrowly lost the Connecticut primary to former California Governor Jerry Brown. The margin was 37 to 36 percent, a result attributable to Brown carrying the state's white Catholic voters. With the New York primary looming, Clinton accepted an invitation he'd earlier declined: a forum organized by a prominent New York Democrat who envisioned a more central U.S. peacemaking role in Northern Ireland. A former Jesuit seminarian and descendant of a County Tipperary clan, Brown announced before the dinner that, as president, he'd appoint a special envoy to Northern Ireland, investigate British human rights abuses, and issue a visa to Sinn Fein leader Gerry Adams—all a reversal of existing U.S. policy. Clinton quickly followed.

As president, Clinton followed through—and more. The first five years of his presidency included many post-midnight calls to political principles in Northern Ireland, and when the stalemate was finally broken in 1998, British and Irish leaders gave Clinton much of the credit in an emotional White House gathering. "If I played a positive role," Clinton responded, "I'm grateful to have had the chance to do so."

The people of Northern Ireland, in turn, were grateful for the attention Bill Clinton had given their troubles. In 1995, when he visited Derry, a huge throng assembled at Guildhall Square. Seeing him on the dais, the crowd went into a chant, "Bull! Bull! Bull!" Perplexed, Clinton turned to Irish statesman John Hume. "Why are they saying that?" he asked. Hume, familiar with the local dialect, smiled and said, "They are saying your name."

WELFARE AND HEALTH CARE REFORM

When the Clinton record is assessed, a sweeping welfare overhaul bill is invariably put in the plus column, while his administration's unsuccessful attempt to expand access to health care insurance is invariably cited as a flameout. This conventional view is understandable, but the actual story is more nuanced.

When he ran in 1992, Governor Clinton vowed "to change welfare as we know it." Although the line was vague, it got loud applause, even among liberal audiences. Actually, Clinton didn't have a fixed idea of what he wanted to do, and when he turned the issue over to the White House domestic policy shop, what emerged was a blueprint that cost more money and would have *expanded* government assistance. Produced by a president who won only 43.5 percent of the popular vote—and to whom no member of Congress owed their victory—it was dead on arrival on Capitol Hill.

After Democrats lost Congress in the 1994 midterm elections, Republicans resurrected the idea with a plan that adhered more closely to Clinton's 1992 campaign rhetoric than his 1993 policy proposals. Under Speaker Newt Gingrich, Congress passed welfare reform legislation that Clinton vetoed twice. Finally, with his own 1996 reelection campaign in full swing and his political Svengali Dick Morris whispering in his ear that it would be folly to hand Bob Dole a potent campaign issue, Clinton signed the Personal Responsibility and Work Opportunity Act. The measure essentially required most welfare recipients to seek work as a condition of receiving relief. At the August 22, 1996, bill-signing ceremony, Clinton pronounced the bill "far from perfect," criticizing the legislation he was signing.

Three Department of Health and Human Services officials resigned over the law, saying it cut the social safety net too deeply. When the legislation proved successful and popular, Gingrich took credit for it. This was understandable, but it was Clinton who rhetorically softened Democratic Party opposition to the idea—and who ultimately signed it into law.

Health care reform was a different story entirely. In September 1991, Clinton told a group of Arkansas newspaper editors who asked him about health care that he didn't yet have a plan, but would have to formulate one "because Bob Kerrey is running on it." The Nebraska Democrat had made expansion of health care a cornerstone of his campaign; in time, the Clinton campaign offered some broad policy principles—but few details—on how to achieve universal health care coverage.

The details would come after the election—and then some—in the form of a massively complicated proposal produced by a 500-person committee headed by First Lady Hillary Rodham Clinton. Conventional wisdom holds that her plan was so intrusive and unwieldy that the Democratic leadership that controlled Congress wouldn't even bring it to a vote; that it spawned the notorious "Thelma and Louise" ads that established the narrative leading to the Democrats' ballot box debacle in 1994; and that a chastened Bill Clinton was forced to concede in the aftermath that "the era of Big Government is over."

All of that happened, it's true. But it's also apparent two decades later that the era of Big Government was only taking a nap. Mrs. Clinton's task force rekindled a nascent desire for universal health care within the Democratic Party—one dating to Harry Truman's time in the White House—and when Hillary Clinton ran for president in 2008, both she and Barack Obama resurrected the issue. By that time the principles of "Hillarycare" had even been incorporated into Massachusetts law under Republican Governor Mitt Romney. They are now codified in federal law.

SPLIT PERSONALITY

It has often been said that Bill Clinton possessed great talents and great flaws. To some observers, it was as if "Bad Bill" and "Good Bill" coexisted uneasily in the same body. "We all have a lot of experience of Bill Clinton—the good Bill and the bad Bill, the charming, brilliant politician and the liar," conservative columnist Roger L. Simon wrote. "When Clinton is at his most relaxed and spontaneous, he appears—and possibly is—the most truthful. When he is enraged and tense (as in the Monica finger-wagging episode), he has Pinocchio beaten around the block."

Another way of looking at it is that Clinton's gifts and flaws are rooted in the same outsized personality traits, which produced both great failure and success.

Monica Lewinsky has just turned twenty-two years old on July 10, 1995, when she accepted an unpaid internship as the White House. By Veterans Day, Miss Lewinsky was pressed into service during a government shutdown in the West Wing. The same qualities of risk-taking and chutzpah that allowed his ill-considered relationship with young Lewinsky to flourish after only the briefest of contact with her also served him well in the tense standoff with House Republicans.

Those attributes of the Clinton personality include charm, an ability to read people, a habit of personalizing every encounter, a willingness to push limits to the breaking point, and a preternatural level of self-confidence. Throw into that mix a tendency toward verbal expediency, and you have a formidable political operator. Indeed, two years before the sex scandal broke—and two years before Clinton lied about it to his wife, his cabinet, and his county—then-Senator Bob Kerrey told journalist Martha Sherrill, "Clinton is an unusually good liar. Unusually good. Do you realize that?"

All of those qualities also came into play in his games of budget brinkmanship with Gingrich and the Republicans in 1995 and 1996. The upshot was a balanced budget, which the Republicans demanded, while Democrats protected most of their cherished programs. And through adroit maneuvering and skillful turns at the presidential megaphone, Clinton got credit for both. When it came to fiscal and economic policy, Clinton had one more qualification: his mastery of public policy issues. It was this wonkish expertise in the body of a charming political glad-hander that led to his greatest successes as president.

AN ECONOMIC VISION

When he ran for the presidency the first time, Clinton's handlers described him as "the man from Hope." This was hype. He left Hope, Arkansas, as a small boy and was really raised in Hot Springs. In any event, as a candidate Clinton really was the Man with the Plan—a detailed economic blueprint. His communications team even turned the campaign's budget proposals into a book, *Putting People First*, which became an unlikely best-seller.

There was a coherent thrust to Clinton's proposals consisting of two broad goals: first, strengthening a middle class hard hit by technological displacement, depleted pensions and retirement funds, and the disappearance of traditional well-paying blue collar jobs. Second, helping the working poor ascend the economic ladder into the middle-class—and stay there. His proposed methods included expanding Medicare, funding "lifetime learning" programs and, most importantly, vastly increasing payments to the working poor under the Earned Income Tax Credit. Clinton had also run as a "new kind of Democrat" who understood the limits of deficit spending, meaning that he was obliged to find tax increases to pay for his programs.

Under color of making the wealthiest Americans "pay their fair share," Clinton took aim at the top earners, who were being taxed at a top rate of 31 percent. Two new brackets were created, one for those earning more than $115,000 (36 percent) and one for those making above $250,000 (39.6 percent). The corporate tax rate rose from 34 percent to 38 percent, caps on Medicare were removed, and more of Social Security was means-tested. The only regressive tax in Clinton's plan was a 4.3 cents-per-gallon increase in federal gasoline taxes.

In Washington parlance, Clinton's budget plan was "revenue neutral." It raised a lot of new money, but it spent that money, meaning that the annual federal budget deficit remained at roughly $200 billion. Congressional Republicans unanimously opposed it, with many predicting disaster. Yet the financial markets liked the Clinton plan—a Democratic president had shown fiscal restraint by not increasing the debt—and began to reward the administration by lowering interest rates. But passage was hardly a foregone conclusion. Newt Gingrich, then the GOP House Whip, told his troops that the legislation would cause a recession. Representative John Kasich of Ohio, the ranking Republican member of the House budget committee, told Democrats it would "put the economy in the gutter."

Every Republican in both houses of Congress, and a number of Democrats, voted against the Clinton budget. In the House, the final vote was razor-thin 218–216; in the Senate, Vice President Al Gore was needed to break a 50–50 tie.

"This plan has already begun to work," Clinton said while signing the bill on August 10, 1993. "I say to those Members who took a big chance in voting for this, with all the rhetoric that was thrown against them, if you go home and look your people in the eye and tell them you were willing to put your job on the line so that they can keep their jobs, I think they will understand and reward you with reelection."

He was wrong about that. The Democrats took a bath in the 1994 midterm elections. But more important, Clinton was right about the economy. It got much better.

GAYS, FREE TRADE, AND NATIONAL MOURNING

In 1993, Clinton affixed his signature to the enabling legislation to implement the North American Free Trade Agreement. The idea of a free trade zone encompassing Canada, the United States, and Mexico was first broached by Ronald Reagan during his 1980 presidential campaign. A treaty gradually took shape under George H.W. Bush but had not been ratified in Congress when Clinton defeated Bush. As governor, Clinton was an ardent free trader, even if most Democrats on Capitol Hill were not. Clinton tepidly endorsed NAFTA as a candidate but rarely mentioned it as president unless asked. As it turned out, he was pushing hard behind the scenes.

The Senate was on board, but arrayed against Clinton were the most liberal Democrats and the most conservative Republicans in the House. Rahm Emanuel, miscast as White House political director, was tasked with rounding up wavering Democrats. A master board was prepared, and each member's personal objections noted. Clinton and Vice President Al Gore made some 200 calls to these members. In September, at the White House, Clinton personally asked three living ex-presidents—Bush, Jimmy Carter, and Gerald Ford—for their help. Lining up the support of Carter and Bush was particularly bold: Clinton persuaded the man he'd beaten a year earlier to help him and got Carter to do something the thirty-ninth president had been reluctant to do on his own behalf—namely, lobby members of Congress for their votes.

On December 21, 1993, Clinton also authorized a Department of Defense Directive dubbed "Don't Ask, Don't Tell." The order was designed to finesse the issue of gays in the military. Clinton had criticized the ban during the 1992 campaign but mainly at gay Democratic fundraisers on the West Coast. Later, in the waning weeks of the 1996 campaign, he would sign the Defense of Marriage Act, a bill with a name that would have made George Orwell smile, given that it defined marriage as a union exclusively between a man and a woman, thus excluding homosexuals. Clinton did this in the middle of the night, too, while the traveling White House press corps was stuck in a filing center in a South Dakota cornfield. This was hardly a profile in courage, and Clinton knew it—but he didn't disavow his actions until 2013, when the landscape on the issue of gay marriage had been transformed.

In the aftermath of the 1994 GOP takeover of Congress, Clinton began the second phase of his presidency feeling obliged to proclaim that he still mattered. "I'm relevant," he blurted out at a press conference. "The Constitution gives me relevance." He was right about that. In the United States, the commander in chief is always a significant player. And in the modern presidency, a chief executive with sufficient rhetorical gifts must assume the role of national grief counselor—which is precisely what happened after April 19, 1995, when the Alfred P. Murrah Federal Building in Oklahoma City was destroyed with a truck bomb, killing 168 people and injuring many more.

Four days later, in Oklahoma City, Bill Clinton was an emotional anchor for an unmoored city and country. "It was the nation's first exposure to Clinton as mourner in chief," White House speechwriter Michael Waldman noted later. "In fact, it was the first time Clinton had been a reassuring figure rather than an unsettling one."

When Clinton entered the cavernous hall at a memorial service four days after the bombing, White House photographer Robert McNeely recalled, the only sounds were people in the audience sobbing. After he spoke, the president made himself available to those in the crowd who needed more time with him, almost as though he were a pastor at a large church.

"It's kind of a throwaway line now, 'I feel your pain,' but he literally could," McNeely said. "He could take people and just hug them and connect to them in a way and really listen to them." If Clinton helped the people of Oklahoma City recover from a terrible blow, it can also be said that they helped him recover his voice. The bombing occurred in a time of increasing antigovernment rhetoric that inspired some toward violence. Six weeks later, while delivering the commencement address at Michigan State University, Clinton said, "There is nothing patriotic about hating your country, or pretending that you can love your country but despise your government."

FOREIGN POLICY CRISES

Foreign policy was not a dominant theme in the three-way 1992 campaign between Clinton, Bush, and Texas billionaire Ross Perot. Nonetheless, Clinton took issue with the Bush Administration in three areas: Candidate Clinton said that Bush's reauthorization of most favored nation (MFN) trading status for China put America "on the wrong side of human rights and democracy." He was also "appalled" by the U.S. practice of repatriating would-be Haitian refugees picked up on the high seas. And he vowed to "end" Serbian aggression in Bosnia.

President Clinton, however, said not a peep as China was granted MFN, did not alter Haitian refugee policy, and did little for three years as the war of attrition in the Balkans continued among Serbs, Croats, and Bosnian Muslims. Although Secretary of State Warren Christopher forthrightly described what was going on in the Balkans ("Serbian ethnic cleansing . . . mass murder . . . systematic beatings, and the rape of Muslims . . . prolonged shelling of innocents in Sarajevo . . . forced displacement of entire villages, inhuman treatment of prisoners in detention camps"), the administration's prescription to stop such behavior was anything but bold. Christopher vowed only to bring "the full weight of American diplomacy to bear on finding a peaceful solution."

The rhetorical gap between the problem and the proposed solution amounted to cognitive dissonance, suggesting vacillation in the White House. Soon, Sarajevo was under siege, and France was urging NATO air power be used to relieve the beleaguered defenders. Clinton approved that step, but he vetoed legislation to lift the arms embargo for the region that prevented Bosnians from defending their cities. But in an appearance on CNN's *Global Forum* Clinton termed the fighting in Bosnia "a civil war" instead of genocide or even Serbian aggression.

After CNN correspondent Christiane Amanpour asked Clinton about his "constant flip-flops" on Bosnia, he parried the question testily. Others were harsher. Liberal *New York Times* columnist Anthony Lewis wrote a blistering piece about the president's "waffling and confusion." Fittingly, it was watching the carnage on CNN that finally strengthened Clinton's resolve. Backed by U.S.-led NATO air strikes, American diplomacy kicked into high gear. By December 1995, the Dayton Accords finally ended the fighting. It was a historic achievement, putting an end to the worst atrocities in Europe since World War II, but one tempered by the fact that by then some 200,000 people had lost their lives, most of them civilians.

If Clinton's response to the Oklahoma City bombing was pitch-perfect, his performance in the Balkans crisis was uneven, slow, but ultimately successful. A third crisis arose in those years, in the African nation of Rwanda. Here, the failure was total.

The Rwanda fiasco started, insofar as the United States was concerned, in war-torn Somalia. A humanitarian military mission under George H.W. Bush morphed under Clinton into something more difficult: a nation-building mission involving the search for recalcitrant Somali warlord Mohammed Farrah Aidid. Instead of arresting him, U.S. forces were pinned down in a desperate urban firefight popularized by the book and movie *Black Hawk Down*. Eighteen U.S. servicemen lost their lives in March 1993, and the new commander in chief vowed never again to be trapped into sending American troops into war zones without clear goals and exit strategies. Although entirely understandable, this impulse would, only a year later, essentially condemn 800,000 Rwandans to a violent death.

The killing, most of it done with machetes, was planned in advance and precipitated by the April 6, 1994, shooting down of a Mirage jet—a gift from French President Francois Mitterrand—carrying Rwandan President Juvénal Habyarimana and Burundian President Cyprien Ntaryamira. Canadian Army Major Romeo Dallaire, commander of the UN Assistance Mission in Rwanda, immediately feared the worst. In January he'd sent a fax to New York relaying the warnings of an informant who revealed that Hutu extremists had been ordered "to register" all members of the Tutsi tribe in Kigali. "He suspects it is for their extermination," Dallaire wrote. "Example he gave was that in 20 minutes his personnel could kill up to 1,000 Tutsis."[1]

Thus warned, neither the United Nations nor the United States did anything. Actually, the truth is worse than that: the bureaucracies in Washington and New York actually took steps to prevent Dallaire's UN peacekeepers from saving Rwandans. Dallaire's informant had warned that when the killing started, the first targeted victims were to be Belgian peacekeepers, so as to facilitate the withdrawal of Belgian forces. Alarmed, the Belgians requested reinforcements. They were turned down by UN officials, who'd been told flatly that the United States was adamantly opposed to reinforcements. Determined to prevent any more Somalia scenarios, the United States had taken humanitarian peacekeeping efforts off the table.

As predicted, hours after the plane crash Hutu extremists began seeking out any Rwandan, Hutu or Tutsi, who'd been involved in the peace process that Dallaire's soldiers were supposed to facilitate. This included the country's prime minister, whom ten Belgian peacekeepers tried to protect. She was shot to death, and the Belgians were murdered and mutilated.

Dallaire's total force consisted of just 440 well-equipped Belgians and a poorly equipped force of 2,000 other soldiers, most from Bangladesh and Ghana. But 800 Belgians were an hour's flight away in Nairobi, and 300 U.S. Marines were on alert in neighboring Burundi. But Dallaire's orders were clear: remain neutral and use his forces only to get foreigners out of the country. Dallaire later told journalist (and future Obama Administration diplomat) Samantha Power that when he saw the heavily armed force of some 1,000 French, Belgian, and Italian troops dispatched to the Kigali airport, he thought of how much killing he could have prevented if given authority to use these men for actual peacekeeping. But those troops were there to get their own people out—and then they simply left. It was Day 3 of the genocide.

In the three days it took to evacuate the Europeans and Americans, some 40,000 Rwandans were killed. The slaughter of Tutsis continued unabated until mid-July. In Washington, administration officials refused to reconsider their decision to flee, refused requests from human rights groups to destroy the radio station exhorting Hutus to commit mass murder, and refused even to use the word "genocide." By the time the bloodletting was finished, nearly 1 million Rwandans had perished in one of the worst cases of genocide since World War II. Years later, Clinton conceded that had the U.S. intervened early in the crisis, at least 300,000 Rwandans might have been saved. He called the failure to act one of his biggest regrets. "I do feel a lifetime responsibility," he told ABC News in 2008.[2]

Five years later, with Tutsis in power and Hutu extremists on the run, Clinton visited Kigali and delivered a mea culpa—of sorts. "It may seem strange to you here, especially the many of you who lost members of your family," Clinton said, "but all over the world there were people like me sitting in offices, day after day after day, who did not fully appreciate the depth and speed with which you were being engulfed by this unimaginable terror."

This was disingenuous, the kind of carefully parsed statement that had earned Clinton the unflattering moniker "Slick Willie" back in Arkansas. Although the collective guilt it impugns to the rest of the world is reasonable, any implication that Clinton didn't know what was happening wasn't true: the Rwandan genocide was splashed on the front pages of American news outlets in real time.

Years after the Rwanda crisis, this author spotted Mark Salter, John McCain's chief of staff, near the White House. The shadow of impeachment was then hanging over the White House, a threat Clinton was meeting with customary defiance. Removing the cigarette from his mouth, Salter smiled drolly and said without preamble, "Can this dude take a punch, or what?"

That's a badge of honor in McCain-land. It's a compliment in the rest of the country, too. When he was inaugurated in 1992, Clinton uttered an interesting adage: "There is nothing wrong with America," he said, "that cannot be cured by what is right with America." He was trying to appeal to the best instincts of his countrymen. Yet, with the simplest of substitutions—replacing the word "America" for "Clinton"—the forty-second U.S. president also provided a fitting postscript to his own long and eventful career on the public stage.

♦ ♦ ♦ ♦ ♦

52. George W. Bush: The Decider and Delegator

by Peter Baker

When presidents come into office, they often seem determined to do things differently than their predecessors, especially if their predecessors were from the other party. So perhaps it was no surprise that when President George W. Bush arrived in the White House in January 2001, the phrase often heard in the halls was "ABC"—Anything But Clinton.

That applied to policy, naturally, but also to the president himself. Whether by instinct or inclination, Bush often seemed the opposite sort of leader than Bill Clinton. No more late-night, pizza-fueled brainstorming. No more extended policy seminars with sometimes-indeterminate resolutions. No more fluid compromise or political triangulation. Bush made a point of always wearing a coat and tie in the Oval Office. Meetings started on time and, more important, ended on time, even if there might still be more to be said. Memos were best delivered in a page or two, no more. Decisions were to be made crisply and, once made, not to be second-guessed.

Bush was smarter than his critics assumed and more engaged in policy than many thought, particularly in the areas that most interested him. But he had little of Clinton's voracious appetite for policy detail and nuance. He embraced a management style that he learned at Harvard Business School. A president, he thought, should set broad direction, assemble a capable team to carry out his instructions, and then give them room to operate without micromanagement. His job, as he saw it, was to be the leader, not a policy wonk. It was an approach that seemed to serve him well at times, especially in the days and weeks after the terrorist attacks of September 11, 2001, when he reassured a frightened country with a confident, bullhorn-wielding performance on top of a wrecked fire truck at "ground zero" in New York City. His approval numbers shot up above 90 percent, higher than any president has seen in the history of polling.

Bush's steadfast view of leadership helped steady him through the rockier moments. Even as others in the White House grew panicky in the face of political setbacks or became eager to shift course to overcome obstacles, Bush held firm, stiffening his team and quite often getting much of what he wanted. He was written off many times only to refuse to give in, from his first days in office when he was deemed a weakened figure because of the controversial Florida recount that led to his victory, to his final days in office when his popular standing had crashed to historic lows amid war and financial crises.

DECIDER AND DELEGATOR

When Congress balked at Bush's landmark $1.6 trillion tax cut proposal and his top legislative liaison, Nick Calio, was ready to compromise, Bush took his lesson from Clinton's predecessor, the first George Bush, whose agreement to raise taxes as part of a deficit-cutting plan despite his "read my lips" campaign vow helped undercut his credibility and party support. So Bush told Calio not to give an inch. "Nicky, don't wobble," Bush told him. "One-point-six, keep saying one-point-six." Ultimately, Bush did compromise, of course, bartering down to $1.35 trillion and agreeing to an expiration date for the tax cuts. Moreover, he paid a price by alienating Senator James Jeffords of Vermont, who left the Republican Party to become an independent and caucus with the Democrats, handing control of the Senate to the opposition. But Bush got more than many prognosticators thought he would and that was his goal.

What neither he nor anyone else fully anticipated was just how drastically his young presidency would be transformed before its first year was out when al-Qaeda terrorists struck New York and Washington, killing about 3,000 people in the most devastating attack on the homeland since Pearl Harbor. Bush's presidency was destined to be defined by the "Global War on Terror" and by his national security policies.

When the bombing sorties over Afghanistan seemed to make little headway in their first weeks in the fall of 2001 and the newspapers were already writing about a Vietnam-style "quagmire," for instance, Bush got word that some on his national security team were increasingly anxious. "We're going to stay confident and patient, cool and steady," he counseled them. Within weeks, the Taliban had been ousted from Kabul and Kandahar, although, of course, that was not the end of the story.

But as with many presidents, Bush's strengths could be weaknesses as well. He trusted the people on his team so much that they sometimes led him astray. In delegating to others, he gave them enough room not just to operate but sometimes to fail, and in some cases to fail spectacularly. And even then Bush was often reluctant to step in and make changes. What came across as steely determination in some circumstances could lapse into stubborn inflexibility in others. For a leader who once famously styled himself as "The Decider," he sometimes deferred imposing his own judgment in cases when it potentially could have made a difference.

Bush had also surrounded himself with advisers with extraordinary stature and experience, people like Vice President Dick Cheney, Secretary of Defense Donald Rumsfeld, and Secretary of State Colin Powell, all seasoned veterans of previous administrations. But what seemed like an asset may also have inhibited a relatively unseasoned commander in chief when the domestic presidency he expected was abruptly transformed in an instant into a wartime presidency. "With that kind of experience sitting around the table, maybe it did not leave a lot of room for his own judgment in these matters," offered his longtime Texas friend, Jim Langdon. "His team has been there, done it, seen it all, had the context, while Bush was governor of Texas."

THE FATEFUL DECISION

The most consequential case study, of course, is Iraq. Bush was not the only one to trust the deeply flawed intelligence about Iraqi weapons, but his faith in the judgment of those around him left little room for the sort of doubt that could have averted a profound miscalculation. Though it seems hard to fathom in retrospect, Bush never encouraged a robust debate about whether invading Iraq was a good idea; the debates inside the White House were about how, not whether. At a certain point, once he had started down the road of confronting Saddam Hussein, the journey to war took on a certain self-fulfilling inevitability.

Moreover, Bush left it to others to determine how the operation should be conducted and what would happen after Saddam Hussein was taken out of power, taking his lesson this time from Lyndon B. Johnson. Bush thought LBJ had been too immersed in micromanaging the war in Vietnam by hand-picking bombing targets instead of trusting his generals. At one point in the weeks before the Iraq invasion, Bush convened the nation's top generals and asked if any of them had concerns, but only after opening the meeting with a full-throated endorsement of Rumsfeld, which sent a message to some in the room who were harboring doubts about the defense secretary's strategy. Most of the generals then endorsed the war plan.

When General Eric Shinseki, the mild-mannered Army chief of staff, expressed worries about the flow of forces, long supply lines, and the lack of a northern approach from Turkey, it did not trigger a deeper inquiry. Rumsfeld and the other generals told Bush the plan was solid, and he just accepted that judgment on face value. With that, the course was set. "You could hear the hinge of history turn," recalled Kori Schake, a National Security Council official who was in the room at the time.[1]

For the next three years, Bush would defer to others as Iraq gradually spiraled out of control. Before the invasion, he approved plans for a quick occupation with only a light purge of government ranks and the Iraqi army. After installing Paul Bremer as head of the Coalition Provisional Authority, however, Bush acceded without question to his new viceroy, who proceeded down a very different path.

Bremer swept tens of thousands of members of Hussein's Baath Party out of government, including teachers and bureaucrats who had obtained party membership cards just to work. And he disbanded the entire army rather than just the most elite units loyal to Hussein, sending home hundreds of thousands more Iraqi men without pay but armed with guns and resentment. Bremer reasoned that Iraq's Shiite majority would never trust a new government with remnants of the Sunni Baath Party and that the army had effectively disbanded itself by disappearing from the battlefield in the face of American power. But his decisions on de-Baathification and disbanding the Iraqi army were strongly opposed by the top U.S. military commanders in Iraq, whose advice Bremer simply ignored. Either way, Bush had left the decisions to others who did not necessarily agree with each other and did not step in to be The Decider himself.

Bush likewise stood by Rumsfeld even when advisers like Colin Powell, Condoleezza Rice, Andy Card, Michael Gerson, Joshua Bolten, among others, urged him to make a change as the situation in Iraq worsened. Just as important, Bush stuck with the strategy that Rumsfeld and Generals John Abizaid and George Casey promoted, a lighter-footprint strategy focused on reversing what Bremer had done. Under this approach, United States troops were to pull back to their big bases, increasingly turning the war over to newly enlisted Iraqi forces and drawing down the American presence in Iraq while diplomats encouraged a political reconciliation between the warring Shiite and Sunni factions. The authors of the strategy believed the occupation itself was a spark for the insurgency, and so the more the Americans could pull back and put an Iraqi face on the security force, the sooner the violence would ebb. The idea, Rumsfeld said repeatedly, was to take the hand off the bicycle so the Iraqis could learn to ride for themselves.

The notion had a certain logic to it, and perhaps the strategy might have worked had it been applied more assertively at the beginning of the occupation. But after three years of bloody resistance and a growing civil war between Sunni insurgents and Shiite militias and death squads, it was clearly not working. In nightly reports to Bush, a clutch of White House aides tried to make the case that radical change was now needed.

BUSH TAKES CHARGE

Finally, at this point, frustrated at the out-of-control violence and the lack of visible progress toward resolution, Bush stepped in. More than three and a half years after the invasion, Bush put aside his preference for delegating to others, overcame his fear of repeating the mistakes of LBJ, and forcefully asserted his own judgment about what to do in Iraq.

Over Cheney's objections, Bush replaced Rumsfeld in favor of Robert Gates, who had been his father's CIA director. Abizaid and Casey were replaced as well, and the noted Army counterinsurgency expert, General David Petraeus, was tapped to take over the fighting. To turn things around, Bush concluded that his theory of the case had been backward—rather than fixing Iraq's politics first on the assumption that would defuse the conflict, he came to believe that security had to come first before the politicians could find accommodation and a new working order. That would mean more troops, not fewer, as well as a more aggressive strategy of putting American troops in the field to protect the Iraqi civilian population.

The dilemma for Bush was that almost no one else favored more troops. Coming off a midterm election debacle in which his party lost both the House and Senate, he confronted a new, emboldened Democratic Congress that claimed a mandate to get Americans out of Iraq, not escalate the war. And it wasn't just the other party that bristled at the idea of a troop surge. Republicans in Congress were anxious about Iraq too, and looking for ways out.

Bush's own secretary of state, the Joint Chiefs of Staff, the outgoing commanders in the field, and others on his team all opposed sending more forces.

"I know the decision's unpopular, the decision to surge," he later told aides one day when he was in an uncharacteristically reflective mood. "I made mistakes," he conceded. "All of the mistakes, they rest right here, with me. But you know what? There's great pressure not to lead—not to act. There's pressure to say, 'Oh, well, this is too damn hard, too risky, let's not do it.'" But, he added, "The world needs America to lead. You know why? Because nothing happens if we don't lead."[2]

With the American recommitment to securing Iraq, Sunni sheiks who had begun turning away from the insurgency felt confident in switching sides, Shiite militias commanded by Moqtada al-Sadr stood down, al-Qaeda was finally pushed back, and the violence receded dramatically. As a result of Bush's risky and unpopular troop surge, and under the steady leadership of General Petraeus, Iraq was pulled back from the abyss.

Arguably, Bush confronted a similar situation less than two years later when Wall Street brokerages faced collapse and the world economy suddenly teetered on the edge. "If money isn't loosened up, this sucker could go down," Bush bluntly warned lawmakers during a private meeting. His approach was no more popular than the troop surge to Iraq. Once again Bush decided to go all in. He favored applying the full force of the United States to stop the bleeding, in this case through a $700 billion bailout like never before.

As with Iraq, Bush understood that his own popular standing had sunk so low that he was no longer an effective spokesman for such a toxic idea, and so he put forward someone else with more credibility to lead in making the case to the public. In this case, Treasury Secretary Hank Paulson played the role of a financial David Petraeus. And once again, Bush bulled forward despite the adverse politics of the moment, forcing Congress to finally hold its nose and approve the plan after the House initially rejected it and sent markets into a tailspin.

Neither Bush's troop surge to save the U.S. campaign in Iraq nor his financial bailout to avert an economic meltdown were perfect solutions by any stretch, but in both cases, they arrested a dangerous slide and paved the way for a turnaround. With the American recommitment to its financial institutions, capital was reinfused into the system, banks were stabilized, and a feared depression was staved off long enough for Bush's successor to arrive and take the next step, an economic stimulus plan.

Each decision flew in the face of political self-preservation, amounting to perhaps the boldest presidential decisions in a generation. But as David Frum, a former Bush speechwriter, argued, each proved necessary after years in which the administration failed to act. The same stubborn streak that did not recognize, or accept, the gathering crises yielded to equally fixed determination to resolve them. "Bush made crises through neglect," Frum said, "and then resolved crises through courage."

♦ ♦ ♦ ♦ ♦

53. Barack Obama: "Light Footprint," Heavy Burdens

by David E. Sanger

Barack Obama was elected in 2008 with the promise to lead America out of one of the most severe recessions in modern memory, rein in the excesses of the Bush era, and withdraw America from two bruising wars. Measured by those goals alone, six years into his presidency, Obama was largely a success.

But history will not measure Obama in broad strokes alone, or merely by the enormity of the challenges he faced in 2009. Presidencies are not judged simply by the accomplishment of major objectives. They are measured by how the occupants of the Oval Office handled the unanticipated consequences of American action, the rise of new threats, and the unanticipated consequences of U.S. action. They are measured by the reordering of global power and whether it shifted to America's advantage.

Even after 180,000 U.S. troops returned home from two conflicts that yielded few of the results Americans once hoped for, President Obama's stewardship of American power has triggered renewed debate. In this debate, the picture necessarily grows more complicated. Obama governed at a moment of retrenchment in world affairs, when Americans were deeply ambivalent about the degree to which they wanted to become enmeshed in the chaos abroad. Obama himself often seemed to embody that ambivalence.

It did not take long for Obama's own vision of himself as a transformational figure in American politics to collide with the harsh partisanship at home and a splintering of the established world order. His critics, many of them eyeing a chance to regain Republican control of the White House, looked for any evidence that America was in retreat, any new sign that American interests were being ignored or that respect for the country had declined under the president's watch. They found much to bolster their case.

Still, when pressed, Obama's critics failed to create a unified alternative approach. Traditionalists in the Republican Party—leaders like Senator John McCain, who ran against Obama and lost in 2008—argued for greater use of

American muscle to counter Islamic radicals, Russia's reckless actions in Ukraine, Iran's nuclear ambitions, and China's attempt to seize territory in the Pacific. Others, mostly of the Tea Party conservatives and a left wing of the Democratic Party uncomfortable with Obama's interventionism, echoed public calls for America to retreat from a bitter world. That division gave Obama a chance to seek a middle ground, one in which a wise president avoids the temptations of overreach and harnesses American power—economic, diplomatic, and military—to reshape a world growing ever more hostile to the nation's long-term interests.

It is still too early to tell which of the two sweeping narratives surrounding the Obama Administration will prove most accurate. The first suggests that it was Obama's duty to redress what Thomas Wright of the Brookings Institution calls "the breakdown of the international order."[1] When the Arab Spring began in early 2011, that breakdown seemed quite possible. It seemed as though Barak Obama might preside over an era in which democratization finally came, if haltingly, to the greater Middle East. When that effort collapsed, only to be replaced by a mix of chaos and new dictatorships, Obama was criticized for failing to support fledgling democracies and defend territory that American blood and treasure had been spilt to liberate. Worse yet, his critics argued, he failed to face off against aggressive challengers, from Russia's Vladimir Putin to North Korea's Kim Jong Un.

The second narrative is a reversal of the first: it argues that the United States emerged scathed but essentially unchallenged during Obama's presidency, retaining its role as the sole superpower precisely because it resisted the temptations to leap into every conflict. Russia, in this narrative, was acting out of weakness—and will soon find that restoring past glories is an expensive hobby. Islamic terrorists filled vacuums created by the predictable failure of regional dictators, including some which the United States supported; however, the extremists cannot govern and will eventually burn out.

"DON'T DO STUPID S***"

Confronting that kind of chaos, the president portrayed his strategy as one that followed the doctor's creed: first, do no harm. That was the essence of his salty, and seemingly flip, statement to his staff when speaking to reporters on Air Force One in 2014: "Don't Do Stupid S***." It was not, as Hillary Rodham Clinton later noted, something that would easily translate into a national security strategy.

But to President Obama this was more than a cheeky slogan. It was a first step in preserving American power: to recognize that not every fight is

America's fight and that the country needed to regain its sense of balance. In his view, Iraq and Afghanistan had been more than costly folly; they had been enormously expensive distractions that kept the United States from focusing on long-term threats and core interests. America had taken its eye off of China's rise in Asia, ignored the long-term impact of climate change, and engendered enmity throughout the Middle East with its decade-long antiterrorism and reconstruction efforts in Iraq and Afghanistan.

"Ending two wars was important, not because I was under any illusions that that would mean we wouldn't have any terrorist threat,"[2] Obama said in an interview with *Vox*, an online publication, early in 2015. In what may have been his most pensive public explication of his strategy, he added: "It does mean, though, that by not having 180,000 people in Iraq and Afghanistan," America was free to "more strategically deploy, with a smaller footprint" to focus on the spread of disease and cyber security, and "to look at the new threats and opportunities that are out there. And that, I think, has been the real challenge over the last six to eight years."

To Obama, this was a new form of foreign policy realism—one that avoids getting caught up in frenzied headlines or treating each crisis playing out on CNN as an urgent call for American action. Susan Rice, his national security adviser, argued that such a realistic approach would keep the administration from being "buffeted by alarmism in nearly instantaneous news cycles."[3]

Obama's critics, however, believed that approach was based on a misunderstanding of what happens when America cedes its role as the world's indispensable nation. Condoleezza Rice, President George W. Bush's secretary of state, argues that five years of signaling that others need to step in and stressing that America can no longer police the world have taken a toll. "There was a view that if the United States pulled back and stopped 'imposing' and 'insisting' in the world, the vacuum would be filled by good things: the international community and the allies," Rice said in 2014, when I asked her to evaluate the Obama legacy. "But what has filled that space has been brutal dictators; extremist forces, especially in Iraq and Syria; and nationalism."[4]

So was that Obama's fault, or the world's?

THE BUSH "INHERITANCE"

The president's first term was about stemming the bleeding. Initially, he felt drawn into every international crisis, whether it was the lengthy debate over the Afghan surge, the overt and covert efforts to neuter the Iranian nuclear program, the Arab Spring and its ugly aftermath, the failure of the Russian reset, or the arrival of new leadership in China. Each foreign policy challenge generated Situation Room meetings, crisis phone calls to foreign leaders, and relentless questions from journalists, born of a 24/7 news cycle, who demanded answers—and who often equated silence with indecision.

Obama himself quickly came to resent the expectation that America was the solution to all foreign policy crises. His first priority was restoring the domestic economy and winning the battle over health care reform. Foreign policy initially ranked a distinct third. "It fascinated him, but he resented the mindshare it took up," one of his closest national security aides told me later. "He felt he had been elected for a domestic agenda, and he wanted to get back to it."

One could hear that emotion in his speeches: whenever he spoke of America's mission in Afghanistan, he would usually conclude by saying that he wanted to get to "nation building at home." He kept looking for ways that others could be compelled to share the burdens of leadership that America traditionally shouldered, especially in areas around the world where the United States' interests were remote. When a disaster struck in Asia he once asked aides, out of exasperation, why some issues were not China's responsibility to solve instead of his. The easy answer, of course, was that China did not have America's global reach, even if it harbored the desire to flex its muscles. The more complex answer, of course, was that if America let China fill that void, it would only be a short while before alarms would be raised that China was molding the world to its liking. No wonder Obama felt he was being sucked into a national security vortex that he could not escape.

Indeed, in 2013, as he was about to be sworn in for a second term, he told visitors to the White House that he had spent his first four years dealing with his "inheritance," the burden of a crashed economy and two wars that would never come to a satisfying conclusion. Now he wanted to focus anew on domestic renewal. The problem was that he had lost the majorities needed to get almost anything through Congress unscathed.

"Sometimes the best you can hope for is to move the needle," he said during a conversation about gun control. Some of those who left the White House wondered, what had happened to the man who had come to Washington talking of transformational change?

The answer was that he had realized the limits of his powers—as all presidents who come to the Oval Office with grand ambitions eventually must. Obama's first hope had been that the world would respond to him for the mere fact that he was not George W. Bush—that America's allies would join in a new sense of partnership, and its adversaries would respond to his early invitation that, "we will extend a hand if you are willing to unclench your fist."

Neither friend nor foe responded as Obama had hoped. The Europeans, even more eager to exit Iraq and Afghanistan, retreated to deal with problems at home, including an economic implosion that threatened the European Union. Iraq's Shia-dominated government turned on the Sunni population that had ruled with such brutal force under Saddam Hussein, bringing parts of the country to the brink of civil war.

The troop surge that Obama ordered into Afghanistan at the end of 2009—short in duration, he promised, whether successful or not—proved a disappointment. His generals thought it was too small to be effective; Obama thought that the Pentagon had lived too long in a world of endless timelines and bottomless budgets.

The essence of his surge decision in Afghanistan was to send a message that America's effort to rewire the country would be given one last chance. In 2009, he spoke publicly about how Afghanistan was a "war of necessity" for preventing another terrorist attack on the United States. By 2010, the reality of Afghanistan was best reflected in the name of the secret committee Obama set up to work out the terms of the U.S. disengagement, the "Afghan Good Enough Committee." The name said it all: Don't expect a Jeffersonian democracy, just settle for some stability. America's goal was no longer to transform Afghan society. The aim was simply to achieve some equilibrium so that the United States could pull back, wean the country from aid, and pray for the emergence of a stable government. Obama took the same approach in Iraq, declaring as troops were withdrawn in 2011 that the country would be "stable, secure, and self-reliant."[5]

LEADING FROM BEHIND

That same instinct to keep a light hand informed many other decisions in 2011, the year of the Arab Spring. As revolution swept the region, Obama decided, reluctantly, to join the European intervention in Libya to oust Muammar al-Qaddafi. His justification was humanitarian, and in an address to the nation he stated that while "some nations may be able to turn a blind eye to atrocities in other countries, the United States of America is differ-ent."[6] He ordered U.S. forces to help save Benghazi from an attack that many predicted would kill 10,000 Libyans. However, he insisted that France and Great Britain take the lead in the NATO bombing campaign, a defensible approach to alliance burden sharing that an unnamed Obama aide regrettably characterized as "leading from behind." After Qaddafi fell, NATO pulled back. Instead of a burgeoning democracy, chaos filled the streets. It was, as Obama himself later admitted, a mistake.

"Had we not intervened, it's likely that Libya would be Syria," he said in one interview in the summer of 2014 with my colleague Thomas Friedman.

"And so there would be more death, more disruption, more destruction. But what is also true is that I think we [and] our European partners underestimated the need to come in full force if you're going to do this. Then it's the day after Qaddafi is gone, when everybody is feeling good and everybody is holding up posters saying, 'Thank you, America.' At that moment, there has to be a much more aggressive effort to rebuild societies that didn't have any civic traditions."[7]

He concluded: "So that's a lesson that I now apply every time I ask the question, 'Should we intervene, militarily? Do we have an answer [for] the day after?'"

In many places around the world, Obama never found that answer. Syria became the most notable example—and the one most likely to haunt members of the administration as they write their memoirs. In his first term, the president rejected a plan from Secretary of State Hillary Rodham Clinton and CIA director General David Petraeus to arm the "moderate" opposition, although even Mrs. Clinton conceded, in a conversation at the time, that "they are hard to identify, and hard to trust." President Obama was concerned, understandably, that weapons would fall into the wrong hands—exactly what happened in Afghanistan in the late 1980s. Still, the result in Syria was years of seeming paralysis that appeared to violate the president's own standard that the United States could not turn away from atrocities around the world: in Syria, the casualties were twenty times greater than in Libya.

Over time, the Obama doctrine became clear. In Libya, Obama intervened because it was quick and casualty-free; the war could be fought from the air or offshore. The Syrian conflict, on the other hand, was simply too difficult to confront. That war was on the ground, in crowded cities, where the "light footprint" weapons of the first term—drones, cyber bugs, and Special Forces—were ineffective. The use of ground troops was a political pitfall—not just for the president but also for a casualty-weary Congress.

The result of this new reality was that the president found himself repeatedly making statements he could not back up. In August 2011, for instance, he stepped into the Rose Garden to declare that Syrian dictator Bashar al-Assad must "step aside." But there was no plan in place to ensure that he would, and as of this writing three and a half years later, Assad remains in power. To the United States, and its allies, a dictator dropping barrel bombs, although horrific, was better than the risk of intervention or the chaos resulting from Assad's overthrow.

When Obama briefly threatened in the summer of 2013 to strike at Syria's power centers for Bashar al-Assad's use of chemical weapons against his own people, he reversed himself at the last minute and threw the question to

Congress, which clearly would not vote for another U.S. intervention. He was widely criticized for drawing a "red line" and then failing to follow through on his threats. "It may have been one of our worst moments," said one aide who was involved in those discussions. "Not because of what it meant in Syria—eventually we got the chemical weapons out [thanks to a deal partly brokered by the Russians]. But we hurt American credibility."

FAMILIAR FOES

Credibility became critical when President Obama turned to a major goal: seeking a nuclear deal with Iran. Obama knew that if could bring thirty years of enmity to an end, if he could fundamentally change the nature of the U.S. relationship with a country that still held "Death to America" rallies, it would be the greatest alteration of the geopolitical landscape since Nixon went to China. But it would also be harder than the China initiative. The Chinese were willing to alter their system, at least around the edges, to enter the global economy. But to do so, they did not need to give up their regional influence; it would only grow. Iran remained ruled by traditionalists who believed they were still fighting a revolution and could hardly justify their existence without the presence of the American "Great Satan." The Iranian leadership equated a nuclear capability—if not a weapon—with regional power.

Just months into his tenure, Obama began writing to Iran's supreme leader, Ayatollah Ali Khamenei, arguing that once the two countries were beyond their nuclear differences, they could begin to discuss a partnership that would change the dynamics of the Middle East. Khamenei's response was a diatribe, a litany of now-familiar Iranian complaints about past offenses that Tehran blamed on the United States. But over time, even as he ramped up the pressure of sanctions and covert activity, Obama sensed a change in Iran. A new government was elected in Tehran on a platform of ending the crushing economic embargoes against the country. A secret mission was sent to explore a temporary accord that would freeze Iran's nuclear progress while the two countries engaged in talks.

What followed was nearly two years of shadowboxing, as the two sides tried to negotiate just how large a capability to make nuclear fuel Iran would retain, and for how long. But an agreement, Obama knew, would be the easy part: distrust on both sides renewed fears of deception. Hardliners in Iran saw secret plots to prevent the reemergence of Persian power. Opponents in Congress saw a grand deception in which Iran would secretly seek weapons elsewhere. It quickly became clear this was not one negotiation, but three:

The United States and its allies versus Iran, President Hassan Rouhani against the military and the clerics in Iran, and Obama versus the Congress. It made an already difficult negotiation process nearly impossible.

Nonetheless, scores of negotiators, nuclear experts, and outsiders made the talks a full-time occupation. Many in Washington wondered whether Obama and his second-term Secretary of State John Kerry wanted the agreement too desperately; after the collapse of Middle East peace talks, it was Kerry's best bet for a signature breakthrough.

A deal with Iran was also President Obama's greatest hope of demonstrating that he could fulfill the promise he made in 2008 to move the United States toward the elimination of nuclear weapons. He had enjoyed two years of moderate success, including a minor nuclear accord with Russia, called New START, which modestly limited the number of nuclear weapons each side could hold. The accord was the main achievement of the Russian "reset" that Obama and Hillary Clinton hoped for. But when Vladimir Putin retook the Russian presidency in 2012, progress halted. Suddenly, Iran became Obama's best hope for a legacy-making success.

By early 2015, it was still impossible to say whether President Obama would achieve breakthroughs in either arena. After the annexation of Crimea and the attacks into Ukraine in 2014, any real discussion with Russia seemed off the table for as long as Vladimir Putin remained in power. A preliminary accord with Iran was struck in early April 2015, but the fate of the final deal depended in part on implementation—which is fraught with risks. Obama knew that at best the Iran deal would extend the country's timeline to a bomb by ten to fifteen years, much-needed breathing space but not the kind of permanent solution previously envisioned. Sometimes in foreign policy, buying time is the best alternative.

LIGHT FOOTPRINT, HEAVY BURDENS

Historians will debate how Obama's promising start in foreign policy seemed to unwind in the second term. Perhaps the answer lies in the fact that the strategy that served Obama so well at the beginning of his presidency— epitomized by the aggressive counterterrorism campaign that decimated the core leadership of al-Qaeda and led to the raid that killed Osama bin Laden— proved insufficient to the broader challenges.

Certainly the administration's problem was not shyness from using force, as many critics argued. Whereas President Bush had ordered roughly fifty drone strikes in Pakistan, the home of the core al-Qaeda leadership at the time, Obama ordered roughly 300 in his first term alone. And he approved the "Olympic Games," the code name for the secret cyber-attacks on Iran's nuclear enrichment facilities, which wiped out roughly 1,000 nuclear centrifuges before the computer code became public and the operation was shut down.

Special Forces, drones, and cyber-attacks were all part of a strategy that, in the first term, was described as the "light footprint." The phrase was meant to connote a lightning-quick strike that made maximum use of American technological superiority. "Dumb wars" of occupation by large numbers of ground troops—how Obama once described Iraq—were out. America's approach would be to accomplish its goals through remote control whenever possible and by the quickest possible involvement on the ground whenever the use of direct force was unavoidable. The president also learned to play the long game. The Treasury Department became his favorite noncombatant command by refining the art of the economic squeeze on Iran, eventually forcing the mullahs to the negotiating table. The light footprint approach undeniably fit the national mood at the time.

In retrospect, however, a "light footprint" approach to every international crisis was essentially a defensive strategy, and a bit unsatisfying, at least in historical terms. Roosevelt and Truman had solidified America's post–World War II role by helping create the United Nations, the international financial institutions, and the Marshall Plan to rebuild Europe; Kennedy emerged from the Cuban Missile Crisis with treaties limiting the spread of nuclear weapons; George H.W. Bush, whose foreign policy Obama admired, engineered a peaceful ending to the Cold War and lured new allies from the ruins of the Soviet Union. President Obama wanted to add to that list of executive success. The question was how to do it in the midst of austerity and retrenchment.

The light footprint approach also had an illusory element. It was satisfying in the short term but did not put a stake in the ground or create lines that the world knew America would defend. It was suited to certain conflicts, but not others.

Vladimir Putin, among others, seemed to understand this. The chaos he unleashed in Ukraine by sending in irregular forces, tanks, and arms to support Russian-speaking separatists couldn't be contained with a light-footprint solution primarily dependent on economic sanctions. At least for a time, Putin seemed immune to the pressure of sanctions, although at this writing, many believe the crash in oil prices and the sanctions together may unexpectedly hurt Putin's standing.

America's adversaries saw the light footprint strategy as an opportunity to test the nation's commitment to global leadership. "We're seeing the 'light footprint' run out of gas," said one of Obama's former senior national security aides. "No one is arguing for military action, for bringing back George W. Bush's chest-thumping."[8] At the same time, he said, the president's oft-repeated lines that those who violate international norms will be "isolated" and "pay a heavy price" over the long term have sounded "more like predictions" and "less like imminent threats."

A MIXED LEGACY

That is a central irony of the Obama presidency. Under his stewardship the country is, by nearly all qualitative measures, much stronger today than at the beginning of his tenure. The economy has recovered. Energy independence is in sight. No other country can match American innovation or technology.

And yet Obama faced what his former national security adviser, Thomas Donilon, called "a challenge to the post–Cold War order in Europe, an order that we have a lot to do with."[9] Obama himself clearly wanted to be the president who built on that postwar order rather than see it fray at the edges.

Obama "understands that being a transformative president on a global stage is about more than good intentions and good plans," said Jeffrey Bader, a close Obama adviser on Asia during the first two years of the administration. "It's about finding places where you are not dependent on adversaries who refuse to budge, or who benefit from demonstrating their hostility to the United States."[10]

President Obama has acknowledged critics who see his foreign policy as too accommodating to adversaries. But in public, at least, he has been unapologetic. His response to criticism has been that America elected him to show a caution that had been missing from national security policy for a decade.

"We do nobody a service when we leap before we look," Obama said in 2013, just after his second inauguration. "A big chunk of my day is occupied by news of war, terrorism, ethnic clashes, violence done to innocents. And what I have to constantly wrestle with is where and when can the United States intervene or act in ways that advance our national interest, advance our security, and speak to our highest ideals and sense of common humanity. And as I wrestle with those decisions, I am more mindful probably than most of not only our incredible strengths and capabilities, but also our limitations."[11]

All modern American presidents have to make life-and-death decisions that seek equilibrium between complex, and in some cases opposing, national interests. "You make the decisions you think balance all these equities, and you hope that, at the end of your presidency, you can look back and say,

I made more right calls than not and that I saved lives where I could," said Obama. "And that America, as best it could in a difficult, dangerous world, was, net, a force for good."[12]

Here was a president clearly struggling with two overwhelming imperatives: putting out fires and a desire to build something lasting. He had succeeded in the first. The second turned out to be far more difficult to achieve.

Presidential Scandals

54. Watergate: Dirty Tricks and Cover-Ups

by John Aloysius Farrell

Richard Nixon's ruin began on Sunday, June 13, 1971, on the morning after his daughter, Tricia, married Edward Cox in the Rose Garden at the White House. On its front page that day, next to a photograph of the bride, the *New York Times* carried the first installment of what came to be known as "The Pentagon Papers," a secret Defense Department study of the duplicitous government activity that led the United States into the Vietnam War.

Nixon was at the nadir of his first term, a moment, he recalled, when his troubles were "so overwhelming and so apparently impervious" as to snuff his hopes for reelection. His approval rating had plummeted; less than half the country thought he was doing a good job. His foes were legion: in late April and early May, a half million antiwar protesters had gathered in Washington. The economy was uncooperative. "If the prospects are that dire," Nixon told adviser George Shultz, after getting a gloomy report, "maybe we all better turn in our suits and run for the hills."[1]

In the Oval Office on Saturday, fretting as he waited for the rain to lift and give Tricia the outdoor wedding she so wanted, Nixon had raged, sequentially, about his foes. It was an extensive list, that included "long-haired, dirty looking" protesters; the Eastern Establishment; feminists; teachers' unions; Jews ("Goddamn, they are a vicious bunch"); African Americans ("We don't do well with blacks. . . . We don't want to do so damn well with blacks"); the "softies" of the Ivy League; the "ass kissers and butter uppers" in the bureaucracy; and the "lousy, dirty . . . cowardly bastards" in the press.

Nixon's hopes rested with three potentially transformative initiatives: the secret Vietnam peace negotiations, back-channel talks on a strategic arms limitations treaty (SALT) and other issues with the Soviet Union, and an historic diplomatic opening to China. The prospects for a stunning turnaround, the greatest Nixon comeback of all, were tantalizing—and terribly stressful. His thoughts about China reflected his mood and said much about his troubled character. "Nixon was excited almost to the point of euphoria," Henry Kissinger recalled. "But he also was assailed by his chronic anxiety that no enterprise of his would ever come to a totally satisfactory ending."[2]

LIGHTING A FUSE

So things stood when at 12:18 PM a voice-activated tape machine clicked into motion as a White House operator connected Nixon to his deputy national security adviser, General Alexander Haig. After a brief discussion about casualties in Vietnam, Nixon, distracted, asked: "Nothing else of interest in the world today?" Haig, the eager adjutant, lit a match. The "goddamn *New York Times*" had published "an expose of the most highly classified documents of the war," Haig said. It was "a devastating security breach of the greatest magnitude of anything I've ever seen."[3]

The leak was the work of Daniel Ellsberg, a summa cum laude graduate of Harvard, defense scholar, and former Marine, whose views had been transformed by the two years he spent in Vietnam as a counterinsurgency operative. For months after his return, he had trudged around Capitol Hill, towing Top Secret chapters from a swollen briefcase, trying to persuade antiwar lawmakers to hold hearings or read the material into the *Congressional Record*. None summoned the courage to do so. By the time Ellsberg approached the *Times*, his expectations had plummeted. The study's publication, he believed, might at best cause a minor stir—"close to zero." He could not have been more wrong.[4]

Nixon could have left well enough alone, for the timeframe covered by the Pentagon Papers ended before he took office. The study was "a tough attack on Kennedy" and "brutal on President Johnson," Haig told the president. "They're gonna end up in a massive gut fight in the Democratic Party on this thing." As Nixon's chief of staff, H.R. Haldeman, wrote in his diary that evening, "The key now is for us to keep out of it, and let the people that are affected cut each other up."

Instead, Nixon commandeered the gut fight, lurching into a colossal confrontation with his enemies in the press. As the courts ruled against him, Nixon worked himself into a frenzy—and personally launched the calamitous initiatives that would culminate in the Watergate scandal.[5]

On Monday evening, Nixon spoke to Attorney General John Mitchell, who was seeking permission to put the *Times* on formal notice: the paper could be prosecuted under the Espionage Act if it continued to publish state secrets. Mitchell told him that the administration would look "silly" and "foolish" if it failed to act. Nixon gave his blessing. "He's a strong man, that Mitchell," Nixon told Kissinger after the attorney general hung up. "A lot of people will say this is trying to suppress the press and the rest. But so be it. We'll go down fighting." The decision made, he went bowling.

The *Times* ignored the warning. On Tuesday, the Justice Department urged the federal courts to suppress the newspaper's continued publication of the study—the first time a U.S. government had ever demanded such "prior restraint."

Things went south quickly. Johnson and the Democrats were, wisely, lying low. The press and public focused instead on Nixonian repression of the press. "People believe that we are covering something up," a colleague, Charles Colson, warned Haldeman. By Thursday night, Nixon realized the fix he was in. "It's all blurred," he griped, in frustration. The nation's editors rallied around the *Times*, and the courts rebuffed the administration. The Supreme Court heard the case on an expedited basis and, in a 6 to 3 decision on June 30, handed the administration a humiliating defeat.

A free press had the duty "to prevent . . . the government from deceiving the people and sending them off to distant lands to die," wrote Justice Hugo Black, in one of the majority opinions. The restraining orders were "a flagrant, indefensible and continuing violation of the First Amendment."[6]

CROSSING THE LINE

Nixon had commandeered a relatively minor incident and transformed it into a political crisis. He focused his fury on Ellsberg and the Left. In a manic scene in the Oval Office, he and his aides whipped themselves into ascending states of wrath about this left-wing troublemaker. Haldeman then reported that their antagonists at the Brookings Institution, a liberal think tank, were sitting on other secret files.

"Bob? Now you remember Huston's plan?" Nixon said, referring to White House aide Tom Huston's proposal to use burglary and bugging and other illegal counterintelligence tactics against antiwar protesters. "I want it implemented on a thievery basis. Goddamn it, go in and get those files. Blow the safe and get it."[7]

Colson drew the assignment. A plan was concocted to start a fire at Brookings and ransack the building in the resulting chaos. Cooler heads, recognizing the dangers of arson—and, potentially, homicide—prevailed, and the plan was abandoned. But a line had been crossed, and principles were jettisoned.

Nixon viewed Senator Edward Kennedy as a likely opponent in 1972. With remarkable moral agility, he ordered his aides to pass around the Kennedy chapters of the Pentagon Papers—the very material they were asking the courts to keep secret. "Leak it to some other paper," Nixon said, with no apparent irony. "The public is entitled to know."[8]

Nixon ordered up a "declassification project" in which evidence of transgressions by Democratic presidents—Franklin Roosevelt's responsibility for

Pearl Harbor, John Kennedy's actions in the Bay of Pigs, and the like—would be excavated from government files and publicized. He needed "a small group of tough guys," to do it. "I really need a son of a bitch . . . who will work his butt off and do it dishonorably. . . . I'll direct him myself," the president told his aides.

Colson had just the man: a retired CIA agent named Howard Hunt, who was hired as a White House consultant. When he couldn't unearth proof that Kennedy had ordered the assassination of South Vietnam President Ngo Dinh Diem, Hunt forged State Department cables, which Colson peddled to *Life* magazine. Nixon came up with another assignment for his "tough guys"—to smear leakers like Ellsberg.

Thus was born the Special Investigations Unit, led by David Young, thirty-two, and Egil Krogh, thirty-one. Lacking any expertise in black operations, they brought on a kooky former FBI agent: G. Gordon Liddy. They were given a wad of money, high-tech toys, and a suite on the ground floor of the Executive Office Building. They called themselves the Plumbers, because they stopped leaks. Soon, Colson had Hunt join them, and Nixon aide John Ehrlichman telephoned the CIA, instructing the agency to give them "carte blanche."[9]

It was an awful notion. The last thing Richard Nixon needed were "tough guys" like Hunt and Liddy, governed by spaniels like Colson, Young, and Krogh, who would salute at 2 AM and, as Nixon put it, "go out and do a few" dirty tricks on their own.[10]

Hunt and Liddy drew CIA disguises and equipment and jetted off to Los Angeles over Labor Day weekend, to burglarize the Beverly Hills offices of Ellsberg's psychiatrist, Dr. Lewis Fielding. They broke windows, jimmied locks, and threw files and pills around to make it look like a drug-related crime but failed to find the evidence they wanted to defame or blackmail their target.

Ehrlichman and Krogh were stunned when they reviewed the report that Hunt and Liddy submitted upon their return from California. Ehrlichman had signed off on a "covert" operation with the express caveat that it not be traced to the White House and claimed later that he thought they would obtain Ellsberg's file through more subtle means, like bribing a nurse. To give Nixon the desired deniability, Ehrlichman did some tap-dancing when he reported to the president. "We had one little operation. It's been aborted out in Los Angeles, which, I think, it is better that you don't know about."[11]

In a classic bureaucratic maneuver, Liddy was then made someone else's problem—shipped to Nixon's campaign committee with the responsibility of gathering political intelligence on the president's foes in the antiwar movement and the Democratic Party. (Haldeman and Attorney General Mitchell feared that Yippies and Weathermen might disrupt the GOP convention in Miami, as they had the Democrats in Chicago in 1968.) Liddy quickly recruited Hunt. Different address, different boss, but the bad boys were back in business.

APPETITE FOR DIRTY TRICKS

From the beginning of his presidency, the White House staff had toiled to meet Nixon's appetite for political sabotage and subterfuge.

"I want, Bob, more use of wiretapping," he told Haldeman in May. "Why don't you put your money . . . on surveillance and so forth."

"Maybe it's the wrong thing to do, but I've got a feeling that if you are going to start, you have to start now," Nixon said. "Maybe we can get a real scandal on any one of the leading Democrats."

"Scandal or improprieties," Haldeman echoed. "The leading Democrats."

"Now you're talking," said Nixon.[12]

Soon, Nixon's men had phony newspaper reporters, under the code name "Chapman's Friend," collecting information on the Democratic presidential campaigns. A spy called "Ruby I" infiltrated the campaign organization of Senator Edmund Muskie and copied sensitive documents, including the floor plan of its headquarters, a prerequisite for bugging. An office was rented nearby for use as a listening post. The "Sedan Chair I" and "Sedan Chair II" operations disrupted the Democratic campaign events and ultimately landed a mole in Senator George McGovern's inner circle. And Hunt, under "Ruby II," put a spy in McGovern headquarters to do the groundwork for a break-in and bugging operation there.[13]

With Nixon's personal approval, one dirty tricks campaign grew to encompass two-dozen agents in eleven states. The men were told, at first, to target Muskie, who was seen as Nixon's likely opponent. Many of the tricks were harmless: releasing mice at a Muskie press conference, and ordering limousines carrying baffled African diplomats to arrive unbidden at a Muskie campaign dinner. Other capers, like the forgeries they produced on counterfeit campaign stationery, spreading racial and sexual slurs to divide the Democrats, were clearly unlawful.[14]

By the fall of 1971, it was hard to find a White House aide with a political portfolio who wasn't involved in a dirty tricks campaign. Mitchell and Haldeman met to try and bring order to the chaos surrounding their "covert activities." The two chiefs passed on one proposal, called "Operation Sandwedge," that would have set up a private investigative agency. Liddy then proposed an in-house project called "Gemstone." The plan was rife with burglary, bugging, and blackmail and, in its early iterations, with prostitutes, spy planes, thuggery, and kidnapping. When he presented this abomination to the Attorney General of the United States in his offices in the U.S. Department of Justice, with the Counsel to the President at his side, using charts prepared by the Central Intelligence Agency, Liddy was not fired or scolded. Instead, Mitchell told him to come back with something a little cheaper.[15]

Liddy did. And on June 17, 1972, a team of burglars led by Hunt and Liddy broke into the Watergate office building, where they were arrested in the midst of bugging and photographing files at the headquarters of the Democratic National Committee. Nixon's men never even considered coming clean about their true activities. The break-in at Dr. Fielding's office and the other "White House horrors," as Mitchell called them, made a cover-up inevitable.

"Apparently . . . they used the same people for a wide range of things," Haldeman told Nixon. "You've got cross ties in your leading people and all that. If these guys were only on this thing, you could cut them loose and sink them without a trace."[16]

ALL THE KING'S MEN

Watergate opened a wider window on government misbehavior. Subsequent investigations inspired by the scandal revealed that the FBI, the CIA, and other security agencies had employed such tactics, and worse, for decades, and that all the Cold War presidents had conspired to keep the knowledge from an oblivious public. Stashed in the government's files were records of massive domestic surveillance programs; hundreds of "black-bag" jobs; CIA drug experiments conducted on unsuspecting citizens; and the attempted assassinations of foreign leaders. The Kennedy Administration had joined hands with Mafia gangsters in its plots to murder Castro and authorized the FBI's surveillance of Martin Luther King Jr., with bugs in his hotel rooms recording his extramarital affairs. When civil rights demonstrators threatened to disturb Lyndon Johnson's coronation at the 1964 Democratic convention, he sent the FBI to eavesdrop.

Nixon failed to appreciate, however, something the long-haired kids in the streets could have told him—namely, that the times indeed were changing. Vietnam had shattered the Cold War consensus, polarized a generation, and primed Americans to mistrust their presidents and their government. Nixon's wily old pal FBI Director J. Edgar Hoover had read the tides of public sentiment and balked when he was asked to do what he had done for other chief executives. So Nixon brought the black ops into his White House, to be run by raw amateurs and klutzy has-beens. The distinction between national security and political expediency predictably blurred and then swiftly disappeared altogether.

"Who will rid me of this meddlesome priest?" mused Henry II, and a knight seeking royal favor murdered Archbishop Thomas Becket in the cathedral at Canterbury. Did Nixon order each specific breach of the law? No. But in June 1971 he had instructed Haldeman and Colson: "You've got to really have a sophisticated assault upon the Democrats. Humphrey must be destroyed. Muskie must be destroyed. Teddy Kennedy must be."[17] It wasn't hard for Nixon's knights to discern what their sovereign wanted. Nixon's mutterings led not to Canterbury, but to Watergate.

Nixon's White House taping system furnished the evidence his enemies needed. In the summer of 1974, the Supreme Court ruled that the president had to surrender his tapes to the courts. One of them—the so-called smoking-gun tape of June 23, 1972—captured Nixon conspiring with Haldeman to obstruct the Watergate investigation. Nixon's popular support dwindled. A House committee voted to impeach him. On August 9, 1974, Nixon resigned—the only American president to achieve such disgrace.

◆　◆　◆　◆　◆

55. Iran-Contra: Saving Reagan's Presidency

by David M. Abshire

On an ominous November 3, 1986, a Lebanese periodical, *Al-Shiraa*, reported that the United States sold weapons to Iran. The story spread like wildfire in the American press. One shocking headline read, "Reagan Trades Arms for Hostages." After three days of White House silence, President Reagan denied it all. "We will never pay off terrorists because that only encourages more of it," he declared in his reassuring manner.

Iran had troubled the counsels of U.S. leaders virtually since the inception of the Islamic Republic in 1979. In November 1979, 400 Iranian radicals, many of them members of the Iranian Revolutionary Guard, broke into the walled grounds of the U.S. Embassy in Tehran, taking fifty-two U.S. employees hostage. The failed hostage rescue launched in April 1980—which led to the death of eight U.S. service members—essentially destroyed Jimmy Carter's presidency.

With Reagan's inauguration in January 1981, the fifty-two U.S. hostages held in Tehran were finally released, but troubles with Iran continued. In 1984, the Lebanese terrorist group Hezbollah, a Shiite movement closely allied with the Iranian Revolutionary Guard, seized three U.S. citizens. In 1985, the group abducted four more Americans, including the CIA station chief in Lebanon. The National Security Advisor at the time, Robert "Bud" McFarlane, backed by CIA Chief William Casey, convinced the president to become involved in a highly secret arms-for-hostage deal. Iran needed arms for its war against Iraq, and the hostages held by Hezbollah were the special bait. The secret U.S. scheme run out of the National Security Council (NSC) contradicted the much publicized program called "Operation Staunch"—a high-profile effort led by Secretary of State George Shultz—to ensure that no U.S. allies gave any arms to Iran, a country publicly labeled as supporting terrorism.

In the ensuing days of late November 1986, more revelations of arms sales to Iran shook the president's credibility. To the Congress and the press, it became increasingly clear that the Reagan Administration had violated its own no-concessions policy of withholding weapons from all nations that sponsored terrorism. It had also contradicted its own embargo on arms sales to Iran specifically.

The situation soon got worse. The mishandled initial White House investigations and the guidance of the national security advisor led to Reagan making a disastrous speech on November 13. His address was filled with inaccurate statements, such as his pronouncement that all the weapons and spare parts shipped to Iran "could easily fit into a single cargo plane." Actually, the first two shipments in August and September of 1985 totaled 504 tube-launched, optically tracked, wire-guided antitank missiles (TOWs). An uncharacteristically defensive Reagan also declared in the speech that the "unprecedented speculation" and countless press reports had been not only wrong, but also "potentially dangerous to the hostages." The president assured the American people that "our no-concessions policy remains in force."

After the speech, polls showed that only 14 percent of the public believed the president's story. And the crisis continued to spiral downward. At the time of Reagan's speech, an NSC staffer, a very aggressive, free-wheeling U.S. Marine Lieutenant Colonel named Oliver North, was still trying to trade *more arms* for hostages. On November 19, an even more confused President Reagan conducted a primetime press conference filled with more inaccuracies, including a monstrous one—the United States, he insisted publicly, had not been involved with Israel as an intermediary in supplying weapons to Iran.

Attorney General Edwin Meese was worried enough to launch an investigation into what Reagan's subordinates had actually done in the Iranian arms deal. Then, a second shoe dropped like a concrete block: that investigation turned up a telltale memo by Lt. Col. North, who was operating directly out of the executive office of the president. The memo revealed that North had inflated the price of arms going to Iran to illegally divert the profits to the Nicaraguan contras, the anti-Sandinista forces opposing the Marxist regime of Nicaragua. When Meese informed President Reagan of this memo, the president was devastated. The blood drained from his face.

Funding the Nicaraguan rebels—whom Reagan proudly called "freedom fighters"—defied the Boland Amendment, a congressional restriction passed to explicitly prevent just such support. While the Boland Amendment had some ambiguities, a Reagan authorization of the diversion of funds to the contras clearly could have been a heinous offense. If Reagan knew of the diversion, he could have been guilty of a cover-up and obstruction of justice, which were grounds for possible impeachment.

By 1986 the Reagan Presidency was unraveling. The Iran-Contra revelations raised questions about the president's judgment, credibility, and management style. Simply put, the survival of the Reagan presidency was at stake, and I soon found myself drawn into the unfolding drama when I was asked to serve as a Special Counselor to the President on Reagan's cabinet, with a charge of managing the White House response to the Iran-Contra investigations. My task was to restore trust so that it could once again become the basis of Reagan's leadership. It was not going to be an easy task. On December 31, 1986, I picked up a copy of the *Washington Post* and read an op-ed by the popular columnists Rowland Evans and Robert Novak. It was titled "The Reagan Presidency Is Dead."

SEEDS OF SCANDAL

The seeds of the Iran-Contra crisis were planted in the spring of 1983, when Secretary of State George Schultz initiated a major diplomatic campaign to dissuade other countries from selling arms to Iran. As the U.S. ambassador to NATO at the time, I was instructed by the State Department to become a lead spokesperson of this antiterrorist policy at NATO meetings. The unequivocal message I and others delivered was "absolutely no dealings with terrorists."

Then in the early morning of October 23, 1983, a disguised truck driven by terrorists was able to penetrate the headquarters complex of U.S. Marines serving as peacekeepers in Lebanon's increasingly bloody civil war. Tragically,

241 Marines were killed, and the rest of the U.S. peacekeeping contingent was later withdrawn from Lebanon.

After the bombings of the Marine barracks and, later, the U.S. Embassy in Beirut, it became clear that those responsible were Hezbollah terrorists—Lebanese Shiites financed by Shiite Iran. On January 18, 1984, Iran was thus placed on the State Department's public list of terrorist states. Then Hezbollah began a campaign of kidnapping Americans, and on March 16, 1984, they hit the jackpot by seizing CIA Station Chief William Buckley. CIA Director Bill Casey, a consummate spymaster who traced his service back to the World War II–era OSS, had personally picked Buckley for the sensitive assignment in Beirut. Not surprisingly, the news of Buckley's capture and torture shook Bill Casey. This was his own man who held a sacred bond to the agency that Casey led and loved.

Three months later a videotape was passed to an American journalist in Beirut that in turn was secretly sent over to the State Department. In it, three kidnapped Americans, including the emaciated William Buckley, pleaded for the release of seventeen Islamist terrorists being held by Kuwait. Casey took the tape to the White House for a tearful Ronald Reagan to view. It contained images of an abused, weakened, but courageous Buckley. In total contradiction to state policy, Ronald Reagan was setting the emotional stage for the trade of arms for hostages.

As it happened, National Security Advisor Bud McFarlane was at this time in contact with a freelance consultant named Michael Ledeen. He had shadowy connections to both the Israelis and some Iranians and argued that there was a "moderate" cabal in Iran who were willing to arrange for the release of the U.S. hostages in exchange for U.S. weapons transfers. Soon after, Israeli officials came to McFarlane with the clever idea that they ship the weapons to the Iranians, and the Americans replace the shipped weapons. McFarlane liked the idea, as did Casey. This theory eventually evolved into the plan of hostages being released to show the clout of the "moderate" faction in Iran in return for arms being shipped from Israel and replaced by the United States.

At a National Security Planning Group meeting at which, irresponsibly, no notes were taken, McFarlane, strongly backed by Bill Casey, pushed the arms idea against the opposition of the other principals present. Although Casey's own CIA operatives knew that the principle Iranian interlocutor in the deal was a discredited character, Casey did not reveal this critical information. This omission was disastrous and truly inexcusable, for the principle mission of the CIA director is to fairly represent the intelligence community and its findings to the president, and not to twist or omit critical information to fit the director's personal views on U.S. policy.

The hostage issue played on Reagan's conscience until, tragically, he relented in his principled opposition to the scheme. He gave in to McFarlane's plan.

CIA Director Casey also had problems on another front. With many lawmakers furious over what they saw as the CIA's earlier and unauthorized mining of the Nicaraguan harbor and charges that Casey himself had dissembled to the Senate Intelligence Committee on the issue, Congress passed the Boland Amendment. It stipulated that no appropriated funds for the CIA or any other "department, agency, or entity of the United States involved in intelligence activities may be obligated or expended for the purpose . . . of supporting directly or indirectly military or paramilitary operations in Nicaragua."

As befitted a clever tax attorney, Casey spotted a loophole in the Boland Amendment. The NSC at the White House was not involved in "intelligence activities," as prohibited in the amendment, and therefore could be the coordinating body for the effort to support the Contras. As it happened, Casey knew and admired a young, gung-ho marine who worked at the NSC, and was willing to think and act outside the box. His name was Oliver North.

Of course, North would not—could not—officially be working for Casey, because that would constitute breaking the Boland law. He would be working for National Security Advisor Bud McFarlane. It was a "neat" arrangement designed to outfox Congress. After passage of the Boland Amendment, President Reagan had said that the "freedom fighters" in the contras must nevertheless be held together "body and soul." McFarlane repeated those words to the zealot Ollie North, who took them to mean that anything goes. And thus was a dangerous initiative launched.

A CONFEDERACY OF DECEPTION

In the Watergate hearings, Senator Howard Baker had famously posed the central question: "What did the president know, and when did he know it?" He was referring to President Nixon, but now his question applied to President Reagan.

The national security advisor, Vice Admiral John Poindexter, sat just steps away from the Oval Office. The big question was whether he had explicitly told the president about Lt. Col. Oliver North's illegal diversion of funds from the arms sales to Iran to the contras of Central America? In danger of being swept away in the confusion and chaos of the moment, President Reagan and his chief of staff Don Regan made dramatic moves and instituted three short-term remedies to try and get ahead of the crisis.

First, the president asked for the resignation of Poindexter and North—that is, he fired them. Second, the president set up his own bipartisan board of three eminent individuals: former senator John Tower, former national security advisor Brent Scowcroft, and former senator and secretary of state Edwin Muskie. This panel became known as the "Tower Commission," after its chairman. The administration hoped the commission could quickly turn out a report detailing what went wrong and how to fix it, even as a newly appointed independent counsel, Judge Lawrence Walsh, and two congressional committees proceeded at a more deliberate pace to investigate the matter.

Finally, President Reagan pledged not to exert executive privilege in the investigation that would follow, a point the president made when he called requesting that I become his Special Counselor for managing the Iran-Contra investigation process. "David, I want your help in carrying out my commitment to get out all of the facts. There is no holding back through executive privilege. I want to get to the bottom of things. I want to ensure that there will be no cover-up."

Those words were permanently etched in my mind. I reflected on the summons I had received in 1973 from a besieged Nixon White House, which wanted my help in managing the Watergate crisis. I refused; my fear at that earlier time was that Nixon might be leading a cover-up. Nixon in many ways was more brilliant than Reagan and was an artful schemer and global strategist. I believed that Reagan had probably been very naive in the Iran-Contra affair, but I felt he was incapable of leading any kind of conspiracy. His words about openness and not invoking executive privilege turned out to be historic in the saga of restoring Reagan's presidency.

I later learned about the critical period from November 5 to November 20, 1986. Beginning with the first inkling that a major scandal was about to break, National Security Advisor John Poindexter had invited his predecessor, Bud McFarlane, back to work with Oliver North to prepare a chronology of events. All three had apparently put aside their pledge to the U.S. Naval Academy honor code about truth. They created more than a dozen versions of a chronology, none of which were accurate. Their intention was to prepare a version that would best protect the president and the White House, thus wrongly moving the administration into a cover-up.

Bud McFarlane, who later had an aching conscience that the self-righteous Colonel North never shared, described this process to the Tower Commission as an attempt to create "a chronology that obscured essential facts." McFarlane confessed that this chronology did not present a "full and completely accurate account" of the events, and he admitted that he knew that the account was "misleading, at least, and wrong, at worst." Soon afterward, CIA Director Bill Casey gave misleading testimony on the matter on Capitol Hill, the blatant inaccuracy of which so infuriated Secretary of State George Schultz that he threated to resign.

If these early attempts to shield the president and gild his motives were aimed at helping Reagan, they actually did the exact opposite. The deliberate distortion of the record made the president's press conference of November 19 disastrous. Storylines had already been changed by the staff so often that they compounded the president's confusion and soon made him publicly appear incompetent or even dishonest. Part of President Reagan's confusion was driven by Poindexter's and North's impassioned plea to him that the lives of the hostages were at risk and the truth could thus not be told.

THE TOWER COMMISSION SPEAKS

On the morning of February 26, 1987, the Tower Commission released its report. The report was broken down into five parts: the introduction; a section on the arms transfers to Iran; then one on the diversion and support for the Nicaraguan Contras; then a narrative of the affair; and finally, the commission's recommendations and conclusions. The commission noted that the NSC system had served the White House well for more than forty years, and, had it been used in this case, it could have "help[ed] prevent bad ideas from becoming presidential policy."

Tower stressed that the commission unanimously agreed that attempts were made to trade arms for hostages and that there was evidence of a diversion of funds. The best news of the report was the commission found no evidence to suggest that the president knew of the diversion. The commission was also convinced that the president wanted the full story to be told. On the other hand, the report highlighted the misleading statements of North, McFarlane, Poindexter, and (White House Chief of Staff Don) Regan in their attempts to "distance" or protect Reagan from the scandal.

While the Tower Report exonerated the president of any cover-up, it criticized his management style and provided a devastating analysis of his presidential leadership and policy during this period. As commission member Muskie said at the press conference releasing the report, "The policy was a wrong policy, and it was the president's policy." The report held the president fully responsible for not seeing that the successful processes of the NSC were effectively utilized.

Ultimately, Iran-Contra's notorious failure was indeed the fault of the president, made possible by his evasion of the NSC process. This lasting lesson for the future raises an all-important question: when will presidents fully learn from history? The NSC process had been avoided before—most notably by President Lyndon Johnson during the critical decision-making period between October 1964 and February 1965, when U.S. participation in the Vietnam War escalated with ground troops. President John F. Kennedy also circumvented the process of the NSC, previously used by President Dwight Eisenhower, which resulted in the disastrous Bay of Pigs affair. In December 2002, before the second Iraq war, the NSC process was again aborted and the State Department excluded; preparation and execution of both the fighting and reconstruction were turned over to the Defense Department.

The National Security Act of 1947 was inspired by the wise men who had crafted the winning strategies of World War II. These men knew that all elements of national power, departments, and agencies had to be coordinated to achieve success. Organizing these constituents creates checks and balances by bringing in different points of view to bear on key policy discussions. The Tower Commission emphasized this important fundamental lesson, one that commission member General Brent Scowcroft understood during the first Bush Administration and the Gulf War, when he was National Security Advisor. The result was the successful use of the NSC process during that conflict, which still serves as a model of coordinated strategies and diplomatic action.

In hindsight any flaws of the Tower Commission report are minor compared with the commission's landmark achievement. After many months, during which the government was in crisis and the Cold War at a critical phase, the Tower Commission produced a credible and broadly accepted document that created the foundation for restoring the Reagan Presidency.

Reagan noted the commission's critical role in a seminal March 4 speech on its findings. "I've studied the board's report. Its findings are honest, convincing, and highly critical, and I accept them," Reagan said. "A few days ago, I told the American people I did not trade arms for hostages. My heart and my best intentions tell me that was true, but the facts and the evidence tell me it is not." He said that he did not know about the diversion of funds to the contras, "but as president, I cannot escape responsibility." Reagan went on to criticize his own management style and said that he had met with the entire NSC staff. "And I told them that there'll be no more freelancing by individuals when it comes to our national security."

I thought the speech was just right, and so did the national press. Veteran *New York Times* journalist R.W. Apple, Jr., wrote that "President Reagan spoke to the American people tonight in a spirit of contrition that has not been heard from the White House in a quarter of a century; . . . not since

John F. Kennedy took the blame for the catastrophic Bay of Pigs invasion in 1961 has any president so openly confessed error."

The parallels were not coincidental. As early as the previous January, we had studied what President Kennedy had said publicly after the Bay of Pigs disaster: "It was all my fault." That was our model for President Reagan's speech. Afterward, the president had an immediate approval-rating jump of nine points in the CBS News polls. Respondents once again approved of his job performance by a 51–42 margin. Reagan clearly had his shortcomings and failings, but he was still the leader.

THE CURSE OF IRAN-CONTRA

Bill Casey, the famed spymaster at the center of the Iran-Contra scandal, was struck down by a seizure related to brain cancer just before he was to testify a second time on the Iran-Contra affair. He took his Iran-Contra secrets to the grave and was never dragged through humiliating inquiries and inquisitions—a true blessing for the indefatigable cold warrior. Tragically, CIA station chief William Buckley died in the hands of his Hezbollah torturers in June 1985, before the Iran-Contra scandal even broke into the press. Buckley was honored with a star on the agency's Memorial Wall and the Distinguished Intelligence Cross, the highest CIA honor.

Oliver North was convicted of destroying NSC documents, aiding and abetting in the preparation of false chronologies for congressional testimony, and accepting an illegal gratuity. He was sentenced to a three-year suspended prison term, two years of probation, $150,000 in fines, and 1,200 hours of community service. An appeals court overturned the convictions, however, on the basis that North's immunized congressional testimony had been used against him because witnesses were called who had heard that previous testimony. A reinvigorated North went on to write his autobiography, run unsuccessfully for the U.S. Senate, and become a television commentator.

Admiral Poindexter was convicted of five felony charges related to obstruction of Congress and perjury, and he was sentenced to a six-month prison term. An appeals court later likewise overturned the conviction on the basis that North's immunized testimony might have tainted the Poindexter trial. Admiral Poindexter disappeared from public sight for a while before reappearing at the Pentagon in the early 1990s.

Robert McFarlane pleaded guilty to four misdemeanor counts related to withholding information from Congress and was sentenced to two years' probation, a $20,000 fine, and 200 hours of community service. Heroically, he had not sought immunity during his congressional testimony, and he paid the price. He served his sentence and applied himself wholeheartedly to his community service. Despite his public acceptance of responsibility, Bud McFarlane developed bitterness toward his commander in chief, an antipathy that was shared by most of the Iran-Contra codefendants. "We should have expected that Congress would be angry and disagree with our actions, but since those actions had been undertaken in good faith and with the President's approval, they should never have led to criminal prosecution," McFarlane later wrote. "But Ronald Reagan lacked the moral conviction and the intellectual courage to stand up in our defense and in defense of his policy."

The curse of Iran-Contra played on through its mixture of patriotism, passion, and deceit. The morality play had many facets. Bud McFarlane was in on the very inception of trading arms for hostages, the violation of congressional restrictions, and the misleading of Congress; he tried to stop the operation when he realized it was failing. He was lied to by Oliver North, and, of course, he never knew of the diversion of funds to the contras. He took responsibility for his acts and paid a price that North and Poindexter, the other two Annapolis graduates, never did. He had a conscience and carried guilt, often wearing it on his own sleeve. At the lowest point that guilty conscience drove him to attempt suicide.

When the nightmare ended, however, Bud McFarlane established a new and successful career for himself in international consulting. At his fiftieth birthday party, a wide range of friends rallied around him, including former President George H.W. Bush, former national security advisors Brent Scowcroft and Zbig Brzezinski, and Chief of Naval Operations Admiral James Watkins. At that moment, it was possible to believe the Iran-Contra curse had finally been lifted.

◆ ◆ ◆ ◆ ◆

56. The Clinton Impeachment: Washington's Scorched Earth Politics

by Kirk Victor

The image is burned into the national political consciousness: President Bill Clinton, just one day before his 1998 State of the Union address, staring into the cameras and flatly denying allegations that he had carried on an affair with a young White House intern. "I did not have sexual relations with that woman, Miss Lewinsky," Clinton insisted.

Allegations of a scandalous affair between Clinton and Monica Lewinsky had made headlines for a week and would dominate the news throughout the entire year. Independent Counsel Kenneth Starr had been granted authority to broaden his initial mandate from investigating Clinton's late 1970s investment in an allegedly fraudulent land deal in Arkansas—called "Whitewater"—to also include whether the president had obstructed justice and perjured himself about an alleged affair.

The "I" word—impeachment—was even being bandied. Somehow Clinton had to show that he could still govern and to persuade the public to focus on upbeat economic news and not be distracted by salacious talk of a sex scandal. Robert Shrum, one of Clinton's advisers on the speech to be delivered on January 27, told the president that this State of the Union address would attract attention as never before. He told the president that "if he could command that chamber, if he looked and sounded presidential—well, that was a critical test he had to pass."[1]

"What I didn't say explicitly, but believed, was that the country would decide if he could still be President," Shrum later recalled.[2]

Throughout a year of investigations that included grand jury testimony, Clinton's eventual admission of an inappropriate relationship with Lewinsky, impeachment, trial, and eventual acquittal by the Senate, Clinton continued to focus publicly on managing a robust economy and demonstrating that he could still serve effectively in the Oval Office. He simply refused to surrender to the myriad embarrassments, humiliations, and allegations of the Lewinsky scandal. His strategy worked, as public support for the president never wavered despite months of profound political turbulence.

In the process Clinton showed that the president's bully pulpit, front and center on such occasions as a State of the Union address, can be used to sway the public in a way that no member of Congress, or even an independent counsel pursuing perjury charges, can match. Of course, booming economic times were critical to building public goodwill that proved impervious even to a tawdry sex scandal. In that sense, Clinton benefitted greatly from the first balanced budget in thirty years, the lowest inflation rate in many years, the lowest unemployment in twenty-four years, and a steeply declining crime rate.

From President Clinton's point of view, the push for impeachment was nothing more than an exercise of raw political power—and one that he put in the context of other episodes in recent history, from questionable tactics used in torpedoing Robert Bork's nomination to the Supreme Court in 1987 to the charges used to make the case against John Tower to be Defense Secretary in 1989.

"This was about power, about something the House Republican leaders did because they could, and because they wanted to pursue an agenda I opposed and had blocked," Clinton wrote in his memoirs, *My Life*. "In the partisan wars that had raged since the mid-1960s, neither side had been completely blameless. I had thought the Democrats wrong to examine the movie tastes of Judge Bork and the drinking habits of Senator John Tower. But when it came to the politics of personal destruction, the New Right Republicans were in a class by themselves."[3]

A RARELY USED TOOL

Agree or not with Clinton's analogies, there is no denying that impeachment is a rarely used tool. Before Clinton, only one other president, Andrew Johnson, had been impeached. That case, shortly after the Civil War, was precipitated by a battle over the exercise of presidential powers in an official personnel decision—specifically whether Johnson could fire the Secretary of War. Johnson was acquitted in 1868 when the Senate fell a single vote shy of the two-thirds margin that the Constitution requires to convict a president and remove him from office.

Unlike Clinton's case, that earlier impeachment involved a constitutional showdown over the official duties of the president and questions about whether he exceeded his authority. By contrast, Clinton's impeachment revolved around a sexual affair about which the president lied, including while under oath in the deposition of a case brought by Paula Jones, a former Arkansas state employee who charged that Clinton had sexually harassed her.

In the days before the 1998 State of the Union address, the news was consumed by Starr's issuance of subpoenas to White House staffers and his moves to obtain presidential records. All the while, Clinton hoped to demonstrate that despite the frenzy all about him, he was still the president, focused on doing the nation's business.

As Clinton himself reflected in his memoirs, when he entered the packed House chamber, "the big question was whether I would mention the controversy."[4] By then, of course, he had decided to take the advice of Shrum and other advisers not to refer to the unfolding scandal.

"The strategic purpose here was to rise above the frenzy, not to feed it," Shrum wrote. The speech was, Shrum added, a "consciously strategic document," in which, as always, the target audience was the broad public. But "for the first time in years, the imperative was to reach out to congressional Democrats. In short, Clinton had to prove to the country that he could be President and he had to hold his base."[5]

As he rattled off the country's good economic numbers, Clinton was repeatedly interrupted with applause. It was obvious that Democratic lawmakers, who would be critical to the survival of his presidency in any ensuing impeachment and trial, were with him.

And much to the consternation of Clinton's critics, especially House Republican lawmakers determined to pursue impeachment, the public continued to give the president sky-high approval ratings. The public had clearly decided to distinguish between Clinton's personal conduct, which they disapproved of, and his performance on the job. The public simply had no stomach to oust this president from office for his personal conduct in a sexual liaison, however disgraceful.

A *Chicago Tribune* poll put the president's favorable numbers at 72 percent after the speech. When the year began, Clinton's approval was 59 percent—and it never went lower than that even amid all the revelations that culminated in his impeachment.[6]

A FLAWED IMPEACHMENT

Clinton's ability to carry on through this firestorm, as well as the public perception that GOP lawmakers were more interested in scoring political points than in pursuing justice, made the chances for removing him from office virtually zero. With his deft political skills, Clinton outflanked, outmaneuvered, and outgunned Starr as well as Republicans on the House Judiciary Committee, who were leading the charge for impeachment.

Proponents of impeachment contended that Clinton had crossed the line when he took the oath and lied during his deposition in the sexual harassment case brought by Paula Jones. Jones's lawyers were given wide latitude by federal judge Susan Webber Wright to quiz Clinton about his relationships with other women during both his time as governor and as president.

At that deposition on January 17, the president was caught off guard when Jones's lawyers peppered him with questions about Monica Lewinsky. They asked if he had "sexual relations" with her, to which he said no.

In fact, on ten occasions, Clinton and Lewinsky had had sexual encounters. Still, for the next seven months, the president continued to deny the affair. "I went on doing my job, and I stonewalled, denying what had happened to everyone: Hillary, Chelsea [his daughter], my staff and cabinet, my friends in Congress, members of the press, and the American people. What I regret the most, other than my conduct, is having misled all of them," Clinton wrote in his memoirs.[7]

"I was embarrassed and wanted to keep it from my wife and daughter," he continued. "I didn't want to help Ken Starr criminalize my personal life, and I didn't want the American people to know that I'd let them down. It was like living in a nightmare. I was back to my parallel lives with a vengeance."[8]

Meanwhile, two days after the State of the Union address, Judge Wright ordered that evidence related to Lewinsky be excluded from the Jones lawsuit as "not essential to the core issues." On April 1, she tossed the case out altogether.

Still, Starr was undeterred and would continue to pursue his investigation. Starr's tenacity fueled Clinton's deep hostility toward what he saw as an out-of-control prosecutor, "trying to create a firestorm to force me from office."[9] The independent counsel's persistence, at this point, "exposed the raw political nature of Starr's investigation," Clinton wrote in his book. "Now he was pursuing me on the theory that I had given a false statement in a deposition the judge had said was not relevant, and that I had obstructed justice in a case that had no merit in the first place."[10]

Starr countered during his testimony before the House Judiciary Committee in November's impeachment hearing that lying under oath is a serious matter. "Sexual harassment cases are often 'he said–she said' disputes," he noted. "Individuals take an oath to tell the truth, the whole truth and nothing but the truth. And no one is entitled to lie under oath simply because he or she does not like the questions or because he believes the case is frivolous or financially motivated or politically motivated. The Supreme Court . . . has stated that there are ways to object to questions; lying under oath is not one of them."[11]

When Starr's investigation produced incontrovertible evidence of the affair—Lewinsky's blue dress stained with Clinton's DNA—the president, finally, acknowledged on August 17, in a nationally televised statement, that he had engaged in "a relationship with Miss Lewinsky that was not appropriate. In fact, it was wrong. It constituted a critical lapse in judgment and a personal failure on my part for which I am solely and completely responsible."

In the statement, he also admitted that his "public comments and my silence about this matter gave a false impression. I misled people, including even my wife. I deeply regret that."

PROSECUTORIAL OVERREACH

But even in those brief remarks, Clinton left no doubt that he had nothing but contempt for Starr and his investigation. "I had real and serious concerns about an independent counsel investigation that began with private business dealings 20 years ago, dealings, I might add, about which an independent federal agency found no evidence of any wrongdoing by me or my wife over two years ago.

"The independent counsel investigation moved on to my staff and friends, then into my private life. . . . This has gone on too long, cost too much, and hurt too many innocent people."

Clinton's public comments came after he had given four hours of testimony in the Map Room of the White House while the grand jury viewed the proceedings on closed-circuit television in the courthouse. He began his testimony with a brief statement acknowledging inappropriate intimate contact with Lewinsky. He was then quizzed at length by prosecutors about his denial of having had "sexual relations" and his parsing of words over the meaning of that phrase.

Clinton wrote in his memoirs that Starr's lawyers were trying to get him "on videotape discussing things in graphic detail that no one should ever have to talk about publicly." They were "trying hard to turn my interrogation into admissions that were humiliating and incriminating. That's what the, to date, whole four-year, $40 million investigation had come down to: parsing the definition of sex," Clinton wrote.[12]

The next day—after his admission of the affair—Clinton's approval number was 66 percent. It would remain in that political stratosphere until he was finally acquitted. Still, a few weeks later, on September 9, Starr delivered to the House of Representatives a 445-page report, filled with graphic details of Clinton's sexual relationship with Lewinsky, along with eighteen boxes of supporting evidence. His investigation had found "substantial and credible" evidence of wrongdoing by the president related to his affair with Lewinsky and efforts to conceal it—actions that the independent counsel found constituted eleven impeachable offenses.

Clinton again put Starr's action in historical context with that of Special Prosecutor Leon Jaworski, who had investigated President Richard Nixon's actions in the Watergate affair that ultimately led to Nixon's resignation in 1974. Starr, Clinton argued, had exceeded his role by alleging impeachable offenses—a job that the Constitution gives Congress.

"The independent counsel was supposed to report his findings to Congress if he found 'substantial and credible' evidence to support an impeachment; Congress was supposed to decide whether there were grounds for impeachment," Clinton wrote in his book. "The report was made public on the eleventh [two days after it was delivered]; Jaworski's never was. In Starr's report the word 'sex' appeared 500 times; Whitewater was mentioned twice. He and his allies thought they could wash away all their sins over the last four years in my dirty laundry."[13]

HOUSE VERSUS SENATE REPUBLICANS

The House overwhelmingly voted to release the report—a stunning move that meant it was made public before Clinton's lawyers, or even lawmakers themselves, had reviewed it. If their hope was to build support for impeachment and conviction to boot the president from office, they once again badly misread the public mood. While Clinton's approval numbers remained high, the public increasingly saw Starr and the House Republicans as driven by partisan fury against Clinton. Critics saw the report not as a serious, reasoned legal document that built the case for impeachment, but rather as a political document designed to embarrass the president.

Starr defended the report and wrote that perjury and obstruction of justice are "profoundly serious matters" and that "when they are committed by the President of the United States, we believe those acts may constitute grounds for impeachment."

The report's tone even put off lawmakers who were viewed as perhaps undecided on impeachment. The report had a "fluid narrative style that read to many like soft-core pornography," Senator Arlen Specter (R-PA) wrote in his book, *Passion for Truth*.[14]

That the House Republicans were out-of-step with the country also came home on Election Day in 1998, when the president's party gained House seats in a midterm election, which had not happened since 1934. Democrats gained five House seats and held their own in the Senate, preserving the status quo. Speaker of the House Newt Gingrich (R-GA) had tried to nationalize the campaign by running ads for impeachment. In the aftermath of that failed strategy and GOP setbacks at the polls, Gingrich made the stunning decision to resign as Speaker.

Even in the face of clear evidence that the public was not with them, House GOP lawmakers continued to pursue impeachment and to reject a middle course such as censure. Ultimately, after a rancorous, bitter debate, the chamber, on December 19, 1998, voted out articles of impeachment on perjury and obstruction of justice, almost entirely along party lines.

Senate leaders were determined not to follow the House's lead, but rather to maintain the Upper Chamber's reputation as a deliberative body. "As we approached Clinton's trial, I believed that the honor of Congress was at stake: the power of the presidency was threatened, and the reputation of the Senate could be won or lost during this last act of the impeachment melodrama," Senate Majority Leader Trent Lott (R-MS) wrote in his autobiography.[15]

Lott and Senate Democratic Leader Tom Daschle (D-SD) agreed that the Senate must have a more decorous proceeding and they agreed on rules to govern the trial. The House managers' effort to call Monica Lewinsky to provide live testimony was rejected on a 70–30 vote.

In fact, the Senate's proceedings were anticlimactic after the acrimony that had marked the House's impeachment vote. Two days of questioning and speeches by nearly every member were followed by a vote, on February 12, 1999, to acquit Clinton of the perjury article by a 55–45 margin. Ten Republicans joined all forty-five Democrats. Similarly, the Senate voted down the obstruction of justice article on a 50–50 vote, with five Republicans joining all the Democrats. Those votes fell far short of the sixty-seven required to convict the president and remove him from office.

The wrangling, partisanship, and tawdry details of this scandal that had so dominated the headlines for more than a year did little to improve the every-day lives of the American people, or to make the public more respectful of their political leaders. In fact, public disapproval of the federal government has grown markedly in the years since Clinton was impeached. There's little doubt that this sordid chapter in the nation's political history contributed to that overwhelming disdain for Washington. The outstanding question is whether these events ushered in a new era in which political posturing is un-bridled and prone to spin out of control.

◆ ◆ ◆ ◆ ◆

Notes

CHAPTER 1

1. Signing Statement for H.R. 4567, the Department of Homeland Security Appropriations Act of 2005 (P.L. 108-334), available at http://georgewbush-whitehouse.archives.gov/news/releases/2004/10/20041018-7.html.

CHAPTER 3

1. Arthur M. Schlesinger, Jr., *The Imperial Presidency* (Boston: Houghton Mifflin, 1973); Andrew Rudalevige, *The New Imperial Presidency: The Resurgence of Presidential Power after Watergate* (Ann Arbor: University of Michigan Press, 2006); Charlie Savage, *Takeover: The Return of the Imperial Presidency and the Subversion of American Democracy* (Boston: Little, Brown, 2007); "The Imperial Presidency 2.0," *New York Times*, January 7, 2007. For an early appearance of the thesis—at least as predicted—see the fifth letter by the pseudonymous antifederalist "Cato" in 1787.

2. Schlesinger, *Imperial Presidency*, 252. But he also excoriated efforts to centralize administrative powers and impound appropriated funds, to build up a large, politicized staff, and to broaden the "secrecy system" and executive privilege; and the House majority leader released a report entitled *The Imperial Presidency* in 2012 that nearly ignored foreign policy while attacking the president's use of administrative orders in domestic areas. For a broader view of the term, see Mark J. Rozell and Gleaves Whitney, eds., *Testing the Limits: George W. Bush and the Imperial Presidency* (Lanham, MD: Rowman & Littlefield,

2009); and Stephen Skowronek, "The Imperial Presidency Thesis Revisited," in Skowronek, *Presidential Leadership in Political Time*, 2nd ed. (Lawrence: University Press of Kansas, 2011).

3. Quoted in Louis Fisher, *Presidential War Power* (Lawrence: University Press of Kansas, 1995): 6. Another author of the Constitution, James Wilson, noted in its defense that the system it put in place "will not hurry us into war. . . . It will not be in the power of a single man, or a single body of men, to involve us in such distress" (Fisher, 7). See also Robert Kennedy, *The Road to War* (Praeger, 2010): 36–42; Chris Edelson, *Emergency Presidential Power* (Madison: University of Wisconsin Press, 2013): ch. 1. For a diverging view that places much emphasis on the rarity of formally "declared" wars, see John Yoo, *The Powers of War and Peace* (Chicago: University of Chicago Press, 2005).

4. Alexander Hamilton, *Federalist No. 69*; U.S. Constitution, Article I, Section 8.

5. *New York Trust Co. v. Eisner*, 256 U.S. 345 (1921). See more broadly Mariah Zeisberg, *War Powers: The Politics of Constitutional Authority* (Princeton, NJ: Princeton University Press, 2013).

6. See Schlesinger, *Imperial Presidency*, 135–40; Garry Wills, *Bomb Power: The Modern Presidency and the National Security State* (Penguin, 2011). Presidential scholar Richard Neustadt went so far as to argue that "when it comes to action risking war, technology has modified the Constitution" (quoted in Schlesinger, 166.)

7. *Federalist No. 70*; see also the Supreme Court's (rather extreme) dicta in *U.S. v. Curtiss-Wright Export Co.*, 299 U.S. 304 (1936).

8. Rudalevige, *New Imperial Presidency*, ch. 4; James Sundquist, *The Decline and Resurgence of Congress* (Washington, DC: Brookings Institution, 1981).

9. David Gray Adler, "The Clinton Theory of the War Power," *Presidential Studies Quarterly* 30 (March 2000): 155.

10. Office of Legal Counsel, "The President's Constitutional Authority to Conduct Military Operations against Terrorists and Nations Supporting Them," September 25, 2001, available at http://www.usdoj.gov/olc/warpowers925 .htm.

11. The scope of the interrogation program was made public only in December 2014 (and only in part), when the Senate Select Committee on Intelligence released a 500+ page executive summary of a 6,000-page report on the matter.

12. U.S. Department of Defense, "Working Group Report on Detainee Interrogations in the Global War on Terrorism: Assessment of Legal,

Historical, Policy, and Operational Considerations, April 4, 2003, 21 and Section III generally. See also U.S. Department of Justice, "Re: Standards of Conduct for Interrogation under 18 U.S.C. §§2340-2340A," Office of Legal Counsel, August 1, 2002.

13. White House Press Secretary, "President's Statement on Signing of H.R. 2863," December 30, 2005.

14. White House Press Secretary, "Remarks by the President on National Security," May 21, 2009.

15. An early directive, for instance, limited interrogation techniques and expressly prohibited torture (defined far more broadly than the Bush administration had done). He also set aside a number of the legal opinions noted earlier that had made such expansive claims about executive authority.

16. For a link to some of the arguments, see Andrew Rudalevige, "Six Degrees of al-Qaeda?" The Monkey Cage, *Washington Post*, September 12, 2014, available at http://www.washingtonpost.com/blogs/monkey-cage /wp/2014/09/12/six-degrees-of-al-qaeda/. For a useful overview of the drone war, see David E. Sanger, *Confront and Conceal: Obama's Secret Wars and Surprising Use of American Power*, paperback ed. (New York: Broadway, 2013).

17. Attorney General Eric Holder's March 2012 speech, quoted here, led satirist Stephen Colbert to quip that "due process just means that there's a process that you do. The current process is, apparently, first the president meets with his advisers and decides who he can kill. Then he kills them."

18. Andrew Rudalevige, "Signing Statements and Sgt. Bergdahl," The Monkey Cage, *Washington Post*, June 3, 2014, available at http://www .washingtonpost.com/blogs/monkey-cage/wp/2014/06/03/signing -statements-and-sgt-bergdahl/.

19. Charlie Savage and Mark Landler, "U.S. Defends Ongoing Role in Libya Operation," *New York Times*, June 16, 2011; Office of the White House Press Secretary, "Press Conference by the President," June 29, 2011.

20. Quoted in Rudalevige, *New Imperial Presidency*, 195.

21. White House Press Secretary, "Address to the Nation Announcing Military Action in Panama," December 20, 1989.

22. White House Press Secretary, "Remarks of the President Announcing the Deployment of United States Forces in Grenada," October 20, 1983.

23. Interestingly, too, when Republicans took over the House in 2010, even with a Democratic president, they tended to favor a *more*, not less, aggressive posture abroad. The only war seen as an overreach in the 2012 House document noted earlier was the "war on coal." On recent oversight efforts, see Norman Ornstein and Thomas Mann, "When Congress Checks Out," *Foreign Affairs* 85 (November/December 2006).

24. See Robert M. Pallitto and William G. Weaver, *Presidential Secrecy and the Law* (Baltimore: Johns Hopkins University Press, 2007); Michael Colaresi, *Democracy Declassified* (New York: Oxford University Press, 2014).

25. *Hamdi v. Rumsfeld*, 542 U.S. 507 (2004).

26. See, among others, *Rasul v. Bush*, 542 U.S. 466 (2004); *Hamdan v. Rumsfeld*, 548 U.S. 557 (2006); *Boumediene v. Bush*, 553 U.S. 723 (2008).

27. And even in *Hamdi*, the Court noted that the breadth of the AUMF was such that presidents could detain U.S. citizens in the first place, so long as they received a fair hearing.

28. Quoted in David Nather, "New Handshake, Same Grip," *CQ Weekly* (December 17, 2007): 3702.

29. See, e.g., Jack Goldsmith, *Power and Constraint: The Accountable Presidency after 9/11* (New York: Norton, 2012); Eric A. Posner and Adrian Vermeule, *The Executive Unbound* (New York: Oxford University Press, 2010).

30. See Jack Goldsmith, *The Terror Presidency* (New York: Norton, 2007); Steven Calabresi and Christopher S. Yoo, *A History of the Unitary Executive* (New Haven, CT: Yale University Press, 2008): 411–12.

CHAPTER 4

1. George C. Edwards III, *On Deaf Ears: The Limits of the Bully Pulpit* (New Haven, CT: Yale University Press, 2003).

2. George C. Edwards III, *Governing by Campaigning: The Politics of the Bush Presidency*, 2nd ed. (New York: Longman, 2007).

3. George C. Edwards III, *Overreach: Leadership in the Obama Presidency* (Princeton, NJ: Princeton University Press, 2012).

4. George C. Edwards III, *The Strategic President: Persuasion and Opportunity in Presidential Leadership* (Princeton, NJ: Princeton University Press, 2009); Edwards, *On Deaf Ears*.

5. Edwards, *On Deaf Ears*, ch. 5.

6. Robert S. Erikson, Michael B. MacKuen, and James A. Stimson, *The Macro Polity* (New York: Cambridge University Press, 2002). See also Stuart N. Soroka and Christopher Wlezien, *Degrees of Democracy* (New York: Cambridge University Press, 2010).

7. This discussion relies on Edwards, *Overreach*, 30–34.

8. George C. Edwards III, *At the Margins: Presidential Leadership of Congress* (New Haven, CT: Yale University Press, 1989); Edwards, *The Strategic President*; Jon R. Bond and Richard Fleisher, *The President in the Legislative Arena* (Chicago: University of Chicago Press, 1990): ch. 8; Richard Fleisher, Jon R. Bond, and B. Dan Wood, "Which Presidents Are Uncommonly Successful in Congress?" in *Presidential Leadership: The Vortex*

of Presidential Power, eds. Bert Rockman and Richard W. Waterman (New York: Oxford University Press, 2007).

9. This discussion relies on Edwards, *The Strategic President,* ch. 4.

10. James MacGregor Burns, *Roosevelt: The Lion and the Fox* (New York: Harcourt, Brace and World, 1956): 310–15, 321, 337–52, 366–70.

11. Lawrence O'Brien in *The Johnson Years: The Difference He Made,* ed. Robert L. Hardesty (Austin, TX: Lyndon B. Johnson School of Public Affairs, 1993): 76. See also comments by Nicholas Katzenbach in *The Johnson Years,* p. 81.

12. See James L. Sundquist, *Politics and Policy: The Eisenhower, Kennedy, and Johnson Years* (Washington, DC: Brookings Institution, 1968).

13. Randall B. Woods, *LBJ: Architect of American Ambition* (New York: Free Press, 2006): 668.

14. Quoted in Mark A. Peterson, *Legislating Together* (Cambridge, MA: Harvard University Press, 1990): 69–70.

15. O'Brien in *The Johnson Years,* 76–77. Nicholas Katzenbach in *The Johnson Years,* 81. Barefoot Sanders in *The Johnson Years,* 83. Lee White in *The Johnson* Years, 84.

16. Carl Albert, interview by Dorothy Pierce McSweeny, July 9, 1969, interview 3, transcript, 7, 11, Lyndon Baines Johnson Library, Austin, TX; Carl Albert, interview by Dorothy Pierce McSweeny, August 13, 1969, interview 4, transcript, 22, 25, Lyndon Baines Johnson Library; Carl Albert interview by Dorothy Pierce McSweeny, June 10, 1969, interview 2, transcript, 14, Lyndon Baines Johnson Library; Henry Hall Wilson, interview by Joe B. Frantz, April 11, 1973, transcript, 6–7, Lyndon Baines Johnson Library, Austin, TX; Mike Manatos, interview by Joe B. Frantz, August 25, 1969, transcript, 13–14, Lyndon Baines Johnson Library, Austin, TX; John McCormack, interview by T. Harrison Baker, September 23, 1968, transcript, 20, 39–40, Lyndon Baines Johnson Library; Carl Albert, interview by Dorothy Pierce McSweeny, July 9, 1969, interview 3, transcript, 4, Lyndon Baines Johnson Library; Goldman, *The Tragedy of Lyndon Johnson,* 68; Charles Halleck, interview by Stephen Hess, March 22, 1965, transcript, 27, John F. Kennedy Library, Boston; O'Brien, *No Final Victories,* 106, 145–49, 188–89; Richard Bolling, *Power in the House* (New York: Capricorn, 1974): 218, 229; Joseph A. Califano, *A Presidential Nation* (New York: Norton, 1975): 155; Manatos, interview by Frantz, 14, 29–30, 57–58 (see also 32); James L. Sundquist, *Politics and Policy* (Washington, DC: Brookings Institution, 1968): 476–82; Joseph Cooper and Gary Bombardier, "Presidential Leadership and Party Success," *Journal of Politics* 30 (November 1968): 1012–27; Aage R. Clausen, *How Congressmen Decide* (New York: St. Martin's, 1973): 146. See also Rowland Evans and Robert Novak, *Lyndon B.*

Johnson: The Exercise of Power (New York: New American Library, 1966): 364; Arthur M. Schlesinger, Jr., *Robert Kennedy and His Times* (New York: Ballantine, 1978): 742.

17. Albert, interview 4, 23–24. See also Califano, *A Presidential Nation* (New York: Norton, 1975): 155.

18. David A. Stockman, *The Triumph of Politics* (New York: Harper & Row, 1986): 79–80; see also 120.

CHAPTER 5

1. Michael Nelson, *A Heartbeat Away: Report of the Twentieth Century Fund Task Force on the Vice Presidency* (New York: Priority Press Publications, 1988): 21.

2. Joel K. Goldstein, *The Modern American Vice Presidency: The Transformation of a Political Institution* (Princeton, NJ: Princeton University Press, 1982): 4–5.

3. Jody C. Baumgartner, *The American Vice Presidency Reconsidered* (Westport, CT: Praeger Publishers, 2006): 72.

4. Walter F. Mondale, "Memorandum to Jimmy Carter Regarding the Role of the Vice President in the Carter Administration," Walter F. Mondale Papers, Minnesota Historical Society, December 9, 1976, available at http://www.mnhs.org/collections/upclose/Mondale-CarterMemo-Transcription.pdf (accessed Nov. 19, 2014): 2.

5. Richard Moe, "The Making of the Modern Vice Presidency: A Personal Reflection," *Presidential Studies Quarterly* 38, no. 3 (September 2008): 394.

6. Gallup, "Presidential Candidates' Weaknesses in Depth" (April 2, 2008): http://www.gallup.com/poll/105994/Presidential-Candidates-Weaknesses-Depth.aspx.

7. Gallup, "Gallup's Quick Read on the Election" (Oct. 22, 2008): http://www.gallup.com/poll/109759/Gallups-Quick-Read-Election.aspx (accessed Nov. 17, 2014).

8. George Stephanopoulos, "Interview with Joe Biden," *This Week with George Stephanopoulos* (Dec. 21, 2008): http://abcnews.go.com/blogs/politics/2008/12/biden-ill-get-t.

9. Paul C. Light, *Vice-Presidential Power: Advice and Influence in the White House* (Baltimore, MD: Johns Hopkins University Press, 1984): 63.

10. Paul Kengor, "The Vice President, Secretary of State, and Foreign Policy," *Political Science Quarterly* 115, no. 2 (Summer, 2000): 175–76.

11. Baumgartner, *The American Vice Presidency Reconsidered*, 117–18.

12. Ibid., 117–19.

13. Moe, "The Making of the Modern Vice Presidency: A Personal Reflection," 395.

14. Baumgartner, *The American Vice Presidency Reconsidered*, 118.

15. Stephanopoulos, "Interview with Joe Biden."

16. Light, *Vice-Presidential Power: Advice and Influence in the White House*, 75.

17. Ibid., 76.

18. Mark Rathbone, "The US Vice Presidency Today," *Political Insight* (Dec. 2011): 29.

19. Peter Baker, *Days of Fire: Bush and Cheney in the White House* (New York: Doubleday, 2013): 86–87.

20. Moe, "The Making of the Modern Vice Presidency: A Personal Reflection," 396.

21. Kengor, "The Vice President, Secretary of State, and Foreign Policy," 176, 184.

22. Rathbone, "The US Vice Presidency Today," 31.

23. Richard M. Yon, "Vice President Joe Biden: Perpetuating Influence or Restoring Historical Insignificance?" in *The Obama Presidency: A Preliminary Assessment*, eds. Robert Watson, Jack Covarrubias, Tom Lansford, and Douglas M. Brattebo (New York: SUNY Press, 2012): 375–76.

24. Baumgartner, *The American Vice Presidency Reconsidered*, 125.

25. Light, *Vice-Presidential Power: Advice and Influence in the White House*, 1.

CHAPTER 7

1. "Major" regulations are defined according to their impact—most saliently, "major" rules are those expected to have an annual impact on the U.S. economy of $100 million or more.

CHAPTER 10

1. Dan Balz and Haynes Johnson, *The Battle for America 2008* (New York: Penguin Group, 2009): 450.

2. Carl Hulse, "Defense and No Apologies from Author of Fiscal Bill," *New York Times*, Jan. 27, 2009: A-20, http://www.nytimes.com/2009/01/27/us/politics/27obey.html.

3. "Landmark Health Care Overhaul: A Long, Acrimonious Journey." In *CQ Almanac 2009*, 65th ed., ed. Jan Austin, 13-3. Washington, DC: CQ-Roll Call Group, 2010. http://library.cqpress.com/cqalmanac/cqal09-1183-59550-2251513.

4. *Public Papers of the Presidents of the United States: Lyndon B. Johnson, 1963–64*, Volume II, entry 541 (Washington, DC: Government Printing Office, 1965): 1009–1013.

5. Ronald Reagan, "Address Accepting the Presidential Nomination at the Republican National Convention in Detroit," *The American Presidency Project* (July 17, 1980).

6. Richard E. Cohen, "The Impact of Campaigns on Presidential-Congressional Relations," in *Rivals for Power*, ed. James A. Thurber (Rowman and Littlefield Publishers, 2006): 100.

7. Tom Davis, Martin Frost, and Richard E. Cohen, *The Partisan Divide* (Campbell, CA: Premiere, 2014): 33.

CHAPTER 11

1. Josh Earnest, "Press Briefing by Press Secretary Josh Earnest," *The White House* (November 19, 2014).

2. Daily circulation of American newspapers peaked in 1984 and had fallen nearly 13 percent to 55.2 million copies in 2003, according to the Newspaper Association of America. At the same time, advertising revenue, adjusted for inflation, has barely budged. In 1985, newspaper advertising, adjusted for inflation, was $43.04 billion, not much less than the $44.94 billion reported in 2003. That's just 4.4 percent real growth over eighteen years. During that same period, the gross domestic product, measured in current dollars, grew 161 percent.

CHAPTER 12

1. ABC News, *This Week* with George Stephanopoulos, November 23, 2014, interview transcript, http://abcnews.go.com/blogs/politics/2014/11/full-interview-transcript-president-obama-on-this-week.

2. The American Presidency Project, University of California, midterm elections comparative table, http://www.presidency.ucsb.edu/data/mid-term_elections.php.

3. Sean Trende, *RealClearPolitics* political and data analyst, wrote several columns about presidential job approval and midterm election outcomes during 2014: http://www.realclearpolitics.com/articles/2014/03/11/another_look_at_dems_chances_of_losing_the_senate.html; http://www.realclearpolitics.com/articles/2014/11/07/examining_the_polls_and_the_election_results_.html.

4. National 2014 turnout was 36.1 percent, according to the U.S. Election Project, November 25, 2014, http://www.electproject.org/2014g;

see also David Wasserman, *Cook Political Report*, nonpartisan analysis of election results, published in the NYT Nov. 18, 2014: http://fivethirty eight.com/features/why-house-republicans-did-even-better-than-they -expected.

5. Eisenhower lost thirteen. Reagan lost eight.

6. On the basis of interviews since 2009 conducted by the author, who covered the Senate in 2009–2010, when Obama relied on Democratic congressional majorities while enacting signature legislation. The author wrote about Obama's presidential campaigns and has covered the Obama White House since 2011, discussing his presidency with current and former Democratic lawmakers, advocacy group representatives, former Clinton White House advisers, Hill aides, Democratic National Convention/Democratic Senatorial Campaign Committee/Democratic Congressional Campaign Committee staff, and pollsters who work for Democratic candidates.

7. Author interview for this essay with Professor Edwards, via e-mail, October 28, 2014.

8. Sidney M. Milkis, *The President and the Parties: The Transformation of the American Party System since the New Deal* (New York: Oxford University Press, 1993): 8. (Milkis was at Brandeis University when he published his book; he is now at the Miller Center, University of Virginia).

9. House GOP leadership media availability, U.S. Capitol, December 2, 2014. Transcript available from Federal News Service, and video is here: http://www.speaker.gov/video/boehner-president-s-unilateral-action -immigration-undermines-americans-trust.

10. National Press Club, Schumer speech, November 25, 2014, C-SPAN video: http://www.c-span.org/video/?322914-1/senator-charles-schumer -dny-november-midterm-elections.

11. Example of this analysis: http://www.nytimes.com/1996/08/02 /us/clinton-s-welfare-shift-ends-tortuous-journey.html.

CHAPTER 13

1. Paul Light, *The President's Agenda* (Baltimore: Johns Hopkins University Press, 1982): 52.

CHAPTER 15

1. Edwin McDowell, "1,300 Letters of Truman's Made Public," *The New York Times*, March 14, 1983.

2. Harry Truman, "President Truman's Address Before a Joint Session of the Congress," Harry S. Truman Library & Museum, April 16, 1945.

3. Harry Truman, "Letter from Harry S. Truman to Bess W. Truman," *Truman Papers—Family, Business, and Personal Affairs Papers*, July 12, 1945.

4. Harry Truman, "Letter from Harry S. Truman to Bess W. Truman," *Truman Papers—Family, Business, and Personal Affairs Papers*, June 6, 1945.

CHAPTER 18

1. Robert Dallek, *Flawed Giant: Lyndon Johnson and His Times, 1961–1973* (New York: Oxford University Press, 1998): 278.

2. Jeffrey K. Smith, *Bad Blood: Lyndon B. Johnson, Robert F. Kennedy, and the Tumultuous 1960s* (Bloomington, IN: AuthorHouse, 2010): 186.

3. Robert Dallek, *Flawed Giant: Lyndon Johnson and His Times, 1961–1973* (New York: Oxford University Press, 1998): 190.

CHAPTER 19

1. Raymond Price, *With Nixon* (New York: Viking Press, 1977): 77.

2. *Congressional Record: Proceedings and Debates of the 93rd Congress, First Session, Volume 119, Part 8* (Washington, DC: U.S. Government Printing Office, 1973), 9546.

3. Price, *With Nixon*, 77.

CHAPTER 20

1. Yanek Mieczkowski, *Gerald Ford and the Challenges of the 1970s* (Lexington: The University of Kentucky Press, 2005): 30.

CHAPTER 21

1. David S. Broder, "Inaugural Day: Looking Ahead," *The Washington Post*, January 20, 1977.

2. Meg Greenfield, "Jimmy the Engineer," *The Washington Post*, April 20, 1977.

CHAPTER 23

1. John P. Burke, *Presidential Transitions: From Politics to Practice* (Boulder: Lynne Rienner Publishers, 2000): 251.

CHAPTER 24

1. Charles O. Jones, *Clinton and Congress, 1993–1996: Risk, Restoration, and Reelection* (Norman: University of Oklahoma, 1999).

CHAPTER 25

1. *Days of Fire: Bush and Cheney in the White House* (New York: Doubleday, 2013): 5.1.

CHAPTER 28

1. Warren Kimball, *Churchill and Roosevelt, The Complete Correspondence*, Volume III: *Alliance Declining* (Princeton, NJ: Princeton University Press, 1984): 230–32.

2. Warren Kimball, *Churchill and Roosevelt, The Complete Correspondence*, Volume II: *Alliance Forged* (Princeton, NJ: Princeton University Press, 1984): 748–51.

3. Benn Steil, *The Battle of Bretton Woods: John Maynard Keynes, Harry Dexter White, and the Making of a New World Order* (Princeton, NJ: Princeton University Press, 2013): 58–59.

4. Robert Skidelsky, *John Maynard Keynes*, Volume 3: *Fighting for Freedom* (New York: Viking, 2001): 124.

5. International Monetary Fund, *International Monetary Fund Factsheet, 2014*, p. 1: https://www.imf.org/external/np/exr/facts/pdf/globstab.pdf.

6. Dennis Appleyard and Alfred Field, *International Economics* (New York: McGraw Hill, 2014): 752.

7. Ronald McKinnon, *The Unloved Dollar Standard: From Bretton Woods to the Rise of China* (New York: Oxford University Press, 2013): 31.

8. Harry S. Truman Library and Museum, *Biographical Sketch: Harry S. Truman, 33rd President of the United States* (n.d.), http://www.truman library.org/hst-bio.htm.

9. Alfred E. Eckes, *A Search for Solvency: Bretton Woods and the International Monetary System, 1941–1971* (Austin: University of Texas Press, 1975): 218.

10. Barry Eichengreen, *Exorbitant Privilege: The Rise and Fall of the Dollar and the Future of the International Monetary System* (New York: Oxford University Press, 2011): 47–49.

11. Ruth Judson, "Crisis and Calm: Demand for U.S. Currency at Home and Abroad from the Fall of the Berlin Wall to 2011," International Finance

Discussion Paper 2012-1058 (Washington, DC: Board of Governors of the Federal Reserve System, November 2012): 26.

12. McKinnon, *Unloved Dollar Standard,* 44.

13. Ibid., 43.

14. Judith Goldstein, *Ideas, Institutions and Trade Policy* (Ithaca, NY: Cornell University Press): 164.

15. Richard Toyle, "The International Trade Organization," in *The Oxford Handbook of the World Trade Organization*, M. Daunton, E. Narlikar, and R.M. Stern, Eds. (New York: Oxford University Press, 2012): 95–96.

16. Todd Allee, "The Role of the United States: A Multilevel Explanation for Decreased Support Over Time," in *The Oxford Handbook of the World Trade Organization*, M. Daunton, E. Narlikar, and R.M. Stern, Eds. (New York: Oxford University Press, 2012): 237.

17. Eckes, as quoted by Allee, "Role of the United States," 237.

18. Ernest Preeg, "The Uruguay Round Negotiations and the Creation of the WTO," in *The Oxford Handbook of the World Trade Organization*, M. Daunton, E. Narlikar, and R.M. Stern, Eds. (New York: Oxford University Press, 2012): 123.

19. U.S. Census Bureau, *US Trade in Goods and Services—Balance of Payments (BOP) Basis,* 2015, https://www.census.gov/foreign-trade /statistics/historical/gands.pdf.

20. Preeg, "The Uruguay Round Negotiations," 131.

CHAPTER 29

1. Medicare spending and total spending have been grossed up by the amount of Medicare premiums that are counted in the budget as negative outlays.

2. For a more detailed history, see Sylvester J. Schieber and John B. Shoven, *The Real Deal* (New Haven, CT: Yale University Press, 1999).

3. A more detailed discussion of the commission can be found in Penner (2014).

4. Charlotte Twight, "Medicare's Origins: The Economics and Politics of Dependency," *Cato Journal*, 16, no. 3 (Winter 1997): 309–338.

5. David Blumenthal and James A. Morone (*The Heart of Power: Health and Politics in the Oval Office,* Berkeley: University of California Press, 2009) believe that President Johnson played a crucial role in designing a compromise. This conclusion is questioned by Paul Starr ("The Health-Care Legacy of the Great Society," in *Reshaping the Federal Government: The Policy and Management Legacies of the Johnson Years,* Norman J. Glickman et al., Eds., 2014, available at: https://www.princeton.edu/~starr/articles/articles14

/Starr_LBJ_HC_Legacy_1-2014.pdf.), who cites Mills as claiming the compromise was worked out within his committee.

6. This is sometimes reported as 138 percent because some of a recipient's income is disregarded.

CHAPTER 30

1. See James Madison, "The Structure of the Government Must Furnish the Proper Checks and Balances between the Different Departments," *Federalist Paper No. 51*; John Hart Ely, *Democracy and Distrust: A Theory of Judicial Review* (Cambridge: Harvard University Press, 1980).

2. U.S. Const. Article II, Sec. 2.

3. See *Clinton v. City of New York*, 524 U.S. 417 (1998).

4. See Richard Neustadt, *Presidential Power and the Modern Presidents: The Politics of Leadership from Roosevelt to Reagan* (New York: Macmillan, 1981).

5. See U.S. Const. Am. XIII–XV.

6. See Taylor Branch, *Parting the Waters: America in the King Years 1954–63* (New York: Simon and Schuster, 1988).

7. See Richard Kluger, *Simple Justice: The History of* Brown v. Board of Education *and Black America's Struggle for Equality* (New York: Vintage Books, 2003).

8. See Sherilyn Ifill, *On the Courthouse Lawn: Confronting the Legacy of Lynching in the Twenty-first Century* (Boston, MA: Beacon Press, 2007).

9. See C. Vann Woodward, *The Strange Career of Jim Crow* (New York: Oxford University Press, 2001).

10. Ibid.

11. Jo Ann Robinson, *The Montgomery Bus Boycott and the Women Who Started It: The Memoir of Jo Ann Gibson Robinson* (Knoxville, TN: University of Tennessee Press, 1987).

12. Aldon Morris, *The Origins of the Civil Rights Movement* (New York: The Free Press, 1986).

13. 347 U.S. 483 (1954).

14. 163 U.S. 537 (1896).

15. See *Cherokee Nation v. Georgia*, 30 U.S. (5 Peters) 1 (1831).

16. See U.S. Const. Art. III.

17. Nadine Cohodas, *Strom Thurmond and the Politics of Southern Change* (New York: Simon & Schuster, 1993).

18. Ibid.

19. Ibid.

20. Ibid.

21. See Thomas Purdum, *An Idea Whose Time Has Come: Two Presidents, Two Parties, and the Battle for the Civil Rights Act of 1964* (New York: Henry Holt, 2014).

22. Ibid.

23. Ibid.

24. See Robert Caro, *Master of the Senate: The Years of Lyndon Johnson* (New York: Vintage, 2003).

25. Joseph Califano, *The Triumph & Tragedy of Lyndon Johnson: The White House Years* (New York: Touchstone, 2015).

26. Ibid.

27. Ibid.

28. Ibid.

29. See David Garrow, *Protest at Selma: Martin Luther King, Jr. & the Voting Rights Act of 1965* (New Haven, CT: Yale University Press, 1978).

30. Ibid.

31. Joseph Califano, *The Triumph and Tragedy of Lyndon Johnson*.

32. Ibid.

33. Ibid.

34. Ibid.

35. Ibid.

36. Ibid.

37. Ibid.

CHAPTER 31

1. President John F. Kennedy, "Special Message to the Congress on Urgent National Needs," May 25, 1961.

2. Jeff Foust, "NASA's Need to Win Hearts and Minds," *The Space Review* (March 8, 2010).

CHAPTER 32

1. President Richard Nixon, "Statement about the National Environmental Policy Act of 1969," January 1, 1970.

CHAPTER 35

1. Synonyms include "Schumpeterian competition" and "creative destruction."

2. Culture is a web of beliefs and values that ties society together. See generally Clifford Geertz, *The Interpretation of Cultures: Selected Essays* (New York: Basic Books, 1973). That web is suspended on the architectures of

technology, law, and demographics. See generally, Reed E. Hundt, *In China's Shadow: The Crisis of American Entrepreneurship* (New Haven: Yale University Press, 2006): 25–26. Every important new technological architecture, or platform, changes culture.

3. The surplus rattled those who wanted government to play a diminishing role in the economy and took any government failure as more evidence that government should be smaller. Faced with the success of the Clinton Administration's policies, Fed Chairman Alan Greenspan recommended in 2001 that the Bush Administration cut taxes to re-create a deficit. That was irrational: better to have spent the new revenue on infrastructure and research on clean energy solutions, both stimulating the economy and creating the public goods that would now be driving growth. Greenspan and the other Republicans had their way: still another effect of the outcome of the election of 2000. The Internet and the dot.com boom that it caused had created choices, even if the wrong ones were made.

4. Firms like Covad and Northpoint soared with the NASDAQ index and suffered near or total collapse when the dot.com market bubble popped. But the FCC, more than the stock market, curtailed the growth of new firms in Internet access when it abandoned the "leasing" regulations during the Bush Administration. That move empowered the cable industry to become the dominant provider of Internet access that it is today.

5. These early exploiters of the Internet platform deserve huge credit for forging new business models and creating massive value, but they could not have succeeded so well or so quickly if Internet use had not grown so rapidly in the United States.

6. See Taylor Branch, *The Clinton Tapes: Wrestling History with the President* (New York: Simon & Schuster, 2009): 349–50, for the President's trust in the Vice President's judgment about this information and communications sector.

7. In early 2015, Democratic political advisers were moaning about the fact that voters did not believe the Democratic Party offered policies that could help the middle class in economic terms. See Greg Sargent, "Memo to Dems: Voters you need to win back still really don't like this economy." *Washington Post*, January 20, 2015: http://www.washingtonpost.com/blogs/plum-line/wp/2015/01/20/memo-to-dems-voters-you-need-to-win-back-still-really-dont-like-this-economy. Our technology policy in the 1990s was specifically intended to produce benefits for the middle class; it did so.

8. An administration that trumpets its unwillingness to have any strategic view about a regulated economic sector typically is attempting to disguise its true inclination or is delegating its strategy-making to the firms in the sector that it chooses to favor. In other words, "no plan" is an unrevealed or

outsourced plan. Perhaps unregulated sectors do not call for government strategies, but fewer unregulated sectors exist than Washington lobbyists would admit. In most sectors, for example, incumbents seek regulation to further their status as incumbents.

9. This was the middle of the era of belief in the Great Moderation, a concept that did not survive the financial crisis of 2008–9.

10. Paul Romer, "Endogenous Technological Change," *Journal of Political Economy* 98, no. 5 (1990): 71–102.

11. I vividly recall Gore staffer Greg Simon summoning me to the Old Executive Office Building to show me the Louvre on the computer, displayed there by the Internet instead of software hand-inserted into the computer. This was in that winter, not many weeks after Mosaic had hit the market.

12. See Reed E. Hundt, *You Say You Want a Revolution: A Story of Information Age Politics* (New Haven: Yale University Press, 2000): 9, and more generally passim.

13. Al Gore's father, also a Congressman and Senator from Tennessee, supported the TVA and the interstate highway system; Al Jr.'s application of these two initiatives to information was a conscious homage to his father.

14. An argument for net neutrality, the current hot issue at the FCC as of this writing, is that broadband access is oligopolized and so regulation is required.

15. See Robert J. Klotz, *The Politics of Internet Communication* (Lanham: Rowman & Littlefield Publishers, 2003): 18.

16. According to one poll, a vast majority of Americans approved of the Internet and a similar percentage did not know what it was.

CHAPTER 36

1. Secretary Ickes was the first influential policy advisor to warn that the United States was "running out of oil," thus beginning a long period during which U.S. Presidents approached energy policy from the perspective of supply scarcity.

2. Program to Insure an Adequate Supply of Clean Energy in the Future. Vito A. Stagliano, *A Policy of Discontent: The Making of a National Energy Strategy* (Tulsa: PennWell, 2001).

3. Nixon Address to the Nation, November 7, 1973.

4. Vito Stagliano, *A Policy of Discontent: The Making of a National Energy Strategy* (Tulsa: PennWell, 2001): 30.

5. Ibid., 35.

6. Ibid., 222.

CHAPTER 37

1. Henry M. Paulson, Jr., *On The Brink: Inside the Race to Stop the Collapse of the Global Financial System* (New York: Business Plus, 2010): 45.

2. Real GDP did not reach its previous peak for twelve quarters, compared with eight quarters in the 1973–75 and 1981–82 recessions.

3. The forecast of real GDP in 2008 (ERBP 2008) was for growth of 2.7 percent (fourth quarter to fourth quarter). The current estimate of the outcome is a contraction of 2.8 percent.

4. The PWG was formed in the wake of the stock market crash of October 19, 1987, as an informal coordinating group chaired by the Treasury Secretary with participation by the heads of Federal Reserve Board, Securities and Exchange Commission, and Commodities Futures Trading Commission. The President of the Federal Reserve Bank of New York and other financial regulators also often participated.

5. "G-7 Finance Ministers and Central Bank Governors Plan of Action," U.S. Department of Treasury (October 10, 2008).

6. Technically, Congress could have voted to disapprove the release, but the Senate defeated a measure to do so 52–42 with the strong support of the incoming Obama Administration.

7. Indeed, the administration included a $750 billion placeholder for more money for financial rescues in its first budget.

8. NAB participants provide extra financing to the IMF.

CHAPTER 38

1. The requirement for an annual presidential budget comes from the Budget and Accounting Act of 1921. The deadline was created by the Congressional Budget and Accounting Act of 1974.

2. Article I, Section 7 of the Constitution allows legislation to become law if the president does not sign it within ten days. A pocket veto occurs when the president does not sign a law within ten days but cannot return it to Congress because it is not in session.

3. Article I, Section 9.

4. Article I, Section 8

5. Pub. L. 67–13, 42 Stat. 20.

6. The Bureau of the Budget, which initially was part of the Treasury Department, was transferred to the Executive Office of the President in 1939. It was renamed the Office of Management and Budget in 1970.

7. In 2004, GAO's name was changed to the Government Accountability Office.

8. The law does establish a legal requirement that the House and Senate agree on an annual budget, but there is no penalty if it's not done. As a result, Congress often has failed to adopt a budget when the two houses have been unwilling or unable to agree.

9. Pub. L. 93–344, 88 Stat. 297.

10. The Congressional Budget and Impoundment Control Act was enacted in 1974 but the first budget it applied to was fiscal 1976.

11. The term "mandatory" is a misnomer; a program can always be changed if Congress and the president agree to do it. "Mandatory" is simply a category of spending that occurs because the previous law that created it remains in place. In accordance with the U.S. Constitution, an appropriation is still needed, but the appropriation is usually "permanent and indefinite" and doesn't have to be reenacted each year. Social Security, Medicare, and interest on the national debt are all examples of mandatory spending.

12. From time to time there have been calls, especially from presidents, to change the law so that the congressional budget has to be a joint rather than a concurrent resolution. A joint resolution would require the president to sign the congressional budget resolution and, therefore, give the White House a way to influence what the House and Senate do. Not surprisingly, even though both Republican and Democratic presidents have proposed this change, Congress has mostly rejected it out of hand.

13. The congressional budget resolution does not make program or line-by-line decisions and so is far less detailed than what the president submits to Congress. Much of the reason for this is that, when the Congressional Budget and Impoundment Control Act was considered, other committees did not want to give the new budget committees the ability to make decisions over programs within their jurisdiction and balked at supporting the new budget process unless they were given safeguards that would not happen. The budget committees often make assumptions about individual programs and line items but the assumptions are not binding and frequently are ignored.

14. The president's budget is supposed to be sent to Congress by the first Monday in February, and the budget resolution is supposed to be adopted by both houses of Congress by April 15. In practice, both deadlines have frequently been missed.

15. "Dead on arrival" was most often used when a different political party than the one that controlled the White House was in the majority in one or both houses of Congress. The existence of a congressional budget made that designation more likely because the House and Senate could indicate that the president's budget was unnecessary: Congress would have its own budget, and what the president proposed was irrelevant. Indeed, after Republicans gained control of the House and Senate in 1994, John Kasich (R-OH), the

incoming chairman of the House Budget Committee, said publicly that the president shouldn't bother submitting a budget because congressional Republicans planned to ignore it when they put their budget resolution together later in the year.

16. There is no official list of which programs or parts of programs are considered essential. This gives the president enormous discretion and power over what federal operations will continue and which ones will cease to operate during a shutdown. Both Presidents Bill Clinton and Barack Obama changed the list of essential programs during the shutdowns that occurred while they were in office as it suited their needs.

17. President Bill Clinton showed this decisively during the two shutdowns that occurred in 1995 and 1996. Even though his primary congressional adversary was Newt Gingrich (R-GA), the charismatic speaker of the House of Representatives, Clinton's ability to communicate effectively turned popular opinion against congressional Republicans.

CHAPTER 39

1. This chapter is taken from excerpts of Juan C. Zarate, *Treasury's War: The Unleashing of a New Era of Financial Warfare* (PublicAffairs Books, 2013).

2. Juan Carlos Zarate, "Prologue," in *Treasury's War: The Unleashing of a New Era of Financial Warfare* (New York: PublicAffairs, 2013).

3. Thomas Erdbrink, "Cleric Calls on Iran to Take U.S.-Led Sanctions Seriously," *Washington Post*, September 14, 2010.

4. Ayman al-Zawahiri to Abu Mus'ab al-Zarqawi, July 9, 2005, Federation of American Scientists, Intelligence Resource Program, http://www.fas.org/irp/news/2005/10/letter_in_english.pdf.

5. "Friday News Roundup." *The Diane Rehm Show*, National Public Radio, October 5, 2012, http://thedianerehmshow.org/audio-player?nid=16725.

CHAPTER 40

1. G. John Ikenberry, *Liberal Leviathan: The Origins, Crisis, and Transformation of the American World Order* (Princeton: Princeton University Press, 2011): xi.

2. Zbigniew Brzezinski, *The Grand Chessboard: American Primacy and Its Geostrategic Imperatives* (New York: BasicBooks, 1997).

3. James Lindsay, "George W. Bush, Barack Obama, and the Future of U.S. Global Leadership," *Council on Foreign Relations*, July 6, 2011.

4. James Kitfield, "An 'Indispensible Nation' No More?" *Yahoo News*, November 18, 2011.

CHAPTER 41

1. Lou Cannon, "Reagan: Action to Rescue Hostages 'Long overdue,'" *Washington Post*, May 1, 1980.

2. Lou Cannon, "Reagan Rejects Military Action to Free Iran Hostages," *Washington Post*, March 28, 1980.

3. Lou Cannon, "What Happened to Reagan the Gunslinger?" *Washington Post*, July 7, 1985. *Wall Street Journal* editorial cited in Brigitte Lebens Nacos, *Terrorism and the Media: From the Iran Hostage Crisis to the World Trade Center Bombing* (New York: Columbia University Press, 1994): 116.

4. David Brooks, "Wise Muddling Through," *New York Times*, July 31, 2009.

5. Mark Rozell, interview with author, April 2014.

6. Charlie Cook, "What Will We Expect of the Next President?" *National Journal*, February 6, 1999.

7. Haynes Johnson, "'62 Crisis with Russia Differed from Today's," *Washington Post*, May 9, 1972.

8. Denise Bostdorff, *The Presidency and the Rhetoric of Foreign Crisis* (Columbia: University of South Carolina Press, 1994): 9.

9. "Text of President's Statement," *Washington Post*, September 2, 1983.

10. "Transcript of President Reagan's News Conference," *Washington Post*, June 19, 1985.

11. Lawrence Freedman and Efraim Karsh, *The Gulf Conflict 1990–1991* (Princeton, NJ: Princeton University Press, 1993): 439.

12. The American Presidency Project. Television and Radio Interview: "After Two Years—A Conversation with the President." December 17, 1962. http://www.presidency.ucsb.edu/ws/?pid=9060.

13. Anne-Marie Slaughter, "Fiddling While Libya Burns," *The New York Times*, March 14, 2011.

14. Mark Rozell, interview with author, April 2014.

15. James David Barber, *Politics by Humans* (Durham, NC: Duke University Press, 1988): 93.

CHAPTER 42

1. "Truman's Special Message to the Congress on Greece and Turkey," March 12, 1947, in Harry S. Truman, Public Papers of the Presidents of the United States: Harry S. Truman, Vol. 3: 1947, 176–80.

2. Diary entry of March 7, 1947, in James V. Forrestal, *The Forrestal Diaries*, ed. Walter Millis (New York: Viking Press, 1951): 250–51.

3. "Truman's Special Message to the Congress on Greece and Turkey."

4. Ibid.

5. Memorandum of Conversation, White House, April 3, 1949, quoted in and paraphrased from Alonzo Hamby, *Man of the People: A Life of Harry S. Truman* (New York: Oxford University Press, 1995): 517, 524. Through their successful espionage efforts, the USSR beat U.S. intelligence estimates and tested their first atomic weapon in August 1949.

6. "Remarks of the President to the Final Session of the C.I.A.'s Eighth Training Orientation Course for Representatives of Various Government Agencies," November 21, 1952, reprinted in Michael Warner, ed., *CIA Cold War Records: The CIA under Harry Truman* (Washington, DC: Center for the Study of Intelligence, Central Intelligence Agency, 1994): 471–73.

7. See the National Security Act of July 26, 1947, P.L. 253, 80th Congress, 61 Stat. (part 1): 495–97.

8. Memorandum by the Secretary of State to the President, February 7, 1947, in "General: The United Nations," Foreign Relations of the United States series, vol. I (1947): 712–15.

9. Diary entry of September 26, 1947, in Forrestal, *Forrestal Diaries*, 320.

10. Truman quoted in Anna Kasten Nelson, "President Truman and the Evolution of the National Security Council," *Journal of American History* 72 (September 1985): 377.

CHAPTER 44

1. Parts of this essay are drawn from the author's latest book, *The Kennedy Half-Century: The Presidency, Assassination, and Lasting Legacy of John F. Kennedy* (Bloomsbury, 2013). Notes have been excised for space reasons but are available in the book.

2. Kenneth P. O'Donnell and David F. Powers, *Johnny, We Hardly Knew Ye; Memories of John Fitzgerald Kennedy* (Boston: Little, Brown, 1972) 383.

CHAPTER 45

1. Lyndon B. Johnson, *The Vantage Point: Perspectives of the Presidency, 1963–1969* (New York: Holt, Rinehart and Winston, 1971): 42.

CHAPTER 46

1. Richard Nixon, Remarks to Midwestern News Media Executives Attending a Briefing on Domestic Policy in Kansas City, Missouri, July 6,

1971, Public Papers of the Nixon presidency. Henry Kissinger, *The White House Years* (Little, Brown, 1979).

2. Margaret MacMillan, *Nixon and Mao: The Week That Changed the World* (New York: Random House, 2007): xxi.

3. Bela Kornitzer, *The Real Nixon: An Intimate Biography* (New York: Rand McNally, 1960): 149.

4. Patrick Tyler, *A Great Wall: Six Presidents and China: An Investigative History* (New York: PublicAffairs, 2000): 147.

CHAPTER 48

1. I was a member of Brzezinski's National Security Council staff with responsibility for Middle Eastern affairs, with primary emphasis on the Arab world and Israel. My colleague Gary Sick concentrated on Iran and the Gulf region.

2. See "Memorandum from the President's Assistant (Jordan) to President Carter," June 1977, "Arab-Israeli Dispute, January 1977–August 1978." In *Foreign Relations of the United States* VIII (Washington, DC: Department of State, 2013): 279–95.

3. For more on Camp David, see William B. Quandt, *Camp David: Peacemaking and Politics* (Washington, DC: Brookings Institution, 1986); and Lawrence Wright, *Thirteen Days in September: Carter, Begin, and Sadat at Camp David* (New York: Knopf, 2014).

4. See Gary Sick, *All Fall Down: America's Tragic Encounter with Iran* (New York: Random House, 1985); and Charles Kurzman, *The Unthinkable Revolution in Iran* (Cambridge, MA: Harvard University Press, 2005).

5. See David Rothkopf, "Setting the Stage for the Current Era," in *Zbig: The Strategy and Statecraft of Zbigniew Brzezinski* (Baltimore: Johns Hopkins, 2013): 63–84.

CHAPTER 51

1. Samantha Power, *A Problem from Hell: America and the Age of Genocide* (New York: Basic Books, 2002): 343.

2. Kate Snow, "Bill Clinton's 'Lifetime Responsibility' to Rwanda," *ABC News*, August 2, 2008.

CHAPTER 52

1. Kori Schake, author interview.

2. Brett McGurk, author interview.

CHAPTER 53

1. Thomas Wright, "Interpreting the National Security Strategy" (Washington, DC: The Brookings Institution, February 6, 2015).

2. Matthew Yglesias, "Obama on the State of the World: The Vox Conversation," *Vox*, February 9, 2015.

3. Susan Rice, Remarks by National Security Advisor Susan Rice on the 2015 National Security Strategy, February 6, 2015.

4. David Sanger, "Global Crises Put Obama's Strategy of Caution to the Test," *New York Times*, March 16, 2014.

5. Barack Obama, Remarks by the President and First Lady on the End of the War in Iraq, December 14, 2011.

6. Barack Obama, Remarks by the President in Address to the Nation on Libya, March 28, 2011.

7. Thomas Friedman, "Obama on the World," *New York Times*, August 8, 2014.

8. David Sanger, "Global Crises Put Obama's Strategy of Caution to the Test," *New York Times*, March 16, 2014.

9. Ibid.

10. David Sanger, "Pursuing Ambitious Global Goals, but Strategy Is More," *New York Times*, January 20, 2013.

11. Franklin Foer and Chris Hughes, "Barack Obama Is Not Pleased," *New Republic*, January 27, 2013.

12. Ibid.

CHAPTER 54

1. White House tape recording, Nixon telephone call with George Shultz, June 14, 1971.

2. Henry Kissinger and Clare Boothe Luce, *White House Years* (Boston: Little, Brown, 1979).

3. White House tape recording, Nixon and Haig, June 13, 1971.

4. Ellsberg, oral history, Richard Nixon Library (RNL).

5. White House tape recordings, Nixon and Haig, June 13, 1971, and Nixon and Kissinger, June 13, 1971; H.R. Haldeman (HRH) Diary, June 13, 1971.

6. HRH Diary, June 24, 1971. White House tape recordings, Nixon and Haldeman, June 17, 1971; and Nixon and Mitchell, Ehrlichman, Haldeman, and Ziegler, June 22, 1971. Colson to Haldeman, June 25, 1971, House Judiciary Committee, Statement of Information, Book III. Nixon toyed with the idea of arguing the case before the Supreme Court himself. Perhaps he should have. The Supreme Court decision is *New York Times Co. v. United*

States, 403 U.S. 713 (1971). See David Rudenstine, *The Day the Presses Stopped* (Berkeley: University of California, 1996) for analysis of the legal arguments and the ruling; the websites of the Miller Center at the University of Virginia; and the National Security Archive for analysis of the White House tapes that week. Ellsberg's oral history at the RNL and his memoir, *Secrets* (New York: Penguin, 2002); and John Prados and Margaret Pratt Porter, *Inside the Pentagon Papers* (Lawrence: University Press of Kansas, 2004) are also helpful.

7. White House tape recordings, Nixon and Ehrlichman, Haldeman, and Kissinger, June 17, 1971; and Nixon and Haldeman, June 24, 1971; see also HRH, *The Ends of Power.*

8. White House tape recordings, Nixon and Haldeman, June 16, 1971; and Nixon and Agnew, June 22, 1971. The president also suggested that Mitchell discredit Ellsberg by leaking testimony from a federal grand jury, a practice that could land the attorney general behind bars. See White House tape recording, Nixon and Haldeman and Mitchell and Ehrlichman and Ziegler, June 22 1971. "If I'm going to jail I want to go in a hurry," Mitchell joked, "so I might get a pardon."

9. Nixon, May 22, 1973, televised address.

10. A July 28 memo from Hunt to Colson includes the plan to collect "overt, covert and derogatory information" to "destroy his [Ellsberg's] public image and credibility." In an August 11 memo, Young and Krogh propose to Ehrlichman that the Plumbers launch "a covert operation . . . to examine all the medical files still held by Ellsberg's psychoanalyst." Ehrlichman initialed his approval "if done under your assurance it is not traceable."

11. White House tape recording, Nixon and Ehrlichman, September 8, 1971. Nixon, doubtlessly worrying that some contrary evidence would surface to contradict him, declined to give an unqualified denial that he had known of the Fielding operation in advance. If he did know about it, Nixon said in his memoirs, he would have approved it because Ellsberg was a threat to national security.

12. White House tape recording, Nixon and Haldeman, May 28, 1971.

13. Senate Select Committee (SSC), final report. Nixon joined in the planning and was kept informed about many of the dirty campaign tricks. See, for example, White House tape recordings, Nixon and Colson, December 23, 1971 (New Hampshire write-in campaign), Nixon and Colson, November 3, 1971 (Hunt and the Cubans), Nixon and Haldeman, September 18, 1971 (Enemies and the IRS), Nixon and Haldeman, May 28, 1971 (Chapman's friend), Nixon and Haldeman, May 5, 1971 (Segretti's network).

14. "Dwight Chapin Oral History Interview," C-SPAN.org, April 2, 2007. White House tape recording, Nixon and Haldeman, May 5, 1971. SSC, final report.

15. G. Gordon Liddy, *Will: The Autobiography of G. Gordon Liddy* (New York: St. Martin's Press, 1980), contains details not found elsewhere, including his fondness for self-mutilation, Nazi nomenclature, and an elaborate account of the January 27 meeting with Mitchell, Dean, and Magruder. At one point, Liddy says, he promised to recruit hit men to handle demonstrators at the Republican Convention. "These men include professional killers who have accounted between them for twenty-two dead so far, including two hanged from a beam in a garage," Liddy told them. "And where did you find men like that?" Mitchell is said to have asked. Organized crime, Liddy told him, and they don't come cheap. "Well, let's not contribute any more than we have to to the coffers of organized crime," Mitchell supposedly replied. It was the closest thing to a rebuke. To the Senate Watergate Committee, Mitchell later lamented: "I should have thrown him out of the window."

16. White House tape recording, Nixon and Haldeman, June 26, 1972.

17. White House tape recording, Nixon, Colson, and Haldeman, June 15, 1971.

CHAPTER 56

1. Robert Shrum, *No Excuses: Concessions of a Serial Campaigner* (New York: Simon & Schuster, 2007): 282.

2. Ibid.

3. Bill Clinton, *My Life* (New York: Alfred A. Knopf, 2004): 836.

4. Ibid., 779.

5. Shrum, *No Excuses*, 285.

6. Jeffrey L. Katz with Jackie Koszczuk, "GOP's Recovery Strategy: Get Back to Legislating," *CQ Weekly* (February 13, 1999): 356–57.

7. Clinton, *My Life*, 775.

8. Ibid.

9. Ibid., 775.

10. Ibid., 784.

11. Carl Cannon and Kirk Victor, "Starr's Last Chance," *National Journal* (November 21, 1998): 2763.

12. Clinton, *My Life*, 802.

13. Ibid., 809

14. Arlen Specter with Charles Robbins, *Passion for Truth* (New York: William Morrow, 2000): 449.

15. Trent Lott, *Herding Cats* (New York: ReganBooks, 2005): 176.

Selected Bibliography

Allee, Todd. "The Role of the United States: A Multilevel Explanation for Decreased Support Over Time." In *The Oxford Handbook of the World Trade Organization*, edited by M. Daunton, E. Narlikar, and R.M. Stern. New York: Oxford University Press, 2012.

Appleyard, Dennis, and Alfred Field. *International Economics.* New York: McGraw-Hill, 2014.

Baker, Peter. *Days of Fire: Bush and Cheney in the White House.* New York: Doubleday, 2013.

Balz, Dan, and Haynes Johnson. *The Battle for America 2008.* New York: Penguin Group, 2009.

Baumgartner, Jody C. *The American Vice Presidency Reconsidered.* Westport, CT: Praeger Publishers, 2006.

Blumenthal, David, and James A. Morone. *The Heart of Power: Health and Politics in the Oval Office.* Berkeley, CA, University of California Press, 2009.

Bond, Jon R., and Richard Fleisher. *The President in the Legislative Arena.* Chicago: University of Chicago Press, 1990.

Branch, Taylor. *Parting the Waters: America in the King Years 1954–63.* New York: Simon & Schuster, 1989.

Burns, James MacGregor. *Roosevelt: The Lion and the Fox.* New York: Harcourt, Brace and World, 1956.

Bush, George W. *Decision Points.* New York: Crown Publishers, 2010.

Calabresi, Steven, and Christopher S. Yoo. *A History of the Unitary Executive.* New Haven, CT: Yale University Press, 2008.

Califano, Joseph. *The Triumph & Tragedy of Lyndon Johnson: The White House Years.* New York: Touchstone, 2015.

Caro, Robert. *Master of the Senate: The Years of Lyndon Johnson.* New York: Vintage, 2003.

Clinton, Bill. *My Life.* New York: Alfred A. Knopf, 2004.

Cohen, Richard E. "The Impact of Campaigns on Presidential-Congressional Relations." In *Rivals for Power,* edited by James A. Thurber. Rowman and Littlefield Publishers, 2006.

Cohodas, Nadine. *Strom Thurmond and the Politics of Southern Change.* Macon, GA: Mercer University Press, 1993.

Colaresi, Michael. *Democracy Declassified.* New York: Oxford University Press, 2014.

Connolly, Katie. "Why Liberals Have Grown to Love Joe Biden." *Newsweek* (March 30, 2010). http://www.newsweek.com/why-liberals-have -grown-love-joe-biden-69131?piano_t=1 (accessed Nov. 22, 2014).

Davis, Tom, Martin Frost, and Richard E. Cohen. *The Partisan Divide.* Campbell, CA: Premiere, 2014.

Economic Report of the President (ERP). Washington, DC: U.S. Government Printing Office, 2008.

Economic Report of the President (ERP). Washington, DC: U.S. Government Printing Office, 2010.

Edelson, Chris. *Emergency Presidential Power.* Madison: University of Wisconsin Press, 2013.

Edwards, George C., III. *Governing by Campaigning: The Politics of the Bush Presidency,* 2nd ed. New York: Longman, 2007.

Edwards, George C., III. *On Deaf Ears: The Limits of the Bully Pulpit.* New Haven, CT: Yale University Press, 2003.

Edwards, George C., III. *Overreach: Leadership in the Obama Presidency.* Princeton, NJ: Princeton University Press, 2012.

Edwards, George C., III. *The Strategic President: Persuasion and Opportunity in Presidential Leadership.* Princeton, NJ: Princeton University Press, 2009.

Eichengreen, Barry. *Exorbitant Privilege: The Rise and Fall of the Dollar and the Future of the International Monetary System.* New York: Oxford University Press, 2011.

Fisher, Louis. *Presidential War Power.* Lawrence: University Press of Kansas, 1995.

Gallup. "Gallup's Quick Read on the Election" (October 22, 2008). http:// www.gallup.com/poll/109759/Gallups-Quick-Read-Election.aspx (accessed Nov. 17, 2014).

Gallup. "Presidential Candidates' Weaknesses in Depth" (April 2, 2008). http://www.gallup.com/poll/105994/Presidential-Candidates -Weaknesses-Depth.aspx (accessed Nov. 18, 2014).

Garrow, David. *Protest at Selma: Martin Luther King, Jr. & the Voting Rights Act of 1965.* New Haven, CT: Yale University Press, 1978.

Geithner, Timothy F. *Stress Test: Reflections on Financial Crises.* New York, NY: Crown Publishers, 2014.

Geithner, Timothy F. Financial Stability Plan. Remarks prepared for delivery, February 10, 2009. http://money.cnn.com/2009/02/10/news/econ omy/geithner_remarks/?postversion=2009021011 (accessed January 20, 2015).

Goldsmith, Jack. *Power and Constraint: The Accountable Presidency after 9/11.* New York: Norton, 2012.

Goldsmith, Jack. *The Terror Presidency.* New York: Norton, 2007.

Goldstein, Joel K. *The Modern American Vice Presidency: The Transformation of a Political Institution.* Princeton, NJ: Princeton University Press, 1982.

Goldstein, Judith. *Ideas, Institutions, and American Trade Policy.* Ithaca, NY: Cornell University Press, 1993.

Goodwin, Craufurd D. *Energy Policy in Perspective: Today's Problems, Yesterday's Solutions.* Washington, DC: Brookings Institution, 1981.

Harry S. Truman Library and Museum. Biographical Sketch: Harry S. Truman, 33rd President of the United States. http://www.truman library.org/hst-bio.htm (accessed March 19, 2015).

Hulse, Carl. "Defense and No Apologies from Author of Fiscal Bill." *New York Times,* January 27, 2009.

Ifill, Sherilyn. *On the Courthouse Lawn: Confronting the Legacy of Lynching in the Twenty-first Century.* Boston, MA: Beacon Press, 2007.

International Monetary Fund. *International Monetary Fund Factsheet,* 2014. https://www.imf.org/external/np/exr/facts/pdf/globstab.pdf (accessed March 19, 2015).

Judson, Ruth. "Crisis and Calm: Demand for U.S. Currency at Home and Abroad from the Fall of the Berlin Wall to 2011," International Finance Discussion Paper 2012-1058. Washington, DC: Board of Governors of the Federal Reserve System, November 2012.

Kengor, Paul. "The Vice President, Secretary of State, and Foreign Policy." *Political Science Quarterly* 115, no. 2 (Summer 2000): 175–99.

Kennedy, Robert. *The Road to War.* Santa Barbara, CA: Praeger, 2010.

Kimball, Warren. *Churchill and Roosevelt: The Complete Correspondence,* Volume II: *Alliance Forged.* Princeton, NJ: Princeton University Press, 1984.

Kimball, Warren. *Churchill and Roosevelt: The Complete Correspondence,* Volume III: *Alliance Declining.* Princeton, NJ: Princeton University Press, 1984.

Kluger, Richard. *Simple Justice: The History of Brown v. Board of Education and Black America's Struggle for Equality.* New York: Vintage Books, 2003.

Kurzman, Charles. *The Unthinkable Revolution in Iran.* Cambridge, MA: Harvard University Press, 2005.

"Landmark Health Care Overhaul: A Long, Acrimonious Journey." In *CQ Almanac 2009,* 65th ed., edited by Jan Austin, 13–3—13–14. Washington, DC: CQ-Roll Call Group, 2010. http://library.cqpress.com/cqalmanac/cqal09-1183-59550-2251513.

Light, Paul C. *Vice-Presidential Power: Advice and Influence in the White House.* Baltimore, MD: Johns Hopkins University Press, 1984.

Lott, Trent. *Herding Cats.* New York: ReganBooks, 2005.

McKinnon, Ronald. *The Unloved Dollar Standard: From Bretton Woods to the Rise of China.* New York: Oxford University Press, 2013.

Moe, Richard. "The Making of the Modern Vice Presidency: A Personal Reflection." *Presidential Studies Quarterly* 38, no. 3 (September 2008): 390–400.

Mondale, Walter F. "Memorandum to Jimmy Carter Regarding the Role of the Vice President in the Carter Administration." Walter F. Mondale Papers. Minnesota Historical Society. December 9, 1976. http://www.mnhs.org/collections/upclose/Mondale-CarterMemo-Transcription.pdf (accessed November 19, 2014).

Morris, Aldon. *The Origins of the Civil Rights Movement.* New York: The Free Press, 1986.

Nelson, Michael. *A Heartbeat Away: Report of the Twentieth Century Fund Task Force on the Vice Presidency.* New York: Priority Press, 1988.

Neustadt, Richard. *Presidential Power and the Modern Presidents: The Politics of Leadership from Roosevelt to Reagan.* New York: Macmillan, 1981.

Pallitto, Robert M. and William G. Weaver. *Presidential Secrecy and the Law.* Baltimore, MD: Johns Hopkins University Press, 2007.

Paulson, Henry M., Jr. *On the Brink: The Race to Stop the Collapse of the Global Financial System.* New York: Business Plus, 2010.

Penner, Rudolph G. "Myth and Reality of the Safety Net: The 1983 Social Security Reforms." In *Triumphs and Tragedies of the Modern Congress: Case Studies in Legislative Leadership,* edited by Maxmillian Angerholzer III, James Kitfield, Christopher P. Lu, and Norman Ornstein, Center for the Study of the Presidency and the Congress. Santa Barbara, CA: Praeger, 2014.

Posner, Eric A., and Adrian Vermeule. *The Executive Unbound*. New York: Oxford University Press, 2010.

Preeg, Ernest. "The Uruguay Round Negotiations and the Creation of the WTO." In *The Oxford Handbook of the World Trade Organization*, edited by M. Daunton, E. Narlikar, and R.M. Stern. New York: Oxford University Press, 2012.

Purdum, Thomas. *An Idea Whose Time Has Come: Two Presidents, Two Parties, and the Battle for the Civil Rights Act of 1964*. New York: Henry Holt, 2014.

Rathbone, Mark. "The US Vice Presidency Today." *Political Insight* (December 2011): 28–31.

Robinson, Jo Ann. *The Montgomery Bus Boycott and the Women Who Started It: The Memoir of Jo Ann Gibson Robinson*. Knoxville, TN: University of Tennessee Press, 1987.

Rozell, Mark J., and Gleaves Whitney, editors. *Testing the Limits: George W. Bush and the Imperial Presidency*. Lanham, MD: Rowman & Littlefield, 2009.

Rudalevige, Andrew. *The New Imperial Presidency: The Resurgence of Presidential Power after Watergate*. Ann Arbor: University of Michigan Press, 2006.

Savage, Charlie. *Takeover: The Return of the Imperial Presidency and the Subversion of American Democracy*. Boston: Little, Brown, 2007.

Schieber, Sylvester J., and John B. Shoven. *The Real Deal*. New Haven, CT: Yale University Press, 1999.

Schlesinger, Arthur M., Jr. *The Imperial Presidency*. Boston: Houghton Mifflin, 1973.

Shrum, Robert. *No Excuses: Concessions of a Serial Campaigner*. New York: Simon & Schuster, 2007.

Sick, Gary. *All Fall Down: America's Tragic Encounter with Iran*. New York: Random House, 1985.

Skidelsky, Robert. *John Maynard Keynes*, Volume 3: *Fighting for Freedom*. New York: Viking, 2001.

Skowronek, Stephen. "The Imperial Presidency Thesis Revisited." In *Presidential Leadership in Political Time*, 2nd ed., edited by Stephen Skowronek. Lawrence: University Press of Kansas, 2011.

Specter, Arlen, with Charles Robbins. *Passion for Truth*. New York: William Morrow, 2000.

Stagliano, Vito A. *A Policy of Discontent: The Making of a National Energy Strategy*. Tulsa, OK: PennWell, 2001.

Starr, Paul. "The Health-Care Legacy of the Great Society." https://www.princeton.edu/~starr/articles/articles14/Starr_LBJ_HC_Legacy_1-2014.pdf (accessed February 22, 2015).

Steil, Benn. *The Battle of Bretton Woods: John Maynard Keynes, Harry Dexter White and the Making of a New World Order*. Princeton, NJ: Princeton University Press, 2013.

Stephanopoulos, George. "Interview with Joe Biden." *This Week with George Stephanopoulos* (December 21, 2008). http://abcnews.go.com/This Week/story?id=6499340 (accessed November 17, 2014).

Stockman, David A. *The Triumph of Politics*. New York: Harper & Row, 1986.

Sundquist, James L. *Politics and Policy: The Eisenhower, Kennedy, and Johnson Years*. Washington, DC: Brookings Institution, 1968.

Toye, Richard. "The International Trade Organization." In *The Oxford Handbook of the World Trade Organization*, edited by M. Daunton, E. Narlikar, and R.M. Stern. New York: Oxford University Press, 2012.

Twight, Charlotte. "Medicare's Origins: The Economics and Politics of Dependency." *Cato Journal* 16, no. 3 (Winter 1997): 309–38.

U.S. Census Bureau. *US Trade in Goods and Services—Balance of Payments (BOP) Basis*. 2015. https://www.census.gov/foreign-trade/statistics/historical/gands.pdf (accessed April 4, 2015).

Woods, Randall B. *LBJ: Architect of American Ambition*. New York: Free Press, 2006.

Woodward, C. Vann. *The Strange Career of Jim Crow*. New York: Oxford University Press, 2001.

Yergin, Daniel. *The Prize: The Epic Quest for Oil, Money & Power*. New York: Simon & Schuster, 1991.

Yon, Richard M. "Vice President Joe Biden: Perpetuating Influence or Restoring Historical Insignificance?" In *The Obama Presidency: A Preliminary Assessment*, edited by Robert P. Watson, Jack Covarrubias, Tom Lansford, and Douglas M. Brattebo. New York: SUNY Press, 2012.

Yoo, John. *The Powers of War and Peace*. Chicago: University of Chicago Press, 2005.

Contributors

David M. Abshire—Former President of the "Center for the Study of the Presidency & Congress"; Founder of the Center for Strategic and International Studies; Former Ambassador to NATO; Author, *Saving the Reagan Presidency: Trust Is the Coin of the Realm* and *A Call to Greatness: Challenging Our Next President.*

Jonathan Alter—Author, *The Center Holds: Obama and His Enemies* (2013), *The Promise: President Obama, Year One* (2010), and *The Defining Moment: FDR's Hundred Days and the Triumph of Hope* (2006).

Joseph Amoroso—First Lieutenant, U.S. Army.

Peter Baker—Chief White House Correspondent, *New York Times*; Author, *Days of Fire: Bush & Cheney in the White House* (2013).

Charles Bartlett—Newspaper Journalist; Co-Author, *Facing the Brink* (1967).

Michael Beschloss—Contributor, *New York Times*; Presidential Historian, NBC News; Contributor, *PBS NewsHour*; Author, *Presidential Courage: Brave Leaders and How They Changed America, 1789–1989* (2007), *Jacqueline Kennedy: Historic Conversations on Life with John F. Kennedy* (2011, co-authored with Caroline Kennedy), and two volumes on President Lyndon Johnson's secret White House tapes.

Michael K. Bohn—Author, *Presidents in Crisis: Tough Decisions Inside the White House from Truman to Obama* (2015); *Mount Vernon Revisited, A Photo History of the Mount Vernon Community in Alexandria, Virginia* (2014), *The Achille Lauro Hijacking, Lessons in the Politics and Prejudice of Terrorism* (2004), and *Nerve Center: Inside the White House Situation Room* (2003).

John P. Burke—John G. McCullough Professor of Political Science, University of Vermont; Author, *Honest Broker? The National Security Advisor and Presidential Decision Making* (2009), *Becoming President: The Bush Transition 2000–2003* (2004), and *Presidential Transitions: From Politics to Practice* (2000).

Brian Burnes—Staff Writer, *Kansas City Star*; Author, *Harry S. Truman: His Life and Times* (2003).

Carl Cannon—Washington Bureau Chief, RealClearPolitics; Past Recipient of the Gerald R. Ford Journalism Prize for Distinguished Reporting on the Presidency, and the Aldo Beckman Award.

Lou Cannon—Author, *Governor Reagan: His Rise to Power* (2003), *Official Negligence: How Rodney King and the Riots Changed Los Angeles and the LAPD* (1998), *President Reagan: The Role of a Lifetime* (1991), and *Reagan* (1982).

Guy Caruso—senior adviser in the Energy and National Security Program, Center for Strategic and International Studies; Former Administrator of the U.S. Energy Information Administration (EIA) from July 2002 to September 2008.

Richard E. Cohen—Veteran Washington correspondent who has covered Congress for *National Journal, Politico,* and *Congressional Quarterly*. Coauthor with Tom Davis and Martin Frost, *The Partisan Divide: Congress in Crisis* (2014); Author, *Washington at Work: Back Rooms and Clean Air,* and *Rostenkowski: The Pursuit of Power and the End of the Old Politics.* He has been coauthor of *The Almanac of American Politics*.

Stanley E. Collender—Executive Vice President, Qorvis MSLGROUP; Former staffer on the House and Senate Budget Committees; Author, *The Guide to the Federal Budget.*

Kareem U. Crayton—Professor and Managing Partner, Crimcard Consulting Services, LLC.

Mary Currin-Percival—Associate Research Director for the Survey and Policy Research Institute (SPRI), San José State University.

Kenneth M. Duberstein—Chairman and CEO of the Duberstein Group; former Chief of Staff to President Ronald Reagan in 1988–89.

George C. Edwards III—University Distinguished Professor of Political Science and Jordan Chair in Presidential Studies, Texas A&M University; Editor, *Presidential Studies Quarterly* and *The Oxford Handbook of American Politics* series.

John Aloysius Farrell—Contributing Editor and Correspondent, *The Atlantic* and *National Journal*; Writer, *The Denver Post* and *The Boston Globe*; Author, *Tip O'Neill and the Democratic Century*.

Jeff Foust—Senior Writer, *SpaceNews*.

Sean Gailmard—Professor, University of California—Berkeley; Author, *Learning While Governing: Expertise and Accountability in the Executive Branch*.

Major Garrett—Chief White House Correspondent, CBS News; Correspondent at Large, *National Journal*.

Larry N. Gerston—Professor Emeritus of Political Science, San Jose State University; Author, *Reviving Citizen Engagement: Policies to Renew National Community* (2014).

Fred I. Greenstein—Professor of Politics Emeritus, Princeton University; Author, *The Presidential Difference: Leadership Style from FDR to Barack Obama* (2009), and *Inventing the Job of President: Leadership Style from George Washington to Andrew Jackson* (2009).

Lee Huebner—Airlie Professor of Media and Public Affairs, The George Washington University; Former Publisher and CEO, *International Herald Tribune*.

Reed E. Hundt—Founder and CEO, Coalition for Green Capital; Former Chairman (1993–97), U.S. Federal Communications Commission.

Charles O. Jones—Hawkins Professor Emeritus of Political Science, University of Wisconsin—Madison; nonresident Senior Fellow in the Governmental Studies Program, The Brookings Institution.

Marvin Kalb—Edward R. Murrow Professor of Practice, and Senior Fellow of the Joan Shorenstein Center on the Press, Politics, and Public Policy, Harvard University, John F. Kennedy School of Government; Author, *Haunting Legacy: Vietnam and the American Presidency from Ford to Obama*.

James Kitfield—Senior Fellow, the Center for the Study of the Presidency & Congress; Senior Correspondent, *National Journal*; three-time recipient of the Gerald R. Ford Award for Distinguished Reporting on National Defense. He is the author of *War & Destiny: How the Bush Revolution in Foreign and Military Affairs Redefined American Power*, and *Prodigal Soldiers: How the Generation of Officers Born of Vietnam Revolutionized the American Style of War*.

Yanek Mieczkowski—Professor of History, Dowling College; Author, *Gerald Ford and the Challenges of the 1970s* and *The Routledge Historical Atlas of Presidential Elections*.

Bruce Miroff—Professor and Collins Fellow at the Rockefeller College of Public Affairs and Policy, State University of New York; Author, *Debating Democracy: A Reader in American Politics*, Sixth Edition (2009), and *The Democratic Debate: American Politics in an Age of Change*, Fifth Edition (2010).

Rudolph G. Penner—Institute Fellow, and Arjay and Frances Miller Chair in Public Policy, Urban Institute; former Director of the Congressional Budget Office; Author, *The Moving Pieces of Social Security Reform*.

Garrick L. Percival—Associate Professor and Director of Institute for Public Affairs and Civic Engagement, San Jose State University.

Geoffrey Perret—Author, *Lincoln's War: The Untold Story of America's Greatest President As Commander in Chief* (2004), and *Commander in Chief: How Truman, Johnson, and Bush Turned a Presidential Power into a Threat to America's Future* (2007).

James P. Pfiffner—University Professor of Public Policy, George Mason University; Author, *The Strategic Presidency: Hitting the Ground Running and Power Play: The Bush Presidency and the Constitution.*

Richard M. Pious—Professor of Political Science and Adolph S. and Effie Ochs Chair in History and American Studies, Barnard College; Author, *The American Presidency; The President, Congress, and the Constitution*, and *The War on Terrorism and the Rule of Law.*

William B. Quandt—Edward R. Stettinius, Jr. Professor of Politics, University of Virginia; Author, *Peace Process: American Diplomacy and the Arab–Israeli Conflict since 1967.*

Jesse H. Rhodes—Associate Professor of Political Science, University of Massachusetts-Amherst; Author, *An Education in Politics: The Origin and Development of No Child Left Behind* (2012).

William D. Ruckelshaus—Strategic Director, Madrona Venture Group; Former Administrator of the Environmental Protection Agency from 1970–73 and from 1983–1985.

Andrew C. Rudalevige—Thomas Brackett Reed Professor of Government, Bowdoin College; Author, *The New Imperial Presidency: Renewing Presidential Power after Watergate.*

Larry J. Sabato—Professor of American Politics, University of Virginia; Author, *The Year of Obama: How Barack Obama Won the White House.*

David E. Sanger—Chief Washington Correspondent, *The New York Times.* He has twice been a member of *Times* reporting teams that won the Pulitzer Prize.

Alexis Simendinger—White House Correspondent, *RealClearPolitics.* She won the Aldo Beckman Memorial Journalism Prize in 2008 for excellence in White House coverage.

Elizabeth Edwards Spalding—Associate Professor of Government, Claremont McKenna College; Author, *The First Cold Warrior: Harry Truman, Containment, and the Remaking of Liberal Internationalism.*

Stuart S. Taylor, Jr.—Nonresident Senior Fellow in Governance Studies, Brookings Institution; contributing editor, *National Journal;* coauthor with Richard Sander, *Mismatch: How Affirmative Action Hurts Students It's Intended to Help and Why Universities Won't Admit It;* Coauthor with K.C. Johnson, *Until Proven Innocent: Political Correctness and the Shameful Injustices of the Duke Lacrosse Rape Fraud.*

Katherine Theyson—Assistant Professor of Economics, Sewanee—The University of the South.

Evan Thomas—Editor at Large, *Newsweek;* Author, *Ike's Bluff: President Eisenhower's Secret Battle to Save the World,* and *Being Nixon: A Man Divided.*

Edwin M. Truman—Nonresident Senior Fellow, Peterson Institute for International Economics; Former Assistant Secretary of the U.S. Treasury for International Affairs from 1998–2001; Former Counselor to the Secretary of the Treasury in 2009; Author, Coauthor, or Editor, *Sovereign Wealth Funds: Threat or Salvation?* (2010), *Reforming the IMF for the 21st Century* (2006), and *A Strategy for IMF Reform* (2006).

Kirk Victor—Contributing Editor, *National Journal;* Coauthor on former Senator Ernest F. "Fritz" Hollings memoir, *Making Government Work.*

John T. Woolley—Professor of Political Science, University of California-Santa Barbara; Developed with Gerhard Peters the website, *The American Presidency Project;* Coauthor with Gerhard Peters, *The Presidency A to Z.*

Richard M. Yon—Instructor in American Politics, Policy, and Strategy, United States Military Academy.

Juan C. Zarate—Senior Adviser of Transnational Threats Project and Homeland Security and Counterterrorism Program, Center for Strategic and International Studies; Senior National Security Analyst, CBS News; Visiting Lecturer, Harvard University; Author, *Treasury's War: The Unleashing of a New Era of Financial Warfare* (2013), and *Forging Democracy* (1994).

Julian E. Zelizer—Malcolm Stevenson Forbes, Class of 1941 Professor of History and Public Affairs, Princeton University; Author, *Arsenal of Democracy: The Politics of National Security—From World War II to the War on Terrorism* (2010), *Jimmy Carter* (2010), and *Conservatives in Power: The Reagan Years, 1981–1989* (2010).

Acknowledgments

On Behalf of the Center for the Study of the Presidency & Congress, I would like to thank the following for their contributions to the *Triumphs & Tragedies of the Modern Presidency*:

The late David M. Abshire, whose lifelong commitment to learning from the lessons of history and effort to build consensus in Washington remain driving principles behind the work of this Center.

Our Trustees whose generous support was essential to the book, especially Andrew Barth, Eli Broad, Dr. Malik Hasan, Daniel Lubin, B. Francis Saul III, Pamela Scholl, Gerry Parsky, and Ambassador Robert Tuttle.

Daniel Lubin deserves special thanks for first encouraging us to revitalize the *Triumphs and Tragedies* brand, first in 2014 with *Triumphs & Tragedies of the Modern Congress*, and now, an update to the originally published *Triumphs & Tragedies of the Modern Presidency*. Additionally, I am deeply grateful for funding from the Dr. Scholl Foundation, which enables us to convert the vision into a reality.

Our staff and interns including, Ann Marie Packo, Elizabeth Perch, Hurst Renner, Jeff Shaffer, Sara Spancake, Madeline Vale, Pierre DuBois, Paniz Rezaeerod, Maggie Stanford, Alice Farrell, Alex Morton, Ridvan Pehlivan, Virginia Rayder, Laura Erickson, Devi Modha, Corinne Day, Dominic Leach, Lillie Belle Viebranz, Trevor Falk, and Lia Kapani.

Dan Mahaffee, Collin Odell, and Hurst Renner have been invaluable as the coordinators of this project, spending countless hours to ensure that this book was completed on time—not an easy feat with an edited volume.

Praeger Publishing and its exceptional team, especially Steve Catalano.

The outstanding authors whose contributions of time, experience, and historical knowledge are evident in the final product.

Finally, I would like to thank my very distinguished coeditors, James Kitfield, Norm Ornstein, and Stephen Skowronek, for their leadership of this project. Their complementary experiences and talents make this volume both highly informative and very entertaining.

Maxmillian Angerholzer III
President & CEO
Center for the Study of the Presidency & Congress

Index

About the Editors

MAXMILLIAN ANGERHOLZER III

Mr. Angerholzer serves as the President & CEO of the Center for the Study of the Presidency & Congress (CSPC). He is also Managing Director of the Richard Lounsbery Foundation, a philanthropic institution in Washington, D.C., that awards grants primarily in science and technology policy, education, international relations, and security. Mr. Angerholzer has served as the Special Assistant to the Vice Chairman of the Center for Strategic & International Studies (CSIS) in Washington, D.C., and as an adviser to the CSIS Abshire-Inamori Leadership Academy (AILA). Mr. Angerholzer holds a Bachelor of Arts (magna cum laude) in Political Science from the University of the South in Sewanee, Tennessee, and a Master of Arts from the George Washington University's Elliott School of International Affairs.

JAMES KITFIELD

James Kitfield has written on defense, national security, and foreign policy issues for more than two decades. Currently a contributing editor at the *National Journal*, Mr. Kitfield is a three-time winner of the Gerald R. Ford Award for Distinguished Reporting on National Defense and a five-time winner of the Military Reporters and Editors Association and Medill School of Journalism's top prize for excellence in reporting, largely for his coverage of the wars in Afghanistan and Iraq. His many other awards include the Association of Former Intelligence Officers' Steward Alsop Media Excellence Award, The National Press Club's Edwin M. Hood Award for Diplomatic

Correspondence, and The German Marshall Fund's Peter R. Weitz Prize. A magna cum laude graduate of the University of Georgia's Henry Grady School of Journalism, Kitfield is the author of two books, *War & Destiny* and *Prodigal Soldiers.*

NORMAN ORNSTEIN

A Resident Scholar at the American Enterprise Institute, Norm Ornstien is a contributing editor and columnist for *National Journal* and *The Atlantic.* Named as one of 2012's Top 100 Global Thinkers by *Foreign Policy Magazine,* Mr. Ornstein led a working group that helped shape the campaign finance reform law known as McCain-Feingold. Mr. Ornstein's many books include *The Broken Branch: How Congress Is Failing America and How to Get It Back on Track,* and most recently, *It's Even Worse Than It Looks: How the American Constitutional System Collided with the New Politics of Extremism,* a *New York Times* best-seller. Dr. Ornstein's vast experience includes positions over the past two decades at *USA Today, Roll Call,* the Pew Research Center for People and the Press, CBS News, and the Council of Foreign Relations.

STEPHEN SKOWRONEK

Stephen Skowronek is the Pelatiah Perit Professor of Political and Social Science at Yale University. Dr. Skowronek has been a fellow at the Woodrow Wilson International Center for Scholars and has held the Chair in American Civilization at the École des Hautes Études en Sciences Sociales in Paris. Dr. Skowronek's research concerns American national institutions and American political history. Dr. Skowronek's publications include *Building a New American State: The Expansion of National Administrative Capacities, 1877–1920* (1982), *The Politics Presidents Make: Leadership from John Adams to Bill Clinton* (1997), *The Search for American Political Development* (2004, with Karen Orren), and *Presidential Leadership in Political Time: Reprise and Reappraisal* (2008). Among other activities, Dr. Skowronek was cofounder of the journal *Studies in American Political Development,* which he edited from 1986 to 2007, and he provided the episode structure and thematic content for the PBS miniseries, *The American President* (Kunhardt Productions).